Demystifying Educational Leadership and Administration in the Middle East and North Africa

This volume explores how educational leadership and administration (ELA) is constructed in the Middle East and North Africa (MENA) region and charts the development of ELA as a discipline.

Against the backdrop of rapid growth and interest in the educational restructuring, educational reforms, policy, and leadership landscape of the region, chapters investigate issues concerned with the production and utilization of knowledge in the field and analyze the future of ELA in relation to the educational policies and practices in MENA countries. Featuring a broad range of geographically dispersed specialist contributors involved in leadership, policy, and administration, the volume ultimately sheds light on this little-researched area of study to demystify common tropes and misunderstandings surrounding ELA in the MENA region.

This book will be of use to scholars, researchers, and postgraduate students involved with international and comparative education, higher education management, and education policy and politics more broadly.

Khalid Arar is a Professor of Educational Leadership and Policy in the School Improvement Doctoral Program at the College of Education, Texas State University, USA.

Selahattin Turan is a Professor of Educational Leadership and Policy in the College of Education, Bursa Uludağ University, Turkey and Editor-in-Chief of Leadership and Policy in Schools Journal.

Sedat Gümüş is an Associate Professor in the Department of Educational Policy and Leadership and a Research Fellow of the Asia Pacific Centre for Leadership and Change at the EdUHK, Hong Kong.

Abdellatif Sellami is the Director of the Education Research Centre, College of Education, Qatar University, Qatar.

Julia Mahfouz is an Associate Professor in the Leadership for Educational Organizations program, School of Education and Human Development at the University of Colorado Denver, USA.

Educational Policy and Leadership in the Middle East and North Africa

Series editor: Khalid Arar
Series co-editors: Selahattin Turan, Sedat Gümüş, and Julia Mahfouz

This timely series addresses the need for up-to-date, current literature on educational policy, leadership, and scholarship the Middle East and North Africa (MENA) region to support the work of researchers from developing areas, and give a voice to perspectives rarely heard in the West. The series will offer important insights into the dynamics governing the interplay between global market and education forces in each local context, and will therefore further examine important political, societal, and cultural barriers that continue to hinder the development of education systems in the MENA region. Books in the series will give a critical analysis of the research undertaken and support global understanding of the scope, scale, and complexity of educational policy, politics, and leadership in MENA countries.

Books in the series include:

Higher Education and Scientific Research in the Arabian Gulf States
Opportunities, Aspirations, and Challenges
Khalid Arar, Abdellatif Sellami, and Rania Swalhi

Demystifying Educational Leadership and Administration in the Middle East and North Africa
Challenges and Prospects
Edited by Khalid Arar, Selahattin Turan, Sedat Gümüş, Abdellatif Sellami and Julia Mahfouz

For more information about the series, please visit https://www.routledge.com/Educational-Policy-and-Leadership-in-the-Middle-East-and-North-Africa/book-series/EPLMENA

Demystifying Educational Leadership and Administration in the Middle East and North Africa

Challenges and Prospects

Edited by Khalid Arar,
Selahattin Turan, Sedat Gümüş,
Abdellatif Sellami, and
Julia Mahfouz

LONDON AND NEW YORK

First published 2024
by Routledge
4 Park Square, Milton Park, Abingdon, Oxon OX14 4RN

and by Routledge
605 Third Avenue, New York, NY 10158

Routledge is an imprint of the Taylor & Francis Group, an informa business

© 2024 selection and editorial matter, Khalid Arar, Selahattin Turan, Sedat Gümüş, Abdellatif Sellami and Julia Mahfouz; individual chapters, the contributors

The right of Khalid Arar, Selahattin Turan, Sedat Gümüş, Abdellatif Sellami and Julia Mahfouz to be identified as the authors of the editorial material, and of the authors for their individual chapters, has been asserted in accordance with sections 77 and 78 of the Copyright, Designs and Patents Act 1988.

All rights reserved. No part of this book may be reprinted or reproduced or utilised in any form or by any electronic, mechanical, or other means, now known or hereafter invented, including photocopying and recording, or in any information storage or retrieval system, without permission in writing from the publishers.

Trademark notice: Product or corporate names may be trademarks or registered trademarks, and are used only for identification and explanation without intent to infringe.

British Library Cataloguing-in-Publication Data
A catalogue record for this book is available from the British Library

Library of Congress Cataloguing-in-Publication Data
Names: Arar, Khalid, editor. | Turan, Selahattin, editor. | Gümüş, Sedat, editor. | Sellami, Abdellatif, editor. | Mahfouz, Julia, editor.
Title: Demystifying educational leadership and administration in the Middle East and North Africa : challenges and prospects / edited by Khalid Arar, Selahattin Turan, Sedat Gümüş, Abdellatif Sellami, Julia Mahfouz.
Identifiers: LCCN 2023034098 (print) | LCCN 2023034099 (ebook) | ISBN 9781032369907 (hardback) | ISBN 9781032369914 (paperback) | ISBN 9781003334835 (ebook)
Subjects: LCSH: Educational leadership--Middle East. | Educational leadership--Africa, North. | School management and organization--Middle East. | School management and organization--Africa, North.
Classification: LCC LB2965.M628 D46 2023 (print) | LCC LB2965.M628 (ebook) | DDC 371.2/0110956--dc23/eng/20230814
LC record available at https://lccn.loc.gov/2023034098
LC ebook record available at https://lccn.loc.gov/2023034099

ISBN: 978-1-032-36990-7 (hbk)
ISBN: 978-1-032-36991-4 (pbk)
ISBN: 978-1-003-33483-5 (ebk)

DOI: 10.4324/9781003334835

Typeset in Galliard
by MPS Limited, Dehradun

This inaugural volume of our book series is dedicated to our late colleague Professor Kadir Beycioğlu in recognition of his legacy and his unique inspiration in the field of educational leadership and policy while trying restlessly to make the world a better place.

Contents

List of Figures ix
List of Tables x
List of Editors and Contributors xi

1 Demystifying Educational Leadership and
 Administration in the Middle East and North Africa/
 Editorial Introduction 1
 KHALID ARAR, SELAHATTIN TURAN, SEDAT GÜMÜŞ,
 ABDELLATIF SELLAMI, AND JULIA MAHFOUZ

2 Educational Leadership and Management in Türkiye:
 A Critical Review of Policy, Practice, and Research 12
 MEHMET ŞÜKRÜ BELLIBAŞ, İBRAHIM HAKAN KARATAŞ, AND
 ELIF AYDOĞDU

3 Examining the Knowledge Base in Educational
 Administration and Leadership in Egypt: A Systematic
 Review of Published Research Literature 37
 WAHEED HAMMAD, EMAN AHMED, AND MAYSAA BARAKAT

4 Educational Leadership and Administration in Iraq:
 Challenges and Prospects 62
 MAYAMIN ALTAE

5 Educational Leadership and Administration in Morocco:
 Recent developments and growth prospects 75
 MOHAMMED ELMESKI

Contents

6 Educational Leadership and Administration in Algeria: Policy, Development, and Reflective Practice   95
FELLA LAHMAR AND FATIMA ZAHRA ABBOU

7 Educational Administration and Leadership in Jordan: A Retrospective-Prospective Approach   114
AREF AL-ATTARI AND EIMAN ESSA

8 Principalship in Lebanon: The Unsung Heroes   140
JULIA MAHFOUZ AND RIMA KARAMI

9 The State of Art of Educational Leadership in Palestine: The Two Faces of the Coin   154
SOHEIL SALHA AND SAIDA AFFOUNEH

10 Educational Administration and Policy in Kuwait: A Reflection on Decades of Reform   166
AMAL ABDULWAHAB ALSALEH

11 K-12 Educational Leadership and Administration in Qatar: Lessons Learned   187
ABDELLATIF SELLAMI, RANIA SAWALHI, AND ASMAA E. AL-FADALA

12 Exploring the Omani Educational Administration and Leadership Literature: Hidden Gems or Concerns to Be Addressed?   209
YARA YASSER HILAL AND MUNA KHAMIS AL-ALAWI

13 Revisiting and Reimagining Educational Leadership and Administration in the Middle East and North Africa   233
KHALID ARAR, SELAHATTIN TURAN, SEDAT GÜMÜŞ, ABDELLATIF SELLAMI, AND JULIA MAHFOUZ

Index   *237*

Figures

3.1	Pattern of EAL journal publications from Egypt (2001–2021)	44
3.2	Distribution of articles by type of study	46
3.3	Distribution of articles by school level	47
3.4	Distribution of articles by research methods	49
3.5	Distribution of articles by data collection methods	49
3.6	Distribution of articles by level of statistical analysis	50
5.1	The evolution of NIDE as a composite of three sub-indices	76
5.2	A summary of TIMSS scores of Morocco's fourth and eighth graders in 2011–2019	77
5.3	School development project internal and external stakeholders	81
5.4	Local, regional, and central stakeholders involved in the design, funding, and quality assurance of the SDP	82
5.5	Potter and Brough's hierarchy of system capacity-building needs	85
9.1	The structure of the Ministry of Education	160
10.1	The organizational structure of the Ministry of Education (MoE, 2021)	170
10.2	Policy planning for the MoE	171
10.3	Proposal for the future development of the MoE structure (MoE, 2013)	173
11.1	MoEHE unified school structure in 2016 (developed by the researchers)	196
11.2	MoEHE structure 2016 taken from Koç & Fadlelmula (2016)	199
12.1	Distribution of articles by research methods	218
12.2	Distribution of articles by data collection methods	219
12.3	Overall distribution of articles by level of statistical analysis	220
12.4	The distribution, by percentage, of articles in Arabic and English journals by level of statistical analysis	220

Tables

2.1	Schooling rates by education level in the 2019–2020 academic year	15
2.2	Budget of MoNE	15
2.3	Number of universities and faculty in education by years	23
2.4	Number of educational management graduate programs and graduates by years	25
3.1	Topical coverage	48
7.1	Themes generated from the document analysis	116
7.2	Findings disaggregated by a number of quantitative indicators	118
11.1	MoEHE school teachers' responsibilities compared to those of independent school teachers 2004–2010	194
11.2	Samples of continuous changes and decisions made by the SEC 2004–2015 (adopted from Sawalhi, 2019)	195
12.1	Authorship trends in the review	216
12.2	Gender authorship trends in the review	221
12.3	Topical coverage (the total number of topics exceeded 132, because most of the articles addressed more than one topic)	223

List of Editors and Contributors

Khalid H. Arar, PhD, is a Professor of Educational Leadership and Policy in the College of Education at Texas State University. Dr. Arar's international and comparative research program is rooted at the nexus of social justice, equity, and diversity in K-12 and Higher Education. Using this academic prism he has conducted studies in the Middle East, Europe, the Mediterranean, and North America. He was a winner of Routledge's prestigious Choice Outstanding Academic Title in 2021, and received CIES Study Abroad Best Book Award in 2022. At Texas State, he received Presidential Award for Excellence in Scholarly/Creative Activity, from the College of Education, and was nominated as a finalist in 2022. In 2023, he was awarded the title of Honorary Professor of International Studies, and recently AERA Division A honored him with the Excellence in Research Award, 2023. Dr. Arar is the Associate Editor of the *International Journal of Leadership in Education*; *Journal of Equity in Education and Society*, and editor-in-chief of the book series *Educational Leadership for an Equitable, Resilient and Sustainable Future* (Routledge).

Selahattin Turan, PhD, is a Professor of Educational Leadership and Policy at Bursa Uludağ University, Turkey. He received his MA and PhD degrees from the Ohio University, the Gladys W. and David H. Patton College of Education in Educational Leadership in 1998. He was past president of the International Society for Educational Planning, past chair of the Division A-Ad Hoc International Committee of the AERA, founding president of ECO Educational Institute, and the dean of College of Education at Eskisehir Osmangazi University. His primary professional interests are theory in leadership, educational policy, and sociology of technology and alternative perspectives in education. Dr. Turan has published widely in a variety of scholarly journals and presented papers at the annual meetings of AERA, ISEP, NCPEA, and UCEA.

Dr. Sedat Gümüş is an Associate Professor in the Department of Educational Policy and Leadership and a Research Fellow of the Asia Pacific Centre for Leadership and Change at the EdUHK. Before moving to Hong Kong, he was an Associate Professor at Aarhus University, Denmark. He received his PhD from the Department of Educational Administration at Michigan State University, USA, in 2012 and his Master's from the same institution in 2010. He currently serves on the Rowman & Littlefield School Leadership Book Series advisory board and undertakes editorial responsibilities in several academic journals.

Dr. Abdellatif Sellami is the Director of the Education Research Center, College of Education at Qatar University in Qatar. Previously, he served as an Educational Programs Manager at Qatar Foundation in Qatar and a senior researcher and a faculty member at Qatar University. Prior to that, he had served as a faculty member at different universities in the UAE, the UK, and North Africa. His current research interests include K-12 education, higher education, STEM, and critical discourse analysis. He has published numerous journal articles and book chapters on STEM, higher education, and STEM. Currently, he is working on several large-scale research projects on K-12 STEM education, students' career aspirations, education and well-being, and education for sustainable development.

Julia Mahfouz, PhD, is an Associate Professor and Director of the Prosocial Leader Lab in the School of Education and Human Development at the University of Colorado Denver. Her research explores the social, emotional, and cultural dynamics of educational settings placing specific emphasis on mindfulness-based programs and adult social and emotional competencies, specifically that of school administrators and the integration of systemic SEL into principal preparation programs. Her research also examines the relationships among policy, school improvement, social and emotional learning, and international education. Her research has been published in journals such as *Journal of Educational Administration, Educational Management Administration and Leadership, International Journal of Leadership in Education, Education and Urban Society, Mindfulness, College Student Affairs Journal*, and in practitioner outlets such as *The Learning Professional and Education Canada*.

Dr. Mehmet Şükrü Bellibaş is currently working as an Alexander von Humboldt Senior Researcher at Leuphana University in Lüneburg, Germany and as an Associate Professor in the Department of Educational Administration at Adıyaman University, Turkiye. His research interests include comparative and international education, educational leadership, school improvement, and teacher professional learning.

Dr. İbrahim Hakan Karataş, after his BA and MA in Turkish Language and Literature, earned his PhD in Educational Leadership. Karatas is currently working as an Associate Professor in the Department of Educational

Administration, College of Education Sciences, Istanbul Medeniyet University, İstanbul, Turkiye. His research interests include educational leadership, educational policies, educational planning, and non-governmental organizations.

Dr. Elif Aydoğdu graduated from Primary Education Science Teaching program at Eskişehir Osmangazi University. She earned her PhD degree in the field of Educational Administration. She is currently working as an Assistant Professor in the Department of Educational Administration, College of Education, Eskişehir Osmangazi University, Eskişehir, Turkiye. Her research interests include school administrators and teachers professional development, school culture, organizational socialization, organizational change, and leadership.

Dr. Waheed Hammad is an Associate Professor of Educational Administration and Leadership in the College of Education at Sultan Qaboos University (Oman) and Damietta University (Egypt). He received his PhD in School Management from the University of East Anglia, UK. The focus of his PhD research was on institutional and cultural barriers to shared decision-making in Egyptian schools. His research interests include educational leadership and management, instructional supervision, systematic reviews, and teachers and principals' professional development. His international publication outlets include *Educational Administration Quarterly*; *Educational Management, Administration & Leadership*; *School Leadership & Management*; *International Journal of Leadership in Education*; *Leadership and Policy in Schools*; and *Compare*. Dr. Hammad is a member of the British Educational Leadership, Management and Administration Society, and the Gulf Comparative Education Society.

Dr. Eman Ahmed is an Associate Professor in Educational Leadership and Management in the College of Education at Menoufia University (Egypt). She received her PhD from the Pennsylvania State University. Throughout her career, she has worked as a lecturer, researcher, and professor in the USA and Egypt. Her research interests include educational leadership and management, organizational development, ethical decision-making in organizations, and issues on equity and diversity. She has published in leading educational research journals including *Educational Management Administration and Leadership*, *School Leadership and Management*, *International Journal of Leadership in Education*, *Management in Education*, and *Education, Citizenship and Social Justice*. Her most recent research publication includes a systematic review of authentic leadership literature in educational research from 1997 to 2021.

xiv List of Editors and Contributors

Dr. Maysaa Barakat is an Associate Professor in the Department of Educational Leadership and Research Methodology at Florida Atlantic University (FAU) and the President of the Florida Association of Professors of Educational Leadership (FAPEL). She received her Master's and PhD degrees in Educational Leadership from Auburn University, Alabama. She has over 15 years of school leadership experience, both in Egypt and the USA. Dr. Barakat's research focuses on issues of cultural competence, identity, social justice, educational leadership preparation, and international education. Dr. Barakat coordinates a partnership between Egypt and FAU and has been leading professional development opportunities for educators in Egypt since 2016.

Dr. Rania Sawalhi has more than 20 years of experience in education (K-12 and higher education) as she worked as a teacher, vice principal, principal of an international school, strategic manager, researcher, and lecturer. Rania has won several awards such as ICSEI/JPCC 2020 Innovation Award for designing a female empowerment program that included career readiness and social innovation. She was a Study UK alumni awards finalist for social impact. In 2019, Rania completed her PhD Educational Leadership from the University of Warwick (UK) and published a number of research and books in peer-reviewed journals. Rania is a co-founder of Eduenterprise, a non-profit organization registered in the USA and has launched the Educational Leadership Lab applying the design thinking approach and launched Rushd educational leadership coaching e-platform. She is co-founder of WomenEdMENA, LIFE, and ICSEI_ELN co-coordinator. Currently, she is the Deputy Director of Learning and Outreach at the Children's Museum of Qatar.

Dr. Yara Yasser Hilal is a lecturer (Assistant Professor) at the School of Education and Social Work in Sydney University-Australia. She holds a PhD in Education from the University of Leicester, UK, and a Masters degree in Educational Leadership from McGill University, Canada. She comes from a practitioner background with more than 16 years experience in school leadership. She has led and participated in a number of funded research projects in the areas of principal and teacher agency and teacher leadership and knowledge production in the field of educational leadership in the Arab world. Her areas of research include school-based improvement, educational leadership, and management, teachers and principals' continuous professional learning, and critical and cultural approaches to leadership. Her international publication outlets include *Educational Management, Administration & Leadership; International Journal of Leadership in Education; Educational Action Research, and International Journal of Educational Research*.

List of Editors and Contributors xv

Ms. Muna Khamis Al-Alawi is PhD candidate at the College of Education, Sultan Qaboos University, where she specializes in educational administration. Ms. Alawi holds the position of a school administration supervisor in the Ministry of Education, Sultanate of Oman since 2018. Her current research focuses on teacher leadership and commitment to change.

Dr. Amal Abdulwahab Alsaleh is an Associate Professor in the Department of Educational Administration in the College of Education at Kuwait University. She earned her PhD from Pennsylvania State University. Her research focuses on educational leadership, school improvement and reform studies, professional development, and educational policy.

Dr. Mayamin Altae holds PhD from The University of Leicester in Education, MA in Educational Technology from The University of Manchester, and BA in English Language and Literature & Qualified UK Teacher Status (QTS) from Bradford University. She also holds a Qualified FE Teacher Training and Skills Status (QTLS) from Calderdale College in West Yorkshire, UK. Mayamin has more than 20 years of professional experience in teaching and researching in the higher education sectors in the UK and the Middle East and North Africa (MENA). Dr. Mayamin has been advocating for the embedding of technology in the teaching practices at both the university and the school levels and she has designed and delivered educational technology projects in the UK, Kazakhstan, Algeria, Saudi Arabia, Iraq, and the UAE. Dr. Mayamin is also a member of highly prestigious educational research associations in the UK. Dr. Mayamin is currently advising government departments and associations across the Middle East on supporting the implementation of the United Nations Sustainable Development Goals (2030), mainly Goal 4 Quality Education.

Aref Al-Attari is a Professor in the Department of Educational Administration and Foundations, Faculty of Education, Yarmouk University, Jordan. He worked at various institutions such as Sultan Qaboos University, Oman, and International Islamic University Malaysia. He holds PhD in Educational Leadership from University of Durham, UK. His research interests include Educational Leadership, Higher Education, and Foundations of Education.

Dr. Soheil Salha is an Associate Professor of Curriculum and Instruction with specialization in the field of Educational Technology (Math Education). His studies focus on teacher education, curriculum analysis, using software in learning and teaching Mathematics, school design, and higher education issues.

Dr. Saida Affouneh is an Associate Professor working as Deputy President for digitalization and e-learning. She is also the Dean of the Faculty of Education. Her research interest include quality of education and online learning in crisis situations.

Dr. Mohammed Elmeski is a Comparative International Development Education Senior Policy Advisor. His most recent positions include Clinical Associate Professor at Arizona State University, and Senior Researcher at American Institutes for Research. In 2020, Dr. Elmeski was the Co-Chair of the 2020 edition of the International Congress for School Effectiveness and Improvement held in Morocco. His professional expertise includes the design and implementation of educational reform, operational management, change leadership, monitoring and evaluation, and capacity development. His research interests include community engagement, educational leadership, teacher preparation, social-emotional learning, and school transformation in marginalized neighborhoods. Dr. Elmeski earned his PhD in Comparative International Development Education and Program Evaluation from the University of Minnesota, Twin Cities. He has led a diverse career that includes teaching, research, evaluation, technical assistance, and project leadership in the USA, Africa, Central America, MENA, and South Asia.

Dr. Asmaa E. Al-Fadala is the Director of Research and Content Development at the World Innovation Summit for Education (WISE) and a Visiting Fellow at Cambridge University. She has over 25 years of experience in K-12 education, higher education, and policy development. She is leading a number of projects and initiatives at Qatar Foundation, including the Empowering Leaders of Learning (ELL), the Agile Leaders of Learning Innovation Network (ALL-IN), and the WISE Innovation Hub Project. Her research interests include leadership for learning, entrepreneurship education, teacher professional development, educational reform, innovation in education and SDGs. She is a widely published author in the field of educational leadership and policy. Dr. Alfadala holds PhD and MPhil degrees in Educational Leadership and Policy from Cambridge University.

Dr. Rima Karami is an Associate Professor of Educational Administration, Policy, and Leadership at the American University of Beirut. She is the Chairperson of the Department of Education AUB and the Program Advisor for the Educational Management and Leadership program. She holds a Doctorate in Education from Portland State University with a specialty in K-12 Educational Administration and Supervision with a focus on school principalship, organizational change, and educational policy. Karami is the Director and the Principal Investigator of the TAMAM project that has partners in more than 72 schools in nine Arab countries. TAMAM is funded through a grant by the Arab Thought Foundation and received additional funding from the LORE Foundation, Taawon Association, and Al Maymouna organization and was one of the recipients of the 2021–2022 UNESCO-HAMDAN prize for teacher development. Karami currently serves as the Chairperson of the executive committee of Shamaa (Arab Information Educational Network) and as the coordinator for the education sector in Khaddit Beirut.

1 Demystifying Educational Leadership and Administration in the Middle East and North Africa/Editorial Introduction

Khalid Arar, Selahattin Turan, Sedat Gümüş, Abdellatif Sellami, and Julia Mahfouz

Introduction

In the 21st century, educational systems are continually required to adapt to new changes and challenges and, many times, even to contradicting demands from the public and policy-makers, given the globalization of the world economy (Arar et al., 2021; Brooks & Normore, 2010; Lingard, 2021). This trend is blurring the boundaries of the knowledge of what used to be discrete at local or national levels of educational systems (Arnova et al., 2013; Waite et al., 2015). In particular, the globalization of education is having a tremendous impact on what is taught and tested in less developed countries, their policy formation, and organizational forms of schooling (Arar et al., 2021; Mazawi & Sultana, 2010; Oplatka & Arar, 2017; Waite, 2010). While many scholars discuss the effects of globalization on education in general, less work has explored the impact of globalization on education systems in the Middle East and North Africa (MENA) region. Some have lauded its benefits as a means of promoting understanding and learning within the world community, while others have warned against intellectual and cultural colonization and the potential commodification of education (Abdeljalil, 2004; Arar et al., 2021; Darling-Hammond & Lieberman, 2012; Giroux, 2005; Kelly, 2009; McLaren, 2007; Suárez-Orozco & Qin-Hilliard, 2004; Waite et al., 2005). These macro processes radiate onto education systems in different world states and regions either directly, in states that take an active part in the formation of globalization, or indirectly and passively, in states influenced at different levels by these global processes in designing their national educational policy, and its implementation and enactment by educational leaders in different levels (Arar et al., 2017; Oplatka & Arar, 2017). The significance of these processes is examined at length in this book.

In *Demystifying Educational Leadership and Administration in the Middle East and North Africa*, the first volume of our book series, we aimed at twofold: (1) to examine how educational policy and leadership is constructed and enacted in the context of the MENA region, by examining educational policy, leadership, and administration dynamic and scholarship in this distinctive upheaval context; and (2) to explore how educational leadership tries to engender the gap between national, social-cultural context, and global values or contested political projects, with a concern for social justice, equity, and political inclusion. This region is chosen as it presents a distinctive culture with numerous political and contextual challenges (e.g., war, political turmoil, glocal contested projects). Although the label "Middle East and North Africa" (MENA) is used to denote a large area spanning the regions between Africa and Asia, the MENA region encompasses many diverse ethnic groups with different religions, languages, and cultures including Arabs, Turks, Persians, Kurds, Azeris, Copts, Muslims, Christians, Marronites, Jews, Druze, and so on. The educational systems in these lands were formed out of this colorful and multitudinous landscape (Abdeljalil, 2004). As a result, educational leaders and policy-makers in these countries face serious challenges in responding to the diverse populations they serve. These challenges are inevitably attenuated during the political and social upheavals that rock MENA periodically, especially over the last two decades (Akin, 2016; Arar et al., 2017; Arar et al., 2019; Korany, 2011).

Historically, during the 19th and the beginning of the 20th centuries, most countries of the region were under European colonization and that of the Ottoman Empire. Though the colonizing authorities were the first to introduce compulsory education, access to modern (European-style) education was restricted to political and religious elite groups (Abdeljalil, 2004). Colonial education in many ways was designed to shape local intellectual development and to limit the ability of local actors to challenge the colonizers' political control, while enhancing the influence of Western culture (Oplatka & Arar, 2016). Its purpose was to support the colonizer's major interest to advance a dominant and superior Western culture, while annexing further territories in the MENA imposing restrictions on national movements (Arnova et al., 2013; Heyneman, 1997). Often, "Western" initiatives to promote education have ignored particular realities (Arar et al., 2017; Arnova et al., 2013). During the postcolonial era, education spread as a result of significant social changes and the rise of indigenous elites as ruling powers (Mazawi & Sultana, 2010). The willingness of national governments to build a strong nation made the acquisition of literacy a necessity for maximizing human capital. Most scholars and policy-makers in the region have stressed the importance of investing in education in order to promote sustained economic development (Sellami et al., 2022).

In light of popular notions of globalization, the MENA region has always been a place where the informal "soft" inter-cultural exchange of knowledge has taken place. Thus, the educational systems of MENA countries clearly reflect the struggle between advocates of the globalization of education and those who view globalization as a threat to national identity and culture (Arar et al., 2017; Arnova et al., 2013). The educational arena has witnessed multiple schisms (Arar, 2020; Hallinger & Hammad, 2017; Ibrahim, 2010) representing the different ideologies existing within many countries in this region. These schisms are manifested in the division which exists between:

> modern secular education and religious education, and between traditional teaching and learning methods, and extreme versions of French centralization, a deformed version of British inspection and exams, a socialist legacy of "free" and equitable access to education, and Western capitalist (neoliberal) notions of privatization and active-learning pedagogies.
>
> (Ibrahim, 2010, p. 510)

The ability and legacy of knowledge produced in the field of educational administration in the West to solve problems that educational systems and schools face have been critically discussed and analyzed since the early 1950s. All these discussions and critical reviews of educational administration have revealed a serious intellectual accumulation about the usefulness of the knowledge produced in the field (Boyan, 1988; Foster, 1986; Oplatka, 2010). On the other hand, the knowledge produced, research, and scholarship in the field of educational administration in the MENA region seem disorganized and not critically reviewed. That is, the relationship between the knowledge produced in educational policy and leadership and its relation to practice has been a subject of critical examination in the context of the larger social, political, and economic arrangement of the region. It is observed that the knowledge in the field of educational administration produced by scholars in the MENA region has reached a certain point (Hallinger & Hammad, 2017; Oplatka & Arar, 2017). However, there are no scholarly associations, organized bodies, and academic/research journals where the scholars and researchers of the MENA region will come together. One of the aims of this book series is to bring together the academic works and knowledge produced by scholars in the MENA region.

As noted in many landmark studies, the emergence of educational administration as a science in the West coincides with the beginning of the 19th century. However, the birth and maturation of the field of educational administration as a science await the end of the 1950s. The origin of these developments was shaped by the widely known *theory movement* in educational administration (Culbertson, 1988). The leap in the development of the field, especially in the Anglo-Saxon countries these days, corresponds to the breakthrough between 1951 and 1966, the academic studies, associations, and annual meetings produced research and scholarship in educational administration in these years caused the field to develop even faster (Culbertson, 1988; Hallinger, 2013; Hoy, 1982). Educational administration and leadership (EAL) have also encountered issues of credibility within the academy. Educational leadership has a rich history of epistemological debate. The "Theory Movement" of the 1950–1960s and Greenfield's critique of logical empiricism in the 1970s contributed positively to the field and hoped to establish credibility. However, both pieces also had many questions focused on what represents useful knowledge in EAL. As a result of these associations, scholarly works and the production of the book called *Administrative Behavior in Education* (Campbell & Gregg, 1957) and the research and scholarship produced within this framework contributed to the institutionalization of the field of educational administration. As mentioned before, the theory movement claimed that theories have the power to define, explain, and predict the problems in the field of educational administration. In this respect, the problems in practice can only be solved under the guidance of the theory. However, since 1970s, the field of educational administration has brought debates and the boundaries of the field have been questioned and opened to discussion (English, 2002, Foster, 1986; Gumus et al., 2021; Hallinger, 2013).

The paradigm wars of the late 20th century did not exclude EAL (Waite, 2002). The influence of the work is best described in the germinal work of Thomas Barr Greenfield (1973). Thomas Barr Greenfield opposed logical positivism and argued for a humane science of educational administration (e.g., Greenfield & Ribbins, 1993). The rise of Bates' and Foster's critical theory of educational administration in the 1980s, and Evers' and Lakomski's naturalistic coherentism from 1990 to the present time and various forms of post-modernism (English, 2003; Maxcy, 1993), post-structuralism (Niesche, 2014; Niesche & Gowlett, 2019), feminism (Blackmore, 1999; Fuller, 2022), anti-racism (Diem & Welton, 2020; Lopez, 2021; Miller & Callendar, 2019), postcolonialism (Samier, 2021), and relationality (Eacott, 2018), debates about ways of knowing, doing, and being in the social world have been essential to advancing scholarship. In summary, since the 1970s, there has been great diversity in EAL. The last 40 years have observed the division of school effectiveness and school improvement, and educational change not connected to educational administration (e.g., Chapman et al., 2016; Hargreaves et al., 2009) and leadership as the core focus of the field (Thomas, 2006). The shift has had critique (e.g., Eacott, 2018; Lakomski et al., 2017), but questioning of leadership remains marginalized in the field as the core continues to prosper works of literature. Contrary to the West, scholars of the MENA region have not been able to critically evaluate and situate the knowledge produced in the field of administration and educational leadership in the context of large societal arrangements (Oplatka & Arar, 2017; Oplatka & Arar, 2016), and there is no opportunity created so far for the scholars of the region to come together and critically examine the knowledge and scholarship produced. The knowledge produced and developments about research and scholarship in the field of educational administration in other countries and their effects on scholarship and educational administration in terms of theoretical, ontological, and methodical issues are subject to critical examination and discussion in the MENA region.

Thus, *Demystifying Educational Leadership and Administration in the Middle East and North Africa*, as presented in its first-hand chapters, is an international volume that aims to contribute to the understanding of *how* educational leadership and administration (ELA) is constructed in this distinctive region; it explores the development of ELA as a discipline. While the MENA is not a unified entity but is rather composed of a mix of different countries with distinct traits that differ in terms of culture, society, organization, and educational arrangements, we believe that some commonalities and valuable patterns might also emerge. Through each chapter, we seek to understand *How* ELA as a field of study has been developed? *How* the related knowledge base has contributed to policy and practices? *What* are the current state of the art, the shortcomings, and the expectations for the future both in terms of the field and its relation to the policy and practice? *How* ELA in each country bridges the gap between particular and universal values? Especially with the challenges in the socio-political context of those countries, how ELA contribute and navigate education systems, and yet continue to concern themselves with social justice, equity, and political inclusion; *How* has recent political turmoil in the MENA influenced local ELA? What are the lessons to be learned in terms of policy, leadership, and practice?

Scholars from the MENA region whom we believe can move the knowledge base on schools and leadership, policy, and administration in this challenging school contexts were invited for contribution, seeking a geographic representation of each state in this region, whenever it is possible.

This book showcases a collection of contributions that yield inside perspectives on the ELA landscape in the context of the MENA region. The selection of chapters for inclusion in this edited book was deliberate, emanating from the need to provide a rich, informed, and multi-perspective vista on school leadership and administration in the MENA region, bringing together multiple research, policy, and practice insights. In order to reach a wide-ranging audience, the authors tackle salient issues and offer suggestions for educational policy and practice.

The case studies presented in this edited book portray vivid examples of some of the key challenges facing ELA in many MENA countries while identifying important strengths and weakness in the areas of research and scholarship, which may guide and inform policy and practice. The significance of the studies presented in this book lies in their treatment of the dynamics and intricacies of international and local forces. Against the backlash of these influences, the chapters illustrate examples of contextualized educational policy and leadership. The book has direct relevance to educators, policy-makers, researchers, and others.

This chapter provides a context for the remainder of the book and sets the scene for many of the issues tackled in the following chapters. This chapter takes the reader on a journey spanning boundaries, presenting background information on the construction and enactment of educational policy, leadership, and administration in the MENA region. The chapter details how educational leadership is influenced by myriad pressures in the region, which continues to be fraught with myriad social, political, religious, and ethnic conflicts. The chapter further engages the reader by delving into the ways in which educational leadership is positioned at the intersection of local, regional, and global forces.

Focusing on educational leadership and management (EDLM) in Türkiye, Chapter 2 critically evaluates policy, practice, and research in the country. After setting the tone to the remainder of the chapter based on background information related to the education system in Türkiye, Bellibaş, Karataş, and Aydoğdu examine the establishment and development of EDLM as a new field of research. In discussing the tensions between competing elements and the various factors that shape the system of education in Türkiye, the authors further analyze the state of research on EAL and probe the missing links between policy, practice, and research. In this chapter, the authors take the reader a step further by also discussing the evolution and characteristics of higher education in Türkiye.

In Chapter 3, "Examining the Knowledge Base in Educational Administration and Leadership in Egypt: A Systematic Review of Published Research Literature", Hammad, Ahmed, and Barakat provide a systematic review of EAL in a different Middle Eastern setting, Egypt. In looking at the research published on EAL over the past two decades, the authors employ content analysis to draw a portrait of EAL in Egypt and highlight dominant themes and features that characterize existing research on EAL in the Egyptian context. The chapter also engages in an informed discussion of the findings against the backdrop of the international EAL knowledge base with a view to suggesting policy recommendations.

Chapter 4 looks closely at ELA in modern Iraq. Here, Altae gives the reader a detailed account of the development of ELA as an important field of study and practice in the country and examines salient challenges and future prospects for ELA in Iraq. Altae digs into how ELA has undergone fundamental transformations in Iraq over the past 50 years, ascribing these changes to a range of internal and external crises the country has been embroiled in. The reader gets to learn how the paucity of research evidence on ELA in Iraq thwarts attempts by successive governments to ascertain that the implementation of ELA in real-life situations is guided by research. The author then proceeds to argue that current leadership practices in the country are not driven by innovation and creativity, thus resulting in ineffective leadership.

In Chapter 5, Elmeski provides an alternative, North African perspective on ELA in the context of Morocco and presents an informed rich account of the evolution of ELA in the country. He provides a detailed description of ELA reforms that have taken place in Morocco's education. Following a general overview of the available ELA literature, Elmeski discusses the development of ELA in Morocco and how it has been affected by the processes of educational decentralization and governance. Drawing on Potter and Borough's (2005) capacity building model, Elmeski proposes tangible suggestions for the improvement of ELA in Morocco and contemplates key lessons learned which could benefit ELA policy, practice, and research.

In Chapter 6, the reader gets to know about ELA in another North African setting, i.e., Algeria. Here, Lahmar and Abbou examine different aspects of both policy and practice, discussing the various changes and educational reforms that Algeria's education system has witnessed since the country gained its independence in 1962. Using semi-structured interviews conducted with female academics at five different universities in Algeria, the authors decipher participants' views of policy implementation at the levels of administrative and pedagogical leadership. In so doing, Lahmar and Abbou help us better understand ELA and the gap between Algeria's educational policy reforms and practitioners' practices. The chapter also shows the impact of local social and political influences on ELA and stresses the importance of taking these influences into account in future educational reforms.

Chapter 7, "Educational Administration and Leadership in Jordan: A Retrospective-Prospective Approach", by Al Attari and Bani Eissa overviews the education system in Jordan and addresses the way EAL has been redirected to respond to the needs of the country's transition to the knowledge society. The chapter enhances our understanding of EAL by furnishing a critical assessment of the official discourse surrounding educational reforms in Jordan as well as demonstrating the different transformations characterizing EAL. Using a content analysis of official EAL documents, the authors problematize the discourse surrounding EAL and identify key themes underlying these documents, including decentralization, the devolution of authority, and theories of leadership.

Chapter 8, "Principalship in Lebanon: The Unsung Heroes", by Julia Mahfouz demonstrates key defining characteristics of the roles of school principalship in Lebanon, including expectations, responsibilities, and policies. She paints a picture of the roles and experiences of school principals in the country and offers an analytical review of the themes of mentorship, induction, and licensure of principalship in Lebanon and reflects on important barriers and enablers affecting principalship in the country. Building on informal discussions with practicing school principals and experts in Lebanon, Mahfouz provides a critical analysis of her findings and identifies salient gaps in the existing policies and practices, and proposes recommendations for educational policy.

In Chapter 9, Affouneh and Salha write about educational leadership from a Palestinian standpoint, first offering a historical perspective on the education system in Palestine while also outlining how political forces causing tensions between ownership, policy, and leadership in the country. The authors then discuss the main advantages associated with the educational leadership model established in Palestine following the founding of the country's Ministry of Education and further explain existing challenges that call for pertinent crisis management policies. Affouneh and Salha elaborate on the disconnects and the ongoing discrepancies between national policies and experiences and the global norms and practices and go on to propose relevant policy recommendations to address existing leadership issues.

Chapter 10, "Educational Administration and Policy in Kuwait: A Reflection on Decades of Reforms and Challenges", by Alsaleh examines educational administration and policy developments in the Gulf State of Kuwait. To give readers background information, he first provides a historical overview of the evolution of education and discusses the current reality, role, and structure of the Ministry of Education (MoE). Following a close look at school leadership and school structure in Kuwait, Alsaleh examines the country's successive political reforms, disputing their effective role and arguing that they have laid the ground for multiple challenges to education policy. The author's contention, nonetheless, is that the MoE policies played an important part in the promotion of public education in Kuwait and the growth of EDLM as a discipline. The MoE policies, Alsaleh suggests, have also played a key role in contributing to knowledge production at the national and international levels.

In Chapter 11 titled "K-12 Educational Leadership and Administration in Qatar: Lessons Learned", Sellami, Sawalhi, and Al-Fadala take an analytical look at the concepts of leadership and administration in another Arabian Gulf State, Qatar, focusing more specifically on educational policy and practice. Drawing on semi-structured interview data collected from a pool of educators, educational leaders, and policy-makers in Qatar, the authors investigate the expectations and roles of educational leaders and take us through the practices they engage in as is portrayed in the individual voices of the leaders. Their findings raise concerns that despite a series of professional development programs integral to numerous educational reforms, confusion still governs the usage of the concepts of EDLM, policies, and guidelines. Stressing the value of developing teacher and student agency and well-being, the authors stress the need for an environment that empowers teachers and supports teacher leadership.

Chapter 12 focuses on another Gulf State example as it explores EAL in Oman. Hilal and Al-Alawi present a systematic review of literature that has addressed EAL in the context of Oman, considering their present chapter as a response to calls from within the field of EAL which emphasize the need to produce localized scholarship. The authors' main argument is that there is a demand for contextualized research on EAL in Oman. In this chapter, the authors present a review of research articles that have been published in Oman in both English and Arabic over the past two decades. Based on their quantitative analysis, Hilal and Al-Alawi's findings echo those reported in other research conducted on EAL in the broader Arab region.

References

Abdeljalil, A. (2004). Education in the Middle-East and North Africa: The current situation and future challenges. *International Education Journal*, 5(2), 144–153.

Akin, U. (2016). Innovation efforts in education and school administration: Views of Turkish school administrators. *Eurasian Journal of Educational Research*, 63, 243–260.

Arar, K. (2020). Educational Administration in the Middle-East. In R. Papa (Eds.), *Oxford research encyclopedia*, Oxford Encyclopedia of Education,Oxford University Press (pp. 1–26). 10.1093/acrefore/9780190264093.013.672

Arar, K., Brooks, J., & Bogotch, I. (2019). *Education, immigration and migration: Policy, leadership and praxis for changing world*. Emerald.

Arar, K., Orucu, D., & Wilkinson, J. (2021). *Neoliberalism and education systems in conflict: Exploring challenges across the globe*. Routledge.

Arar, K., Turan, S., Barakat, M., & Oplatka, I. (2017). The characteristics of educational leadership in the Middle East: A comparative analysis of three nation-states. In D. Waite, & I. Bogotch (Eds.), *International handbook of leadership in education*. (pp. 355–373). John Wiley & Sons.

Arnova, R.F., Torres, C.A., & Franz, S. (2013). *Comparative education: The dialectic of global and local*. Rowan & Littlefield.

Blackmore, J. (1999). *Troubling women: Feminism, leadership and educational change*. Open University Press.

Boyan, N. J., & Boyan, N. (1988). *Handbook of research on educational administration: A project of the American Educational Research Association*. Longman Publishing.

Brooks, J. S., & Normore, A. H. (2010). Educational leadership and globalization: Literacy for a glocal perspective. *Educational Policy, 24*(1), 52–82.

Campbell, R. F., & Gregg, R. T. (Eds.). (1957). *Administrative behavior in education*. Harper.

Chapman, C., Reynolds, D., Muijs, D., Sammons, P., Teddlie, C., & Clarke, P. (Eds.). (2016). *The Routledge international handbook of educational effectiveness and improvement: Research, policy and practice*. Routledge.

Culbertson, J. A. (1988). A century's quest for a knowledge base. *Handbook of research on educational administration* (pp. 3–26). Longman Publishing.

Darling-Hammond, L., & Lieberman, A. (2012). *Teacher education around the world: Changing policies and practices (teacher quality and school development)*. Routledge, Taylor & Francis.

Diem, S., & Welton, A. D. (2020). *Anti-racist educational leadership and policy: Addressing racism in public education*. Routledge.

Eacott, S. (2018). *Beyond leadership: A relational approach to organizational theory in education*. Springer.

English, F. W. (2002). The point of scientificity, the fall of the epistemological dominos, and the end of the field of educational administration. *Studies in Philosophy and Education, 21*(2), 109–136.

English, F. W. (2003). *The postmodern challenge to the practice of educational administration*. Charles C Thomas Publisher.

Foster, W. (1986). *Paradigms and promises: New approaches to educational administration*. Prometheus Books.

Fuller, K. (2022). *Feminist perspectives on contemporary educational leadership*. Routledge.

Giroux, H. A. (2005). The terror of neoliberalism: Rethinking the significance of cultural politics. *College Literature, 32*(1), 1–19.

Greenfield, T. B. (1973). Organizations as social inventions. Paper presented at the 58th Annual Meeting of the American Educational Research Association, New Orleans, LA.

Greenfield, T. B., & Ribbins, P. (Eds.). (1993). *Greenfield on educational administration: Towards a humane science*. Routledge.

Gumus, S., Arar, K., & Oplatka, I. (2021). Review of international research on school leadership for social justice, equity and diversity. *Journal of Education Administration & History, 53*(1), 81–99.

Hallinger, P. (2013). A conceptual framework for systemic reviews of research in educational leadership and management. *Journal of Educational Administration*, *51*(2), 126–149.

Hallinger, P., & W. Hammad. (2017). Knowledge production on educational leadership and management in Arab societies: A systematic review of research. *Educational Management Administration and Leadership*, Online First, *47*(1), 20–36.

Hargreaves, A., Lieberman, A., Fullan, M., & Hopkins, D. (Eds.). (2009). *Second international handbook of educational change*. Springer.

Heyneman, S. P. (1997). The quality of education in the Middle-East and North Africa (MENA). *International Journal of Education*, *17*(4), 449–466.

Hoy, W. K. (1982). Recent developments in theory and research in educational administration. *Educational Administration Quarterly*, *18*(3), 1–11.

Ibrahim, A. S. (2010). The politics of educational transfer and policymaking in Egypt. *Prospects: Quarterly Review of Comparative Education*, *40*(4), 499–515.

Kelly, A. (2009, March). Globalization and education: A review of conflicting perspectives and their effect on policy and professional practice in the UK. *Globalization, Societies & Education*, *7*(1), 51–68. 10.1080/14767720802677333

Korany, O. M. (2011). Reformative changes in educational leadership in post-revolutionary Egypt: A critical appraisal. *Educational Research*, *2*(10). 17–31. Retrieved from http://www.interesjournals.org/full-articles/reformative-changes-in-educational-leadership-in-post-revolutionary-egypt-a-critical-appraisal.pdf?view=inline.

Lakomski, G., Eacott, S., & Evers, C. W. (Eds.). (2017). *Questioning leadership: New directions for educational organizations*. Routledge.

Lingard, B. (2021). *Globalisation and education: Theorising and researching changing imbrications in education policy*. Routledge.

Lopez, A. E. (2021). Examining alternative school leadership practices and approaches: A decolonising school leadership approach. *Intercultural Education*, *32*(4), 359–367. 10.1080/14675986.2021.1889471.

Maxcy, S. J. (1993). *Postmodern school leadership: Meeting the crisis in educational administration*. Praeger.

Mazawi, A., & Sultana, R. (Eds.) (2010). *Education and the Arab 'World': Political projects, struggles, and geometries of power*. Routledge.

McLaren, A. C. (2007). Designing distance instruction for the Arab world. *Distance Learning*, *4*(3), 17–21.

Miller, P., & Callendar, C. (Eds.). (2019). *Race, education and educational leadership in England: An integrated analysis*. Bloomsbury.

Niesche, R. (2014). *Deconstructing educational leadership: Derrida and Lyotard*. Routledge.

Niesche, R., & Gowlett, C. (2019). *Social, critical and political theories for educational leadership*. Springer.

Oplatka, I. (2010). *The legacy of educational administration: A historical analysis of an academic field*. Peter Lang.

Oplatka, I., & Arar, K. (2016). The field of educational administration as an arena of knowledge production: Some implications for Turkish field members. *Research in Educational Administration & Leadership*, *1*(2), 2–18.

Oplatka, I., & Arar, K. (2017). The research on educational leadership and management in the Arab world since the 1990s: A systematic review. *Review of Education*, *5*(3), 267–307.

Samier, E. A. (2021). Critical and postcolonial approaches to educational administration curriculum and pedagogy. In E. A. Samier, E. S. Elkaleh, & W. Hammad (Eds.), *Internationalisation of educational administration and leadership curriculum* (pp. 47–68). Emerald Publishing.

Sellami, A., Arar, K., & Sawalhi, R. (2022). *Higher education and scientific research in the Arabian Gulf States: Opportunities, aspirations, and challenges.* Taylor & Francis.

Suárez-Orozco, M. M., & Qin-Hilliard, D. (Eds.). (2004). *Globalization: Culture and education in the new millennium.* University of California Press.

Thomas, A. R. (2006). New waves of leadership: A retrospect. In L. Smith, & D. Riley (Eds.), *New waves of leadership: Australian Council for Educational Leaders yearbook 2006* (pp. 10–15). Australian Council for Educational Leaders.

Waite, D. (2002). "The paradigm wars" in educational administration: An attempt at transcendence. *International Studies in Educational Administration, 30*(1), 66–81.

Waite, D. (2010). On the shortcoming of our organizational forms: With implications for educational change and school improvement. *School Leadership & Management, 30*(3), 225–248.

Waite, D., Moos, L., Sugrue, C., & Lew, C. (2005). Globalization and its effects on educational leadership, higher education and educational policy. In: J, Zada (Ed.), *International handbook on globalization, education & policy* (pp. 279–292). Springer.

Waite, D., Rodríguez, G., & Wadende, A. (2015). Globalization and the business of educational reform. In J. Zajda (Ed.), *Second international handbook in globalization, education and policy research* (pp. 353–374). Springer.

2 Educational Leadership and Management in Türkiye

A Critical Review of Policy, Practice, and Research

Mehmet Şükrü Bellibaş,
İbrahim Hakan Karataş, and Elif Aydoğdu

Introduction

This chapter focuses on the past and current policy, practice, and research within the field of educational leadership and management (EDLM) in Türkiye. Scholars agree that when interpreting current educational developments, researchers should also analyze the formation phases of each society's own past dynamics and current issues with respect to the specific local conditions and context. In addition, the national and global aspects of these developments should be analyzed holistically according to social, cultural, philosophical, economic, political, and anthropological perspectives. Therefore, in the first part of this chapter, we present extensive background information on Türkiye's social and cultural context before introducing the education system in the course of its historical development. Then, we examine current teacher and administrator training and appointment processes.

A more accurate depiction of current indicators of the field of EDLM in Türkiye can be provided when considering the government's higher education policy over the past two decades. While many new universities have been established since the founding of the Turkish Republic, there has been a tremendous change in the higher education system over the last two decades, with the number of universities more than doubling since the turn of the century. Along with this rapid growth, many graduate students have been trained both in Türkiye and abroad through various programs initiated by the Council of Higher Education (CoHE) and Ministry of National Education (MoNE) to meet the need for teaching staff in higher education institutions. As a result, universities have hired a large number of new personnel in the process. The second part of the chapter discusses the structure and development of higher education in Türkiye. The discussion then shifts to the development of EDLM as a research area in the Turkish context. While the emergence of EDLM in Türkiye can be traced back to the 19th century, it truly transformed as a discipline in the second half of the 20th century. The developments in the field can be divided into the following periods: the establishment era (1953–1983), expansion era (1983–1997), deepening era (1997–2012), and questioning era (2014–present).

DOI: 10.4324/9781003334835-2

With the growth in the field of higher education, both national and international studies in the field of educational management expanded considerably, especially in the last 20 years. Thus, since the beginning of the new millennium, many researchers have conducted studies to examine the state of knowledge production in education management and leadership in Türkiye (e.g., Balcı & Apaydın, 2009; Bellibaş & Gümüş, 2019; Gümüş et al., 2020; Turan et al., 2014, 2016; Yılmaz, 2018). In the third part of the chapter, we synthesize previous reviews of EDLM work presented in theses/dissertations, conference presentations, and articles in both national and international journals. The relevant studies are examined in terms of the scope, topical foci, theoretical framework, and methodological features of the research; while the current state of this knowledge base is defined in terms of social, cultural, and organizational contexts. Finally, we analyze the relevant studies in terms of the relevance/disconnection of three components: current policy, practice, and research in EDLM.

The Social, Cultural, and Political Context

Following the collapse of the Ottoman Empire and the emergence of modern Türkiye, the TBMM government was established based on national sovereignty on April 23, 1920. Then, after the abolition of the sultanate on November 1, 1922, the Republic was proclaimed on October 29, 1923. Various reforms were initiated in many areas throughout this process. Although debates continue to surround the decentralization perspective of Prince Sabahaddin, a sociologist and educator who is considered one of the founders of Turkish education (Akyüz, 2010; Aytaç, 2018; Ergün, 2008; Güneş, 2016; Ünal & Kavuncuoğlu, 2015), the centralist philosophy of the Ottoman Empire was inherited by the Republic of Türkiye and continues to dominate public management to this day (Lamba, 2010). Despite efforts to promote governance, accountability, delegation of authority, and decentralization in Türkiye, centralism remains prominent in the design and implementation of administrative processes. Hierarchy, as a foundational principle of this centralized management approach, clearly impacts the structuring process of institutions and organizations nationwide.

Comparative studies on cultural values (Hofstede, 1980, 2001; Hofstede et al., 2010) have classified Turkish culture as high in power distance, femininity, uncertainty avoidance, and collectivism. Türkiye typically scores average points in the dimension of long- and short-term orientation, which emphasizes the commitment of societies to traditions and norms or to support change in the face of trouble; and in the dimension of indulgence and restraint, which emphasizes the relative freedom or excessive control of social norms in fulfilling individuals' pleasures and desires. Türkiye tends to accept the unequal distribution of power in society and is marked by cultural dimensions that emphasize subordinates' dependence on superiors, adherence and obeyance to overarching values and authority, and moderation of expectations within a hierarchical structure. Turkish society has a feminine culture that embraces values such as tolerance, benevolence, modesty, and sensitivity; attaches importance to relationships and quality of life; and shares the roles of financial gain and care within the family. Turkish society sees uncertain or unpredictable situations as threats and requires explicit or implicit rules to reduce the anxiety that arises in such situations. Türkiye also has a collectivist culture in which people belong to extended families and/or groups that ask them to protect group members in exchange for loyalty, think and act as a unified whole, prioritize interpersonal harmony, and avoid conflict.

From 2007 to 2019, the elderly population and median age in Türkiye increased due to a decrease in fertility and mortality rates. The median age in Türkiye, which was 32 in 2018, increased to 32.4 in just one year (TÜİK, 2021a). Recent mass immigration to the country has also affected national population dynamics. According to international migration statistics, the number of migrants settling in Türkiye increased by 17.2% between 2018 and 2019, with 677,042 individuals migrating to Türkiye that year (TÜİK, 2021b). Türkiye is a dynamic country with a dense young population, a large part of whom live in cities at present.

Educational Context

Education has played a critical role in the history of the Republic of Türkiye. On March 3, 1924, the Law of Unification of Education was enacted, and all schools, including religious schools, were brought under the governance of MoNE. This law ended divisions in education that had existed since the proclamation of the *Tanzimat* during the Ottoman period. On November 1, 1928, the country shifted to using the Latin alphabet, and education became widespread through literacy studies throughout the country (Erdem, 2011). The Republican period brought with it innovations and reforms in the context of higher education. In the first years of the *Tanzimat* Period, officials in the predecessor to the MoNE presented the idea of structuring a *Darülfünun* (university) for teaching all sciences and knowledge in a suitable place in Istanbul (Akyüz, 2010; Binbaşıoğlu, 2019). This institution was transformed into a modern university with the University Reform in 1933. Many new faculty members from Germany began building new frameworks for understanding higher education at that time (Akyüz, 2010; Erdem, 2011). During this period, Atatürk's aims for national, rational, humane, democratic, and contemporary schooling formed the basic principles of education (Akyüz, 2010). Efforts for innovation and change came to the fore at every level of education, grounded in the development and enlightenment of Turkish society.

Türkiye is a democratic, secular, and social state. In accordance with the decisions of the European Union Education Commission, and for the purpose of maintaining harmony with the European Union, compulsory education was increased to 12 years during the 2012–2013 academic year, with the implementation of a 4+4+4 system divided into primary school (1st, 2nd, 3rd, and 4th grade), secondary school (5th, 6th, 7th, and 8th grade), and high school

Table 2.1 Schooling rates by education level in the 2019–2020 academic year

Education levels		Total (%)
Preschool	Age 3–5	41.78
	Age 4–5	52.41
	Age 5	71.22
Primary school		93.62
Secondary school		95.90
High school		85.01
Higher education		43.37

Source: This table was created using MoNE net enrollment rate statistics for 2019–2020.

(9th, 10th, 11th, and 12th grade), respectively. The CoHE confers undergraduate, graduate, and doctorate degrees through state and private universities (National Education Basic Law, 1973). The statistical data given in Table 2.1 demonstrate that the dissemination efforts in education continue, as opportunity gaps persist, particularly at the preschool and higher education levels.

Decisions about education in Türkiye are largely made by the central government. OECD (2018) data indicate that 72.9% of the decisions in public secondary schools in Türkiye are made at the central or state level, 18.8% at the regional or sub-regional level, and 8.3% at the school level. OECD averages for these levels are 34.2%, 5.1%, and 33.7%, respectively. While there is no decision-making at the local level or one shared across multiple levels in Türkiye, these decision rates are at 12.9% and 14.1% on average across OECD nations (OECD, 2018). MoNE's budget for 2021 is 125,396,862,000 TL, which represents 2.57% of the gross domestic product (GDP), or 11.45% of the central government budget. 72.94% of this educational budget is allocated to personnel expenditures, 11.46% to insurance premium expenditures, 7.94% to goods and service purchasing expenditures, 2.98% to current transferals, 4.66% to capital expenditures, and 0.02% to capital transferals (MEB, 2020) (Table 2.2).

Table 2.2 Budget of MoNE

Type of appropriation	Budget of year 2020 (TL)
Ministry of National Education (MoNE)	125,396,862,000
Personnel expenditures	91,467,345,000
Insurance premium expenditures	14,367,680,000
Goods and service purchasing expenditures	9,956,271,000
Current transferals	3,739,169,000
Capital expenditures	5,836,918,000
Capital transferals	29,479,000
Central government budget	1,095,461,000,000
GDP (gross domestic product)	4,872,000,000,000

Source: This table was created using MoNE budget statistics for 2019–2020.

The Teaching Profession and School Principalship

The teacher training process in Türkiye has a deep-rooted history. Today, teaching is the basis of educational management. Selection processes for the teaching profession in Türkiye differ between public and private schools. In order to be appointed as a contract teacher in public schools, a candidate must first obtain a minimum base score from the "Public Personnel Selection Examination." Then, they must participate in the oral exam and are assigned to a vacant position based on their score (MoNE Regulation on Appointment and Relocation of Teachers, 2015; Regulation on Contracted Teacher Employment, 2016). In areas or times where there are not enough teachers, paid teachers are contracted to work only for the course fee for the specified period (The Decision Regarding the Course Hours and Additional Course Hours of the Managers and Teachers of the MoNE, 2006). Private schools, which operate under the control of MoNE through the "Private Education Institutions Law," differ from public schools in that they require payment of tuition and fees. Contracts for teachers working in these institutions are made with the school founder or founder's representative for at least once per calendar year (Private Education Institutions Law, 2007). Private schools solicit and collect job applications themselves and recruit candidates within the criteria they identify such as written exams, oral exams, professional experience, and sample lectures (Ekmen Türkmen, 2014; Ülgen, 2018). However, these criteria and procedures may vary from school to school.

According to Article 43 of the National Education Basic Law No. 1739, teacher training programs must cover three areas: general culture, field education, and professional knowledge. In addition, the Teacher Training and Development Directorate updated the General Competencies for Teaching Profession in 2017 to transform into a triple classification encompassing professional knowledge (field knowledge, field education knowledge, and legislation knowledge), professional skills (planning education and training, creating learning environments, managing the teaching and learning process, and measurement and evaluation), and attitudes and values (national, moral and universal values, approaches to students, communication and cooperation, and personal and professional development).

The number of students in Türkiye pursuing higher degrees in the educational field is quite high. In the 2019–2020 academic year, 214,441 students studying in education programs constituted 11.6% of the total number of students studying for undergraduate degrees nationwide (ERG, 2020). According to the 2018 OECD Teaching and Learning International Survey (TALIS), Türkiye is the country with the youngest average age of teachers (35.5 years old, respectively). The average age of secondary school teachers is 44.1. In addition, while an average of 68.3% of teachers in OECD countries are female, only 55.8% of teachers in Türkiye are female. Furthermore, on average, 49.3% of OECD teachers have undergraduate degrees, 44.2% have master's degrees, and 1.3% have earned a doctorate or equivalent education.

In Türkiye, 92.3% of teachers have undergraduate degrees, 6.9% have master's degrees, and 0.2% have earned a doctorate degree or equivalent education. With regards to principals in OECD countries, 62.8% reported that they hold a master's degree, while 3.5% have a doctorate degree. By contrast, 78% of the school principals in Türkiye have a bachelor's degree, while only 17.7% have a master's degree, and 0.3% have a doctorate degree (OECD, 2018).

The school principal performs many duties involving education and training, management, personnel, accrual, movable property, correspondence, educational and social activities, boarding schools, scholarships, transportation, security, nutrition, care, protection, cleaning, maintaining order, keeping guard, and public relations. They ensure the fulfillment of the duties assigned to them by the Ministry and provincial/district national education directorates, alongside other duties specified in their job description. Positions with additional managerial status – such as "assistant head principal," "assistant principal," and "teacher authorized as principal" – are also authorized to manage schools or act in the absence of a principal (MoNE Regulation on Preschool Education and Primary Education Institutions, 2014). Managers working in educational institutions defined in this way in legal texts are appointed by the Regulation on Selecting and Assigning Administrators to Educational Institutions, which is affiliated with the MoNE. This regulation has changed many times over the years, and according to the updated information as of May 2021, such educational managers must meet the following requirements:

a be a graduate of higher education;
b work as a teacher in MoNE staff;
c have an Educational Management Certificate;
d be successful in the exams specified in the Regulation, if s/he is seeking a managerial appointment for the first time;
e be qualified and appointed as a teacher to one of the educational institutions of the same type as the educational institution to which s/he will be assigned, and have a course that s/he can teach in exchange for a monthly fee in one of the educational institutions of the same type with the educational institution to which s/he will be assigned;
f not have lost his/her managerial position as a result of a judicial or administrative investigation within the last four years as of the last day of the written exam application; and
g have completed, postponed, or been exempted from the compulsory work obligation for those who will be assigned to the managers of educational institutions that do not contain this condition.

Apart from the general conditions stated above, special conditions for the positions of principal, assistant head principal, and assistant principal are also defined in the regulation. In addition, this regulation also detailed the specifics of the Educational Management Certificate Program prepared by the General Directorate of Teacher Training and Development. Those seeking employment in the management of an educational institution must attend this program and receive an Educational Management Certificate, valid for eight years. Candidates who meet these conditions and pass the exam are evaluated by the Provincial Evaluation Commission with the Evaluation Form. Those who want to be reassigned as a manager can only be evaluated through the Evaluation Form. For those seeking an appointment for the first time, the candidates are called for the oral exam according to their ranking from the arithmetic average of the scores of the written exam and the Evaluation Form. Those who score 60 and above in the oral exam are considered successful. The candidates who succeed in the oral exam are appointed to vacant positions according to their preference and score, considering 50% of the written exam score, 30% of the evaluation form score, and 20% of the oral score for those who are applying for assignment for the first time. In addition, administrators who have completed a four-year term of office can apply to the same position in their current institution or different educational institutions. Administrators who have completed their eight-year term of office in the same educational institution with the same title can apply to different educational institutions within the scope of reassignment with the same title.

According to 2018 TALIS data, the average age of school principals across the OECD was 52.2. The average age of secondary school principals in Türkiye is 43.1, making it the country with the youngest school principals after Saudi Arabia (42.9). In addition, while principals have an average of 17 years of teaching experience across the OECD, this figure is only 10.9 years in Türkiye. The average years of administrative experience of school principals are 9.7 years across the OECD and 6.7 years in Türkiye. As evident from these statistics, both the average amount of teaching experience, which is a prerequisite for school principals, and subsequent principal experience in Türkiye, are below the overall mean of other OECD countries. While the gender balance of principals is relatively equal across the OECD, with 47.3% of principals being female, this number drops to 7.2% in Türkiye.

According to the TALIS 2018, OECD school principals reported devoting 21.3% of their working time during the school year to leadership tasks and meetings. For Türkiye, this rate is 15.1%. In effective schools, principals are instructional leaders; thus they spend most of their time planning and managing educational processes and consequently exhibit behaviors aimed at increasing the quality of education (Balcı, 2014; Hallinger, 2003; Hallinger & Murphy, 1985; Robinson et.al., 2008; Şişman, 2020). In this respect, although the field of educational management outlines the possible required competencies and standards of principals (Ağaoğlu et.al., 2012; Aslan & Karip, 2014; Turan & Şişman, 2000), Türkiye exhibits problems in this area, such as the disregard for merit in the principal appointment system (Arar et al., 2017).

The Emergence and Development of EDLM in Türkiye

Since the second half of the 19th century, when modern education began to become widespread in Türkiye, the issue of educational leadership and management emerged as a practical need. Planning, organization, and management of education at the macro level should be addressed within the scope of these discussions, including practical needs as well, such as the establishment and inspection of schools. The developments of more than two centuries of school management and educational leadership were devised into an academic field in the second half of the 20th century. Today, Turkish educational management departments have gained a prominent place in the broader global discipline with their research, publications, journals, and books. The following section discusses the development of educational management in Türkiye through the interaction between practice and academia over the past two centuries.

The Emergence of the Field of EDLM as a Result of Modernization Efforts in Education (1773–1869)

The modernization of Türkiye education took root in the last quarter of the 18th century and began to connect with the field of EDLM in the mid-19th century. The first Educational Regulations, enacted in 1869, aimed to structure secondary and higher education as well as establish widespread basic education. In fact, it was during these periods that provisions regarding school management entered legal documents for the first time. Although school management was directed by the headteacher (*muallimievvel*) in primary schools (*ibtidai*) and defined as "manager" or "principal" in teacher schools and higher education at the time, the understanding that *the essence of the profession is teaching* dates back to these periods. Principals at the secondary level and below were teachers who oversaw the functioning of education, with responsibilities limited to instructional issues (Batır, 2007; Çağır & Türk, 2017; Özalp & Ataünal, 1977). This arrangement reflects a Bonapartist political understanding of the nation state and political approach in which the overall educational system is strictly centralized and individual schools are bureaucratic. Thus, school management in Türkiye was managed as a practical problem in the second half of the 19th century, but had yet to come to the fore as an academic field of study and specialized training.

The Need for Organization and Management of the Mass and Compulsory National Education (1869–1953)

The education policies of the Republican period took shape with the rise of the Union and Progress Party after the Second Constitutional Era. The German influence of academics who fled Nazi Germany to Türkiye, alongside the invitation of John Dewey from the United States with the establishment of the Republic, blended with earlier French influences that continued throughout the 19th century.

The policies designed to disseminate mass education since the first days of the Republic bear traces of all these countries. While the school had been considered to be one of the main tools for the construction of the nation-state at the time, the principal was the head teacher who guided and lead the implementation of central education policies at the school level (Maarif Teşkilatına Dair Kanun, 1926). During earlier periods, since most village schools only had one teacher, the subject of school management only came to the fore in a small number of secondary and high schools.

The perspective of school management depicted in the legal regulations made in this period reflects a continuing Bonapartist approach. Law 739 of 1926 contains a provision that *"the essence of the profession is teaching,"* pre-dating the modern education experience by over a century. According to this provision, school management is a temporary duty. The main task of principals is to ensure that the teaching-learning processes in schools are carried out in accordance with the determined criteria and qualifications, which continues to this day.

In brief, since the first years of the Republic, after the convening of the National Assembly in Ankara in 1920 and the establishment of the Ankara Government, a critical importance was attached to education. However, the subject of education and school management was not yet considered a professional or academic field.

Quotation

The section titled "Duties and Authority of the Principal" of the High School and Secondary Schools Regulation of 1964:

Article 5: The principal manages the school. The principal is asked to act as an example to his friends and students and to cooperate with the school staff.

Assistants to the director in administrative affairs; assistant principals, teachers and trainee teachers. In addition to these, there are chief of internal services, clerk and account officer, lesson equipment officer, library clerk, stock custodian and administrative officers in schools, depending on the need. The Director is authorized to distribute the duties of management to these officers and to make suggestions to the Ministry through the Governor's Office in order to change their duties as necessary.

Article 6: The principal is authorized to translate, regulate and supervise all the affairs of the school within the limits of laws, regulations and orders. In addition, the principal is also responsible for ensuring the protection, good use, cleanliness and order of the school's buildings and furniture, and closely monitoring the relevant homeworkers.

Article 7: The principal carries out the teaching work without causing any disruption.

Scientification of Education and School Management and Educational Management within the Framework of the Education-Development Relationship (1953–present)

After World War II, interest in education increased globally thanks to the emergence of scientific research indicating a strong relationship between economic growth and schooling. Policies for the dissemination of education throughout the world also precipitated the education planning movement. In this context, the UN and OECD also initiated studies in Türkiyeduring this period. This process formed the main motivation for the development of educational management as both a field of practice and academic area of study in Türkiye.

The United States, which rose to prominence as a global superpower in the 1950s, weakened the European influence of nearly two centuries to usher in a new era for Türkiye. As a result of the US influence, the quality of schools opened in this period increased, and the teaching of the English language and culture proliferated nationwide. Almost a quarter of a century later, in the 1950s, the Turkish population doubled from 13 million to 26 million, leading to an increasing student population and subsequent expansion and deepening of the education system. Secondary education became more diversified and specialized with a variety of school types (public, private, vocational, and technical [VET], etc.), and higher education spread across regions as well. This diversification transformed the school management approach, which previously only involved the monitoring and coordination of education and training processes, into the management of schools, which function as the elements of a large and multidimensional bureaucratic structure. Thus, the dominant identity for school management evolved from being a mere "head teacher," which is responsible for prioritizing educational responsibilities, to serving as an "administrator," which is responsible for prioritizing bureaucratic responsibilities.

Efforts to refine management processes and administrators to increase the efficiency of the state emerged in Türkiye, as in developed countries globally, in the 1950s. For this purpose, the Türkiye Middle East Public Management Institute (TODAIE) was established as the first site of graduate education in the field of educational management, representing a milestone for EDLM in the country (Balcı, 2008). Continuing to exist as an autonomous institution until it had been absorbed into Hacı Bayram Veli University in 2018, TODAIE has been essential to the academic development of the field of educational management in Türkiye.

During this period, interest in public management and efforts to increase its quality were piqued as students in management, planning, and development traveled abroad, primarily to the United States and United Kingdom, for study and research. Students who were sent abroad for postgraduate education in educational management in the 1950s and 1960s became the founders of the field in Türkiye when they returned. The invitation of professor Joseph

Lauwerys from England to plan the establishment of the first faculty of education (Mıhcıoğlu, 1989; Topçuoğlu, 1968) combined academic foundations of Turkish educational sciences and management with the Anglo-Saxon frameworks.

In summary, after nearly two centuries of modernization and a century of institutionalization efforts, the Turkish education system completed its quarter-century adventure and entered a new phase with the planned development period. This 75-year process, which has been continuing from the 1950s to the present, saw the solidification of educational management in Türkiyeas an academic field as well as a practical need. We conceptualize this period in four phases.

Establishment and Search Years (1953–1982)

The second quarter-century of the Republic can be defined as the years of organizational and academic establishment and research around education and school management, as well as for the Turkish education system at large. The main purpose of the policies of this age marked by spreading higher education throughout Türkiye was to train technical manpower, the main factor inciting development throughout the country. This period saw the establishment of technical universities (e.g., KTÜ, Ege, Atatürk, ODTÜ), the opening of science high schools (circa 1965), the expansion of foreign language schools (from 1954 onward), and an emphasis on vocational high schools and education, clearly demonstrating how education was considered a development tool.

Foundational laws reorganizing the Turkish education system according to new conditions – such as the Primary Education Law (1961), National Education Basic Law (1973), and Universities Law (1973) – were passed during this period. Moreover, the duties of school principals increased as a result of an amendment made in the high school and secondary school regulations (1964). Both the coordination of widespread educational service management and newly established objectives for increasing efficiency at the school level increased the prominence of the subject of school management in Türkiye, elevating its educational facilities and personnel closer to those of developed countries.

While the 12 new universities established in Türkiye between 1960 and 1980 brought the total nationwide to 19, most contributions in the field of educational management had been made by TODAIE, the Ankara University (AU) Faculty of Educational Sciences, and the Educational Sciences Department at Hacettepe University (Balcı, 2008). An academic infrastructure was established in the field of educational management in Türkiye, thanks to the limited but fundamental contributions of TODAIE and the experts trained in Educational Sciences at AU (Table 2.3).

Table 2.3 Number of universities and faculty in education by years

	1950	1960	1970	1980	1990	2000	2010	2020
Number of universities	3	7	8	19	28	71	149	207
Number of faculty in education	0	0	1	1	17	51	75	101

Years of Spread (1982–1996)

Although the military coup of September 12, 1980, is regarded as the breaking point of Türkiye's late 20th-century political and social history, the decisive factor shaping the deep transformation of the 1980s was the inevitable spread of neoliberalism globally. After three decades following World War II, the social welfare state weakened and the myth of development began to give way to disappointments. Thus, new economic and market-oriented policies came to the fore in education, including many other fields in Türkiye.

Türkiye continued its educational progress with policies aimed at increasing the diversity and prevalence of schools through several legislative amendments, particularly in the national Constitution. The Religious Culture and Moral Knowledge course became compulsory in primary and secondary education, and the number of religious high schools increased. Additional policies focused on expanding vocational and technical education and increasing the number of schools offering foreign language education. However, the government fell short of its goal to extend basic education to eight years through the inclusion of a three-year secondary school on top of the existing compulsory five-year basic education. In a reflection of neoliberal policies, leading a school began to evolve from "management" as a bureaucratic task, to "management" as an identity suitable for the requirements of the market.

Although education and school management was defined as an additional task given to teachers by the National Education Basic Law, this transformation impacted the legal regulations around the appointment of principals that began occupying the agenda more in the 1980s. The six changes made between 1980 and 1999 in the policies regarding the appointment and relocation of school principals signaled a quest for transformation in the education system. Regulations were issued to define and organize the qualifications of principals, the method of their selection and assignment, and their period of office.

The articles quoted below under *the qualifications for preference to be considered for those who will be appointed to the managerial positions*, in the *Directive on the Appointment and Dismissal of Provincial Organization Administrators of the MoNE, Youth and Sports* published in the March 24, 1986 *Journal of Announcements* (*Tebliğler Dergisi* Volume 49, number

2207), reflect the dominant understanding of education and schools during this period. This passage notably depicts the perspective of school management:

Quotation
Article 5: Candidates to be appointed to school and institution managers within the scope of this directive;
  a) Having a master's degree or doctorate,
  d) Having studied in the field of management or having completed an in-service training course on this subject,
  e) Having a work published in the fields of education, training, management, business management or profession.
Training of managers:
Article 41. To gain the knowledge and skills required by the management, to increase efficiency and to convey the innovations in the field of management, managers are given in-service training within the principles to be determined by the Ministry.

The provisions of this directive recognize that school management is a field of expertise, prioritize those who have received specialized training, and relate the task of school management to the concepts of business management, productivity, and innovation.

Since the 1980s, the fast-paced establishment of many universities and education departments necessitated the proliferation of a large number of teaching staff from a variety of fields. This period saw the inception of graduate programs in the field of educational management in many universities. While the Department of Education (Sciences) in AU conferred around 200 postgraduate degrees in 1995, this number reached 900 in the 2000s. The field of education management has since advanced some of the most popular graduate degree programs in Türkiye (Table 2.4).

Deepening Years (1997–2014)

The turn of the century was a period of constant change in education and school management across Türkiye, with six revisions made in the executive appointment regulation between 1999 and 2014 alone. The most important change made in 1999 was the introduction of a 120-hour basic education requirement for school management, thus ushering in a new era for school management which replaced the *educational sciences model* with a combined *mastery-apprenticeship* and *examination model* (Balcı, 2008). Five years later, the 120-hour training requirement had also been abolished, and the qualifications for managing an educational institution became more exam-based.

The establishment of the 120-hour principal training program requirement for principal appointment, coupled with an increased emphasis on graduate education in the field of educational management, led principals and teachers

Table 2.4 Number of educational management graduate programs and graduates by years*

	1967–1990	1991–2000	2001–2010	2011–2020
Number of master's degree programs	7	17	45	82
Number of PhD degree programs	7	11	17	27
Number of master's degree graduates	40	235	2251	3773
Number of PhD degree graduates	24	59	215	580

Note
* The author assembled these figures on programs and graduates by reviewing information from the database of the National Thesis Center. The field of educational management goes by different names in Türkiye as a major, branch of science, department, and/or program. Within the scope of this research, data were compiled from the database of the National Thesis Center based on the keywords of *education, educational institutions management, supervision, inspection, planning, economy, management,* and *higher education management*, as well as theses published in the field of *education and training*. Programs related to business, public management, management, organization, and other fields related to education such as health education, vocational education, technical education, art education, physical education, and foreign language education were not included in this review. The number of programs represented here includes any programs that graduated students in any given year within the specified years. The number of graduates is not cumulative but rather represents only the number of graduates in the specified range of years.

to education management programs. While this orientation brought the research and theses in these programs closer to practice, the theoretical knowledge in the academy had also been expanded through the work of the teachers and school principals who advanced to further graduate programs. The distance between theory and practice became evident as principals and teachers became more involved in increasingly prevalent scientific and professional organization meetings nationwide. The amendment of the MoNE Organization Law in 2011 and the inclusion of provisions to encourage young managers with master's and doctoral degrees and legal experts started a new era in the MoNE focused on academic quality. During this period, compulsory education was extended to 12 years, basic education was divided into primary and secondary schools, and the number of preschool institutions and kindergarten classes increased. These changes heightened the need for a greater number of principals, as well as increased diversity in educational leadership. On the other hand, as neoliberal policies continued to impact schools, the financial responsibilities of principals also increased.

Constant changes in the hiring regulations for school principals prevented standardization of the appointment processes. The compounding pressures of workload and financial responsibilities for principals, alongside the frequent shifts in appointment regulations, caused disappointment among university educational management faculty and K-12 principals alike. In both practice and theory, questions arose regarding the disconnect between scientific studies in the field of educational management, the national culture and sociology of Türkiye, and the real needs of principals. The quotation below shows how the appointment processes of school principals and related terminology changed in the early 21st century:

Quotation
***The Management** Titled Section of **the Regulation on Secondary Education Institutions of MoNE Published** in 2013*
Management
Article 77- (1) Principals; It leads teachers, students, parents and the environment in education and training, works towards increasing productivity, creating team spirit, integrating the school with the environment and developing the corporate culture, keeping the school ready for service. It constantly renews and develops the school in line with scientific and technological developments, efficiency and transparency principles, and uses time and all opportunities to achieve the school's goals.
(2) School management is responsible for
a) Research and planning,
b) Organizing,
c) Guidance,
ç) Monitoring, inspection and evaluation,
d) Communication and governance.
Manager, duties, authority and responsibilities
Article 78- (1) The principal is responsible for the effective and efficient use of all resources and management with a team spirit in order to achieve the school's purposes in accordance with the general objectives and basic principles of Turkish national education, in line with the provisions of the Constitution, laws, statutes, regulations, directives, circulars and other relevant legislation. S/He is the education and training leader who is primarily responsible for and representative of school. The principal manages the school in cooperation with the boards, commissions and teams within it.

Years of Inquiry (2014–present)

Regulations in 2014 gestured toward a new phase for school management in Türkiye. The search for school principals was transformed by the definition of school principalship as a temporary task, the appointment of school principals through an interviewing process, the setting of four-year terms, and the requirement that a school principal move back into teaching after completing their term. The longstanding tradition of frequent changes in school management legislation has been continuing since 2014 as well, with six amendments in the regulation over the past eight years.

In academia, more questions arose about both educational methods/processes and the scope of research in educational management programs.

Consequently, the volume of research investigating the educational management knowledge base began increasing (Balcı, 2011; Beycioglu, at al., 2019; Kısa, at al., 2021; Oplatka & Arar, 2016; Örücü & Şimşek, 2011; Turan & Şişman, 2013). Perceptions of insufficiency of the scope and methods of education management programs led to the creation of programs with new names, alongside certificate programs.

It is important to note the influence of dimensions of research and practice beyond Türkiye during this period. Globalization and neoliberalism, increasing inequalities worldwide, and transnational problems such as forced migration, global warming, and digitalization strengthened the epistemological and ontological debates about school, education, and educational management (Bates, 1982; Eacott & Evers, 2015; English, 2002; Hyung, 2001). Social justice movements have also turned their attention to non-Western countries, while far-right, nationalist, and occasionally fascist movements, discourses, and policies in the West and developed countries have raised questions about imported information and methods.

With the data-based management and learning analytics included in the MoNE's (MEB's) 2023 Education Vision, the objectives of reducing the bureaucratic workload, transforming school management into a profession of expertise, developing professional skills at the graduate level, and improving personal rights (MEB, 2018) were welcomed by both the field and the academy. MoNE's modification of the content of the principal selection exam in favor of leadership and managerial skills, coupled with a new education manager certificate requirement (MEB, 2021), forms critical improvements that will strengthen the scientific foundations of school management. However, the MEB's regulation published in 2021 also holds the potential to further increase the distance between the academy and practicing educational leaders, since the education management certificate training will be designed and facilitated by the Ministry, excluding universities from the process.

State of the Art in Research on EDLM in Türkiye

As stated previously, many new universities have been established in Türkiye since the foundation of the Turkish Republic, particularly over the last 20 years, when the total number of postsecondary institutions has more than doubled (Ozoglu et al., 2016). With such rapid growth in higher education, the CoHE and MoNE have designed various staff development programs to meet the need for teaching personnel in universities. As a result of the increase in the number of academic personnel, research in the field of educational management expanded, at both the national and international levels, especially in the last two decades (Gümüş et al., 2020; Yılmaz, 2018). Researchers have conducted systematic reviews of these studies on school leadership and management in Türkiye to create a picture of the overall knowledge base in the field (Balcı & Apaydın, 2009; Bellibaş & Gümüş, 2019; Gümüş et al., 2020; Turan et al., 2014, 2016; Yılmaz, 2018). In this section, we examine the status of research in the field of educational management and leadership in Türkiye by reviewing studies produced in the past ten years. Most of the current reviews deal with the relevant research in terms of scope, topical focus, theoretical framework, and methodological features. In this section, we summarize the general trends in these reviews and interpret their findings according to social, cultural, and organizational context.

We first examine the available papers according to their topical focus. Turan et al. (2014) examined educational management studies in national journals published between 2003 and 2013 and found that these studies largely focused on organizational behavior and psychological dimensions such as leadership and organizational culture, burnout, conflict resolution, and organizational citizenship. Organizational factors and leadership issues were among the most studied topics in the conference papers presented during this decade (Turan et al., 2016). Bellibaş and Gümüş (2019) investigated educational management and leadership studies from Türkiye published in internationally respected journals, in terms of their subject, theoretical framework, and method. Their analysis revealed that these articles tended to focus on organizational behavior – consisting of self-efficacy, organizational trust, culture, and climate – followed by leadership. Leadership studies largely focused on leadership styles, such as instructional leadership, collaborative leadership, transformational leadership, academic leadership, teacher leadership, and servant leadership.

It is surprising that leadership has been one of the most studied topics in this area since the discretionary power of school principals is quite limited in Türkiye due to the centralized structure of the education system. Researchers who see this situation as problematic may research leadership to amplify the importance of the concept and attract the attention of practitioners and/or policymakers. The most studied subjects after organizational behavior and leadership involve emotional variables related to the organization such as motivation, job satisfaction, stress, and burnout (Bellibaş & Gümüş, 2019). This shows that the field of educational management and leadership, which has long been criticized for devoting a disproportionate amount of attention to the mechanical and technical dimensions of an organization (Yılmaz, 2018), has now shifted its focus toward the psychological dimensions.

While Turkish scholars frequently examine leadership, organizational, and psychological variables in the context of educational management, they largely ignore key issues emphasized in the international community, including cultural context, gender, social justice, family and environmental factors, educational economy, and educational policies (Bellibaş & Gümüş, 2019). In a similar review of Türkiye's educational leadership literature, Turan et al. (2016) argued that the field excludes alternative perspectives such as feminist, critical, interpretive, and postmodern educational management perspectives. Yılmaz (2018), on the other hand, stated that research in Türkiye should focus on issues such as language, culture, power relations, and social context to better understand the social reality of the country. These topics, which should have been prioritized considering the socio-demographic characteristics of Turkish society, indeed receive little attention due to the hierarchical and centralized public structure and unified education system (Çelik et al., 2017).

The theoretical frameworks of the studies originating from Türkiyealso tend to reflect the limited subjects that they examine (Bellibaş & Gümüş, 2019). About a quarter of the studies focus only on leadership and its characteristics, while another quarter examine only organizational variables (e.g., organizational behavior and emotional factors). Similarly, many studies have been designed to answer the question of how principals' leadership behaviors affect processes and individuals (mostly teachers) in the organization, aiming to link specific leadership types to organizational variables, despite the previously mentioned low likelihood of school principals' enactment of leadership behaviors due to the centralized nature of the education system. However, researchers' focus could reflect a desire for principals to enact greater leadership practices to better shape organizational processes, alongside individual and psychological factors in schools.

Studies on educational outcomes, which have dominated the educational literature in the Western world over the last half-century, have not received significant attention in Turkish studies. For example, the effect of school principals on student achievement and school improvement is largely ignored in the Turkish context (Bellibaş & Gümüş, 2019). This likely stems from the difficulties of gathering student achievement data, since developing an exam protocol and questions can be quite costly and time-consuming for an individual researcher or team. Moreover, the reluctance of Turkish authorities to share central exam data with researchers in Türkiye could also pose barriers to studies on how school principals might influence student outcomes.

Another area of research that has been largely ignored is how contextual variables shape school principals' skills and practices (Bellibaş & Gümüş, 2019). The educational management literature frequently emphasizes how the behaviors of school principals are largely shaped by social, cultural, and organizational structures (Hallinger, 2018). This context may go ignored in Türkiye because Turkish researchers tend to borrow from the educational management knowledge base of the Western world (Balcı, 2008). Research in this field directly adapts the concepts and knowledge developed by countries such as the United States, Canada, and the United Kingdom, where the field was born and developed (Turan & Özkan, 2016; Turan & Şişman, 2013). Efforts to develop theories suitable for the Turkish culture and education system remain limited.

Examining the methods and methodologies of educational management research in Türkiye also holds the potential to provide important information about the nature of the field. In a review of 42 articles, 25 book chapters, and 11 theses, Yılmaz (2018) emphasized that quantitative methods dominate educational management and leadership in Türkiye. Similarly, the majority (2/3) of the studies from Türkiye published in international journals use quantitative methods (Bellibaş & Gümüş, 2019). In addition, Turan et al.

(2016) found that about 45% of the papers presented at educational management conferences consisted of quantitative studies, while 35% were qualitative. These demonstrate a similar pattern; Coşkun-Demirpolat (2016) found that 58.2% of the 282 doctoral dissertations published in the field between 2005 and 2015 used quantitative research designs, 23.8% employed mixed methods, and 17.4% used qualitative methods. It is therefore reasonable to conclude that the positivist paradigm is dominant in educational management research in Türkiye (Balcı, 2008; Turan et al., 2016). Furthermore, cross-sectional survey designs dominate quantitative studies (Balcı & Apaydın, 2009; Bellibaş & Gümüş, 2019). Such studies often aim to acquire descriptive information about current and popular concepts or examine the relationship between these concepts (Balcı, 2009), and therefore are less likely to infer causal relationships (Bellibaş & Gümüş, 2019). This indicates the need for building additional knowledge based on experimental and longitudinal studies.

Quantitative studies in the Turkish context published in international journals are mostly based on regression and correlation (Bellibaş & Gümüş, 2019), while national studies are more likely to employ descriptive and basic level analyses such as t-tests and ANOVA (Turan et al., 2014). Advanced statistics (for example, multilevel analysis) are used in only a small proportion of both national and international quantitative research. While using advanced methods alone should not be the main purpose of a study, the use of single-level correlational analyses rather than multi-level analyses in studies poses a problem, since current studies largely focus on the relationship between school principals' leadership skills and practices and the psychological characteristics of individuals and organizational processes (Bellibaş & Gümüş, 2019). Further research should consider that while leadership skills and practices are a school-level variable in such studies, teachers' psychological states (e.g., stress, job satisfaction, self-efficacy) mostly consist of individual variables.

Compared to quantitative research methods, qualitative research, mixed-method, or theoretical studies are rarely conducted by educational management researchers. Such studies have the potential to make significant contributions to the field, especially in developing theory (Gümüş et al., 2020). The main reason why these studies are not valued may be due to the limited interest in developing a theory suitable for the Turkish educational context; indeed, researchers appear more eager to directly integrate the concepts developed in the Western World into the Turkish context, as previously emphasized by many Turkish academics (e.g., Balcı, 2008; Turan et al., 2016; Turan & Şişman, 2013; Yılmaz, 2018). While researchers tend to test the concepts borrowed from developed countries through quantitative research (Yılmaz, 2018), there are very few studies on the development of theories and concepts suitable for the country's education system (Gümüş et al., 2020). Indeed, these qualitative studies tend to simply describe participants' thoughts on current practices or problems, rather than trying to develop a theory derived from the context.

The majority of the education management and leadership studies (86%) utilized data collection tools like scales and interviews, which enable relatively fast and easy data collection and publication (Turan et al., 2016). This is also the case for Turkish studies published in international journals (Bellibaş & Gümüş, 2019). While this situation could be attributed to a number of factors, one of the most likely reasons is related to academic promotions in the Turkish higher education system, which largely rely on quantitative indicators (e.g., number of studies, citation count, indexing) (Gümüş et al., 2020; Özkok, 2016). As a result, the knowledge produced in the field of educational management focuses on certain topics that typically reflect everyday and popular themes, to the detriment of articles related to the ontology, epistemology, and methodology of the field (Turan et al., 2016). Scarcity of research funds also encourages "quick" and "easy" studies (Balcı, 2008). This may cause a disconnect between the knowledge accumulated in the field of educational management and the realities and context of the education system, further limiting this scholarship's effectiveness for solving practical problems in schools (Bellibaş & Gümüş, 2019; Yılmaz, 2018).

Summary

The Republic of Türkiye is a democratic, secular, and social state. With a young population that largely lives in cities, the country has also received substantial waves of immigration throughout its history, particularly in the past decade. The dominance of high power distance and high uncertainty avoidance in Turkish society foster well-structured rules and job definitions. Turkish culture is collectivist and strongly emphasizes values such as respect, loyalty, and belonging. The education system is centrally structured and MoNE, at the top of the hierarchy, is responsible for making and implementing educational decisions. The national constitution guarantees 12 years of compulsory education free of charge to every Turkish citizen, regardless of gender, race, religion, or language.

Although teacher training has a deep-rooted history in Türkiye, education and school management have primarily been considered a practical need. Consequently, the idea that teaching is the main profession and principalship is a part of the teaching profession has always prevailed. Until the 1950s, EDLM was not considered an academic field in Türkiye. Postgraduate education in EDLM emerged through three main institutions: TODAIE, Ankara University, and Hacettepe University. Post-1950, students who were sent abroad to other countries for graduate education played a key role in the establishment of the field.

In the 1980s, the market-based understanding of neoliberalism's impact on the world showed its effects in the field of education, and as a result, vocational and technical education and foreign language education practices became widespread, and education management assumed an identity shaped by market requirements, with an emphasis on total quality management. Twin understandings of the importance of training for school principal candidates and the need for graduate education in this area have motivated principals and teachers to attend educational management master's and PhD programs. While these programs were initially theoretical in nature, they soon shifted to emphasize practical issues. However, 2014 brought with it frequent changes in the regulations regarding the appointment of principals. The newest law emphasized that school principalship is to be a temporary task rather than a profession, with appointments based on interviews. Along with these policies, the field faces issues regarding the quality of certificate programs and the increased number of graduate programs opened in higher education institutions.

Despite the significant problems associated with policy, practice, and research in the field, substantial strides have been made in human resources and personnel development, with approximately 20% of school principals completing a graduate degree program. About 2500 master's and 600 doctoral students gain their degrees every year from around 70 master's and 20 doctoral programs across the country. Many students attend universities abroad to complete their graduate degrees or conduct research. Approximately 3000 master's students (without a thesis requirement) graduated from university EDLM programs in Türkiye in 2020. These significant numbers demonstrate that the field of EDLM in Türkiye has entered a new phase of finding its own identity after the establishment, deepening, expansion, and questioning periods.

Conclusion

This chapter provided an overview of policy, practice, and research within the field of EDLM in Türkiye. Taking together all these parts, we conclude that a considerable disconnect remains between policy, practice, and research. The practice of EDLM has developed thanks to the educational efforts towards increasing student attendance across the past two centuries, dating back to the pre-Republican era in Türkiye. EDLM as an academic field was born and developed in line with the mission attributed to education in the pursuit of development plans and with the methods and concepts generated in developed Western countries. In addition, national social, political, and economic developments, followed by rapid changes and transformations in education, schools, and teaching after the 1950s have led decision-makers to produce policies designed to overcome daily problems in schooling. These three elements combine to impede consistency between policy, practice, and research within the field of EDLM. Although connection and cooperation between practitioners, academics, and policy-makers is a worthy goal, the rules, habits, and institutional disconnections between bureaucracy, schools, and universities make it difficult for this ideal to actually materialize.

This disconnect is exacerbated by research that ignores the realities of the local context. As discussed, EDLM research in Türkiye is generally conducted using quantitative methods, indicating the dominance of the positivist paradigm. These studies tend to rely upon tools like scales and interviews, which enable fast and easy data collection. The produced knowledge reflects popular themes and aims to replicate frameworks directly from the Western world. Qualitative studies are often based on the descriptive presentation of participant views rather than theory development efforts, thus producing information that is unsuitable for the Turkish context, fails to solve practical problems, and provides poor guidance for educational policymaking (Turan et al., 2016). Thus, there is a critical need to adapt research to fit the Turkish culture and education system; to include alternative research perspectives such as critical, confrontational, and feminist frameworks alongside positivist methodologies; and to analyze the produced information without ignoring the social context such as language, culture, and power relations.

The current research bears only limited potential to inform policymakers about effective practices. In fact, from the policymaker perspective, it seems extremely difficult to successfully implement research findings that are based on theories and practices of Western countries, which may directly conflict with the historical, social, political, economic, and cultural characteristics of Turkish society (Şişman, 1996). For instance, research produced in the field of EDLM in Türkiye mostly focuses on leadership and organizational behavior, but the studied topics are relatively disconnected from the Turkish context. Contextual differences are important as they can differentiate the expectations of principals as either managers or leaders. For example, the tendency towards high power distance and uncertainty avoidance in collaborative cultures puts the leadership in a more charismatic position by assigning different missions to managers, when compared with more individualistic cultures (Sargut, 1994). With a similar approach, Turan and Şişman (2013) mentioned that leadership conceptualizations in the field of EDLM aim to solve the cultural problems of the society; thus, the theories developed in societies that prioritize the individual may not be meaningful and valid in collectivist societies. The development of culturally relevant educational theories and practices could help bridge the gap between policy, practice, and research.

References

Ağaoğlu, E., Altınkurt, Y., Yılmaz, K., & Karaköse, T. (2012). Okul yöneticilerinin yeterliklerine ilişkin okul yöneticilerinin ve öğretmenlerin görüşleri (Kütahya ili). *Eğitim ve Bilim, 37*(164), 159–175.

Akyüz, Y. (2010). *Türk eğitim tarihi. M.Ö. 1000 – M.S. 2010*. Pegem Akademi.

Arar, K., Turan, S., Barakat, M., & Oplatka, I. (2017). The characteristics of educational leadership in the Middle East: A comparative analysis of three nation-states.*The Wiley international handbook of educational leadership*, Waite veI. Bogotch (ed.) (pp. 355–374). John Wiley & Sons.

Aslan, H., & Karip, E. (2014). Okul müdürlerinin liderlik standartlarının geliştirilmesi. *Kuram ve Uygulamada Eğitim Yönetimi, 20*(3), 255–279.
Aytaç, Ö. (2018). Türk sosyolojisinde bir öncü isim: Prens Sabahattin. *Çekmece İzü Sosyal Bilimler Dergisi, 6*(12), 75–120.
Balcı, A. (2008). Türkiye'de eğitim yönetiminin bilimleşme düzeyi. *Kuram ve Uygulamada Eğitim Yönetimi, 54*(54), 181–209.
Balcı, A. (2011). Eğitim yönetiminin değişen bağlamı ve eğitim yönetimi programlarına etkisi. *Eğitim ve Bilim, 36*(162), 196–208.
Balcı, A. (2014). *Etkili okul ve okul geliştirme.* Pegem Akademi.
Balcı, A., & Apaydın, Ç. (2009). Türkiye'de eğitim yönetimi araştırmalarının durumu: Kuram ve Uygulamada Eğitim Yönetimi dergisi örneği. *Kuram ve Uygulamada Eğitim Yönetimi, 15*(59), 325–343.
Bates, R. J. (1982). Towards a critical practice of educational management. *Paper presented at the Annual Meeting of the American Educational Research Association* (New York, NY, March 19–23, 1982).
Batır, B. (2007). *İkinci Meşrutiyet'ten Tevhid-i Tedrisat'a Türkiye'de ilköğretim (1908–1924).* Yayınlanmamış Doktora Tezi, İstanbul Üniversitesi.
Bellibaş, M. Ş., & Gümüş, S. (2019). A systematic review of educational leadership and management research in Türkiye. *Journal of Educational Management, 57*(6), 731–747.
Beycioglu, K., Kılınç, A. Ç., & Polatcan, M. (2019). The 'westernised' map of the field of educational management in Türkiye and dominant perspectives in school leadership education. In E.A. Samier, & E.S. ElKaleh (Eds.), *Teaching educational leadership in Muslim countries* (pp. 135–151). Springer.
Binbaşıoğlu, C. (2019). *Öğretmen yetiştirme açısından Türkiye'de eğitim bilimleri tarihi üzerine bir araştırma.* MEB Destek Hizmetleri Genel Müdürlüğü.
Çağır, M., & Türk, İ. C. (2017). 1869 Statute on general education and its role on the history of Turkish education. Maarif-i Umumiye Nizamnamesi ve Türk eğitim tarihindeki yeri. *Avrasya Sosyal ve Ekonomi Araştırmaları Dergisi/Eurasian Journal of Research in Social and Economics (EJRSE), 4*(11), 62–75.
Çelik, Z., Gümüş, S., & Gür, B. S. (2017). Moving beyond a monotype education in Türkiye: Major reforms in the last decade and challenges ahead. In Y. K. Cha, J. Gundara, S.H. Ham, & M. Lee (Eds.), *Multicultural education in glocal perspectives* (pp. 103–119). Springer.
Coşkun-Demirpolat, B. (2016). Türkiye'de eğitim yönetimi disiplininin paradigmatik duruşu. In K. Beycioğlu, N. Özer, D. Koşar, İ. Şahin (Eds.), *Eğitim yönetimi araştırmaları* (pp. 156–179). Pegem Akademi.
Eacott, S., & Evers, C. (2015). New frontiers in educational leadership, management and management theory. *Educational Philosophy and Theory, 47*(4), 307–311, DOI: 10.1080/00131857.2014.977530
Ekmen Türkmen, S. (2014). *Özel zincir ve butik okulların öğretmen işe alımlarındaki benzerlik ve farklılıklara ilişkin öğretmen ve okul yöneticilerinin görüşleri.* Yayımlanmamış yüksek lisans tezi, Bahçeşehir Üniversitesi.
English, F. W. (2002). The point of scientificity, the fall of the epistemological dominos, and the end of the field of educational management. *Studies in Philosophy and Education, 21*(2), 109–136.
Erdem, A. R. (2011). Atatürk'ün eğitim liderliğinin başarısı: Türk eğitim devrimi. *Belgi, 2,* Yaz, 163–181.
ERG (2020). *Öğretmenler: Eğitim izleme raporu 2020.* ERG Eğitim Gözlemevi.

Ergün, M. (2008). "Prens" Sabahattin Bey'in eğitim üzerine düşünceleri. *Kuramsal Eğitimbilim*, *1*(2), 1–9.

Gümüş, S., Bellibaş, M. Ş., Gümüş, E., & Hallinger, P. (2020). Science mapping research on educational leadership and management in Türkiye: A bibliometric review of international publications. *School Leadership & Management*, *40*(1), 23–44.

Güneş, H. N. (2016). Türkiye'nin yönetsel yeniden yapılandırılması hakkında Prens Sabahattin'in adem-i merkeziyet kavramına atıfla bir değerlendirme. *The Journal of Academic Social Science Studies*, *50*, 125–139.

Hallinger, P. (2003). Leading educational change: Reflections on the practice of instructional and transformational leadership. *Cambridge Journal of Education*, *33*(3), 329–352.

Hallinger, P. (2018). Bringing context out of the shadows of leadership. *Educational management administration & leadership*, *46*(1), 5–24.

Hallinger, P., & Murphy, J. (1985). Assessing the instructional management behavior of principals. *The Elementary School Journal*, *86*(2), 217–247.

Hofstede, G. (1980). *Culture's consequences: International differences in work-related values*. Sage.

Hofstede, G. (2001). *Culture's consequences: Comparing values, behaviours, institutions, and organizations across nations*. Sage.

Hofstede, G., Hofstede, G. J., & Minkov, M. (2010). *Cultures and organizations: Software of the mind*. McGraw-Hill.

Hyung, P. S. (2001). Epistemological underpinnings of theory developments in educational management. *Australian Journal of Education*, *45*(3), 237–248.

Kısa, N., Badavan, Y., & Houchens, G. (2021). Eğitim yönetimi alanındaki kuram-uygulama boşluğunun giderilmesi için çözüm önerileri. *Başkent University Journal of Education*, *8*(1), 220–237.

Lamba, M. (2010). Osmanlı'dan günümüze Türk kamu yönetimde merkeziyetçilik-adem-i merkeziyetçilik üzerine bir inceleme. *Süleyman Demirel Üniversitesi Vizyoner Dergisi*, *2*(1), 131–156.

Maarif teşkilatına dair kanun (1926). *Resmi Ceride*, 3/IV/1926, sy. 338.

MEB (2020). *Millî Eğitim istatistikleri, örgün eğitim, 2019/20*. T.C. Millî Eğitim Bakanlığı Strateji Geliştirme Başkanlığı.

MEB (2021). Millî Eğitim Bakanlığına bağlı eğitim kurumlarına yönetici seçme ve görevlendirme yönetmeliği. *Resmi Gazete*, 5 Şubat 2021, sy. 31386.

MEB (2021). *Millî Eğitim istatistikleri, örgün eğitim, 2020/21*. T.C. Millî Eğitim Bakanlığı Strateji Geliştirme Başkanlığı.

MEB (2018). *2023 eğitim vizyonu*. Milli Eğitim Bakanlığı. http://2023vizyonu.meb.gov.tr/doc/2023_EGITIM_VIZYONU.pdf

Mıhcıoğlu, C. (1989). Eğitim (Bilimleri) Fakültesinin kuruluşu üzerine. *Ankara University Journal of Faculty of Educational Sciences (JFES)*, *22*(1), 347–391.

OECD (2018). *TALIS indicators*. https://stats.oecd.org/ adresinden 13.07.2021 tarihinde alınmıştır.

Oplatka, I., & Arar, K. (2016). The field of educational management as an arena of knowledge production: Some implications for Turkish field members. *Research in Educational Management and Leadership*, *1*(2), 161–186.

Örücü, D., & Şimşek, H. (2011). The state of educational management scholarship in Türkiye from the scholars' perspectives: A qualitative analysis. *Educational Management: Theory and Practice*, *17*(2), 167–197.

Özalp, R., & Ataünal, A. (1977). *Türk millî eğitim sisteminde düzenleme teşkilatı: Talim ve terbiye kurulu, millî eğitim şûrası.* Millî Eğitim Basımevi.
Özkok, E.İ. (2016). *Eğitim yönetimi ve denetimi Türkçe alanyazınının durumu: akademisyen bakış açısı.* [Unpublished master's thesis, Eastern Mediterranean University, Gazimağusa].
Robinson, R.M.J., Lloyd, C.A., & Rowe, K.J. (2008). The impact of leadership on student outcomes: An analysis of the differential effects of leadership types. *Educational Management Quarterly, 44*(5), 635–674.
Sargut, A.S. (1994). Bireycilik ve ortaklaşa davranış ikileminde yönetim ve örgüt kuramları. *Ankara Üniversitesi SBF Dergisi, 49,* 321–332.
Şişman, M. (1996). Yönetim kuramı ve kültürlerarası farklılaşma açısından yönetim uygulamaları. *Kuram ve Uygulamada Eğitim Yönetimi, 2*(2), 295–308.
Şişman, M. (2020). *Eğitimde mükemmellik arayışı (etkili okullar).* Pegem Akademi.
Topçuoğlu, H. (1968). Ankara Üniversitesinin bir "eğitim fakültesi" vardir!. *Ankara University Journal of Faculty of Educational Sciences (JFES), 1*(1), 289–299.
TÜİK (2021a). Adrese dayalı nüfus kayıt sistemi sonuçları, 2019. https://data.tuik.gov.tr/Bulten/Index?p=Adrese-Dayali-Nufus-Kayit-Sistemi-Sonuclari-2019-33705 adresinden 13.07.2021 tarihinde alınmıştır.
TÜİK (2021b). Uluslararası göç istatistikleri, 2019. https://data.tuik.gov.tr/Bulten/Index?p=Uluslararasi-Goc-Istatistikleri-2019-33709 adresinden 13.07.2021 tarihinde alınmıştır.
Turan, S., & Şişman, M. (2000). Okul yöneticileri için standartlar: eğitim yöneticilerinin bilgi temelleri üzerine düşünceler. *Balıkesir Üniversitesi Sosyal Bilimler Enstitüsü Dergisi, 3*(4), 68–87.
Turan, S., & Özkan, M. (2016). Uyarlayan uyarlayana geliştiren geliştirene: Ölçeklere sayılarla bakış. In A. Balcı ve, & İ. Aydın (Eds.), *Prof. Dr. Ziya Bursalıoğlu'na armağan* (pp. 227–244). Ankara Üniversitesi Eğitim Bilimleri Fakültesi Yayını.
Turan, S., & Şişman, M. (2013). Eğitim yönetimi alanında üretilen bilişsel bilgi ve batılı biliş tarzınının eleştirisine giriş. *Kuram ve Uygulamada Eğitim Yönetimi, 19*(4), 505–514.
Turan, S., Bektaş, F., Yalçın, M., & Armağan, Y. (2016). Eğitim yönetimi alanında bilgi üretim süreci: Eğitim yönetimi kongrelerinin rolü ve serüveni üzerine bir değerlendirme. *Kuram ve Uygulamada Eğitim Yönetimi, 22*(1), 81–108.
Turan, S., Karadağ, E., Bektaş, F., & Yalçın, M. (2014). Türkiye'de eğitim yönetiminde bilgi üretimi: Kuram ve Uygulamada Eğitim Yönetimi Dergisi 2003–2013 yayınlarının incelenmesi. *Kuram ve Uygulamada Eğitim Yönetimi, 20*(1), 93–119.
Ülgen, M. (2018). *Kurum kimliği öğelerinin öğretmenlerin özel okul tercihi üzerindeki etkisi: TED Antalya Koleji üzerine bir araştırma.* Yayımlanmamış yüksek lisans tezi, Akdeniz Üniversitesi, Antalya.
Ünal, F., & Kavuncuoğlu, S. (2015). Prens Sabahattin ve adem-i merkeziyetçilik anlayışı. *Dumlupınar Üniversitesi Sosyal Bilimler Dergisi, 45,* 118–129.
Yılmaz, K. (2018). A critical view to the studies related to the field of educational management in Türkiye Türkiye'deki eğitim yönetimi alanı ile ilgili çalışmalara eleştirel bir bakış. *Journal of Human Sciences, 15*(1), 123–154.

3 Examining the Knowledge Base in Educational Administration and Leadership in Egypt

A Systematic Review of Published Research Literature

Waheed Hammad, Eman Ahmed, and Maysaa Barakat

Introduction

Recent reviews of educational administration and leadership (EAL) research indicate substantial growth and development in the knowledge base in the field across the globe. This can be seen, for example, in the dramatic increase in the volume of EAL research coming from non-Western and developing societies (e.g., Ahmed, 2020; Attari & Essa, 2021; Flessa et al., 2018; Hallinger & Bryant 2013; Hammad & Hallinger, 2017). These developments have been fueled by a growing realization among EAL scholars and practitioners of the limitations of Western (mainly Anglo-American) EAL models and the subsequent calls for expanding the existing knowledge base in the field by exploring how EAL is conceptualized and practiced in different cultural contexts (Belchetz & Leithwood, 2007; Dimmock & Walker, 2005: Oplatka & Arar, 2017).

Despite the steady growth of the knowledge base on EAL in Arab societies, several concerns have been raised regarding the quality and relevance of this scholarship and its ability to inform current educational developments in the region (see Attari and Essa, 2021; Hammad & Hallinger, 2017; Hammad et al., 2022; Oplatka & Arar, 2017). This includes Egypt, the focus of the current chapter. Egypt has the largest and one of the oldest educational systems in the Middle East and North Africa and has contributed significantly to the overall development of educational systems in the neighboring countries (Arar et al., 2017). This is despite severe problems that have resulted in the poor performance of Egypt's education system. These problems include lack of resources, low teacher quality, high drop-out rates, poor curricula, gender disparities, and ineffective management and leadership practices (Elbadawy, 2015; OECD, 2015). In order to address these shortcomings, many reform programs have been implemented since the early 1990s, with little evidence of a significant impact on education quality (Barakat, 2019; OECD, 2015).

We argue that exploring the EAL scholarship in Egypt is crucial, not only to accomplish our shared goal of expanding the global knowledge base in the field but also to examine its relevance in the current context of rapid educational changes in the country. This is particularly important considering the significant role that EAL can play during the implementation of change (Gunter, 2011; Hauge et al., 2014). Therefore, the aim of this chapter is to analyze the existing EAL research in Egypt and consider how it may be strengthened to better inform ongoing educational reforms. We believe that this is a timely endeavor since, to date, no attempts have been made to unearth this literature. Having a wider geographical remit, prior reviews of the Arab EAL literature were either "Pan-Arab" (i.e., covering all Arab societies) (Atari & Outum, 2019; Hallinger & Hammad, 2019; Oplatka & Arar, 2017), or region-focused (Hammad et al., 2022; Hammad & Alazmi, 2022), thus ignoring country-level analyses of EAL research. We agree with Hallinger and Bryant's (2013) proposition regarding the need to analyze local EAL literatures across societies as part of the effort to understand "more of the contours in the regional landscape of knowledge production" (p. 324).

The review reported in this chapter covers the EAL research literature published in both English and Arabic journals in the past two decades (2001–2021). Core EAL journals as well as the international journals indexed in the Scopus database are used to identify English-language literature, while the EduSearch and Shamaa databases are searched for Arabic sources. Systematic review methods are employed to identify the key features of the EAL literature under investigation, namely publication volume, authorship trends, types of research studies, the composition of research topics, and the research methods employed.

The first section of the chapter introduces the Egyptian education context, focusing on its structure, administration, as well as its current challenges and reform initiatives. The second section describes the methodology used to conduct the review, including the identification of sources and data analysis procedures. The third section reports the review results, while the last section interprets these results in the light of existing global literature, discusses their implications and proposes a future agenda for improvement.

Educational Administration and Leadership Context in Egypt

In this section we introduce the Egyptian education context, focusing on its structure, administration, as well as its challenges and reform initiatives.

Context

Egypt is among the ten most populous countries in the world (UNESCO, 2006), consequently the country holds a strategic role "in determining the stability of the Middle East and southern Mediterranean area" (Sayed, 2005, p. 67). Egypt has gone through major political and societal changes over the last decade, where education has been conceptualized as one of the pillars of The Sustainable Development Strategy (SDS): Egypt Vision 2030

(Abdel Latif et al., 2018). The Egyptian education system has historically been "the center of Islamic scholarship", secular education, and thought throughout the region (Cochran, 2012, p. 1). Importantly, Egypt's education system has the largest student enrollment in the MENA region (PWC Middle East, 2018). Currently, pre-university education in Egypt serves over 21 million students enrolled in approximately 47,000 schools (MOETE, 2018).

Structure and Administration

The Ministry of Education and Technical Education (MOETE) has centralized control over all of Egypt's Pre-K-12 complex educational structures. These include two years of preschool education (Kindergarten), six years of primary education, three years of preparatory education, and three years of secondary education. Together, the primary and preparatory stages comprise what is known as mandatory or compulsory education. It is important to note that free public education (including higher education) is considered a constitutional right for all Egyptians (Soror, 1997). The MOETE authority also spans across wide regional, cultural, and socioeconomic variations (OECD, 2015). These include government schools, private (Arabic, languages, religious, and international) schools, and technical/vocational (industrial, commercial, and agricultural) schools.

The EMOETE oversees all of these public and private schools and is responsible for curricula development and implementation; supervision of instruction; provision of textbooks and instructional material; licensure and standardized testing; developing educational policies and strategic planning; monitoring and evaluating students, educators, and schools; and controlling all human resources aspects of hiring, firing and the professional development of teachers and administrators (OECD, 2015). In order to manage these thousands of diverse schools, the MOETE employs approximately two million teachers, school leaders, school counselors, district administrators, and support staff members (MOETE, 2017), including 947,282 teachers in public schools and 70,284 teachers in 8171 private schools (MOETE, 2018).

The Route to Educational Leadership

The Professional Academy for Teachers (PAT) is the designated entity responsible for the preparation of educational leaders in Egypt. It was established in 2008 by presidential decree number 129 and falls under the leadership of the EMOETE; however, on the official website, it is stated that "the academy is a local, regional and international center that ensures quality and sustainable professional development for educators in collaboration and effective partnership with colleges of education, schools and other relevant institutions" (Professional Academy for Teachers, n.d.). Teachers in Egyptian public schools can seek gradual leadership appointments following these successive hierarchical promotions from teacher to: (1) Premier Teacher, (2) Premier Teacher (level A), (3) Expert Teacher, and (4) Master Teacher. To move from one level of leadership to the next, there is a two-year on the job minimum requirement. Any Premier (level A) Teacher with two years on the job experience would be eligible to apply for the position of Assistant Principal and for the position of School Principal with four years of experience. In addition, Expert Teachers are eligible to apply for school principalship or for some district-level positions. To become a Principal or Assistant Principal, the candidate must successfully pass a three-day school leadership training course offered by the PAT, which grants a certificate of completion that remains valid for three years (Elbasel & Lashin, 2016; Professional Academy for Teachers, n.d.). To successfully complete the training, candidates go through formative assessment of knowledge attainment of content covered. Upon completion of the school leadership training course, the candidate becomes eligible to apply for school leadership positions. Open positions are advertised within districts through, at least, two well-circulated local newspapers. After which, a district-level committee conducts interviews and selects the best qualified candidate (As per education law 139, issued in 1981 and as modified by law 155, issued in 2007, and law 93, issued in 2012). The selected candidate will be hired or promoted to school principal for two years eligible for renewal based on performance and evaluation. It is apparent that the system for educational leadership preparation is relatively new; Colleges of Education are not directly involved in the process of educational leadership preparation, no advanced degrees are required for assuming school leadership positions and "very few people have the chance to participate in long term programs of administrative training given in universities and specialized institutes" (Hassan, 1980, p. 162), which adds to the many challenges of educational leaders in Egypt.

Current Challenges to Educational Leaders

> The training of leaders must aim at refining their intellectual skills, improving their ability to perform and make sound decisions, and transforming them into creative leaders with far-reaching visions that bring about desired change. The actual reality of the preparation programs for school principals in Egypt suffers from many shortcomings, whether in the process of planning, implementation, follow-up and/or evaluation.
>
> (Abdel Mola, 2014, p. 1)

School leaders in Egypt hold many responsibilities, yet currently, they do not receive the necessary preparation to successfully take on these responsibilities and address associated challenges. This is in part due to (1) the disconnect between colleges of education and school leadership preparation (2) the absence of licensure or certification requirements aligned with formal educational leadership degrees, (3) current training programs not being based on recent educational research and being isolated, one-time events that lack sustainability, (4) lack of follow up on the application and evaluation of school leaders' training programs and its impact (Abdel Mola, 2014; Barakat, 2019; OECD, 2015).

Centralization and control over decision-making at the top level is another problem that educational leaders face in Egypt. High-ranking district and governorate-level leaders seem to be stuck on routines, inflexible in dealing with rules and regulations and resistant to change (Hammad & Norris, 2009). Rigidity of leadership selection mechanisms which are still heavily based on age and seniority is a major challenge for education in Egypt. Another common consequence of top-down centralized bureaucratic systems is a lack of transparency, which could lead to favoritism, inequity, and frustrations (Barakat, 2019). School leaders are also challenged by a lack of autonomy, and especially financial autonomy (OECD, 2015), and the devaluing of opinions and input from younger administrators in a system that values seniority over competency and skills (Hammad, 2010).

Reform Initiatives

Egypt has witnessed an ebb and flow of educational movements and reform initiatives; however, "once a national project for reforming education begins and becomes fruitful, circumstances – economic, political, or of other types – intervene to neutralize or dismantle it" (Ibrahim, 2010, 509). Two major reforms took place in Egypt in the second half of the 20th century, which were the right to a free education and the compulsory education that required every Egyptian child to attend six years of primary and three years of preparatory schooling (Cochran, 2012; Ibrahim, 2010; OECD, 2015; Soror, 1997). These reforms impacted social mobility and resulted in more equitable social outcomes. However, this trajectory was derailed by the "open door" policy of Anwar Sadat (Cochran, 2012; Ibrahim, 2010), a neoliberal ideology that encouraged privatization of the Egyptian education system.

Between 1980 and 2011 the Egyptian education sector received large amounts of foreign aid to support the construction and maintenance of school buildings, the provision of resources, and the development of educators (El Berr, 2004; Ibrahim, 2010). During that time, a substantial focus was placed on the education of girls, bringing basic education to geographically remote and marginalized areas, and developing teachers' capacity (El Berr, 2004). Decentralization initiatives have also been implemented to grant schools greater autonomy and encourage participation and community involvement in the management of schools, yet with modest evidence of such reforms being successful (Ginsburg et al., 2010; Hammad, 2013). Many of these reform efforts remain driven by foreign-aid agencies, have little input and support from stakeholders, and continue to be unevaluated and viewed by many Egyptians as political propaganda (Habaka, 1999; Hammad, 2016). This demonstrates the importance of examining EAL research in the current context of rapid educational changes in the country and its significance in informing ongoing educational reforms.

Reviewing the Egyptian EAL Knowledge Base

Guided by prior EAL research reviews (e.g., Hallinger, 2013; Hallinger & Bryant 2013; Hammad & Hallinger, 2017), this chapter adopted the systematic review method (Hallinger, 2013; Pettigrew & Roberts, 2006). Since the purpose of the chapter is to illuminate patterns of EAL knowledge production rather than synthesize research findings, we employed a topographical approach aimed at identifying the salient features characterizing the body of literature under investigation (Hallinger, 2013). In this section, we describe the methodology used in this review chapter, starting with the identification of potential sources, through to data extraction and analysis.

Identification of Sources

For the purpose of the current review, we limited our search to published EAL literature (i.e., research articles). Since the available English-language EAL literature about Egypt is very limited (Hallinger & Hammad, 2019), we decided to analyze both Arabic and English literature. Therefore, several search techniques were used to locate possible sources. For Arabic articles, we chose to limit our search to the most established, well-known Arabic journals that publish EAL research in Egypt. We started with the two journals affiliated with the Egyptian Society for Comparative Education and Educational Administration (ESCEEA): the *Journal of Educational Administration* which is the only publication specialized in EAL in the Arab region, and the *Journal of Comparative Education* which publishes EAL research that has a comparative dimension. Our list also included six other publications affiliated with Ain Shams University, Cairo University, Al-Azhar University, Alexandria University, and Assiut University. These are cross-disciplinary educational journals that publish research covering a wide range of educational fields including EAL. We chose these journals because they are published by well-known universities and are highly ranked by the Supreme Council of Universities (SCU) in Egypt. In addition, they have been publishing regularly since 2000 and are available online via the EduSearch database. To find relevant sources within these journals, we scanned the titles (and sometimes the abstracts) of all published articles between 2001 and 2021. More than 10,000 titles were scanned at this stage. The inclusion criteria used to filter the articles were: (1) articles about/from Egypt; (2) articles that have a clear focus on EAL; (3) articles that are not about EAL in higher education; (4) articles that are not excerpts from students' dissertations; and (5) articles that are available in full-text format. This search strategy yielded 174 articles that met our criteria.

For identifying English-language sources, a two-stage search strategy was used. The first stage involved searching within ten well-known international EAL journals, namely: *Educational Administration Quarterly (EAQ), Journal of Educational Administration (JEA), School Effectiveness and School Improvement (SESI), Educational Management, Administration and Leadership (EMAL), International Journal of Leadership in Education (IJLE),*

International Journal of Educational Management (IJEM), School Leadership and Management (SLM), Leadership and Policy in Schools (LPS), International Journal of Educational Administration & History (IJEAH), and *International Studies in Educational Administration (ISEA).* Using the same parameters set for the Arabic journals, the titles and abstracts of all articles published in these international journals were scanned to locate relevant sources. This stage yielded a dataset of only 8 articles.

We then moved to the second stage in which we searched for articles within the Scopus database, the rationale being to ensure an acceptable level of article quality. Since it was an open search, we used a set of keywords to locate relevant articles. These included "educational leadership/administration", "school leadership/administration", "principal", "school leader", "organizational", "decision-making", and "Egypt". In this stage, we were able to locate eight additional articles published in eight journals other than those mentioned above, thus bringing the number of English-language sources to 16, and the overall size of the dataset to be reviewed to 190 articles.

Data Extraction and Analysis

The 190 articles identified were scanned to extract data relevant to the research questions. These included article titles, authors' names, year of publication, types of studies, school level, research topics, research methods, data collection tools, and statistical analyses. While it was possible in many cases to extract the necessary data by only reading the abstracts, many other cases required reading specific sections of the articles to find relevant information. Extracted data were then entered into a Microsoft Excel spreadsheet and codes were employed to facilitate subsequent analysis. For example, article topics were coded as follows: leadership = 8, principals = 9, human resources = 5, etc.). Similarly, research methods were assigned the following codes: quantitative = 1, qualitative = 2, and mixed = 3.

Data analysis was conducted quantitatively using descriptive statistics to highlight modal trends and illuminate the salient features of the literature under review. Patterns identified in the dataset were benchmarked against those found in prior reviews of EAL research in the Arab region (Atari & Outum, 2019; Hallinger & Hammad, 2019; Hammad & Hallinger, 2017; Hammad et al., 2022; Oplatka & Arar, 2017) as well as reviews of EAL research from other societies (Adams et al., 2021; Bridges 1982; Gumuş et al., 2020; Hallinger & Chen 2015; Hallinger, 2018).

The Current State of the EAL Knowledge Base in Egypt

The goal of this review is to explore the existing research trends in EAL in Egypt. Using quantitative review methods, we analyzed 190 articles published in Arabic language and Scopus indexed EAL journals over the past two decades (2001–2021). In this section, we present and discuss the key patterns of EAL knowledge production in Egypt as revealed by our analysis.

Volume of Publication

We examined the volume of the Egyptian EAL literature published in the period 2001–2021. Our search identified 174 articles published in eight Arabic language journals and 16 articles published in international journals. Taken together, these numbers suggest that the size of the published Egyptian EAL literature is very small compared, for example, to that of other developing countries such as Turkey (Gumuş et al., 2020) and Malaysia (Adams et al., 2021). Specifically, when compared to the total number of articles published in the same set of Arabic journals over the same period (more than 10,000 articles), the EAL scholarship on Egypt turns out to be very thin indeed, representing only about 1.7% of the overall published educational research. In alignment with Hallinger and Hammad's (2019) observation regarding Arab scholars' limited contribution to global EAL scholarship, the published English language EAL literature from Egypt is even thinner. This imbalance in terms of Arabic versus English-language literature may be attributed to limited English language proficiency among educational researchers in Egypt, in addition to other difficulties associated with academic writing and access to international journals experienced by Arab scholars generally (Getahun et al., 2021).

Despite the small size of the published Egyptian EAL knowledge base, our analysis reveals a significant increase in the publication volume over the period under study. As displayed in Figure 3.1, approximately 83% of the papers in our database have been published since 2010. Similar patterns were reported for EAL research from other developing countries (Ahmed, 2020; Hallinger, 2018; Hallinger & Chen, 2015; Gumuş et al., 2020).

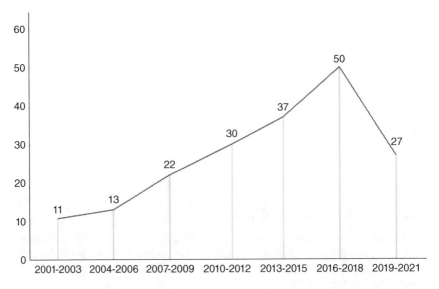

Figure 3.1 Pattern of EAL journal publications from Egypt (2001–2021).

Regarding journal distribution, we found 48% ($N = 84$) of the Arabic articles to be published in the two journals affiliated with the ESCEEA, i.e., *Educational Administration*, and *Comparative & International Education*, thus indicating a preference for Egyptian EAL scholars to publish in these two journals. This is understandable considering ESCEEA being the only academic society that specializes in EAL research in the Arab world and that academic promotion rules in Egypt favor publication in specialized rather than cross-disciplinary journals. The 16 English language articles were found to be dispersed across 14 international journals.

Authorship Trends

Analysis of authorship trends shows that 80% of the articles were single-authored and 20% were co-authored. This is consistent with Hammad and colleagues' (2022) findings regarding authorship patterns in EAL research from the Gulf region. In terms of gender, half of the EAL papers from Egypt were written by men researchers, while 43% of the articles were written by women researchers and the remaining 7% were written by teams of men and women scholars, which reflects a well-balanced representation of both men and women researchers in EAL scholarship in Egypt. This finding aligns with the noticeable increase in the number of women scholars within the EAL discipline in Egypt over the past two decades and the overall direction to empower academic women in all fields (Egyptian Women's Observatory, n.d.). Different results were reported in prior reviews where the Arab EAL literature was found to be "male dominated" (Atari & Outum, 2019; Hammad et al., 2022).

We were also interested in analyzing the institutional affiliations of authors to determine who is involved in conducting EAL research in Egypt and to identify potential "centers of EAL excellence". The analysis reveals that almost all articles were written by faculty members working in colleges of education and other educational research centers. Apart from a few English-language articles that involved non-Egyptian contributors, all articles were written by Egyptian scholars. We also noticed that the articles were scattered across more than 45 academic institutions, thus indicating the absence of centers of research excellence in EAL in Egypt. This aligns with features of EAL research from Arab societies (Hallinger & Hammad, 2019).

Types of Studies

We also focused on analyzing the composition of the EAL scholarship in Egypt in terms of study type. We employed a typology of (1) empirical studies, (2) conceptual/commentary papers, and (3) research reviews to classify the papers identified in this review. As shown in Figure 3.2, 67% of the literature was classified as empirical, 32% as conceptual/commentary, and 1% as research reviews. Similar trends were observed in recent reviews from other

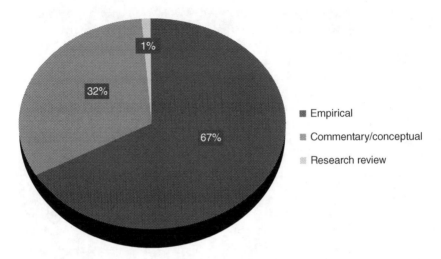

Figure 3.2 Distribution of articles by type of study.

developing societies (Ahmed, 2020; Hallinger, 2018; Hallinger & Hammad, 2019) (Figure 3.2).

Research Topics

Our review focused on identifying the range and concentration of research topics addressed in the EAL literature on Egypt. We started by examining the school level studied in the articles. Consistent with findings reported for EAL scholarship in developing countries (Hallinger, 2018; Hallinger & Bryant, 2013; Hammad et al., 2022), Egyptian EAL scholars showed a preference for studying EAL practices and processes in multiple levels of schooling (34%) and secondary schools (30%), rather than in pre-school institutions (4%), primary (5%), or middle schools (1%) (see Figure 3.3).

Next, we examined the composition of research topics covered in the identified literature. Topical coverage is used to explore the "research front" which highlights the current topics in a given literature (Hallinger & Kovačević, 2019). Drawing on typologies developed in previous EAL reviews (Atari & Outum, 2019; Bellibaş & Gümüş, 2019; Hallinger & Chen, 2015; Hallinger & Hammad, 2019), we classified the topics into 28 categories. Data displayed in Table 3.1 indicated that school leadership was the most studied topic in the Egyptian EAL literature with a total number of 35 articles. This category included studies of different leadership styles such as ethical leadership (Othman, 2017), servant leadership (Salahuddin, 2016), transformational leadership (Jawhar, 2002; Qarni, 2014), distributed leadership (Al-Harthi & Al-Mahdy, 2017; Radwan, 2019), and teacher leadership (Emira, 2010). Indeed, research on leadership in K-12 schools has gained greater prominence in the field since the beginning of the century (Hallinger & Chen, 2015). Governance has also

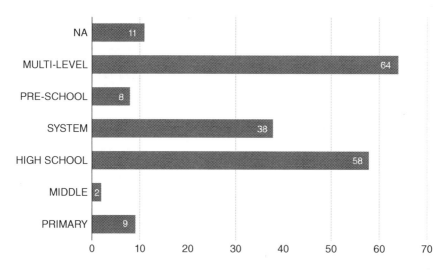

Figure 3.3 Distribution of articles by school level.

been a frequent focus in Egyptian literature. Articles in this category included various topics such as accountability (Abdul Rahman, 2015), decentralization (Hammad, 2013; Nasr, 2010), school-based management (Elmeligy, 2015), and empowerment (Al-Mahdy, 2007; Hassan, 2013). Governance was followed by other topics including school performance and improvement (Alhusayni & Ahmad, 2005; Barakat, 2019; Mandor, 2018) and organizational behavior. Studies in the organizational behavior category included investigations of topics such as organizational climate (Gad Alkarim, 2018), organizational culture (Qarni, 2014), organizational trust (Alhusayni A & Ahmad, 2005; Mahmoud & Barakat, 2006), organizational health (Mohamed & Azeb, 2017), and organizational citizenship (Hashem, 2005; Radwan, 2020). Egyptian researchers have also demonstrated an interest in studying human resources management, with studies addressing issues such as human resource selection (Hasanin, 2019), training (Shubeer, 2008), and job performance appraisal (Mahmoud & Barakat, 2006). Interestingly, we found that three of the most studied topics in the Egyptian EAL scholarship, namely leadership, organizational behavior, climate, and culture, and human resources received similar emphasis in the Gulf and Turkish EAL literatures (Hammad et al., 2022; Bellibaş & Gümüş, 2019).

Research Methods Employed in the Egyptian EAL Literature

As shown in Figure 3.4, within the subset of 127 empirical studies, 85% of the articles used quantitative methods ($N = 108$), and 11% employed qualitative methods ($N = 14$), while mixed methods were employed only in five studies

Table 3.1 Topical coverage[1]

Topics	Total	%
Leadership	35	18.42
Governance (SBM, decentralization, accountability, empowerment)	34	17.89
School performance and improvement	31	16.31
Organizational behavior, climate, and culture	31	16.31
Human resources (selection, preparation, and development)	30	15.78
Principals	29	15.26
Administrative roles, practices, and processes	26	13.68
Administrative and organizational development	26	13.68
Proposed frameworks and models	26	13.68
Quality and accreditation	23	12.10
Comparative administration and leadership	21	11.05
Emotions: commitment motivation, satisfaction	20	10.52
Decision-making	9	4.73
Knowledge management and knowledge society	9	4.73
ICT	9	4.73
Instructional supervision and teacher evaluation	7	3.68
Parents and community	6	3.15
Values and ethics	6	3.15
Entrepreneurship	4	2.10
Gender	3	1.57
Social justice and diversity	3	1.57
Time management	3	1.57
Crisis management	3	1.57
Creative management and leadership	3	1.57
EDLM research	3	1.57
Cultural contexts	2	1.05
Middle-level leadership	1	0.52
Finance	1	0.52

[1] The total number of topics exceeded 190 because most of the articles addressed more than one topic.

(e.g., Barakat, 2019; Ismail, 2008). While this pattern is consistent with what Hammad et al. (2022) found in their recent review of the Arabic EAL scholarship in the Gulf region, it contrasts with findings reported in Hammad and Hallinger's (2017) review of English-language EAL literature which revealed a better balance between quantitative and qualitative methods.

In terms of the data collection methods employed by Egyptian EAL scholars, and consistent with the predominance of quantitative methods, 89% of the empirical studies ($N = 113$) used surveys. Interviews were employed in 19 studies (15%) (e.g., Barakat & Brooks, 2016; Ginsburg et al., 2010; Hammad & Norris, 2009;) and document analysis was used in five articles (e.g., Barakat & Maslin-Ostrowski, 2019; Ginsburg et al., 2010). None of the studies used observation as a data collection technique (see Figure 3.5). Interestingly, it was noticed that most of the occurrences of using qualitative data collection methods were found in the articles published in international

Examining the Knowledge Base in Educational Administration 49

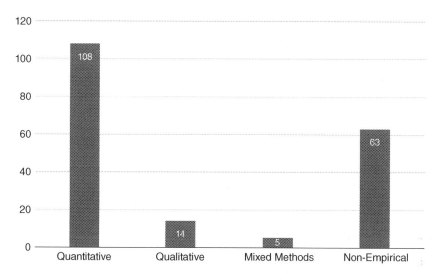

Figure 3.4 Distribution of articles by research methods.

journals. This heavy reliance on surveys is expected given the scarcity of funding resources available for Egyptian scholars, which results in researchers favoring survey-based papers for their relatively low cost (Asuga et al., 2016).

In order to classify the subset of quantitative and mixed methods studies according to their statistical tests, we employed a four-level rubric developed by Bridges (1982) and used in previous EAL reviews (Hallinger & Chen, 2015; Hammad & Hallinger, 2019). As displayed in Figure 3.6, 63% of the

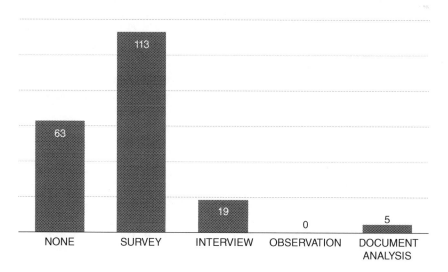

Figure 3.5 Distribution of articles by data collection methods.

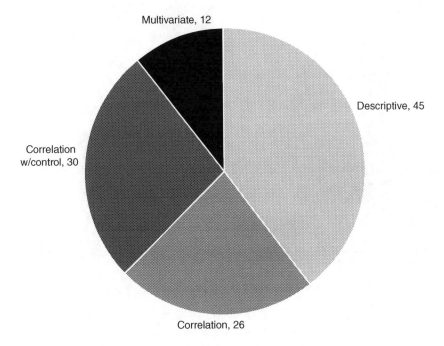

Figure 3.6 Distribution of articles by level of statistical analysis.

quantitative and mixed methods articles ($N = 71$) used Level I and Level II statistical analyses, while 30 articles (26.5%) employed Level III tests (e.g., Othman, 2020; Radwan, 2020). Advanced statistics (Level IV) were only used in 12 studies (10.6%) (e.g., Al-Harthi & Al-Mahdy, 2017; Hammad et al., 2021). This reflects the prevalence of simple quantitative methods in Egyptian EAL studies. In contrast with findings reported for the EAL literatures from Turkey (Bellibaş & Gümüş, 2019), Malaysia (Adams et al., 2021), and the English language scholarship from other Arab societies (Hammad & Hallinger, 2017), the EAL studies from Egypt relied more on descriptive statistical methods rather than on multivariate techniques.

Discussion and Implications

Prior EAL research reviews (e.g., Hallinger & Bryant, 2013; Hallinger et al., 2015; Hammad & Hallinger, 2017) have called for country-level analyses of EAL research as part of the broader goal of diversifying the existing global knowledge base in the field. The current review was conducted with these calls in mind. It sought to examine the EAL scholarship in Egypt in terms of publication volume, authorship trends, types of articles, topical foci, and research methods, drawing on a database of 190 Arabic and English language research articles published in the period 2001–2021. In this section, we discuss the implications of the findings and provide recommendations for development.

The most striking finding emerging from this review concerns the small size of the Egyptian EAL knowledge base compared to what we were expecting from a country like Egypt which has the largest educational system in the MENA region, in addition to a higher education system that is rapidly expanding. This small volume of research output suggests that EAL research in Egypt is still in its infancy despite its steady growth over the past decade. This aligns with the characterization of the Arab EAL literature as an "emerging literature" that is yet to reach maturity (Atari & Outum, 2019; Hallinger & Hammad, 2019). This could be attributed to the fact that educational leadership as a unique discipline that includes an open-ended body of knowledge, which focuses on central concerns and involves a mastery of procedures and distinctive forms of judgment or explanation, is yet to be fully understood and appreciated within the overarching umbrella of the Egyptian public education system. It is also important to view this pattern within the broader context of knowledge production in the Arab world at large. There is evidence suggesting that, due to political, cultural, institutional, and financial constraints, research output from Arab research institutions is generally low, thus causing Arab contributions to global scientific knowledge to be insignificant (Abouchedid & Abdelnour, 2015; Hanafi & Arvanitis, 2015), especially in the social sciences and humanities sector (Ibrahim, 2018).

Low research productivity seems to have been compounded by lack of collaboration. Analysis of authorship trends found most of the articles (80%) to be single-authored, thus reflecting a general tendency among Egypt's EAL researchers to write and publish individually. This is not surprising given the existing evidence concerning the prevalence of an individualist institutional culture in Arab higher education institutions (Getahun et al, 2021). However, in the case of Egypt, lack of collaborative research is totally understandable considering existing academic promotion rules which discourage this practice as they give less weight to co-authored papers (Supreme Council of Universities, 2019). This needs to be changed before we can see more Egyptian scholars engaged in collaborative EAL research. One way to foster collaboration is to encourage EAL scholars in Egypt to develop informal networks and establish connections with colleagues both inside and outside Egypt. This will not only promote collaborative research but also contribute to capacity development by linking EAL scholars in Egypt "with human and financial resources beyond their borders" (Gumuş et al., 2020 p. 40). The ESCEEA can play an important role in facilitating this. As Attari and Essa (2021) argue, such academic associations "play a fundamental role in overcoming the institutional limitations, opening research avenues and integrating practitioners and other stakeholders in scholarly activities" (p. 14).

Analysis of the types of studies revealed that the vast majority of the Egyptian EAL literature was empirical. This aligns with features reported for the EAL scholarship in the Arab region generally (Atari & Outum, 2019; Hammad & Hallinger, 2017). On the positive side, this could be seen as a promising practice since "grounded literature depends on generating a sufficient body of empirical research" (Hallinger & Chen, 2015, p. 11). Nonetheless, a balanced distribution of study types is needed to build a mature EAL knowledge base (Atari & Outum, 2019; Hallinger & Hammad, 2019). Specifically, conceptual research facilitates the generation of relevant EAL knowledge that better fits local contexts. It also enables researchers to ground their empirical research in the socio-cultural contexts of their own societies rather than overly relying on imported conceptual models (Gumuş et al., 2020; Mertkan et al., 2017). Moreover, conceptual studies are particularly needed as they facilitate the critique and contextualization of EAL practices in the Arab region, especially during this time of rapid educational development (Hallinger & Hammad, 2019). This becomes even more important in the Egyptian context where EAL scholars need to contextualize their research in light of the national culture and institutional structures and challenges in order to make it more responsive to current policy changes and national development needs.

Our analysis of topical foci reflected many of the features typifying EAL scholarship in Arab/Muslim countries (see Ahmed, 2020; Atari & Outum, 2019; Hammad et al., 2022; Oplatka & Arar, 2017). First, the current review found "diffuse" coverage of research topics, a feature that was also observed in reviews of early North American literature (see Bridges, 1982; Heck & Hallinger, 2005). Second, in alignment with Oplatka and Arar's (2017) findings, we noted that some topics that have attained significance in the broader EAL literature were either ignored or received minimal attention in this literature. These included social justice, gender, cultural context, middle management, and educational finance. We also noticed that Egyptian EAL scholars were not interested in exploring the relationship between leadership practices/behaviors and school outcomes, especially student learning. This is despite leadership being an important focus for EAL research in Egypt and enhancing student learning being a priority in current educational reform initiatives in the country (Ministry of Education, 2014). Moreover, despite notable interest among Egyptian EAL scholars to study school principals, very little of their research addressed how these principals are prepared and appointed. We see this as a lacuna that needs to be rectified, given the challenges facing school leaders in Egypt at present (Abdel Mola, 2014; Arar et al., Barakat, 2019). Understanding the importance and nuanced complexity of educational leadership and the process of leadership preparation has been the focus of research for decades now. In a recently published study, Grissom and colleagues (2021, p. ix) state:

> based on research since 2000, the impact of an effective principal has likely been understated, with impacts being both greater and broader than previously believed: greater in the impact on student achievement and

broader in affecting other important outcomes, including teacher satisfaction and retention (especially among high-performing teachers), student attendance, and reductions in exclusionary discipline.

Accordingly, to get the most impact on school and student outcomes, there needs to be an intentional focus in EAL research in Egypt on developing effective educational leaders. This is particularly important given the emphasis placed by ongoing reform initiatives on the school as a unit of change, with rising expectations of school principals as leaders of change (Ministry of Education, 2014). Hence, forging a national EAL research agenda that addresses these issues becomes an urgent priority. This can be useful in bridging the apparent disconnect between EAL research and policy reforms.

Our review also identified a number of methodological weaknesses. First, Egyptian EAL scholars produced an overly high proportion of quantitative studies, with surveys being the sole data collection method. Such excessive reliance on quantitative methods is problematic as it limits the researcher's ability to capture the complexities of the phenomenon under investigation, thus posing a challenge to building a mature knowledge base. It also raises concerns about the quality of the Egyptian EAL research (Bellibaş & Gümüş, 2019). The predominance of quantitative research could be attributed to the impact that globalization and imported models and research methods have had on Arab societies. These models are characterized by heavy emphasis on positivistic approaches, thus resulting in a large percentage of quantitative studies (Altbach, 2015). Therefore, we recommend that EAL scholars in Egypt make efforts to rectify this by alternative approaches that can enhance the quality of their research and increase its ability to unravel the complex issues associated with EAL practices and processes. We specifically highlight the importance of qualitative research because, as Hallinger and colleagues suggest, it is "particularly useful for developing rich descriptions of practice, and can play an especially important role during the early stages of building a knowledge base" (Hallinger et al., 2015, p. 451)

Another methodological limitation emerged when we analyzed the statistical tests employed in the studies. The analysis revealed that Egyptian EAL scholars relied mostly on simple (descriptive and correlational) rather than advanced (multivariate) statistical analyses. While consistent with trends found in the EAL literature from Africa (Hallinger, 2018) and the early North American scholarship (Bridges, 1982), the predominant use of weak, mostly descriptive, statistical analyses as problematic as they fail to capture the complex nature of the relationships among the variables influencing EAL practices and processes (Bridges, 1982). Hallinger and colleagues (2015, p. 451) highlighted this as a serious limitation of the EAL in Vietnam, indicating that "reliance on theoretically barren, unsubstantiated survey instruments and weak statistical methods represented a persisting constraint on theory-building, policy analysis, and validation of effective practice". Similarly, in their reviews of EAL literatures from Arab societies, Hammad et al. (2022)

and Oplatka and Arar (2017) argued that Arab scholars' reliance on simple statistical tests caused their investigations to stay on the "descriptive level", thus limiting their ability to fully understand EAL processes and associated challenges and to produce meaningful results that can inform effective practice. Thus, it is important that future EAL research in Egypt adopt more sophisticated designs that use advanced statistical analyses to address this shortcoming.

Conclusion

In this chapter, we tried to sketch a broad picture of the EAL knowledge base in Egypt, hoping to highlight its strengths and weaknesses and provide suggestions to improve it to increase its ability to inform current educational developments in the country. We expect that the findings of this review will draw the attention of educational research institutions, EAL scholars, and policy-makers in Egypt to the importance of EAL research for educational reform and encourage them to consider ways to develop it in terms of quantity, quality, and relevance. Our findings suggest that in its current state, the Egyptian EAL knowledge base is largely disconnected from educational policy and practice. For example, while current policy changes focus on raising education quality and improving school outcomes, there continues to be a lack of research that explores how school leadership practices and processes enable or hinder such endeavors. In addition, despite decentralization being a recurrent theme on the reform agenda, there is thin empirical evidence on the impact of decentralization initiatives on school effectiveness. As for practice, the existing knowledge base fails to provide a clear picture of leadership practices in Egyptian schools. For example, despite a large number of studies exploring school leadership and principals' administrative roles and practices, these studies often remain at the descriptive level and ignore the complex relationships between these practices and other important school variables (see also Oplatka & Arar, 2017). We argue that without addressing these shortcomings the existing EAL knowledge base will remain unable to inform educational policy and practice in Egypt.

We believe that developing the existing EAL research in Egypt into a mature scholarship that is better connected to policy and practice is a huge endeavor that requires collaboration, coordination, establishing connections and partnerships, and providing adequate resources and training. Also important is intellectual leadership that can guide these efforts and direct them toward the common goal of building a solid national EAL knowledge base that is contextually relevant and at the same time linked to global EAL scholarship (Hallinger & Hammad, 2019). This is particularly important because, with EAL increasingly growing into a more "internationalized" field of research (Mertkan et al., 2017; Samier et al., 2021), more contributions are expected from Middle Eastern societies, especially from Egypt considering its massive education system as well as its position as one of the key actors in the region.

In concluding this review chapter, it is appropriate to highlight its limitations. The first limitation relates to the limited scope of the database, especially with regard to Arabic-language sources; our database included 173 articles published in eight Egyptian journals, thus ignoring other articles that might have been published in other Arabic journals inside or outside Egypt. This review also did not consider EAL literature published in other formats such as books, book chapters, or postgraduate dissertations. While this might raise concerns about the generalizability of our findings to the full EAL scholarship in Egypt, we argue that the dataset analyzed in this review provides a reasonable representation of the existing EAL literature in Egypt. Another limitation concerns our analytical approach. This review employed a quantitative, topographical approach aimed at identifying general patterns of EAL knowledge production rather than synthesizing substantive research findings. However, we consider this review as a preliminary investigation providing future directions for capacity development aimed at strengthening the EAL knowledge base in Egypt.

References

Abdel Latif, A., Magdy, D., El Sharkawy, K., William, M., & Maguid, M. (2018). *Egypt SDS 2030: Between expectations and challenges to implementation.* Retrieved from: https://fount.aucegypt.edu/cgi/viewcontent.cgi?article=1063&context=studenttxt

Abdel Mola, K. A. (2014). Developing school principal preparation programs in the primary stage in light of some contemporary global trends. Masters Theses, Fayoum University.

Abouchedid, K., & Abdelnour, G. (2015). Faculty research productivity in six Arab countries. *International Review of Education, 61*(5), 673–690.

Abdul Rahman, M. (2015). Educational accounting as an approach to ensure the quality of human resource management processes in public secondary schools in Egypt. *Journal of Scientific Research in Education, Faculty of Women for Arts, Science, and Education, 16*(5), 1–40.

Adams, D., Thien, L. M., Chuin, E. C. Y., & Semaadderi, P. (2021). The elusive Malayan tiger 'captured': A systematic review of research on educational leadership and management in Malaysia. *Educational Management Administration & Leadership, 7*, 1–20. 10.1177/1741143221998697

Ahmed, E. (2020). Systematic review of research on educational and management in Muslim societies. *Educational Management Administration & Leadership, 5*, 1–23. 10.1177/1741143220973658

Al-Harthi, A., & Al-Mahdy, Y. (2017). Distributed leadership and school effectiveness in Egypt and Oman: An exploratory study. *International Journal of Educational Management, 31*(6), 801–813.

Alhusayni, A., & Ahmad, E. (2005). Organizational trust and the effectiveness of school performance in the Arab Republic of Egypt. *Journal of Comparative and International Education, 8*(17), 17–134.

Al-Mahdy, Y. (2007). Empowering teachers in basic education schools in Egypt: An empirical study. *Journal of the College of Education in Educational Sciences, Ain Shams University, 31*(2), 9–56.

Altbach, P. G. (2015). Academic colonialism in action: American accreditation of foreign universities. *International Higher Education*, 32(1), 5–7.

Arar, K., Turan, S., Barakat, M., & Oplatka, I. (2017). The characteristics of educational leadership in the Middle East: A comparative analysis of three nation-states. In: D. Waite, & I. Bogotch (eds), *The international handbook of educational leadership* (pp. 355–373). Wiley.

Asuga, G.N., Scevak, J., & Eacott, S. (2016). Educational leadership, management, and administration in Africa: An analysis of contemporary research. *School Leadership and Management*, 36(4), 381–400. 10.1080/13632434.2016.1247042

Atari, A., & Outum, N. (2019). Research on educational administration published in Arabic language educational journals: A systematic review and analysis. *International Studies in Educational Administration (Commonwealth Council for Educational Administration & Management (CCEAM))*, 47(1). 61–73.

Attari, A. T. A., & Essa, E. B. (2021). Arab scholarship in educational administration, management and leadership: An overview. *Educational Management Administration & Leadership*, 1, 1–19, 10.1177/17411432211012011

Barakat, M. (2019). Perceptions of educational leaders regarding contemporary reform initiatives in Egypt. *Journal of Educational Administration and History*, 51(4), 330–351. 10.1080/00220620.2019.1590323

Barakat, M., & Maslin-Ostrowski, P. (2019). Ripples of hope: Leading educational change for equity in Egypt's public schools. *International Journal of Leadership in Education*, 6, 10.1080/13603124.2019.1690706

Barakat, M., Brooks, J. S. (2016). When globalization causes cultural conflict: Leadership in the context of an Egyptian/American school. *Journal of Cases in Educational Leadership*, 19(4), 3–15. 10.1177/1555458916672707

Belchetz, D., & Leithwood, K. (2007). Successful leadership: Does context matter and if so, how? In C. Day & K. Leithwood (eds), *Successful principal leadership in times of change: An international perspective* (pp. 11–137). Springer.

Bellibaş, M., & Gümüş, S. (2019). A systematic review of educational leadership and management research in Turkey: Content analysis of topics, conceptual models, and methods. *Journal of Educational Administration*, 57(6), 731–747. 10.1108/JEA-01-2019-0004

Bridges, E. (1982). Research on the school administrator: The state-of-the-art, 1967–1980. *Educational Administration Quarterly*, 18(3), 12–33. 10.1177/0013161X82018003003

Cochran, J. (2012). *Education in Egypt (RLE Egypt)* (Vol. 1). Routledge.

Dimmock, C., & Walker, A. (2005). *Educational Leadership: Culture and Diversity*. Sage.

Elbasel, M., & Lashin, S.K. (2016). Strategies for selecting school principals: Introduction to total quality management. Retrieved from https://www.researchgate.net/publication/328675390_astratyjyat_akhtyar_mdyry_almdars_mdkhl_ladart_aljwdt_alshamlt

Egyptian Prime Minister (2013). *Decree number 428, 2013: Executive Policy for Chapter seven of Education Law number 139 of year 1981*. Retrieved from https://manshurat.org/node/1994

Egyptian Women's Observatory (n.d.). *Women's Strategy 2030*. Retrieved September 30, 2021 from https://enow.gov.eg/%D8%A7%D9%84%D8%B1%D8%A4%D9%8A%D8%A9%20%D9%88%D8%A7%D9%84%D9%87%D8%AF%D9%81%20%D9%81%D9%8A%202030

Elbadawy, A. (2015). Education in Egypt: Improvements in attainment, problems with quality and inequality. In R. Assaad & C. Krafft (Eds.), *The Egyptian labor market in an era of revolution* (pp. 127–146). Oxford University Press.

El Berr, S. (2004). *Non-German donor activity in education in Egypt*. ZEF Bildungsstudie (Center for Development Research), University of Bonn. https://www.zef.de/fileadmin/webfiles/downloads/projects/el-mikawy/egypt_non-german-donor.pdf

Elmeligy, R. (2015). School-based management: An approach to decision-making quality in Egyptian general secondary schools. *School Leadership & Management*, 35(1), 79–96. 10.1080/13632434.2014.962499

Emira, M. (2010). Leading to decide or deciding to lead? Understanding the relationship between teacher leadership and decision making. *Educational Management Administration & Leadership*, 38(5), 591–612. 10.1177/1741143210373738

Flessa, J., Bramwell, D., Fernandez, M., & Weinstein, J. (2018). School Leadership in Latin America 2000–2016. *Educational Management Administration & Leadership*, 46(2), 182–206. 10.1177/1741143217717277

Gad Alkarim, U. (2018). Creating the organizational climate for applying knowledge management processes: A case study on the managers of public secondary schools in Qaliubiya Governorate. *Journal of Educational Administration*, 5(20), 243–304.

Getahun, D. A., Hammad, W., & Robinson-Pant, A. (2021). Academic writing for publication: Putting the 'international' into context. *Research in Comparative and International Education*, 16(2), 160–180. 10.1177/17454999211009346

Ginsburg, M., Megahed, N., Elmeski, M., & Nobuyuki, T. (2010). Reforming educational governance and management in Egypt: National and international actors and dynamics. *Education Policy Analysis Archives*, 18(5), 22–37. 10.14507/EPAA

Grissom, J. A., Egalite, A. J., & Lindsay, C. A. (2021). *How principals affect students and schools: A systematic synthesis of two decades of research*. The Wallace Foundation. http://www.wallacefoundation.org/principalsynthesis

Gumuş, S., Bellibaş M.Ş., Gumuş E., & Hallinger, P. (2020). Science mapping research on educational leadership and management in Turkey: A bibliometric review of international publications. *School Leadership & Management*, 40(1), 23–44. 10.1080/13632434.2019.1578737

Gunter, H. M. (2011). *Leadership and the Reform of Education*. Policy Press.

Habaka, A. (1999). *A comparative investigation into technological change and educational reform in secondary schools in England and Sweden: Applications to Egypt* (Unpublished master's thesis). Ain Shams University.

Hallinger, P. (2018). Surfacing a hidden literature: A systematic review of research on educational leadership and management in Africa. *Educational Management Administration & Leadership*, 46(3), 362–384. 10.1177/1741143217694895

Hallinger, P., & Chen, J. (2015). Review of research on educational leadership and management in Asia: A comparative analysis of research topics and methods 1995–2012 *Educational Management Administration & Leadership*, 43(1), 5–27. 10.1177/1741143214535744

Hallinger, P., & Hammad, W. (2019). Knowledge production on educational leadership and management in Arab societies: A systematic review of research. *Educational Management Administration & Leadership*, 47(1), 20–36. 10.1177/1741143217717280

Hallinger, P., & Kovačević, J. (2019). A bibliometric review of research on educational administration: science mapping the literature, 1960 to 2018. *Review of Educational Research*, 89(3), 335–369. 10.3102/0034654319830380

Hallinger, P. (2013). A conceptual framework for systematic reviews of research in educational leadership and management. *Journal of Educational Administration*, 51(2),126–149. 10.1108/09578231311304670

Hallinger, P., & Bryant, D. A. (2013). Review of research publications on educational leadership and management in Asia: A comparative analysis of three regions. *Oxford Review of Education*, 39(3), 307–328. 10.1080/03054985.2013.803961

Hallinger, P., Walker, A., & Trung, G. T. (2015). Making sense of images of fact and fiction: A critical review of the knowledge base for school leadership in Vietnam. *Journal of Educational Administration*, 53(4), 445–466. 10.1108/JEA-05-2014-0060

Hammad, W. (2010). Teachers' perceptions of school culture as a barrier to shared decision-making (SDM) in Egypt's secondary schools. *Compare*, 40(1), 97–110. 10.1080/03057920903374432

Hammad, W. (2013). The Rhetoric and Reality of Decentralisation Reforms: The Case of School-Based Management in Egypt. *International Studies in Educational Administration (Commonwealth Council for Educational Administration & Management (CCEAM))*, 41(2), 11.

Hammad, W. (2016). Conflicting road maps: Cross-cultural professional development for Egyptian educators. *Compare: A Journal of Comparative and International Education*, 46(2), 293–313. 10.1080/03057925.2014.985186

Hammad, W., & Hallinger, P. (2017). A systematic review of conceptual models and methods used in research on educational leadership and management in Arab societies. *School Leadership & Management*, 37(5), 434–456. 10.1080/13632434.2017.1366441

Hallinger, P., & Hammad, W. (2019). Knowledge production on educational leadership and management in Arab societies: A systematic review of research. *Educational Management Administration & Leadership*, 47(1), 20–36. 10.1177/1741143217717280

Hammad, W., Samier E., & Mohammad, A. (2022). Mapping the field of educational leadership and management in the Arabian Gulf region: A systematic review of Arabic research literature. *Educational Management Administration & Leadership*, 1–20. 10.1177/1741143220937308

Hammad, W., & Norris, N. (2009). Centralised control: A barrier to shared decision-making in Egyptian secondary schools. *International Studies in Educational Administration*, 37(2), 60–73.

Hammad, W., & Alazmi, A. A. (2022). Research on school principals in the Gulf states: A systematic review of topics and conceptual models. *Management in Education*, 10.1177/0892020620959748

Hammad, W., Abu Shindi, Y., Morad, H., Al-Mahdy, Y., & Al-Harthi, K. (2021). Promoting teacher professional learning in Egyptian schools: The contribution of learning-centered leadership, *International Journal of Leadership in Education*. 10.1080/13603124.2021.1969038.

Hanafi, S., & Arvanitis, R. (2015). *Knowledge production in the Arab World: The impossible promise*. Routledge.

Hasanin, M. (2019). Suggested procedures for developing the selection process for policy makers education in Egypt. *Journal of Educational Administration*, 6(22), 359–449.

Hashem, N. (2005). Mechanisms for activating organizational citizenship in Egyptian school. *Journal of Comparative and International Education, 8*(14), 243–319.

Hassan, M. A. M. (1980). *Guidelines for the development of programs of preparation of school administrators in Egypt* (Doctoral dissertation) University of Pittsburgh.

Hassan, N. (2013). A proposed vision to improve the performance of training and quality units in the Egyptian school in the light of recent trends. *Journal of Scientific Research in Education, Faculty of Women for Arts, Science, and Education, 15*(20), 65–89.

Hauge, T. E., Norenes, S. O., & Vedøy, G. (2014). School leadership and educational change: Tools and practices in shared school leadership development. *Journal of Educational Change, 15*(4), 357–376. 10.1007/s10833-014-9228-y

Heck, R.H., & Hallinger, P. (2005). The study of educational leadership and management: Where does the field stand today? *Educational Management, Administration, and Leadership, 33*(2), 229–238. 10.1177/1741143205051055

Ibrahim, A. S. (2010). The politics of educational transfer and policymaking in Egypt. *Prospects, 40*(4), 499–515. 10.1007/s11125-010-9173-3

Ibrahim, B. (2018). Arab Spring's effect on scientific productivity and research performance in Arab countries. *Scientometrics, 117*(3), 1555–1586. 10.1007/s11192-018-2935-

Ismail, M. (2008). Professional development for teachers of the first cycle of basic education in the light of the concepts of quality and accreditation: A field study on the qualification program for primary school teachers for the university level. *Journal of Comparative and International Education, 11*(22), 57–138.

Jawhar, Y. (2002). The transformational leadership style as an approach for improving the performance of the school principal in Egypt. *Journal of Comparative and International Education, 5*(7), 139–202.

Ministry of Education and Technical Education [MOETE] (2018). Annual book of statistics, Chapter 2, Schools, classes and students. *The general administration of information systems and decision support.* http://emis.gov.eg/Site%20Content/book/017018/pdf/ch2.pdf

Ministry of Education and Technical Education [MOETE] (2017). *Statistical summary of pre-university education. The general administration of information systems and decision support.* http://emis.gov.eg/Site%20Content/matwaya/2017/matwaya2017.html

Ministry of Education. (2014). *Strategic plan for pre-university education.* https://planipolis.iiep.unesco.org/en/2014/strategic-plan-pre-university-education-2014-2030-5881

Mohamed, A, & Azeb, E. (2017). Organizational health of special education schools in Egypt and job satisfaction among their teachers: An analytical study. *Journal of Educational Administration, 4*(13), 15–132.

Mahmoud, H., & Barakat, S. (2006). The relationship between the confidence of general education school principals and teachers in the accuracy, objectivity and effectiveness of the job performance evaluation system and their sense of organizational justice: A field study. *Journal of Educational Sciences, Cairo university, 14*(2). 2–63.

Mandor, H. (2018). Improving the public secondary school performance in Egypt in the light of organizational slack dimensions. *Journal of Educational Administration, 5*(19), 117–177.

Mertkan, S., Arsan, N., Inal Cavlan, G., & Onurkan Aliusta, G. (2017). Diversity and equality in academic publishing: The case of educational leadership. *Compare: A Journal of Comparative and International Education*, 47(1), 46–61. 10.1080/0305 7925.2015.1136924

Nasr, A. (2010). Decentralization and organizational development of kindergarten in the Arab Republic of Egypt: A proposed model. *Journal of Educational Sciences, Cairo University*, 18(2), 118–224.

Oplatka, I., & Arar, K. (2017). The research on educational leadership and management in the Arab world since the 1990s: A systematic review. *Review of Education*, 5(3), 267–307. 10.1002/rev3.3095

Organisation for Economic Co-operation and Development (OECD). (2015). *Schools for skills: A new learning agenda for Egypt*. http://www.oecd.org/countries/egypt/Schools-for-skills-anew-learning-agenda-for-Egypt.pd

Othman, M. (2017). A proposed model to achieve competitive advantage for the primary school in Egypt in the light of ethical leadership (approach). *Journal of Educational Administration*, 4(13), 133–199.

Othman, M. (2020). The role of school leadership in achieving the dimensions of a knowledge society in pre-university education: A field study in Upper Egypt. *Journal of Educational Administration*, 7(27), 275–351.

Pettigrew, M., & Roberts, H. (2006). *Systematic reviews in the social sciences*. Blackwell.

Professional Academy for Teachers [PAT] (n.d.). http://pat.edu.eg/

Pwc Middle East (2018). *Middle east education: Understanding education sector in Egypt*. https://www.pwc.com/m1/en/industries/education/education-country-profile-egypt.html

Qarni, U. (2014). Strengthening the relationship of transformational leadership and organizational culture with institutional capacity In the Egyptian general secondary schools: A proposed vision. *Journal of Educational Administration*, 1(2), 13–112.

Radwan, O. (2019). Distributed leadership as an approach for accomplishment of professional learning communities in industrial technical schools in the Arab Republic of Egypt. *Journal of Education, Al-Azhar University*, 184(2), 511–553.

Radwan, O. (2020). Democratic practices and behaviors of organizational citizenship among general secondary school teachers in the Republic of Egypt Arabia. *Journal of Educational Administration*, 7(26), 256–345.

Salahuddin, N. (2016). School principals servant leadership and teachers job satisfaction: A proposed structural model for effective school in Egypt. *Journal of the College of Education in Educational Sciences, Ain Shams University*, 40(1), 65–166.

Samier, E. A., Elkaleh, E. S., & Hammad, W. (Eds.). (2021). *Internationalisation of educational administration and leadership curriculum: Voices and experiences from the 'Peripheries'*. Emerald Group Publishing.

Sayed, F. H. (2005). Security, donors' interests, and education policy making in Egypt. *Mediterranean Quarterly*, 16(2), 66–84. 10.1215/10474552-16-2-66

Shubeer, M. (2008). Training needs of primary school principals. *Comparative and Journal of International Education*, 11(22),215–309.

Soror, A. (1997). Egypt: A reform strategy for Egyptian education. Educational reform: An open file – the approach of decision makers. In Arabic. *Futures (Mostkabaliat) Journal*, 27(104), 624–644.

Supreme Council of Universities (2019). *Rules and system of work of scientific committees*. Ministry of Higher Education.

UNESCO. (2006). *Decentralization of education in Egypt* (Country report on the UNESCO seminar on EFA implementation: Teacher and resource management in the context of decentralization, Administrative Staff College of India, Hyderabad, India, 6–8 January 2005). UNESCO.

4 Educational Leadership and Administration in Iraq

Challenges and Prospects

Mayamin Altae

Introduction

Many years of political and authoritarian influences in Iraq changed the perception of educational leadership and administration (ELA) by school leaders who, at times, perceived ELA as a mere process of monitoring teachers' work and arranging records. School leaders should have the power "to influence colleagues to change in ways that they would not otherwise consider" (Altae, 2022: 5), which has not been the case in the Iraqi context. ELA in Iraq has gone through massive turmoil within the last five decades due to the many internal and external conflicts that the country has gone through. The consecutive governments' focus on national security and the militarization of the country hindered the development of the ELA and made the country lag behind in this field compared to other countries in the region. Iraq's geographical location at the heart of the Middle East surrounded by six other countries made it more susceptible to the influences of the progress made by such neighbouring countries due to comparison. Advances in the ELA sector in the neighbouring countries make the Iraqi deficiencies in the field more noticeable. This chapter sheds light on the current situation of the ELA field in Iraq, its shortcomings and prospects through reviewing the government documents in this field and also working with the educational officials at the Directorate General for Educational Planning at the Ministry of Education in Baghdad to explore their vision in this respect.

The current Iraqi government recognizes the importance of building a research-based educational leadership system to ensure that the implementation on the ground is informed by research. This is being done through focusing on "strengthening the capacity of the Ministry of Education to effectively plan, budget, implement and monitor equitable delivery of quality education services" (UNICEF, 2021). However, this does not seem to be an easy journey due to the lack of rigorous research in the country as a result of the chaos that marred the education sector as a whole following the invasion of the country in 2003. The research field in educational administration in Iraq is still in its infancy and is barely connected to the policy and practice in the country. There are no specific educational administration roles within

DOI: 10.4324/9781003334835-4

Iraqi schools, and such roles are being played by inspectors "because it is part of their responsibilities to energise teachers to fulfil their potentials in supporting the schools' performance" (Altae, 2022: 4). Current leadership practices in Iraq seldom draw from innovation and creativity and are often ineffective at meeting objectives due to the lack of "critical education" (UNICEF, 2021). Hence, efforts within the Iraqi MoE are aimed at advancing the roles of educational leaders in schools. These efforts to improve educational leadership programs include the tasks of renewing, evaluating, and developing of the programs offered by schools, in addition to serving the teaching staff as part of the MoE's strategy to adapt to changes (Najm, 2018). The tasks of psychological and educational counselling for teachers to direct and assist them in addressing the problems they face are also on the MoE list. Also, and for the first time in the history of the Iraqi MoE's practices, there is an effort to equip education leaders with the skills necessary to reinforce the relationship of the teacher with the community, and to enable the community to benefit from and improve school work resources.

The war on Iraq in 2003 "resulted in destruction of 80% of the educational institutions and the collapse of the educational process after the invasion" (Issa & Jamil, 2010: 363). However, it introduced a new education system dubbed as the education for "new" Iraq, one that was meant to modernize the Iraqi education provision and make up for the years of chaos that had plagued the system in the post-2003 era. The education leadership and administration sector has been identified as a top priority to achieve a modern and comprehensive education system. (Arar, 2020) The Iraqi MoE has many ELA considerations on the table that need addressing to rehabilitate this important sector, which will contribute to the overall change of the education system. This chapter focuses on the schools' leadership and administration aspect in Iraq, the current challenges, and the prospects of development. School leadership is pivotal to the development of education leadership values in Iraq, a country that has witnessed many internal and external conflicts over the last five decades.

Schools Administrations: Human Aspect and Teachers Inclusion

From the humanistic perspective, the school administration and headteachers' roles are essential to the process of tapping into and maximizing teachers' potential because "principals can influence teacher emotions through several key behaviors: professional respect shown for teacher capability; providing appropriate acknowledgement for teacher commitment, and sacrifice" (Lambersky, 2016: 379). It is the efforts that the administration takes towards the professional development of teachers and other school staff that drive the improvement of outcomes for all. The more awareness that school leadership shows towards such issues, the better outcomes they are able to achieve in bringing everyone together to complete a mutual aim. Historically, Iraqi schools' leadership has not been very effective in implementing "housekeeping" rules. The school leadership has been left to flow in an ad hoc manner in accordance with a set of informal agreements within the internal schools' communities. As long as those communities were adhering to the MoE guidelines in terms of curricula and exam requirements, they were deemed to be in order. The schools ensure

> that students are ready for national examinations and that schools are performing to the standards set up by the Ministry of Education. They report to the local directorate of education and then to the Ministry of Education.
>
> (Altae, 2022: 3)

This has, unfortunately, created a culture of indifference towards the administration of required tasks in a robust and effective way. The result is a lack of purposefully trained school leaders who are unable to move schools beyond solely being a medium for the delivery of information (Arar et al., 2021). Such issues were left to the personal assessment of each leader who applied their understanding of social norms within their communities. The tribal aspect has interfered in this, as most school leaders are appointed from the same area of their schools and are known to the local communities. Many of the school leaders sought tribal affiliation in order to get the "support of the tribe and improve chances for individual advancement" (Crane, 2003: 30). The tribal intervention in education and in other political sectors started at Saddam Hussein's time. Upon emerging into power, Saddam found the tribes in Iraq were excluded from public sector life and saw them as potential supporters of his regime. He started to work on manipulating the tribal *Sheikhs* and making them a socio-political power that could be transformed into docile tools to serve his regime and become authentic associates for power-sharing. Thus,

> the tribal intervention in the state justice system, in the running of the state bureaucracy, and in state education, and the phenomenon of tribal blood feuds being turned against the state's law-enforcement officers—all the result of the tribes' growing self-confidence.
>
> (Baram, 1997: 21)

That policy continued for decades, and the tribes imposed their wish on the MoE in the appointment of education leaders in the schools within their areas, which was part of the Ba'th policy to supervise schools through its local cells. That was done by appointing "one full member as a part of a cell who will act as a full time Ba'thist administrator within each school" (Faust, 2015: 110). The tribal influence in this field continued even after the fall of the regime. Therefore, it was difficult for the schools' leaders to implement any evidence-based management strategies to instil professional development activities in schools. Continuous professional development can establish "a positive relationship between the selected variables of teachers' efficiency and determinants of the human resource management and development strategies" (Hashmi, 2014: 83). Such lack of awareness about the importance of evidence-based management in school leadership has resulted in some members of school communities to feel excluded, especially if they were not from the same area where schools are located. Therefore, it is now time for the Iraqi ELA provision to instil the concepts of modern management in the awareness and practices of school leaders. In the end, school leadership is a humane process, and it is important to provide all of school members with a suitable environment to do their job effectively. Making everyone feel valued and included and applying the same rules to all irrespective of their backgrounds will result in a successful leadership style Oplatka & Arar, 2017. This is a vital point that the Iraqi ELA sector currently lacks and needs in order to make school leadership central to sustainable school performance goals and the creation of a harmonious atmosphere for everyone. School administration in Iraqi urban and rural areas lacks the "ruly" method in dealing with the schools' communities, i.e., it is not controlled and lacks discipline. This is hindering the development of the individuals (teachers and school administrators) within schools and obstructing the government's views in relation to modernizing the school leadership provision. It is worth mentioning here that since the invasion of the country in 2003, many of the training programs that the MoE used to run for school leaders have either stopped or been deleted due to the chaotic scenes that followed the dismantling of previous governments' departments, including the education sector. Hence, such a lack of training of school leaders resulted in many of them restoring to their own initiatives and leading according to their own social backgrounds and being directed by the necessities of the local communities where they serve. It is important to train those leaders to adopt a stance of responding to challenges and drawing a recovery plan by building on experiences that "looks a lot more like learning and adaptation than simply following orders and establishing routines" (Kayes et al., 2013: 193).

Schools Governing Bodies: Choosing What Is Right for Schools

Structurally, school leadership in Iraq functions in a strict top-down approach.

> The leadership process starts from the Ministry of Education and works down through local directorates of education in the provinces to the school inspectors and headteachers. The structure of leadership responsibilities is fixed across all stages of education with no regard to children's changing needs.
>
> (Altae, 2022: 3)

The schools governing bodies' provision is not currently clear in the structure of Iraqi schools. There are what is called parent–teacher councils in some schools, but their functions are far from the real function of the governing bodies; they are only a means "to encourage parents to communicate directly with the school administration in order to follow up their sons/daughters' performance" (Jamil & Sabah, 2021: 277). Indeed, school governing bodies play a massive role in shaping school leadership and administration practices due to their contribution in guiding and advising schools and closely working with leaders. The role of a school governor simply encompasses "appointing and working with the headteacher; acting as a change agent; active participation in the school; organising the governing body; dealing with complaints; working with parents; and chairing meetings" (James et al., 2012: 3). The absence of such governing bodies in the Iraqi education scene has deprived the leadership provision from establishing a cooperative relationship with the schools' communities, and widened the gap between parents and teachers to communicate. There is a clear "lack of communication between teachers and parents" in Iraqi schools because "teachers know nothing about their students' cultural background and did not visit their neighbourhoods or families" (Al-asadi, 2016: 32). Although parents' evening meetings are still in place, such evenings are hardly functional because many parents do not attend them. This has made parents completely unaware of what is happening inside schools and the policies and methods that are being implemented. This has increased the challenges facing school administrations and hindered the government's efforts to engage parents with schools as part of the "new" Iraq requirements.

The "new" Iraq that emerged after the invasion of 2003 with the all-new education department was meant to catch up with the modern educational trends and engage all stakeholders in the leadership of the educational institutions starting from schools to the higher education sector. The whole education system was meant to receive support from the international community (after the invasion) to "enable Iraqi people to renew and reconstruct their education system and achieve the goals" (UNESCO, 2005). Furthermore, the absence of governing bodies has made it difficult for schools to be in close service of their local communities and has, to a certain degree, severed a vital line of connection between such important stakeholders. This connection is important to "build effective working teams of school staff, parents, and community members to promote the academic work" (Dougherty, 2013: 163). There is, undoubtedly, a massive task for the Iraqi MoE here to establish a policy to create schools' governing bodies that work with school leadership teams to uplift the already underdeveloped school administration practices and achieve the government targets of renovating the educational leadership provision. The Iraqi education leadership provision would benefit from such addition to the leadership framework because such governing bodies would secure the support of parents to any changes and/or suggestions to practices that schools would intend to introduce. Schools' leadership teams would also benefit from some parents' experiences in the education field and from their knowledge about the local communities and their needs, which would enable better planning and direction of school policy.

Governing bodies are, therefore, one of the cornerstones in building modern school leadership provisions in Iraq and they are the first line of defence against any social turmoil or unrest especially in a country like Iraq where the social mosaic of the communities makes it difficult for school leaders to fully grasp the needs of each community. In Iraq, it is normal to find many different ethnicities living in the same area side by side, but such cultural and social diversity comes at a cost. The different cultural and mainly religious beliefs might make it impossible for school leaders to address every group's interests. Hence, the school governing bodies can play a vital role in bringing the different viewpoints together for the sake of establishing an equitable education for all.

Educational Leadership and Communities: Creating More Leaders, Not Followers

Following the invasion of Iraq in 2003, many of the local education directorates were dismantled and new educational authorities were formed with new faces in charge. Most of the former local education senior leaders were normally chosen from the loyal circle of the Ba'ath Party that was the catalyst for the propaganda of Saddam Hussein's regime. The Ba'th Party was not only the source of the previous regime's intelligence, but it also was the main on-the-ground provider of the security aspects that the regime had coveted. Ba'th Party had a local branch in every neighbourhood of the 18 Iraqi provinces, and its members were in charge of almost all issues that are linked to the political aspects of everyday life including education. Education was seen by Saddam Hussein's regime as a potential threat to national security and so it became a top priority for the government to have it under the control of the regime's security. In this fashion, no one would be better placed to take control of education other than the Ba'th Party branches that were located in every corner of the country. A Background Paper on Iraq published by the US Department of State mentioned that the Ba'th Party that was close to the Iraqi government controlled all the propaganda outlets (The White House, 1991), and schools were seen as suitable places to promote such agendas. All headteachers of schools were appointed on the recommendation of the Ba'ath Party branches in the areas where schools were located. Although such arrangements were harsh and stringent, it had worked for the previous regime by keeping communities under control and working with them in a coherent manner. The cohesion was the outcome that the previous regime wanted from school leaders no matter what the means. It was not a problem for the Ba'th Party officials if the school leaders were doing what was wanted from them out of fear as long as they ran their schools in accordance with the so-called "national security".

However, the new government that was formed by the American coalition looked at all school leaders as part of the old regime, and they did not want to see them involved in the formation of the "new" Iraqi education system. Among the different reasons for excluding the previous school leaders were concerns about their loyalty to the previous regime as they were appointed on the Ba'th Party's recommendations, and their potential to discreetly work with the remaining Ba'th Party cells to make the schools a source of the communities' destabilization. This approach has worsened the situation even more for the education leadership provision mainly because all those who were brought in to lead the schools had no prior experience in administration and had no education leadership skills. In addition, there have been no training programs in place to prepare these new education leaders for their posts due to the aftermath of the invasion that destabilized the education sector and led to the insufficient supply of educational logistics support, insecurity, and lack of training (Issa & Jamil, 2010).

Most of the new leaders, as a result, were unable to lead their schools effectively at such a very decisive stage of the Iraqi educational leadership change. The new appointees have been on many occasions replaced by others, which exacerbated the situation of the educational leadership in the schools even more. It did not only affect the work inside schools but also severed the links that schools used to have with their surrounding communities. This is a huge challenge for the Iraqi MoE that needs to be addressed in order to restore an acceptable level of connection between school leaders and the local communities. The relationships between them are vital in establishing sound and strong communities because the roles of schools are not only limited to working with students but also working with parents and other members of the communities where schools are located.

Therefore, the prospects are for the MoE to start working with the school leaders on intensive training programmes to enable them to work with their local communities effectively. Such work is important to make these education leaders influential in their surroundings by making their school premises hubs for the communities where everyone can use to learn and develop. School leaders also need to be able to convince their communities about the importance of working with schools to diminish any problems or myths about education and its role in national progress. The image of education in Iraq has already been tarnished following the invasion of 2003, which led to the deterioration of the standards. The invasion of Iraq by the American forces "resulted in destruction of 80% of the educational institutions and the collapse of the educational process after the invasion" (Issa & Jamil, 2010: 363). Extensive work is needed now to restore the image of education. School leaders can do this job by working with communities and addressing the education needs of students and listening to parents and other community leaders. School leaders also need to engage communities in their decision-making process by running consultation sessions and involving them in the education process.

More importantly, school leaders can work with communities to help in establishing settled and resilient local communities in the face of the current challenges facing the Iraqi education provision, mainly the fragile security situation. Many students have been drawn into terrorism by terrorist groups due to their vulnerability that is a result of a poor knowledge of their surroundings and the hidden agendas of the vicious terrorist groups who look at Iraqi schools as an easy target to recruit impressionable students and exploit their parents. There is a need to act on the basis of knowledge as a powerful instrument, and raise awareness among school children about such issues to prevent tragic consequences because "the use of school-aged youth by al-Qaeda in Iraq can also be attributed to situational factors, which could lead young persons to view membership in the group as advantageous" (Bott et al., 2009: 35). Extensive national campaigns are, therefore, needed to stress the importance of the working relationship between school and local community leaders to protect the schools and the students from any external negative influences. This can happen by organizing awareness sessions for parents about the potential dangers surrounding their children and equipping them with the skills needed to detect any unusual practices or concerns that they might come across. This will have a great influence in developing the quality of education provided to students and protecting future generations from distorted ideas in order to build strong communities that are equipped with the knowledge and the education standards needed to make them important contributors to the development of the national education sector as a whole.

Evaluating School Leadership: Creating the Right Environment

One of the obstacles currently facing the Iraqi education leadership provision is the absence of effective and workable assessment tools of school leadership performance. As mentioned earlier, school leadership in the Iraqi education context prior to 2003 has always been led centrally and in accordance with rigid guidelines; in other words, it has always been closely monitored by the previous governments. School leaders were perceived as being capable of doing their job or at the very least, knowing enough to do so. The metrics for knowing "enough" was mainly linked to the national security measures that were imposed on them by the Ba'th Party. They were mainly required to know how to monitor any security breaches in their schools and report any suspicious activity, and to lead by simply adhering to the MoE's guidelines. There was no room for any manoeuvre of designated tasks. School leaders were not offered any support, and their performance had never been audited nor assessed. The education leadership provision, thus, suffered from a great deterioration during the eight-year war with Iran from 1980 to 1988, the invasion of Kuwait in 1990, and the subsequent harsh years of international sanctions from 1991 until the collapse of the regime in 2003. That period of more than 20 years of wars and isolation from the international community threw the education leadership sector into complete turmoil. There were no development leadership programmes and no trainings provided to school heads due to the education sector falling as a priority to the government as compared to the defence and national security sectors.

The post-2003 governments have been working on renovating the education leadership sector and implementing some modern practices in the field with a focus on how to assess the performance of education leaders. Governments promote projects in this respect by encouraging education officials and headteachers to get involved in assessing the needs to rebuild the education leadership provision. To support the rebuilding of the education system,

> Several other changes were implemented or encouraged in teacher instructional methods, retention of students, and student assessment. Teachers were encouraged to revise and reform their classical teaching method, which was based on memorization, and to adopt student-centred teaching techniques, emphasizing the development of creative and analytical skills.
>
> (Vernez et al., 2014: 6)

Governments are focusing on introducing a clear and quality strategy because many "headteachers expressed that one of the main challenges facing reform in the education system is quality assurance and clarity on the management strategy" (Lapcha & Mahdi, 2021: 5).

However, there are no systemic action plans to do this and there is an absence of leadership skills of current school heads. Therefore, there is an urgent need for the Iraqi MoE to rectify the situation and begin by assessing school leadership performances. This can be done by looking at the qualifications of school leaders and matching them with the standards of acceptable levels of education leaders. The teaching qualification has always been accepted as a requirement for school leaders, but "from the late 20th century, there has been a growing realization that headship is a specialist occupation which requires specific preparation" (Bush, 2013: 455). As mentioned earlier in the chapter, most of the current school leaders replaced the previous ones after the invasion in 2003, and they were rushed to the promoted jobs for political reasons, mainly to get rid of the old guards who were allegedly loyal to the previous regime. School leaders also need extensive training programmes to enable them to lead and distribute administration responsibilities across the school leadership team. In addition, more field observation programmes need to be introduced to oversee the performances of school leaders on the ground and assess their abilities to engage teachers in the decision-making process as well as the consulting of parents in the way schools should be run. This is important in the "new" Iraq because, after many years of dictatorial leadership, there should be a more cooperative way to make everyone's voice heard when making decisions and implementing new practices. This is, in the end, the democracy that the new government is promoting in all other sectors of life, and schools should be the first to implement it. In doing so, the government is encouraging the use of the Internet:

From secondary school students who use it to find materials to complete homework assignments to women who gather before computers to learn from the experiences of women elsewhere how to promote their own interests in Iraqi society, the Internet has opened many venues for change.
(Davis, 2005: 12)

The democratic atmosphere in schools, if appropriately implemented, would result in a sense of belonging to the place by the school community, which will have positive outcomes on the teaching and learning process by providing teachers "with the necessary aspects to meet the training needs of different educational settings and organising and executing educational programs in schools" (Altae, 2020). Sharing information with parents and being more transparent about future plans would also promote the work relationships between schools and their local communities. Among other aspects that are currently absent from the scene of school leadership in Iraq is the clarity about the authorities that school heads have. Since the collapse of the previous education system, there have been no definitive guidelines for school administrations about the level of powers that the leading teams possess. This has resulted in the deputy heads currently running a lot of the schools' daily administration tasks including setting up timetables for teachers, meeting with parents, looking at students' disciplinary issues, and even reporting repairs and administrating the purchase transactions, all while the heads tend to look at the legislative issue acting as a link between schools and the MoE. There are also no middle leader roles meaning there is little to share outside the circle of the heads and their deputies. It is important for all Iraqi communities to know about what is happening in their respective schools and share any future plans. School communities have been marginalized for many decades due to previous political regime restrictions and it is now time to make them feel included and empowered. It is also important to educate school leaders about the purpose of their roles. Most of the current school leaders in Iraq are executing their roles in a solely administrative and authoritarian way without paying attention to the core purpose of their role, which is, in the end, to facilitate and achieve quality teaching and learning. School leadership is different from any other context of leadership because schools have many individual differences on the part of teachers and students that need to be considered by the leaders. This is another prospect that the education officials in Iraq require to pay more attention to and provide appropriate training for education leaders to make them understand that leadership in education is not a privilege but a mandate, and it has to be inclusive for all.

True Schools Leaders for Iraq: Selecting the Right People

As stated earlier, the qualifications of the current school leaders in Iraq are far behind the acceptable standards and this is because of the absence of clear and definitive education leadership programmes on the school level. The political aspects are still dominating school environments in the country and most of the current school leaders have connections with politicians of their local MPs who support them no matter what their qualifications and abilities are. The school leaders might be under pressure to satisfy various external parties (Arar, 2015). It is, therefore, imperative for the MoE to start planning and working on reassessing this provision. If the MoE is not able to replace some current school leaders due to their links to senior officials, then a contingency plan needs to be implemented to rehabilitate these leaders and bring them to acceptable standards in order to secure quality education for the upcoming generations. School leaders need to be introduced to modern education leadership patterns to enhance their leadership style. More training is also needed throughout the year to create a kind of momentum for school leaders and make them involved in a continuous development process just as the case in England where many "potential heads undertake leadership training, with a national curriculum, before becoming principals and receive national accreditation on successful completion of the activity" (Bush, 2013: 463). This would empower these leaders and provide them with the skills needed to take their schools to the next level.

The senior officials at the MoE need to draw a policy that allows school administrators and leaders to gain more power in running their schools and to familiarize them with the dimensions of modern leadership styles, which would lead to greater success in their roles. School leaders are not just ordinary employees who look after the daily work inside schools; they are community leaders who could influence their surroundings in a great deal by providing quality education and making schools hubs for knowledge and education activities in their areas. Schools are homes of the smaller communities where the good lives flourish and the struggled ones are redirected to the right path. Hence, true leaders are the ones who can make the best of their surrounding communities by acquiring the leadership skills needed to master their jobs. It is time for Iraqi school leaders to rise above the narrow ideas of politics and focus on their jobs as being responsible for the bringing up of the upcoming generations. Even if some of those leaders are surviving being incompetent due to their political links, their success in their role is what determines their continuity in the end because educational leadership is not limited to the education sector. Educational leadership is the leadership of the communities as a whole including the cultural, economic, and social aspects. The schools are the places where intellectuals, scientists, doctors, soldiers, judges, and other graduates stem from.

Ultimately, the security aspect had had its massive toll on the education leadership provision in Iraq in the last 15 years. It had not only drained the government's resources but also impacted the education leadership sector very badly. The instability of the political process and the fragile security situation resulting from the American invasion in 2003 were like the final straw that brought the educational leadership back. The invasion was quickly followed by the emergence of various militias and groups who became active inside every neighbourhood and used school buildings for their alleged resistance actions without paying any thought to the future of the generations of people whom they were supposed to fight for. Add to that the horrible psychological consequences that such activities of spreading fear among civilians have had on the families and their children. Therefore, it is very difficult to establish a sound and effective school leadership provision in the mid of an atmosphere of horror. This is why, the Iraqi MoE, in cooperation with the local governing councils, needs to work on diminishing any military or terrorist activities around schools and other educational institutions in order to enable school leaders to do their job. School leaders also need to be independent of any political circles and focus on establishing a successful, harmonious and peaceful education environment in their schools.

References

Al-asadi, F. (2016). The role of school-parent relationship in improving Iraqi EFL student's language skills. *International Journal of Humanities and Social Science*, 6(7), 28–33.
Altae, M. (2020). An overview of the stages of development of the Iraqi English language curriculum. *Social Sciences & Humanities Open*, 2(1), 100047.
Altae, M. (2022). Teacher leadership and teacher identity in turbulent times in Iraq. *Management in Education*, 36(4), 178–185.
Arar, K.H. (2015). Leadership for equity and social justice in Arab and Jewish schools in Israel: Leadership trajectories and pedagogical praxis. *International Journal of Multicultural Education*, 17(1), 162–187.
Arar, K. (2020). Educational Administration in the Middle-East. In R. Papa (Eds.), *Oxford research encyclopedia*, Oxford Encyclopedia of Education, Oxford University Press (pp. 1–26). 10.1093/acrefore/9780190264093.013.672
Arar, K., Sawalhi, R., Chaaban, Y., Zohri, A., & Alhouti, I. (2021). School leaders' perspectives towards leading during crisis through an ecological lens: A comparison of five Arab countries. *Journal of Educational Administration and History*, 5, 1–20.
Baram, A. (1997). Neo-tribalism in Iraq: Saddam Hussein's tribal policies 1991–96. *International Journal of Middle East Studies*, 29(1), 1–31.
Bott, C., Castan, W. J., Lark, L., & Thompson, G. (2009). Recruitment and radicalization of school aged youth by international terrorist groups. Retrieved from https://www.eccnetwork.net/sites/default/files/media/file/2009-recruitment-and-radicalization.pdf
Bush, T. (2013). Preparing headteachers in England: Professional certification, not academic learning. *Educational Management Administration & Leadership*, 41(4), 453–465.
Crane, C. C. (2003). *Reconstructing Iraq: Insights, challenges, and missions for military forces in a post-conflict scenario*. Strategic Studies Institute, US Army War College.
Davis, E. (2005). *Strategies for promoting democracy in Iraq* (Vol. 31). United States Institute of Peace.
Dougherty, A. M. (2013). *Psychological consultation and collaboration in school and community settings*. Cengage Learning.

Faust, A. M. (2015). *The Ba'thification of Iraq: Saddam Hussein's totalitarianism.* University of Texas Press.

Hashmi, K. (2014). Human resource management strategies and teacher's efficiency within schools: A co-relational study. *IAFOR Journal of Education, 2*(1), 65–87.

Issa, J., & Jamil, H. (2010). Overview of the education system in contemporary Iraq. *European Journal of Social Sciences, 14*(3), 360–368.

James, C., Jones, J., Connolly, M., Brammer, S., Fertig, M., & James, J. (2012). The role of the chair of the school governing body in England. *School Leadership & Management, 32*(1), 3–19.

Jamil, M., & Sabah, R. (2021). Updating a proposed experiment for parents-teachers councils' work in the Republic of Iraq "Distance education as a model". *LARK Journal for Philosophy, Linguistics and Social Sciences, 4*(43), 276–313.

Kayes, D. C., Allen, C. N., & Self, N. (2013). Integrating learning, leadership, and crisis in management education: Lessons from army officers in Iraq and Afghanistan. *Journal of Management Education, 37*(2), 180–202.

Lambersky, J. (2016). Understanding the human side of school leadership: Principals' impact on teachers' morale, self-efficacy, stress, and commitment. *Leadership and Policy in Schools, 15*(4), 379–405.

Lapcha, H., & Mahdi, Y. (2021). Coalition building for better religious education reform. Retrieved from https://opendocs.ids.ac.uk/opendocs/handle/20.500.12413/15930

Najm, H. A. J. (2018). The role of transformational leadership in achieving administrative creativity: An exploratory research on the views of sample of officials in the office of Iraqi Ministry of Education. *Al-Rafidain University College for Sciences,* (42), 112–135.

Oplatka, I., Arar, K. (2017). The research on educational leadership and management in the Arab world since the 1990s: A systematic review. *Review of Education, 5*(3), 267–307. 10.1002/rev3.3095

UNESCO. (2005). Iraq, education in transition: Needs and challenges. Paris: UNESCO. Retrieved from https://unesdoc.unesco.org/ark:/48223/pf0000138665

UNICEF. (2021). *Education every child in school, and learning.* UNICEF. Retrieved from https://www.unicef.org/iraq/what-we-do/education

Vernez, G., Culbertson, S., & Constant, L. (2014). *Strategic priorities for improving access to quality education in the Kurdistan region – Iraq. Monograph.* RAND Corporation. PO Box 2138, Santa Monica, CA 90407-2138.

5 Educational Leadership and Administration in Morocco

Recent Developments and Growth Prospects

Mohammed Elmeski

In Morocco, the role of educational leadership and administration (ELA) as a school reform accelerator cannot be over-emphasized. Leadership is the linchpin that aligns standards, accountability, human capital, structures, and organizational practices to provide quality learning opportunities for all (Ward et al., 2018). However, little is known, especially internationally, on ELA in Morocco and the extent to which it is leveraged as a system turnaround driver. This chapter is a contribution to fill this gap.

The chapter consists of four sections. Section "The Learning Improvement Imperative for ELA in Morocco" describes the learning improvement imperative of ELA in Morocco, including an overview of the in-country emergent literature. Section "The Evolution of ELA" follows the evolution of ELA from a policy on decentralization to the School Development Project (SDP). Section "Areas for Capacity Building: Building ELA Capabilities to Ensure Effective Decentralization" examines areas of capacity building in ELA. Finally, Section "Policy, Practice, and Research Implications" concludes with policy, practice, and research implications.

The Learning Improvement Imperative for ELA in Morocco

Shifting the focus to leading for results is Morocco's most challenging improvement frontier. According to the World Bank (2019) Learning Poverty report, sixty-six percent of Moroccan youth leave school with too little learning and too few of the skills to be employable, productive citizens (World Bank, 2019). In 2019, the High Council for Education, Training, and Scientific Research (HCETSR) conducted a performance appraisal of the implementation of the 2015–2030 strategic vision for educational improvement. The appraisal evaluated inclusiveness & equal opportunities,[1] education quality,[2] and the advancement of the individual and society. The three indices form the National Index on the Development of Education (NIDE). Figure 5.1 shows incremental progress on NIDE. However, the observed growth remains insignificant and volatile.

DOI: 10.4324/9781003334835-5

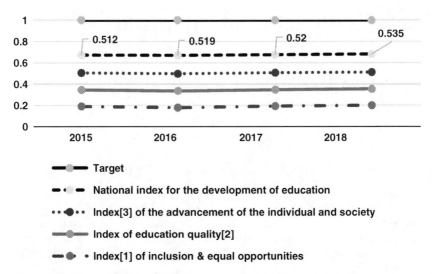

Figure 5.1 The evolution of NIDE as a composite of three sub-indices.

Source: Higher Council for Education and Training 2019 performance monitoring for the strategic vision 2015–2030.

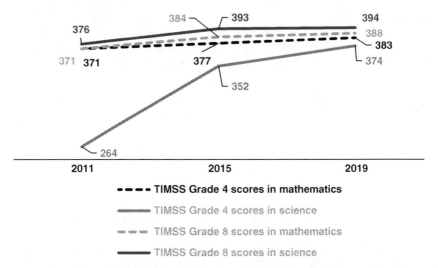

Figure 5.2 A summary of TIMSS scores of Morocco's fourth and eighth graders in 2011–2019.

Another quality red flag are the results from Trends in International Mathematics and Science Study (TIMSS) and Progress in International Reading Literacy Study (PIRLS). Gains in fourth and eighth graders' scores in TIMSS have been steady since 2011. However, as shown in Figure 5.2, Morocco continues to lag by a 116-point gap in science and mathematics and a 159-point gap in reading, compared to the international TIMSS and PIRLS average of 500. In this regard, a close examination of the evolution of reform foci since the rollout of NCET reveals a mounting realization of the importance of ELA as a boundary spanner between input investments and improved student outcomes.

Turning around Morocco's consistently lagging educational performance has gained prominence as the most pressing imperative for strengthening ELA since the launch of the rollout of the National Charter for Education and Training (NCET) in 2000. The evolution of Morocco's reform policy indicates a rising awareness among policy-makers that input investments alone (infrastructure, curriculum, and textbook reform, and staff recruitment and training) are not sufficient to improve learning for all students. This is consistent with the literature on the limitations of the production function model to educational change (Hanushek, 2003, 2020; Hanushek & Woessmann, 2016, & Loeb & Bound, 1996). It also reflects the growing realization of the importance of systems thinking as a holistic approach to school reform. This is reflected in the review of existing literature on ELA in Morocco which indicates a budding realization of the importance of ELA as a boundary spanner between policy and results.

A review of the literature on ELA in Morocco in Arabic, French, and English confirms similar findings in the Arab region reported in Atari and Outum (2019), and Hallinger and Hammad (2019). Studies of ELA in Morocco represent an emerging body of knowledge stretched over a variety of topics. They cover educational policy and school-based leadership (Amghar, 2019 & Lekhsadi, 2000); ELA theory versus implementation (Akhyar, 2016; Betty, 2011, & Dadi, 2014); leadership of place in marginalized urban neighborhoods (Elmeski, 2015); and the role of governance reform in promoting ELA (Bourqia, 2016 & Chafiq, 2019). Other topics include principals' technological readiness (Boqoulou & Berrad, 2016; Laouni, 2021); strategic planning in public schools (Benatou & Chentouf, 2016); and the role of local governance boards in educational leadership (Serhani, 2016).

Taken together, existing studies conducted on ELA in Morocco document a mounting realization that leadership at all levels is critical to navigating the complexity of equity, quality, and inclusiveness demands of educational improvement. They also highlight the need for systems of support and decision-making autonomy to empower school leaders to concretize the country's policy aspirations about ELA. In the next section, I elaborate further on the latter point by situating the evolution of ELA in the larger administration reform agenda pertaining to educational decentralization and school-based improvement.

The Evolution of ELA in Morocco

Policy Inception

A review of Morocco's educational reform policy milestones since the turn of the century indicates that the rise to prominence of ELA seems to build on efforts to bolster the capacity for decentralized educational governance in Morocco's 12 administrative regions. In this regard, four milestones have marked ELA inception and growth in the country. (1) The National Charter for Education and Training (NCET) reform in 2000–2010, (2) the 2015–2030 Strategic Vision for Reform (SVR), (3) the 2019 Education Framework Act (EFA), and (4) the 2021 New Model for Development. Altogether, the four milestones reflect a paradigm shift from a heavily top-down system of administration to a more decentralized governance model.

In this chapter, I posit that the growth of ELA is intertwined with the overarching national policy on decentralization. Decentralization, according to Daun (2007) and Saito (2008), fosters democratization, closer services to people, better governance, and effective development. In this regard, Winkler (1989) and Wolman (1990) argue that when individual preferences are properly considered, social welfare increases. In education, Daun (2007) notes that many developing countries sought to decentralize due to (1) the inability of the government to finance increasing educational costs, (2) cultural factors, (3) low capacity of the state, (4) consistently lagging performance of the education system, and (5) international influence.

Education decentralization was a key priority of NCET (MoE, 2000). The 2000–2010 reform agenda mainly focused on the EA in ELA. Reform lever 15 in NCET was aimed at "Initiating Decentralization and Decentering in the Sector of Education and Training". With this milestone, the emphasis of educational reform shifted from prioritizing access to education to a focus on quality improvement. NCET and the ensuing educational decentralization created the incubation conditions of ELA. The charter explicitly named the school principal as a central actor in educational improvement (Chafiq, 2019). It called for a shift from the old command-and-control administrative paradigm to a leadership that facilitates participatory governance and responds to place-based needs.

More than a decade after the NCET, the 2015–2030 SVR charted a more focused vision on learning equity, quality, and social advancement. It also represents the first time a policy document named leadership and management capacity as key levers of educational improvement. It was only in the 2015–2030 SVR when L in ELA became salient. Reform lever 23 prioritized promoting leadership and efficient management capacity throughout the educational system, with a specific emphasis on school-based leadership. In August 2019, Morocco's parliament ratified the country's first education law since independence. *The EFA 51.17* is historic because it represents a legally binding framework for education reform that defines improvement priorities and the central and regional provisions to achieve them. EFA is an important institutional milestone for ELA because it has provided the legal backing for the implementation of the ELA provisions in the 2015–2030 SVR.

In April 2021, the royally appointed Special Commission on the Development Model released *the New Model for Development (NMD)*. This is the nation's roadmap for integrated and inclusive social and economic progress through 2035. NMD is a key milestone in ELA development because it integrates the improvement of leadership and administration within a systems vision that places ELA as a catalyst of the country's educational, social, economic, and governance reform. The NMD reinforced the centrality of school and system leadership in leading impactful school turnaround. It identified five key levers for closing the quality gap: (1) Strengthening teacher training and motivation, (2) reorganizing the assessment system and school pathways, (3) revamping the curriculum, textbook content, and pedagogical practices, (4) empowering schools to lead change and stakeholders' engagement, and (5) bolstering system capacity to implement school reform. The NMD recognizes that school transformation cannot materialize without the full engagement of all stakeholders. For that reason, it recommends a certification mechanism that evaluates school quality based on the extent to which school principals and their leadership teams create the conditions of effective school management, and improve students' cognitive, socio-emotional, and physical development.

Notwithstanding the rising prominence of ELA on the policy agenda, it is critical to remain vigilant about its viability in practice. In other words, unless systems are in place to enable ELA to span the boundaries of inputs and outcomes, its effectiveness as a school improvement lever will be limited. In this regard, the HCET (2007) reported that school management boards averaged 99% in primary, lower secondary, and secondary schools in Morocco. However, gains in the regulatory framework and governance structures have yet to translate to evidence of genuine engagement of the regional and school leaders to build partnerships around school improvement.

A similar study of educational governance commissioned by HCETSR in 2015 (Co-efficience, 2015) concluded that educational leadership grows when mechanisms of transparency, decision-making, management, leadership, and participation are instituted. These mechanisms evolve at the central, regional, and local levels in accordance with a vision for effective leadership that is coherent in its approach and clear about its intended outcomes.

In 2014, Morocco launched the first principals and administrators' preservice regional training programs (Mili, 2017). As illustrated in the list below, the program is designed to equip school principals and administrators with the knowledge tools to lead school organizations. The new program includes 34-hour courses covering ten areas:

1 The Profession of Educational Administration and School Management
2 The School Development Project
3 Information and Communication Technology
4 Communication and Facilitation
5 Pedagogical Management for School Success
6 Psycho-sociological Aspects of Management
7 Evaluation; Change Leadership; Management and Implementation of School Life (extra-curricular activities)

8 School Law and Administrative and Pedagogical Organization
9 Introduction to Financial and Material Resource Management and
10 Documentation and Archiving.

To summarize, school leadership and administration is nested in Morocco's governance and decentralization reform. The evolution of thinking about school leadership and administration is indicative of the pace of reform in the country. It is incremental and forward looking. However, like any useful change, timing is as important as delivery. The system seems to deliver on infrastructure and input investments but continues to lag on student outcomes. The persistently stagnant NIDE clearly signals that the system needs bold and time-bound action at the central, regional, and school levels to stem learning poverty. Educational leadership then should not just be a decentralization by-product. More importantly, it should drive the battle against learning poverty and hold everybody accountable for winning it.

The latest system performance evidence from the 2019 NIDE suggests that the need is dire for a leadership of proximity that is both attuned to the stewardship of public education resources as well as the quality and equity questions inherent in targeting resources to benefit those who need them most. The ideals of the SDP capture this vision of school improvement.

The School Development Project: The Operational Embodiment of ELA in Morocco

The Ministry of Education (MoE) characterizes the SDP as the enactment mechanism of school decentralization. It constitutes a systematic approach to improving school-based management. In this section, I define SDP. Then, I provide an overview of its rationale, inception, design, and the role of international partners in supporting its development.

To use a familiar nomenclature, the SDP is equivalent to the school improvement plan (Flinspach & Ryan, 1992; Leithwood et al., 2006). In 1994, the MoE issued memo number 73 that called for schools to put together the SDP to undertake action research and pedagogical innovation at the school and community levels. In 1997, the MoE described SDP as a voluntary and coherent plan intended to improve learning outcomes and strengthen the links between schools and their economic, social, and cultural environments. In this regard, the MoE *2006–2007 Orientation Guide for the School Project* described SDP as the school's comprehensive plan that articulates the needs and aspirations of its constituents and fleshes out the strategy for achieving them.

The National Strategy for the School Development Project (MOE, 2011) institutionalized SDP as the school-level tool for implementing decentralization, instituting participatory governance, and project-based approaches to educational reform. SDP is intended to introduce results-based management, integrate strategic management tools, empower school staff and community

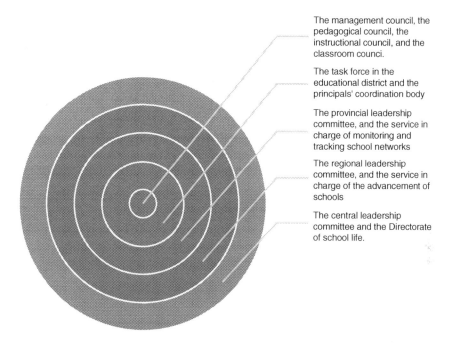

Figure 5.3 School Development Project internal and external stakeholders.
Source: Adapted from the National Strategy for the School Development Project.

members to generate bottom-up solutions to school-specific challenges and place the interests of the students at the center of school improvement efforts.

SDP is also a mechanism for engaging local stakeholders to tap all available place-based assets to improve learning outcomes. Figure 5.3 depicts the level of involvement of the school's internal and external stakeholders as described in the National Strategy for the School Development Project (NSSDP). Headed by the school principal, the Management Council (MC) leads the design, implementation, and monitoring of the SDP. MC consults with the Pedagogical Council, the Instructional Council, and the Classroom Council to incorporate their input during the implementation process. The implementation guide spells out what a school project should look like. The scripted approach to implementing SDP is intended to provide a common language and shared understanding of the innovation process and its success criteria. Figure 5.4 graphs the various roles fulfilled by the local, regional, and central government stakeholders involved in the design, funding, and quality assurance of the SDP as conceptualized in the NSSDP.

At the school level, the school principal oversees the design, implementation, advocacy, and reporting on the improvement work. The MoE provides guidance on the number of people in the principal's leadership team, tips for

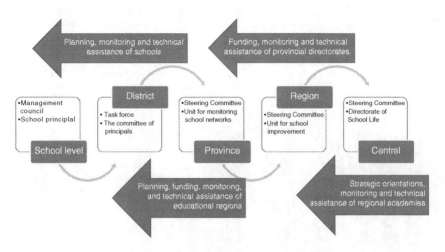

Figure 5.4 Local, regional, and central stakeholders involved in the design, funding, and quality assurance of the SDP.

Source: The National Strategy for the School Development Project, p. 8.

conducting gap analysis, steps for putting together the strategic improvement plan, and the eligibility criteria for funding. The SDP guide leverages lessons learned from multiple international cooperation projects. Morocco's international development partners have clearly supported decentralization and governance reform on their bi-lateral and multi-lateral cooperation strategies (European Training Foundation, 2020; USAID, 2008; UNICEF, 2019) On a larger scale, the World Bank and the Government of Morocco concluded a US$ 500 million loan agreement to support education sector reform in 2019–2024. The loan is aimed at strengthening sector's management capabilities and accountability by strengthening financial and human resources management and school leadership.

In addition to multilateral donors, country development partners such as the United States and Canada have provided technical assistance to bolster system and school leadership and management capabilities. The United States Agency for International Development (USAID) funded technical assistance in pilot projects intended to build capacity for school leaders and administrators to implement SDP. These projects include the Morocco Education for Girls (MEG) 1997–2003, Basic Education Policy Support Activity (BEPS) 2004, Advancing Learning and Employability for a Better Future (ALEF), 2004–2009, and Improving Training for Quality Advancement in National Education (ITQANE), 2009–2014.

Through BEPS (Filion & Rambaud, 2004), school principals had access to two training manuals focused on promoting learning environments that support girls' education and community participation. ALEF's support included training school principals, administrators, and teachers in social mobilization around school improvement, introducing communities of practice as a mechanism of peer-to-peer development and support, and strengthening the skills of school principals and teachers in management and instructional leadership (Muskin, 2012).

ITQANE continued to strengthen principals' and school administrators' capacity to engage the community in designing and supporting school projects (Creative Associates International, 2014). Between 2017 and 2022, the United States, through the Millennium Challenge Account Morocco, has expanded support for strengthening effective governance and leadership through the integrated SDP model called "the Secondary School of Challenge" (MCA, 2021). Areas of capacity building for school leaders in 90 pilot high schools include finance, management, data use, and strategic planning for principals and administrators.

Canada also assisted the MoE in strengthening system and school leadership. Its landmark projects were the Project for the Reinforcement of the Institutional Capacities of the Moroccan Educational System (PROCADEM) and the Project for Assistance for the Management of Schools, PAGESM. Implemented in 2005–2010. PROCADEM was aimed at bolstering the educational system's institutional capacity to decentralize school governance, human resource management, and strategic planning. The capacity-building beneficiaries were regional and provincial system leaders and administrators.

In 2012–2015, Canada funded the PAGESM, the technical assistance project for the management of schools in Morocco (MoE, 2022). The strength of the project lies in its focus on building the capacity of school principals in designing, implementing, managing, monitoring, and evaluating school projects. PAGESM also provided technical assistance in building the leadership and management capacity of provincial, regional, as well as central administrators. This was an important aspect of educational leadership development because it acknowledged the systems nature of school improvement and the importance for all administrators to have a shared language and shared expectations about what improvement means, how it is measured, and the responsibility of each actor in following through.

In summary, the review of the programs undertaken to promote ELA in Morocco indicates that substantial efforts have been invested in building systems capacity in this area. Since 2000, policy-makers remained consistent in structuring leadership and administration development around SDP. This is a well-informed decision in my view because (1) it created a coherent and shared understanding for the rationale of ELA, (2) it helped build the leadership knowledge base around SDP, and (3) it channeled development partners' support to pilot and scale up international evidence-based leadership practices at the school and systems levels.

The combination of efforts at the level of the regulatory framework for the SDP, the concomitant in-service training efforts through international partners, and the pre-service training program in place since 2014 seems to be paying off. The July 28, 2021, issue of the Moroccan newspaper *The Economist* reported that 70% of schools have a funded SDP (Nazih, 2021). At face value, this is an encouraging statistic because it suggests that school principals and management boards have submitted school improvement plans that meet expected funding acceptance criteria. However, further research and evaluation are needed to take stock of the learning uptake from the pilot capacity-building programs and determine where further improvement is needed. In the next section, I elaborate on capacity-building considerations that can deepen ELA implementation and strengthen its focus on learning outcomes.

Areas for Capacity Building: Building ELA Capabilities to Ensure Effective Decentralization

The task of leadership, according to Peter Drucker, is to create an alignment of strengths in ways that make a system's weaknesses irrelevant (Whitney & Trosten-Bloom, 2010). Having established the consistent presence of ELA in the national reform agenda, I posit that strengthening leadership as an improvement driver will help align bolder policies on decentralization with school improvement. I borrow Potter and Brough's (2005) hierarchy of system capacity needs to shine the light on where ELA has taken hold and where deeper improvement is needed.

Figure 5.5 presents the hierarchy's nine components. It indicates that getting to outcomes is not a linear undertaking. Closing the equity-in-learning

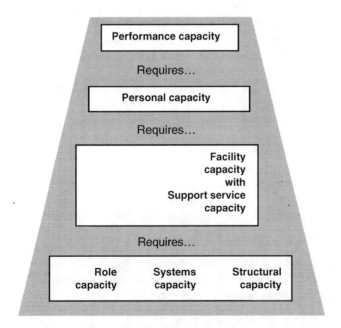

Figure 5.5 Potter and Brough's hierarchy of system capacity-building needs.
Source: Potter & Brough, 2004, p. 341.

gap and providing access to quality learning opportunities is a multifaceted undertaking that requires building and aligning strengths on the nine interdependent capacity components. Performance capacity refers to the extent to which principals, teachers, and teaching paraprofessionals have the needed resources and tools to provide quality and equitable learning opportunities for all students. Personal capacity touches on the extent to which school leadership and instructional staff have the knowledge required to fulfill their missions based on evidence of what works. Personal skills cover pedagogical and management knowledge, know-how, and socio-emotional competencies. Personal skills undergird the needed dispositions and behaviors necessary for forming collaborative teams, managing uncertainty, and leading learning organizations. Performance and personal capacity require workload, supervisory, facility, and support capacity.

Workload capacity gauges the degree to which staff are available in sufficient numbers and complementary skills to meet the demands of learning. Supervisory capacity refers to the mechanisms in place to monitor improvement work, provide guidance, and demand accountability. Facility capacity refers to the extent to which the school infrastructure allows for quality learning to occur. This includes availability, safety, and quality of school facilities (classrooms, school grounds, latrines, access to electricity and water, resource centers, learning labs, equipment, storage, etc.) Support capacity includes all training and assistance services allowing school leaders to deliver on instructional and organizational leadership. The six capacity components require adequate systems capacity, structural capacity, and role capacity. System capacity refers to the transparency, responsiveness, and timeliness of the support available to school principals and local leadership teams to implement SDP. Structural capacity refers to the existence of processes to document action and monitor discharge of duties. Finally, role capacity measures the extent to which school principals and improvement teams are extended decision-making discretion to turn schools around.

The review of the National Strategy for the School Development Project, the multiple international cooperation projects, and the HCETSR study of educational governance (Co-Efficiency, 2015) indicate that the MoE has invested in building system and structural capacity for ELA at least since 2000. Having said that, HCETSR reports (2008 & 2014) and the Human and Institutional Capacity Development (HICD) report (Thompson et.al, 2017) underscore the importance of capacity building to cultivate leadership cultures that are results-oriented, more attuned to local needs and assets, and less burdened by top-down compliance reporting.

In 2008, HCETSR identified system weaknesses in installing supervision, accountability mechanisms, and incentives to promote local leadership. It also pointed to the need for structures that support ELA regionally and in schools. These include an effective and comprehensive information management system for data-based decision-making. The HCETSR (2014) evaluation of the implementation of NCET from 2000 to 2013 took stock of the installation phase of structures of decentralized governance across regions and schools. However, it reported the need for significant capacity building in ELA across all levels of decentralized decision-making in regional education authorities and schools. The report also noted that the push to decentralize was hampered by insufficient action to win local stakeholders buy-in, and the non-translation of decentralization policies into regulations granting local administrators the legal standing to lead. It also reported the lack of incentives to take on the myriad tasks associated with planning, design, consultations, campaigning, winning buy-in, implementation, evaluation, recalibration, and continuous education improvement.

The Human and Institutional Capacity Development (HICD) report (Thompson et.al, 2017) reiterated similar concerns about ELA in its assessment of decentralized governance and school-based management. The report identified challenges in infrastructure, finance, human resources, and pedagogy. Cross-cutting these categories are capacity issues pertaining to information, resources, tools, incentives, knowledge and skills, capacities, and motivation. The HICD report found that too many school leaders lack the tools, financial resources to fund, and staff school improvement mandates (performance capacity). Leaders and administrators need extensive training in building the knowledge, behaviors, and dispositions needed for effective school leadership (personal capacity). The report warns that the MoE will not be able to achieve its strategic improvement goals if the shortage of qualified staff at the central and regional levels is not resolved (workload capacity). The supervisory capacity is not adequate. Inspectors are expected to provide supervision but are not trained, mandated, or assisted to conduct monitoring that enhances ELA. Supervisory capacity can be a key enabler of learning organizations when it is seen as a source of gap and asset analysis, on-the-job information sharing, and capacity building. In this regard, the very culture of inspection will need to be revisited if inspectors are to contribute to the development of ELA as coaches and mentors.

The other findings of the HICD can be grouped under a combination of systems, structural, and role capacity. At the structural level, governance councils are not yet granted decision-making authority to implement improvement plans. The central MoE units still exercise a priori control over regional programs, which undermines the availability and timeliness of local solutions. Issues with decision-making discretion (role-capacity) and control over resources still pose barriers to leadership capabilities at the school level. The policy on autonomy of planning and budget management, personnel management, and the participation of the management councils is not yet supported by school control over budget and personnel.

In summary, building local and regional ELA capacity is Morocco's pressing improvement frontier. Fully cognizant of the cultural, political, ethical, and resource complexity of a change that entails power and accountability redistribution, more studies are needed to examine readiness and capacity for decentralized ELA. As we noted earlier, the importance of ELA as a lever of change is no longer an issue in Morocco. By contrast, strengthening ELA reform with a full understanding of the cultural and resource implications inherent in the change process is Morocco's current wicked problem (Elmeski, 2021). It should galvanize research, policy, and practice if ELA is to truly deliver on its potential as a driver of education reform.

Policy, Practice, and Research Implications

In this section, I discuss the policy, practice, and research growth perspectives of ELA in Morocco. I also reflect on the international implications of the points discussed in this chapter, especially to countries in the Middle East and North Africa (MENA).

At the level of policy, I have noted that the rise to prominence of ELA in Morocco is tributary for the most part to the overarching policy on decentralization and governance reform. I would argue, however, that strengthening ELA should be treated as a key enabler of effective school improvement. In Morocco, the capacity of the system to deliver quality and equitable educational services to all rests on empowered place-anchored leaders who have the agency, capacity, and accountability disposition to act as catalysts of educational improvement. Therefore, policy-makers will need to show more audacity in trusting educators at the regional and local level to be change-makers, not just implementers of top-down reform mandates.

One other policy implication pertains to the urgent need to bridge the gap between anticipated policy reform outcomes and the practical conditions that shape reform implementation. Twenty years of experimentation is ample time for any system to learn, grow, mature, and demonstrate autonomy. If it is not yielding the anticipated results, the reform intervention assumptions should be revisited. Putting in place policies that call for decentralized and place-based decision-making without support provisions that nurture autonomy amounts to half measures that stunt leadership, cultivate cynicism amongst education administrators, and end up hollowing ELA out of its transformative potential.

Strengthening ELA is not simply a policy affair. It is a knowledge base, a set of dispositions, leadership behaviors that are learned and honed by doing, and, most importantly, a change management leadership that walks the talk of participatory decision-making. Ghandi's famous quote that "whatever you do for me but without me, you do against me" is a sobering reminder that even the most technically sound ideas, in this case ELA, will fail the test of viability if they are not accompanied with proper policy analysis that examines considerations of technical feasibility, economic and financial possibility, political viability, and administrative operability (Patton et al., 2013.) In this regard, protests and strikes organized by local and national unions and administrator associations (L'Opinion, 2021) are indicative of their considerable malaise about work overload with few incentives. They are also a cry for recognition, consideration, and engagement in decision-making. Policy-makers at the central level will, therefore, need to exert more effort to engage in the messiness of co-construction of the systems of support with school leaders to win their engagement in the change process.

At the level of practice, the literature referenced in this chapter shows evidence of principals and administrators implementing an inquiry-based approach to the advancement of their profession. Strikes also demonstrate that administrators, through their professional associations, have considerable ability to organize. These are important agency markers that should be seized and cultivated to build an ELA community of practice. In work environments where too many principals are often under-staffed and over-stretched, the ELA community of practice is the convening umbrella that confederates disparate initiatives to build a unified platform for evidence and expertise, set the standards of effective practice, and shape the ELA improvement agenda. Unless principals and administrators show the needed leadership to coordinate access to information, training, and resources, and organize to build research collaboratives that strengthen home-grown evidence of what works, it is likely that the central MoE authorities will continue to operate on the assumption that truly autonomous ELA is unrealistic because the local administrators do not have the capabilities to lead without close central supervision.

From a research perspective, a significant proportion of the knowledge produced on ELA in Morocco consists of evaluations and reports. In this regard, Morocco's higher education institutions have an immense gap to fill in educational research in general, and ELA specifically. For now, it is HCETSR that produces data about ELA in Morocco. The High Council for Education, Training and Scientific Research has played a crucial role in securing what I would term as educational research sovereignty in the country. Its evaluation studies and assessments have helped triangulate the findings of international reports about the country's education performance. In this chapter, I pieced together the picture of ELA in Morocco mostly from various HCETSR reports as well as capstone papers of graduating principals. Building a peer-reviewed national and regional research base should be the priority that will provide home grown-evidence informing decision-maker's understanding of the factors impeding and enabling ELA in Morocco. This is a massive and worthy research undertaking that universities should take the lead in. As of now, their footprint in the field is virtually nonexistent.

Morocco, and for that matter North Africa, remains the terra incognita of academic research on ELA. Atari and Outum (2019) noted that North African scholarship on educational administration is barely visible in the Middle East. One potential explanation that certainly merits further research is that three of these countries, Morocco, Algeria, and Tunisia, have a shared French colonial history, and have, as a result, been imbued with French administration tradition. French continues to remain, at least unofficially, the dominant de facto language of communication, administration, and research in North Africa. It would therefore be reasonable to posit that ELA has not grown as much as it should, at least compared to the Middle Eastern countries, because ELA in France has not been a topic of extensive research as it is in the United States and United Kingdom (Tulowitzki, 2013). Normand (2016) qualified French research literature on educational management as quite poor. It seems, therefore, that the lack of publication in ELA in Morocco and North Africa is partly due to the dearth of research in France on the subject.

An independent research agenda is an important step towards ideological sovereignty that carves a space for Morocco and North Africa in ELA knowledge production. It is important to note here that SDP is not just a Moroccan innovation, it is a key component of school reform in Algeria (Tounsi, 2016) and Tunisia (Baatour, 2005). Collaboration between researchers from North Africa will create synergies that strengthen the evidence base of ELA in the region. Following are illustrative priority areas for research in Morocco that could certainly be relevant to North Africa and other MENA countries.

As shown in this chapter, reports on SDP showed that the policy talk on principals' leadership and participatory governance is not matched by dedicated resources and capacity building in practice. One area of research is to investigate what happens in the leadership black box of schools, educational districts, regions, and even at the level of the central departments. This is an important missing link in the policy-to-practice divide.

Other equally important research topics include investigating ELA capacity landscape, the role of school partners in promoting ELA, systems thinking and ELA improvement, and the role of regional ecosystems in creating differentiated ELA. To begin with a benchmarking appraisal of ELA capacity landscape, such a study could comb through the MENA educational systems, and assess their systems of support for ELA capacity using Potter and Brough's model for example. Investigating the willingness and ability of school partners to support local ELA at the school and regional levels is also very important. This chapter documented where the central government needs to increase its support for ELA. But we also know that unless local partners step-up and collaborate with schools to advance their own initiatives, we cannot talk about partnerships. Conducting such research will help nuance the assumptions about local readiness for effective participatory school governance.

Referencing systems thinking, I posit that no meaningful ELA will take hold if schools and educational systems in Morocco are not operating as learning organizations. Going back to Peter Drucker's definition of leadership as the task of aligning strengths in ways that make the system's weaknesses irrelevant, the agenda of future ELA research in Morocco should also emphasize identifying ELA horizontal and vertical assets that allow leaders and administrators to join up system strengths to ensure that schools live up to their missions as places for quality education for all. Another systems area for further investigation pertains to the cultural, structural, human resources, and political barriers versus enablers influencing ELA deep implementation and growth prospects.

The role of the regional ecosystems in creating capabilities for continuous ELA improvement is an additional research area. Under the practice implications, I highlighted the importance of professional communities as enablers of efficacious ELA. Little is known about the existence or functioning of those communities in Morocco. Little is also known about the role of the regions' flagship universities in spearheading education research that supports school and system improvement at the local and regional levels.

Last, but not least, universities and professional communities seem to be woefully under-tapped in pushing forward school improvement work in Morocco. Unless we know the factors underlying their limited involvement in supporting and sustaining education reform, Morocco's effort in turning around its educational system will remain lopsided in its heavy central management, and hence, deprived of the resources of local and regional partners who feel equally responsible for school improvement implementation and are involved enough to own accountability for its outcomes.

Conclusion

This chapter is probably the first attempt to describe the evolution of ELA in Morocco. Analyzing the Moroccan educational leadership development contributes to filling the gap in ELA research in Morocco as well as French-speaking North Africa, given the shared colonial history, ensuing similarity in heavy centralization, and the dearth of research on ELA in the region.

This chapter began with a review of the school improvement imperative of ELA. I then undertook an overview of the existing literature and discussed the main landmarks that have shaped ELA development. After that, I presented the SDP as a model of ELA implementation at the school level. Next, I highlighted areas of further capacity building using Potter and Brough's model. Finally, I discussed the policy, practice, and research implications of ELA improvement. This overview has shown that ELA is an important policy driver for system reform. However, more efforts are needed to build systems of support that strengthen local ownership and leadership of school development. In this regard, the ambitious policy intentions will need to be substantiated with enabling regulatory frameworks, adequate funding, collaborative practice, and systematic research to ensure that ELA is fully tapped as a transformative engine of education reform that moves the needle on learning outcomes for all students.

Notes

1 The inclusion and equal opportunities are a composite of 50 indicators grouped into nine categories: Preschool education for all, access to basic education for children aged 6–14, expanding access to schooling beyond basic education, combatting school wastage, gender equity, involvement of the private sector in generalizing equitable access to education, regional equity in the supply of educational services, availability of adequate infrastructure in schools, and inclusive education.

2 The index of education quality includes 50 indicators grouped into nine categories: learning outcomes, learning conditions, system efficiency, teacher-student ratio, ending delays in schooling exceeding two years, learning conditions at the school level, teaching conditions, integration of digital technology in schools, and student advising.

References

Akhyar, I. (2016). Alidara Attarbawiya bayna muwakabati alislah wa tahadiyati lwaqi3: Alqa? id tarbawi bi libtida? Inamudajan [School administration between the implementation of reform and the challenges of reality: The education leader in the primary as a model.] Tangier: Regional Center for the Professions of Education and Training.

Amghar, A. (2019). School-based leadership in the education reform agenda in Morocco: An analysis of policy and context. *International Journal of Leadership in Education, 22*(1), 102–115.

Atari, A., & Outum, N. (2019). Research on educational administration published in Arabic language educational journals: A systematic review and analysis. *International Studies in Educational Administration (Commonwealth Council for Educational Administration & Management (CCEAM)), 47*(1), 17–19.

Baatour, A. (2005). Mashou3 almouassa: Tajrbia Tounsia. [School Development Project: Tunisia experience.] *Annashra Attarbawiya*. Retrieved from: مشروع المؤسسة:تجربة تونسية – leblogmouatassim (over-blog.com)

Benatou, S., & Chentouf, M. (2016). *Attakhtit alistratiji bimo?assasati atta3lim al3umumi* [Strategic planning in public schools]. Tangier: Regional Center for the Professions of Education and Training

Betty, M. (2011). Alidarai almadrassiya min madouri alislahi atarbawiyi [School administration from the perspective of educational reform.] *Majallat 3ulu:m Attarbiya* [Education Sciences Journal], *50*, 95–103.

Boqoulou, A., & Berrad, M. (2016). *Tawdifu technologia ali3lam watawasul fi l?idara attarbawiya* [Applying ICT in school administration]. Tangier, Morocco: Regional Center for the Professions of Education and Training.

Bourqia, R. (2016). Repenser et refonder l'école au Maroc: la Vision stratégique 2015-2030. [rethinking and overhauling school in Morocco: The strategic vision 2015–2030]. *Revue internationale d'éducation de Sèvres, 5,* (71), 18–24.

Chafiq, A. (2019). Islah alidara attarbawiya bilmaghrib: Ta3zizu liqudurati alqiyadiya fi ghiabi istiqlaliyati almu?assati atta3limiyati [Reforming educational administration in Morocco: Strengthening leadership capacities in the absence of independent educational institutions. *Majalat Al3ulum Alijtima3iya Journal of Social Sciences, 8,* 524–539. مجلة العلوم الاجتماعية: العددالثامن آذار – مارس 2019 - المركز الديمقراطي العربي retrieved from (democraticac.de)

Co-efficience. (2015). Hakamat manzumat attarbiya wa takwin [the governance of the education and training system.] High Council for Education and Training Retrieved from GOUVERNANCE-AR-Finale-20-05-2016.pdf (csefrs.ma)

Creative Associates International. (2014). Improving training for quality advancement in national education. Retrieved from: https://pdf.usaid.gov/pdf_docs/PA00MTK5.pdf

Dadi, A. (2014). Alidara Attarbawiya wa mashru3 almu?asasa: Ikrahat wa rihanat wa afa:q [School administration and the school development project: Constraints, stakes, and prospects] *Dafatir Attarbiya wa Takwin Notebooks on Education and*

Training. Retrieved from الإدارة التربوية ومشروع المؤسسة: إكراهات ورهانات وآفاق (shamaa.org)

Daun, H. (Ed.). (2007). *School decentralization in the context of globalizing governance: International comparison of grassroots responses*. Dordrecht, The Netherlands: Springer.

Elmeski, M. (2015). Principals as leaders of school and community revitalization: A phenomenological study of three urban schools in Morocco. *International Journal of Leadership in Education, 18*(1), 1–18.

Elmeski, M. (2021). Commentary – Systems thinking and educational leadership: Implications of the special issue to school improvement in development contexts. *Journal of Educational Administration, 59* (1), 132–137.

European Training Foundation (2020). Country strategy paper 2020 update: Morocco. Retrieved on August 1, 2021 from Country Strategy Paper 2017-20 Actions 2020_Morocco - EDITED_ICE (europa.eu)

Filion, L., & Rambaud, M. F. (2004). *Achieving increased attainment of basic education among girls in selected rural schools in Morocco*. Creative Associates International. Report retrieved from: https://pdf.usaid.gov/pdf_docs/PNADQ818.pdf

Flinspach, S. L., & Ryan, S. P. (1992). *Vision and accountability in school improvement planning*. Chicago Panel on Public School Policy and Finance. Retrieved from https://files.eric.ed.gov/fulltext/ED350718.pdf

Hallinger, P., & Hammad, W. (2019). Knowledge production on educational leadership and management in Arab Societies: A systematic review of research. *Educational Management Administration & Leadership, 47*(1), 20–36.

Hanushek, E. A. (2020). Education production functions. In *The economics of education* (pp. 161–170). Academic Press.

Hanushek, E. A. (2003). The failure of input-based schooling policies. *The Economic Journal, 113*(485), F64–F98.

Hanushek, E. A., & Woessmann, L. (2016). Knowledge capital, growth, and the East Asian miracle. *Science, 351*(6271), 344–345.

Laouni, N. (2021). School principals' self-efficacy beliefs for technology integration in Moroccan public schools. *International Journal of Educational Leadership and Management, 6*, 11–17. Retrieved from: https://www.hipatiapress.com/hpjournals/index.php/ijelm/article/view/9154

Leithwood, K., Jantzi, D., & McElheron-Hopkins, C. (2006). The development and testing of a school improvement model. *School Effectiveness and School Improvement, 17*(4), 441–464.

Lekhsadi, M. (2000). *Waqi3 alidarah almadrasiya bilmaghrib bayna attakwin attarbawi wa tandimi l?idari: Dirassa lilqiyadati attarbawiyati bi tta3limi athanawi* [The reality of school administration in Morocco between pre-service training and administrative organization: A study of educational leadership in secondary education]. Casablanca, Morocco: Annajah Aljadida Printing

Loeb, S., & Bound, J. (1996). The effect of measured school inputs on academic achievement: Evidence from the 1920s, 1930s and 1940s birth cohorts. *The Review of Economics and Statistics, 4*, 653–664.

L'Opinion (2021, March 9). *La grogne des cadres administratifs de l'enseignement se poursuit*. [The grumbling of school administrators continue]. Retrieved from: https://www.lopinion.ma/La-grogne-des-cadres-administratifs-de-l-enseignement-se-poursuit_a12458.html

Mili, A. (2017). Instauration d'un cycle innové de la formation initiale des cadres de l'administration scolaire au Maroc. [installing a renvoated cycle for pre-service training for school administrators in Morocco.] Retrieved from عبد السلام ميلي - CRMEF Casablanca Settat

Millennium Challenge Account (2021). Rapport d'activite [activity report]. Retrieved from https://www.mcamorocco.ma/sites/default/files/documents/RAPPORT%20D%27ACTIVITE%20AGENCE%20MCA-MOROCCO%202021%20WEB.pdf

Ministry of National Education (2022). Projet d'appui à la géstion des établissements scolaires au Maroc (PAGESM). [Project for the support of the management of schools.] Retrieved from: https://www.men.gov.ma/Fr/Pages/PAGESM.aspx

Ministry of National Education (2011). Alistratijiya al wataniya limashrou3 ala-moassaa: Addalilu al ijra3i. [The national strategy for the operationalization of the school development project: The operational guide]. Retrieved on May 04, 2021, from: https://www.men.gov.ma/Ar/Documents/guide_procedure2011.pdf

Ministry of National Education, Vocational Training, Higher Education, and Scientific Research. (2000). Almithaqui Alwataniyu littarbiyati wa takwini [The National Charter for Education and Training, NCET]. Retrieved from الميثاق الوطني للتربية و التكوين (men.gov.ma)

Muskin, J. A. (2012). Educating youth for entrepreneurship in work & life: Experience of a junior secondary school project in Morocco. *Journal of International Cooperation in Education, 15*(2), 15–22.

Nazih, A. (2021, July 28). 70% des écoles ont un projet d'établissement financé. [70 percent of schools have a funded SDP]. *L'Economiste*. Retrieved from: https://www.leconomiste.com/article/1079689-70-des-ecoles-ont-un-projet-d-etablissement-finance

Normand, R. (2016). France: Between civil service and republican ethics – the statist vision of leadership among French principals. In *A decade of research on school principals* (pp. 357–374). Cham: Springer International Publishing.

Potter, C., & Brough, R. (2004). Systemic capacity building: A hierarchy of needs. *Health policy and planning, 19*(5), 336–345.

Patton, C. V., & Sawicki, D. S. (2013). *Basic methods of policy and planning* (3rd ed.). Routledge, Taylor Francis Group.

Saito, F. (Ed.) (2008). *Foundations for local governance: Decentralization in comparative perspective*. Seta, Otsu, Japan: Physica-Verlag Heidelberg.

Serhani, A. (2016). *Waqi3 wa Afaq taf3il almajalis ata3limiya bi mo3assasati attarbiya wa tta3lim al3umumi* [The reality and the prospects of the enactment of the instructional councils in public schools.]. Tangier: Regional Center for the Professions of Education and Training.

The High Council for Education and Training (HCETSR) (2015). Aro3ya al istratijiya lil3islah: Min ajli madrasati al insaf wa ljawda wa li3rtiqa3 [For a school of equity, quality, and advancement: Strategic vision for 2015–2030 reform]. Retrieved on July 05 from الرؤية الاستراتيجية للإصلاح: من أجل مدرسة الإنصاف والجودة والارتقاء (csefrs.ma)

The Higher Council for Education and Training (2014). Ataqriru atahlili: Tabiqu lmithaq alwatani littarbiya watakwin 2000 – 2013: Almuktasabat, almu3iqat, wa tahadiyat [Analytical report: The implementation of the National Charter for Education and Training 2000–2013: Achievements, barriers, and challenges.] retrieved from: تطبيق الميثاق الوطني للتربية والتكوين: المكتسبات والمعيقات والتحديات (csefrs.ma)

The High Council for Education, Training, and Scientific Research (2008). Taqrir almajliss Ala3la lita3lim 3an halati almathoumati alwataniyati litarbiyati wa takwini wa afaqiha [the HCETSR report on the state and prospects of the Moroccan education and training system]. Retrieved July 07 from تقرير المجلس الأعلى للتعليم عن حالة المنظومة الوطنية للتربية والتكوين وآفاقها (csefrs.ma)

The High Council for Education and Training. (2007). Almarakaziya wa latarkiz fi qita3 atarbiya lwataniya: Tajribatu alakadimiyati aljihawiyati littaribiyati wa takwin [Decentralization and decentering in the national education sector: The experience of the regional academies for education and training.] Retrieved on June 04, 2021 from: اللامركزية واللاتركيز: تجربة الأكاديميات الجهوية للتربية والتكوين (csefrs.ma)

Thompson, R., Tekeu, R., El Bouazzaoui, H., Benyamna, S., Tamer, B., Baidada, M., Echchotbi, M., Guedira, A., Ezzaki, A., Ennasri, I., & Moustaghfir, K. (2017). *Human and institutional capacity development assessment of the Ministry of National Education, Vocational Training, Higher Education, and Scientific Research.* Morocco: United States Agency for International Development.

Tounsi, M. (2016). La scolarité obligatoire en Algérie: ambitions et défis. [Compulsory education in Algeria: Ambitions and challenges.]. *Revue internationale d'éducation de Sèvres, 2* (73), 47–56.

Tulowitzki, P. (2013). Leadership and school improvement in France. *Journal of Educational Administration, 51*(6), 812–835. 10.1108/JEA-03-2012-0026

UNICEF (2019). *Every child learns: UNICEF education strategy 2019 – 2030.* New York: UNICEF. Retrieved on July 03, 2021, from https://www.gcedclearinghouse.org/sites/default/files/resources/190466eng.pdf

United States Agency for International Development (2008). Country assistance strategy: Morocco. Retrieved on April 3, 2021, from https://pdf.usaid.gov/pdf_docs/Pdacn034.pdf

Ward, C., Metz, A., Louison, L., Loper, A., & Cusumano, D. (2018). *Drivers best practices assessment.* Chapel Hill, NC: National Implementation Research Network, University of North Carolina at Chapel Hill. Based on: Fixsen, D.L., Blase, K., Naoom, S., Metz, A., Louison, L., & Ward, C. (2015). Implementation Drivers: Assessing Best Practices. Chapel Hill, NC: National Implementation Research Network, University of North Carolina at Chapel Hill.

Whitney, D. D., & Trosten-Bloom, A. (2010). *The power of appreciative inquiry: A practical guide to positive change.* Berrett-Koehler Publishers.

Winkler, D. R. (1989). *Decentralization in education: An economic perspective* (Vol. 143). World Bank Publications.

Wolman, H. (1990). Decentralization: What it is and why we should care. In Bennett, R. (Ed.), *Decentralization, local governments, and markets: Towards a post-welfare agenda* (pp. 29–42). Oxford: Clarendon Press.

World Bank (October 2019). *Morocco learning poverty brief.* Retrieved on August 10 from MNAMNC01MARLPBRIEF.pdf (worldbank.org)

6 Educational Leadership and Administration in Algeria

Policy, Development, and Reflective Practice

Fella Lahmar and Fatima Zahra Abbou

Introduction

Literature concerning educational leadership and administration is expanding, lending credence to the experiences, structures, and theoretical frameworks of Western societies. Meanwhile, a growing number of scholars have been calling for the expansion of the knowledge base of educational leadership and administration to encompass other nations' heritage (Baker & Wiseman, 2005; Ball et al., 2011; Oplatka & Arar, 2016; Wiseman, 2009). For Arab countries, literature produced on leadership and administration remains limited, even within the UAE which is identified as the largest producer of knowledge in this field (Hallinger & Hammad, 2019; Oplatka & Arar, 2017). Moreover, research output on educational leadership in Arab countries remains narrowly focused on themes of leadership styles and orientations, the barriers faced by educational leaders or exploring leaders' managerial perceptions and practices (Izhar & Arar, 2017). Similarly, in the Algerian context, the field of leadership and administration (ELA) remains in an embryonic stage (Miliani, 2021). This chapter contributes to literature within an Algerian context by focusing on emergent key dimensions of Algerian HE leadership in terms of vision, structure, and expansion.

To chart these reforms, the chapter is structured into four sections. It begins with a brief sketch of the Algerian educational system to set the context. Emergent key reforms within the established system serve as a basis for clarifying the different mechanisms, policies, and aspects in an Algerian educational setting. Next, the chapter focuses on the HE sector by examining how various policy reforms shaped and reshaped HE touching upon organisational and pedagogical aspects. Accordingly, it explores how two formal leadership styles emerge from the above policies: administrative and pedagogical leadership. Following policy implementation, the interview data of a sample of female HE staff is examined to explore how policies are perceived by agents at the level of implementation across both administrative and pedagogical leadership. A discussion of the findings focuses on the discrepancy between policy reforms and the views and experiences of practitioners holding leadership positions. Finally, the chapter argues for the need to consider the

DOI: 10.4324/9781003334835-6

complexities of the local socio-political Algerian context and the micro-political dynamics of leadership when proposing new educational reforms.

Theoretical Perspectives and Research Methods

Questions over the demarcation of educational administration and leadership form an ongoing debate (Connolly et al., 2019; Oplatka, 2010). Similarly, ontological questions discussing what constitutes educational leadership or educational administration remain controversial (Connolly et al., 2019; Eacott, 2017). Traditional debate on leadership revolves around concepts of authority in relation to the administrative and political system that shapes educational policies at different levels (Birnbaum, 1991). Questions actively discussed include: What is leadership? How does it link to education, values, and the nature of change? And how is it shaped by/and interacts with policy? Answers to these questions closely tie to other foundational issues about the nature and purpose of education at individual, societal, and global levels.

This chapter charts administrative structures and leadership roles within formal policy, along with leaders' perceptions and practical experiences. Analysis is underpinned by Giddens' (1984) "double hermeneutic" notion. Here, whereas structural conditions shape these leaders' roles and restrict their agency, state educational policies are interpreted by subjects who think, feel, and reflect on their conditions and contribute to shaping the structure. Taking leadership as a cultural and social phenomenon, the historical context of the development of the modes of activity becomes essential to understanding participants' views and the institutionalisation process. Accordingly, this analysis reviews key reform policy documents and semi-structured interview data. Policy analysis is primarily based on acts and regulations published in the Official Gazette Algeria (Boudam, 2022) that relate to educational reform. Other consulted documents include Algerian Constitutions, the Ministry of National Education (MEN), and the Ministry of Higher Education and Scientific Research (MESRS) online portals (MESRS, 2022a; MEN, 2022).

Semi-structured interviews were conducted between December 2019 and March 2020, with 18 academics holding permanent positions within Algerian universities; 14 were conducted face-to-face and 4 via telephone and Zoom. Participants were selected through purposive sampling of female university academics who either held formal leadership positions (administrative or pedagogical) or were teaching staff. Each interview lasted between 45 and 60 minutes. Ethical approval from the Institute of Education at the University of Reading was gained prior to collection of fieldwork data. The data were anonymised, coded, and thematically analysed using six stages of thematic analysis in an iterative process (Braun & Clarke, 2006). All names used in this chapter are pseudonyms to protect the confidentiality of participants.

The larger study, from which the fieldwork data emerge, aims to examine female staffs' views on the concept of leadership, organisational/institutional barriers, and opportunities influencing their career progression or willingness to hold senior leadership roles alongside their professional identity construction within Algerian higher education (HE). While gender imbalance in HE leadership is a global issue (Mott, 2022), in Jordan, Syria, Lebanon, and Algeria, it is reported that only about 4–5% of institutions in the HE sector are headed by women. Moreover, a severe underrepresentation of women in decision-making positions in scientific institutions in Algeria is also reported (The European Commission, 2015). Hence, these underrepresented women leaders' voices in Algerian HE remain important to contribute to the debate. A diverse range of topics emerged from this analysis, although this chapter focuses solely on data demonstrating explicit or implicit conceptions of leadership and administration. Analysis centres on how these leaders interpret their leadership roles and agency within a centralised system of HE where autonomy is limited.

Organisation and Administration: Key Features of Algerian Education

The first post-colonial Algerian Constitution 1963 ("Constitution 1963," 1963), endorsed a year after independence in 1962, aims at "building a socialist democracy, resisting human exploitation in all its forms, guaranteeing the right to work and free education, and eliminating all remnants of colonialism" ("Constitution 1963," 1963, Article 10). Similarly, Article 65 of the 1963 constitution held the state responsible for guaranteeing equal education and vocational training access. The central nature of the Algerian educational system was based on this 1963 Constitution. Schools developed for everyone albeit with geographical disparities to close educational access; children of the elite/wealthy shared classes in the public sector. Emphasis lay on achieving state objectives by moulding learners to serve socialist societal and economic visions and frameworks. This developed as a top-down system of education rather than a school-led or profession-led system; the formal educational institutions became entirely controlled by the one-party socialist state. The National Educational system functions within the jurisdiction of the state, and "no individual or group initiative is allowed outside the framework specified in this order" (Boumediene, 1976, Article 10). Hence, the doors for privatisation and market competition were closed. The educational system is perceived to respond to the comprehensive development plan of the country (Boumediene, 1976, Article 11).

Despite the long struggle of Arabisation in education, linguistic duality characterised the newly independent Algerian school system. In HE, the humanities, social and economic sciences are mostly Arabised, while the French language dominates in the scientific and technological university fields, even where officially Arabised. French continued to be the primary prevailing foreign language in the country and the dominant language in core administration and privileged job markets, despite not regulated as such (Taleb-Ibrahimi, 2007). In 2001, the Council of Ministers approved a new reform project that sought to reform the educational system. Accordingly, the National Committee for the Reform of the Educational System, the Benzagho Committee, was created and entrusted with reforming the educational system across the Evaluation and Training Committee, the HE Reform Committee and the Curriculum Reform Committee. Such reform affected both the NE lower-section and HE sectors (Benghabrit-Remaoun, 2016; Bin-Muhammed, 2016; Saidouni, 2021). Yet, the Benzagho Committee, due to its strong consultative links with France, raised national debate over identity tensions and, therefore, questioned the objectives and possible effectiveness in an Algerian context of these reforms (Benghabrit-Remaoun, 2016; Bin-Muhammed, 2016; Saidouni, 2021). In such a politically and culturally-charged context, the educational ministers, as potent leadership and administrative symbols and policies contributing to the national character-building processes, remain ongoing areas of national debate beyond the classroom spaces (Saidouni, 2021).

Due to these historical and evolving processes the education sector subsumed under the direct central tutelage of the state, its public institutions and administration system. The school system is seen as central to citizenship education ("Constitution 1963," 1963, Articles 65). All issues related to quality assurance, such as appointments of staff, curriculum and teacher education, become the direct responsibility of the state's public institutions. Accordingly, reform remains centrally driven by a political government agenda as the whole system is founded on public funding with attached restrictions. Centralisation continued with various constitutional amendments, including the latest Constitution of December 2020 ("Constitution of the People's Democratic Republic of Algeria," 2020).

By 2022, Algeria's education system comprised four key stages: primary, lower-secondary, upper-secondary and HE. The curricula at primary, lower-secondary and upper-secondary schools are standardised across all schools for any given grade. All children must be enrolled in school by age six; pre-schooling is not mandatory. The vast majority of educational institutions in Algeria at the National Education (NE) and the HE levels are publicly funded institutions. In a highly centralised administration system, the NE is led by the MEN, while the HE sector is led by the MESRS (MESRS, 2022a). Private fee-paying schooling and HE sectors, while limited, are gradually growing segments as policies start to decentralise educational provision towards privatisation. The next section details central administrative aspects of the Algerian HE system.

Algerian HE Reforms: Administrative and Pedagogical Leadership

All universities maintained the administrative and pedagogical systems inherited from the colonial era (Miliani, 2021). In 1963, the MEN encompassed the lower part of the national education system and the higher sector of education (Decree No. 121-121 dated April 18, 1963). Since then, changes to HE are diverse and include organisational and pedagogical aspects set within the 1971, 1999 and 2004 key reforms. From 1962 to 1970, some universities were established at the national level within different regions (Bouadam, 2022). In 1970 a separate Ministry for Higher Education and Scientific Research appeared alongside the original MEN (GSoG, 1970). In 1971 this administrative change was followed by drastic reformation of Algerian National Education, within the National Education lower sector and the HE system (GSoG, 1971a; 1971b). Such change included reformed objectives, programmes, and the administration structure along with the HE scientific research curricula, including the Arabisation policy. In 1980 a restructuring project was launched, known as "the University Map," aimed to align HE with the needs of national development. This marked a shift from a conservative socialist system of education towards the labour market. This shift became apparent in the 1989 educational reform which sought to raise national capabilities and competencies and strengthen relations with the labour market (General Secretariat of the Government, 1989).

Key 1999 reform saw universities transform into public institutions of a scientific, cultural and vocational nature (GSoG, 1999). The February 4, 1999, Act No. 05-99 includes the directive for HE and scientific research, which makes the university a public institution of a scientific and cultural nature offering more flexible provision (GSoG, 1999). Reorganisation mainly took the form of colleges, as a unit of teaching and research. The monitoring, follow-up and evaluation processes were conducted by the Ministry of HE (GSoG, 1999, Article 39). Moreover, a body called "National Universities Symposium" and regional bodies called "University Academies" would be established with the Minister in charge of HE. These bodies provide a framework for consultation, coordination and evaluation on the activities of the Higher Education Network and the implementation of the specific national policy in this field (GSoG, 1999, Article 43). The board of directors of the public institution consists of state representatives, elected university representatives drawn from academic staff and key sector representatives involved in programme delivery (GSoG, 1999). In an advisory capacity, the board of directors includes legal or actual persons who financially contribute to funding the institution, and external personalities appointed for their relevant competence. Two key forms of leadership – academic and administrative – emerge from this formal policy structure. Within academic formal leadership, the board of directors' academic staff representatives are elected from the highest-ranking professors. Representatives for state administrative leadership are appointed by high-ranking officials within public administrative offices. Academic leadership assumes roles within the advisory bodies, whereby it is tasked with evaluating scientific research and pedagogical activities of the institution. The rector of the university academy is a member of the board of directors for major universities (GSoG, 1999).

The 1999 reforms reshaped HE administration paving the way for the private sector to establish private institutions for HE with a license handed over by the Minister for Higher Education, provided a set of conditions are met. Conditions include ensuring the quality of education meets the level of free public education, respecting the elements of national identity and national religious and cultural features. Formal justification for the creation of these private institutions derives from narratives responding to "national needs identified in the blueprint for the country's economic, social and cultural development." The Act does not permit the privatisation of public national educational institutions (GSoG, 1999). The framework Act of April 1999 was supplemented by the 2008 and 2016 amendments that specify the terms and conditions for issuing a license to establish a private institution for HE. Medical sciences are excluded from the disciplines allowed in private institutions of HE according to the 2008 amendments (Article 43 bis 2, February 27, 2008). These amendments enabled the opening of private international institutions for HE subjects concordant with a ratified bilateral agreement (Article 43 bis 3, February 27, 2008). Students can complete the apprenticeship stage in a private institution and complete their studies in public institutions with the approval of the Ministry or vice versa; such terms and conditions were also issued in 2016 (Bouadam, 2022).

The Act No. 2000–04 of December 6, 2000 details the guiding provisions for HE, which despite various reforms the system applies mainly top-down policy implementation (MHESR, 2022b). Article 43 of this December, 2000 Act cites an advisory body called the "National Universities Symposium," to be established with the Minister of HE (GSoG, 2008). However, the mission of the regional advisory bodies of HE is still limited to consultation, coordination, evaluation and implementation of the specific national policy in this field. The HE Minister wields central authority on decisions which include: determining HE field lists; divisions and specialisations; the annual determination of the conditions for joining the first cycle (Bachelor) and the second stage (Masters) on the basis of certificates and/or exams; annually determining the modalities of organising the competition for admission to the BA and MA phases (GSoG, 2008, Article 13–19); determining education programmes alongside the modalities of student assessment, transfer and orientation in the first (BA) and second (MA) cycle (GSoG, 2008, Article 16), and annually determining the conditions for admission to the third cycle – the doctoral programme (GSoG, 2008, Article 19). HE teaching staffs' duties are mainly exercised in the following fields: teaching, supervising, directing, monitoring and evaluating students' knowledge, while evaluating supervisors, research, continuous professional development, sharing of experience and consultation, along with the dissemination of knowledge (GSoG, 2008, Article 52). Also, determining research professors and research staffs' competence to supervise students registered for a doctoral degree and/or managing research activities is part of their remit (GSoG, 2008, Article 53). So, university-based educational leadership does not have room for manoeuvre when validating new programmes without attaining central Ministry approval.

Among the recommendations of the 14th Conference of Ministers Responsible for Higher Education and Scientific Research in the Arab

World in 2014, entitled: "Financing Higher Education in the Arab World," was to invite Arab countries to consider the exchange of recognition and accreditation for academic degrees and certificates issued by branches of the Arab Open University, provided that these degrees and certificates are approved by the affiliated country responsible for issuance. Algeria indicated that reforms to its new educational system include the restructuring of the Ministry of Higher Education's central administration. A directorate for university equivalencies, certificates and documentation was created, in addition to the completion of a draft executive decree specifying the conditions and recognition process for the equivalency of degrees and university ranks (The Arab Organization for Education & and Science (ALECSO), 2022). This reform momentum is gradually and fundamentally changing the education system at sector levels alongside its internal motives. The external UN 2030 Agenda for Sustainable Development that the UN Member States are expected to "achieve" strongly drives policy. Meeting those goals form part of the ALESCO conference agendas. Programme restructuring including the September 2004 key reform introduced the LMD (Bachelor-Master-Doctorate) programme to Algerian HE (MHESR). It was a reform structure implemented within the HE system divided into three educational cycles: firstly, leading to a Bachelor's degree (L), secondly, leading to a Master's degree (M), and finally, a doctorate degree (D). HE courses are reorganised into semesters composed of a combination of teaching units. Education and training are evaluated via a credit system, not by years of study. To facilitate student mobility and individual choice, credits can be capitalised and transferred from one course to another.

Algerian HE moves from compulsory fixed paths to more fluid mobility using the credit system. Such reorganisation of education through the LMD system is intended to offer flexible educational design, content of innovative educational programmes, and allow better comparability of qualifications on the job market (MHESR, 2022a). According to Trow's developmental theory of HE classification, Algeria has expanded to a "universal system" with GER of 52.6% in 2019 which increased from 29.9% in 2010 (Liu et al., 2021). In 1963, the Algerian HE was launched with one university and two institutes inherited from the colonial era. By 2021–2022, there were 54 institutions attaining university status, 9 University Centres, 37 National High Schools and 11 High Schools for Teachers. High Schools for Teachers select high-achieving Baccalaureate candidates due to high demand – as this route guarantees employment as permanent teachers within National Education (MESRS, 2022b). Student numbers shifted from 156 postgraduate students registered at the university in 1963 to 80,000 during the 2020–2021 academic year. The number of graduate students enrolled for the 2020–2021 academic year amounted to 1,696,000, of whom, 66% were female. For funding, approximately 7% (6.97%) of the public budget was allocated to the HE sector in 2021, compared to a budget of 2.43 in the 1970s (Liu et al., 2021).

While this expansion of HE and increased enrolment may represent progress, questions over the quality of education and the employability of graduates have risen. Central financial funding carries with it the guardianship of the Ministry of Higher Education. Amounts set for university funding remain dependent on state budgets and the economy status. Key decisions such as determining salaries, summoning international competencies, and coordinating the budget of scientific conferences are dependent on the allocated budget and remain restricted by the approval of the central administration in the Ministry. This centralisation may limit the autonomy of local institutional creativity in aspects of internal management and international research collaboration. The next section examines examples of leadership and administration dynamics enacted by subjects at implementation levels within the Algerian socio-political context.

Educational Leadership and Administration in Algerian HE: Voices from the field.

Leadership, Administration and Bureaucracy

To understand how participants perceive leadership, they were asked to provide a definition. Key subthemes in the data show most participants linked leadership to aspects of influence. Here, Sirine stated:

> *Leadership does not mean that I am holding a senior leadership role; it means when I am teaching a group of students and influencing them to be the best version of themselves both academically and personally, I become a leader ... this is true leadership. Leadership does not need a table and a chair, but it must impact society and direct the visions.*
>
> (Sirine, pedagogical position)

The notions of transformation, enthusiasm and impact were also expressed by Hadjer, a lecturer, who stated:

> *Leadership for me is that you transform ordinary students, and make them unique, ambitious, enthusiastic people who will eventually also impact and leave their fingerprints. This is my message to my students.*
>
> (Hadjer, Lecturer, no formal administrative/pedagogical position)

Hadjer and Sirine's definitions echo the majority of the participants' views about their understanding of leadership. Leadership is perceived as a personal characteristic rather than a formal administrative position:

> *I cannot qualify what I am doing as leadership because it is just administrative and bureaucratic work. Being a leader and having influence comes from my personality, but not from my administrative role.*
>
> (Zeyneb, Vice-Head of Department)

Additionally, due to accompanied bureaucratic duties, holding a senior administrative position is thought to be limited in its influential leadership.

I do not consider someone holding a senior leadership position a leader because leadership is more significant than formal position. Most senior administrators find themselves fulfilling bureaucratic duties rather than influencing their colleagues as they should.
(Leila, Lecturer with no formal leadership position)

Influence as a factor emerges in all participants' accounts as necessary to leadership. Besides, Leila highlighted an organisational/institutional issue in Algerian HE in which the academics holding senior leadership roles find themselves required to carry out various bureaucratic duties instead of leading their entourage. This could be related to the centralised nature of HE in Algeria, which means that leaders have limited autonomy over their decisions.

Working Environment and Conflicts of Interests

Participants expressed a common concern over the paradox surrounding holding a senior leadership position and academic progression. Six participants who held a senior leadership role and subsequently resigned explained how their administrative role negatively affected their academic career progression. According to Zahira, when the working team is not supportive, it can be challenging to manage people with "different mentalities" or different approaches to work commitments.

Now, I've resigned from my administrative role, and I feel better because I can focus on my research. I had many issues when I was the head of the department. I had many issues with my colleagues because I was very strict. I wanted lecturers to bring their marks early and come on time to move quickly and smoothly, but it did not happen, so I quit because of the different mentalities.
(Zahira, Lecturer; Previously Vice-Head of Department and Head of Department)

Zahira described how her health deteriorated due to a heavy administrative workload and the lack of support from her team. Her statement, *I was very strict*, possibly highlights her administrative authority when dealing with staff, an approach that conceivably generated resentment. Besides interpersonal conflict, some participants explained that it might be preferable to avoid these administrative positions due to various ethical issues, including conflicting interests. For example, Zeyneb stated:

My supervisor was a very competent and experienced academic. She was not happy when I told her about my decision to be the vice-head of my department. When I asked why, she replied that people who hold these roles have the reputation that they want them to build a network to look for their interests, not making the department or the university better.

(Zeyneb, Vice-Head of Department)

Participants viewed such exploitation as morally wrong, but all admitted that opportunistic practices exist within their working environments. Meriem and Soumia commented:

Because some lecturers working with us only think about their benefit more than the greater good for the university's students.

(Meriem, Lecturer and a member of the Doctoral Training Team)

[…] this is making the working environment not productive and [negatively affecting] the wellbeing of the academics. Our department is getting worse and worse. However, this does not affect me because I do not care about the head of the department. I do my job the best way possible, but I know that he is negatively affecting the whole department's performance … I do not want to hold a senior leadership role because it is better to focus on my research and more beneficial for my career.

(Soumia, Lecturer with no formal leadership position)

These accounts demonstrate how educational leaders' practices affect their departments' cultural environments, while also being affected by it.

Policy Ambiguity and the Lack of Professional Development Programmes

Other reported key concerns include the lack of training and ambiguous policy. Participants declared that the university/ministry did not provide any training when they were first employed or allocated an administrative or pedagogical position. Besma, as the past department's vice-head, and her university's local journal chief editor at the time of this interview, stated:

We did not have any training programme. Recently, the ministry introduced a training programme for the new academics. However, I observed these training and saw that they do not focus on quality. They do it for bureaucratic reasons. There is no real training, especially in administrative posts, and pedagogical posts do not exist. So, you are appointed to start, and you have to start researching and learning how to do it on your own.

(Besma, Lecturer, her university's Journal Chief Editor, and the past Vice-Head of Department)

Although improvement was noted when the ministry introduced training programmes for new academics, Besma and Cheikha were critical of the inadequate process of leaders' appointments due to the lack of quality training and/or assessment of competence:

The problem in our society and universities is that we do not prepare our leaders. Instead, we give them responsibilities without examining their competence or experience.
(Cheikha, Director of a Research Laboratory, and previously was a Vice-Head of Department)

Cheikha's evaluation was supported by Naima's personal experience as she described the hardships faced once appointed to a pedagogical role of examining the quality of scientific research in her department:

No one told me what my job description was. I asked about it, and I made all the efforts to understand this role.
(Naima, previously held a pedagogical role)

Although the official journal explains the role and duty of every position, Naima believes it is insufficient to support her in fulfilling her job specification. Twelve participants who held or were holding senior leadership positions agreed with Naima and criticised current regulation as ambiguous and open to personal interpretation, which can cause conflict between colleagues. As Besma concludes:

The problem is that we do not have a rule applied everywhere. I know the rules because of my position, but other lecturers do not know, so they need to read about the rules to know their rights and duties; otherwise, we will always be in unnecessary fights that could have to be avoided if we knew our rights and duties; this is one of the problems that we have.
(Besma, Lecturer, her university's Journal Chief Editor, and the past Vice-Head of Department)

Challenges emerge, including the ambiguity in interpreting policies, cultural tolerance to breaking regulations, no strict adherence to deadlines and internal conflicts of interest. Accordingly, the participants' positions, experiences and reflections demonstrate their potential contribution to shaping their organisations through resistance, action and forming social networks. Participants' views, including Zahira's, possibly indicate an unreliable quality assurance system. Moreover, the participants' reflexivity on practice shows some disparities between policymakers' claims of aspired standards and the day-to-day educational realities of policy implementation.

Discussion

Policy, Culture and Leadership

Administrative and pedagogical leadership emerge as two key categories in Algerian HE, which confirms previous literature (Miliani, 2021). Leaders in this study show aspiration for increased autonomy to exact influence and change while constrained by a central administrative bureaucratic system; this reflects what Oplatkaa and Arar's (2017) systematic review highlights in other Arab contexts. Participants observe more opportunities for agency and career development within their academic roles as lecturers or researchers beyond the formal administrative positions.

Descriptions of leadership resonate with transformational leadership (Bass & Avolio, 1994; Burns, 2012). Bass and Avolio's (1994) conceptualisation of transformational leadership includes idealised influence, inspirational motivation, intellectual stimulation of subordinates to fulfil their highest potential, and individualised consideration by taking care of followers' individual needs and development. While several studies show that women tend to adopt a transformational leadership style more than men, this gender difference in transformational leadership and effectiveness remains a controversial area of research examining sex and gender-role traits (Bass, 1999; Bobe & Kober, 2020; Chen & Shao, 2022). While all participants are Muslims, the potential influence of Prophet Muhammad's leadership model (Arar & Haj-Yehia, 2018) embedded within the Algerian Muslim cultural imagination is not to be underestimated in influencing local perceptions on optimal leadership characteristics, even when he is not explicitly mentioned.

In this regard, participants' views lend credence to studies that illustrate the contribution of cultural and social inhibiting factors in the discrepancy between the positive perceptions towards shared, moral and transformational leadership models of educational leaders in the Arab world, and ways in which leaders apply these models in practice (Izhar & Arar, 2017). The participants' reflexive accounts show how decision-making processes become political arenas of competing individuals and group interests where coalition forms of leadership may emerge through the dynamics of change and conflict in organisations. As demonstrated, educators are critically reflecting on their own needs, priorities, objectives, and strategies in the process of implementing policies. While the government rules and state resources shape the educational system at both lower and HE sectors, it is the self-conscious participating agents who decide on ways of enacting those policies within certain circumstances.

The Algerian educational system, including HE, is slowly but gradually heading towards a market-driven model of education. The new policies allow fee-paying private and international educational provisions to penetrate marketisation elements in education to create an internally competing educational market, and to prepare learners and the economy for global competition. With the introduction of the three-cycle LMD system of HE, the Algerian education system furthers the objectives of the Bologna process targeting "the labour market, for further competence building and for active citizenship" ("The Bergen Communiqué," 2005, p. 6). However, Ball & Cohen's (1999) careful analysis highlights how policymakers' lack of evaluation of the complex circumstances of the education system translates to their mistaken assumption that restructuring institutions, educational programmes and curricula will sufficiently achieve the set reform goals. This pre-evaluation is especially important for change as:

> [N]eoliberal reforms rely heavily on obedience to rules, laws, policies, standards of processes and outputs, and meticulous record keeping (e.g., paperwork). But, many traditional societies are relationship-based; that is, employees in this society are more likely to emphasize interpersonal relationships and trust over strict application of regulations and rules. For example, they tend to be tolerant, to some extent, of rule breaking, attaching less importance to record keeping and objective criteria (e.g., learning standards, reporting, standards of efficiency, strict measurement of student achievement).
>
> (Oplatka, 2019, p. 39)

Participants' accounts of their experiences demonstrate such cultural disparities. Educational leaders in Algeria are left to handle the uncertainties of change which policymakers throw at them. Market competition requires cultural contexts that tolerate flexibility, change and risk taking; yet, the Algerian Hofstede's Uncertainty Avoidance dimension remains high with a score of 70 (Hofstede Insights, 2022). In contrast to Western European individualistic societies, from which educational reforms are imported, a hierarchical order in Algeria is socially accepted with a score of 80 for the high power-distance cultural dimension. Algeria is a collectivist society with a low rate of 35 for the individualism cultural dimension (Hofstede Insights, 2022). Additionally, Algeria's low score of 35 on the Masculinity dimension means that society is not driven by individual competition, achievement and success, and that compromise and negotiation are key to resolving conflicts which could be perceived as threatening to the group's well-being. These dimensions may partly explain some head of departments' behaviour to building close networks around their position, not only to advance their personal interests, but also to avoid personal conflicts with unknown members who adopt different approaches to work. Such dimensional effects may contribute to resignations from administrative positions to avoid interpersonal relations conflicts. Many researchers connect organisational culture with leadership behaviour in terms of an exchanging influence; leaders' behaviours contribute to shaping the internal organisational cultures while also influenced by such cultures (Bass, 1985; Connolly et al., 2019).

Emerging challenges may discourage participants from holding senior leadership positions which conflict with their research career progression. When judging the utility of training provision, participants reported this as inadequate to enable staff to effectively conduct their duties. In this regard, Ramdani et al. (2014) survey research on business organisations in Algeria found insignificant links between training and operating efficiency potentially attributed to the design of training programmes which do not account for efficiency. Yet, evaluation of training utility may be influenced by perceived disparity between theoretical knowledge and the work environment which leaders inhabit. This is because "[t]ransfer (or 'on-the-job performance') is a function of both knowledge acquisition and the favorability of the work environment for allowing new skills to be applied" (Alliger et al., 1997, p. 352). The work environment not only affects staff performance but also shapes female staff's decisions towards holding leadership positions or retaining them.

Leadership and the "Ethics of Intimacy"

Educational leaders in Algerian HE function within a socio-political context where personal networks play an important role in navigating conflicting webs of interests (Boubekeur, 2013). Several studies in MENA revealed the permeation of "wasta" (literally means "intermediary" in Arabic) into networks of family relationships and close friendships to circumvent bureaucratic obstacles, facilitate transactions and access jobs (Budhwar & Mellahi, 2016; Smith et al., 2012). The use of *wasta* in Algeria is expressed as "*al-ma'arifa*" ("who you know") referring to the importance of the social network, piston[1], *laktaf* ("shoulders") as a reference to supportive social relationships, "*ras*" (head) – someone at the pinnacle, or *wasel* – describes a person who has wide access to different authority circles and social structure (Smith et al., 2012). The "*ben'ammis*" (literally means "cousins' relationship") concept is commonly used in Algeria as an alternative to *al-ma'arifa/wasta* in referring to networks that favour kinship or friends' interests. This *al-ma'arifa/wasta* practice questions the fragility of modern state bureaucratic structural models, including education, in effectively serving citizens and replacing traditional social ties in MENA contexts.

Algeria's brutal 1990s civil political conflict impacted social network dynamics, even within kinship relations. Consequently, Mellahi and Wood's (2003) research found that employment in Algerian small- and medium-sized companies (SMEs) primarily depends on trusted ties with acquaintances or friends rather than through family connections. Yet, their (2003) research also emphasised that kinship played a key factor in the recruitment of female and older employees. In a conservative social context, "[d]espite deregulation, SMEs in Algeria remain committed to HRM [the human resource management] practices founded not on formalization and rules, but rather on personal networks" and "remains deeply embedded in an 'ethics of intimacy'" (Mellahi & Wood, 2003, p. 379). This context potentially disadvantages women from holding or sustaining positions at decision-making levels due to existing male networking cultures, as some studies reveal in other Arab Middle-Eastern countries such as Lebanon (Budhwar & Mellahi, 2016). In 2021/2022, females represent 66% of enrolled graduate students in Algerian HE (Liu et al., 2021). Yet, female leadership representation in Algerian HE lags behind.

The SHEMERA project report illustrates how women in Algeria are underrepresented at the top of the academic ladder with around 17% of female representation among academics at grade A (The European Commission, 2015). Algerian women as latecomers to jobs in HE, largely derive from traditionally defined family gender roles, have to negotiate their spaces, authority and leadership credibility within this Algerian hierarchical cultural context or what Mellahi and Wood (2003) describes as "chikh"/sheikh (in Arabic means "learned, and/or wise") culture. Moreover, the importance of conflict avoidance within a sense of "in-group" relationships, and the avoidance of risk-taking in Algerian cultural dimensions could potentially propose more challenges for women, traditionally a subordinate group, to gain access or retain authority within their roles as leaders in such a micro-political context of HE, especially where *wasta* networks are absent or weak. Various studies in the Arab world, including Algeria, illustrate how the strongest *wasta*, and not necessarily the strongest profile, precedes in the employment selection process (Budhwar & Mellahi, 2016; Mellahi & Wood, 2003; Ramdani et al., 2014; Smith et al., 2012). While this research does not examine the impact of *wasta* on the employment selection process, it confirms the potential active role that personal network dynamics play in HE leadership circles. This study shows how HE senior leadership personnel are perceived to be building personal networks to primarily serve their personal interests rather than those of their departments or organisations.

This cultural context demonstrates how demarcations between leader and follower are influenced by various societal criteria beyond the formal job position. Considering this networking dimension, these "ongoing social relationships provide the constraints and opportunity that, in combination with characteristics of individuals, issues, and organizations, may help explain unethical behavior in organizations" (Brass et al., 1998, p. 17). Accordingly, whereas central policies restrict educators to the implementation arena, the process of interpretation and implementation produce spaces for agency through power dynamics and social praxis. From this complex background, the deep meanings that educators attribute to key concepts surrounding policy reform could be strikingly different from where they originate due to ontological and epistemological differences in social-cultural understandings about education and leadership issues. There is an urgent need for developing educational environments and leadership systems that instil the best of local heritage, history and sense of belonging, but remain open to learn from others in ways that do not inhibit self-worth. It is a goal that demands political willingness embedded into a democratic transparent system which remains an aspiration in the Algerian socio-political context.

Further research may examine the impact of *wasta* on educational leadership, equal opportunities, educational working environments and transparent productive networking arrangements in the Algerian educational system. Research is required on how the micro-political cultural dynamics are shaping imported programmes, such as the LMD, compared to implementation in its indigenous cultural contexts.

Conclusion

In this chapter, key features of the Algerian education system reforms, organisation and administration have been examined. Discussion of relevant literature contextualised reforms in its historical context, and considered the overall system of education, while focusing particularly on HE reforms. **Algerian HE is conceived in terms of academic objectives to meet university needs and/or professional objectives to address the requirements of the socio-economic sector. These objectives are then translated into teaching programmes built by the lecturers when grouped into research teams, and into human, material and financial resources to be mobilised and presented as programme delivery. Education ministries define the overall strategy for HE and draw up guidelines for the HE national master plan. Hence, HE institutions theoretically retain the power to define and propose, within a central strategy, their own training and research policy by taking into account local skills, specific data and potential of their immediate environments.**

Finally, two formal types of leadership clearly emerge from the policies: administrative and pedagogical leadership which concede with previous research. The participants' accounts expose some of the conflicts, challenges and dilemmas that HE leaders encounter on the ground. Within this context, centralised management of the educational sector leaves room, albeit limited, for leadership at the grassroots level regarding how to translate public policy and vision into pedagogical and administrative areas of praxis which differ from originally conceived plans for reform by policymakers. Here, the educational system becomes both the medium and the outcome of such social praxis.

Note

1 In Algeria, the concept "piston" means knowing someone in some position of influence who could provide assistance.

References

Alliger, G. M., Tannenbaum, S. I., Bennett Jr, W., Traver, H., & Shotland, A. (1997). A meta-analysis of the relations among training criteria. *Personnel Psychology*, 50(2), 341–358. Retrieved July 03, 2022, from https://onlinelibrary.wiley.com/doi/10.1111/j.1744-6570.1997.tb00911.x

Arar, K., & Haj-Yehia, K. (2018). Perceptions of educational leadership in medieval Islamic thought: A contribution to multicultural contexts. *Journal of Educational Administration and History*, 50(2), 69–81. 10.1080/00220620.2017.1413341

Baker, D. J., & Wiseman, A. W. (Eds.). (2005). *Global trends in educational policy* (Vol. 6). Elsevier.

Ball, D. L., & Cohen, D. K. (1999). Developing practice, developing practitioners: Toward a practice-based theory of professional education. In L. D.-H.-G. Sykes (Ed.), *Teaching as the learning profession: A handbook of policy and practice* (pp. 3–32). Jossey-Bass.

Ball, S. J., Maguire, M., Braun, A., & Hoskins, K. (2011). Policy actors: Doing policy work in schools. *Discourse: Studies in the Cultural Politics of Education, 32*(4), 625–639. 10.1080/01596306.2011.601565

Bass, A., & Avolio, B. J. (1994). Introduction. In B. M. Bass, & B. J. Avolio (Eds.), *Improving organizational effectiveness through transformational leadership* (pp. 1–9). Sage Publications.

Bass, B. M. (1985). *Leadership and performance beyond expectations*. The Free Press.

Bass, B. M. (1999). Two decades of research and development in transformational leadership. *European Journal of Work and Organizational Psychology, 8*(1), 9–32. 10.1080/135943299398410

Benghabrit-Remaoun, N. (2016). *Mobiliser la ressource humaine et susciter son engagement pour la cause éducative: Une nécessité vitale [Mobilize human resources and encourage their commitment to the educational cause: A vital necessity]* Forum Mondial de l'éducation de Londres, London. http://www.theewf.org/uploads/pdf/Nouria-Benghebbrit-%E2%80%93-EWF-2016-Presentation.pdf

Bin-Muhammed, A.-H. (2016). *Algerian scholars warn against Westernizing education in the name of reform [Ulama' al-jaza'ir yuhadhirun min taghrib al-ta'lim bi'sm al-islah]*. Al-Jazeera. Retrieved July 13, 2022, from https://www.aljazeera.net

Birnbaum, R. (1991). *How colleges work: The cybernetics of academic organization and leadership*. Jossey-Bass.

Bobe, B. J., & Kober, R. (2020). Does gender matter? The association between gender and the use of management control systems and performance measures. *Accounting & Finance, 60*(3), 2063–2098. 10.1111/acfi.12365

Boubekeur, A. (2013). Rolling either way? Algerian entrepreneurs as both agents of change and means of preservation of the system. *The Journal of North African Studies, 18*(3), 469–481. Retrieved July 14, 2022, from 10.1080/13629387.2013.775870

Boumediene, H. (1976). *Official Gazette of the Algerian Republic: Laws and orders*. Algiers: The Official Press. Retrieved from SGG Algérie (joradp.dz)

Bouadam, R. (2022). Importance of contextualisation in developing university training: Professional Master's degree in "sustainable management of waste in an urban environment" in Algeria. *Humanities & Social Sciences Reviews, 10*, 10–22.

Brass, D. J., Butterfield, K. D., & Skaggs, B. C. (1998). Relationships and unethical behavior: A social network perspective. *The Academy of Management Review, 23*(1), 14–31. 10.2307/259097

Braun, V., & Clarke, V. (2006). Using thematic analysis in psychology. *Qualitative Research in Psychology* (3), 77–101. 10.1191/1478088706qp063oa

Budhwar, P. S., & Mellahi, K. (Eds.). (2016). *Handbook of human resource management in the Middle East*. Edward Elgar Publishing. 10.4337/9781784719524.

Burns, J. M. (2012). *Leadership*. Open Road Integrated Media.

Chen, S.-C., & Shao, J. (2022). Feminine traits improve transformational leadership advantage: Investigation of leaders' gender traits, sex and their joint impacts on employee contextual performance. *Gender in Management: An International Journal*, 37(5), 569–586. 10.1108/GM-06-2020-0167

Connolly, M., James, C., & Fertig, M. (2019). The difference between educational management and educational leadership and the importance of educational responsibility. *Educational Management Administration & Leadership*, 47(4), 504–519. 10.1177/1741143217745880

Constitution 1963 (1963). constit-1963-ar.pdf (premier-ministre.gov.dz)

Constitution of the People's Democratic Republic of Algeria (2020). www.joradp.dz

Eacott, S. (2017). A social epistemology for educational administration and leadership. *Journal of Educational Administration and History*, 49(3), 196–214. 10.1080/00220620.2017.1315380

General Secretariat of the Government (1970). *Acts and Ordinances: Ordinance No. 70-53 Containing the Establishment of the Government*. Algiers: The Official Press. Retrieved from SGG Algérie (joradp.dz)

General Secretariat of the Government (1971a). *Ministry of Primary and Secondary Education – Employment of Contract Teachers*. Algiers: The Official Press Retrieved from SGG Algérie (joradp.dz)

General Secretariat of the Government (1971b). *Specific Basic Act for Laboratory Technicians of Institutions of Higher, Secondary and Technical Education*. Algiers: The Official Press Retrieved from SGG Algérie (joradp.dz)

General Secretariat of the Government (1989). *Executive Decree No. 89-93 regulating the central administration in the Ministry of Education and Training*. Algiers: The Official Press Retrieved from SGG Algérie (joradp.dz)

General Secretariat of the Government (1999). *Act No. 99-05 includes the Higher Education Directive Legislation*. Algies: The Official Press. Retrieved from https://services.mesrs.dz/DEJA/fichiers_sommaire_des_textes/02%20ar.pdf

General Secretariat of the Government (2008). *Act No. 06-08 of February 2008, Containing the Higher Education Directive Legislation*. Algiers: The Official Press. Retrieved from https://services.mesrs.dz/DEJA/Ensemble%20des%20textes%20juridiques%20depuis%20l%27ind%C3%A9pendance%20et%20publie%20dans%20le%20journa%20officiel%20/loi08-06ar.pdf

Giddens, A. (1984). *The constitution of society: Outline of the theory of structuration*. Polity.

Hallinger, P., & Hammad, W. (2019). Knowledge production on educational leadership and management in Arab societies: A systematic review of research. *Educational Management, Administration & Leadership*, 47(1), 20–36. 10.1177/1741143217717280

Hofstede Insights (2022). *Country comparison: Algeria*. Hofstede Insights. Retrieved July 06, 2022, from https://www.hofstede-insights.com/country-comparison/algeria/

Izhar, O., & Arar, K. (2017). The research on educational leadership and management in the Arab world since the 1990s: A systematic review. *Review of Education*, 5(3), 267–307. 10.1002/rev3.3095

Liu, D., Jemni, M., Huang, R., Wang, Y., Tlili, A., & Sharhan, S. (2021). *An overview of education development in the Arab region: Insights and recommendations towards sustainable development goals (SDGs)*. Smart Learning Institute of Beijing Normal University (SLIBNU). http://www.alecso.org/publications/SLIBNU-ALECSO_BOOK.pdf

Mellahi, K., & Wood, G. T. (2003). From kinship to trust: Changing recruitment practices in unstable political contexts. *International Journal of Cross Cultural Management: CCM, 3*(3), 369–381. 10.1177/1470595803003003007

Miliani, M. (2021). Educational leadership in Algeria: A decisive factor in the 2004 Higher Education Reform. In D. Mifsud, & P. Landri (Eds.), *Enacting and conceptualizing educational leadership within the Mediterranean Region* Vol. 2, pp. 101–116. Brill. 10.1163/9789004461871

Mott, H. (2022). *Higher education: Maximising impacts.* T. B. Council. https://www.britishcouncil.org/sites/default/files/gender_equality_in_higher_education_report.pdf

Oplatka, I. (2010). *The legacy of educational administration: A historical analysis of an academic field.* Peter Lang. 10.3726/978-3-653-00936-1

Oplatka, I. (2019). *Reforming education in developing countries: From neoliberalism to communitarianism.* Routledge. 10.4324/9781351234337

Oplatka, I., & Arar, K. H. (2016). Leadership for social justice and the characteristics of traditional societies: Ponderings on the application of western-grounded models. *International Journal of Leadership in Education, 19*(3), 352–369. 10.1080/13603124.2015.1028464

Oplatka, I., & Arar, K. (2017). The research on educational leadership and management in the Arab world since the 1990s: A systematic review. *Review of Education, 5*(3), 267–307. 10.1002/rev3.3095

Ramdani, B., Mellahi, K., Guermat, C., & Kechad, R. (2014). The efficacy of high performance work practices in the Middle East: Evidence from Algerian firms. *The International Journal of Human Resource Management, 25*(2), 252–275. https://www.tandfonline.com/doi/full/10.1080/09585192.2013.826918

Saidouni, N.-E. (2021). *The cultural issue in Algeria: Elites - identity - language (a critical historical study) [Al-mas'alah al-thaqafiyyah fi al-jaza'ir al-nukhab - al-huwayah - al-lugha (dirasat tarikhiah naqdiah)].* Arab Center for Research and Policy Studies.

Smith, P. B., Torres, C., Leong, C.-H., Budhwar, P., Achoui, M., & Lebedeva, N. (2012). Are indigenous approaches to achieving influence in business organizations distinctive? A comparative study of guanxi, wasta, jeitinho, svyazi and pulling strings. *The International Journal of Human Resource Management, 23*(2), 333–348. 10.1080/09585192.2011.561232

Taleb-Ibrahimi, K. (2007). *L'Algérie: Coexistence et concurrence des langues* [Algeria: Coexistence and competition of languages]. In F. Abécassis, G. Boyer, B. Falaize, G. Meynier, & M Zancarini-Fournel. (Eds.), *La France et l'Algérie: leçons d'histoire: De l'école en situation coloniale à l'enseignement du fait colonial [France and Algeria: lessons in history: From school in a colonial situation to teaching the colonial fact].* ENS Éditions. 10.4000/books.enseditions.1253

The Arab Organization for Education, C., & and Science (ALECSO) (2022). *Education Ministers Conference.* ALECSO. http://www.alecso.org/nsite/ar/

The Bergen Communiqué (2005). *The European higher education area – Achieving the goals* The Bologna process: European ministers responsible for higher education.

The European Commission (2015). *SHEMERA (Euro-Mediterranean research cooperation on gender and science: SHE Euro-Mediterranean Research Area)* (169195). European Union. https://cordis.europa.eu/project/id/266633/reporting

Wiseman, A. W. (Ed.). (2009). *Educational leadership: Global contexts and international comparisons* (Vol. 11). Emerald. 10.1108/S1479-3679(2009)11

7 Educational Administration and Leadership in Jordan
A Retrospective-Prospective Approach

Aref Al-Attari and Eiman Essa

Introduction

In 2003, Jordan launched ambitious, multi-donor reform projects to redirect education to meet the expectations of the knowledge-based economy. The Jordan Education Initiative (JEI), and Education Reform for Knowledge Economy (ERfKI) (spanning the years 2003–2015) were streamlined to the inter-sectoral "Economic and Social Transformation Plan" (2003) which had been assigned to the Ministry of Planning and International Cooperation. The Ministry of Education Strategic Plan (2006) was devised in response to those initiatives.

Educational administration at the Ministry, Directorates of Education (DoE), and schools were given a pivotal role in the implementation of the education reform agenda. The focus of the reform agenda was on the devolution of important authoritative positions, responsibilities, and decision-making to the DoE and school level. Thus, models of management such as "school-based management", "distributive leadership", and "teacher leadership" were championed. However, landmark official documents issued while ERfKI was winding down in 2015, lamented the fact that education, which was a source of national pride in Jordan, was deteriorating. "Jordan Vision 2025" pointed to the general decline in the education system, particularly in the public school system, as evidenced, among other things, by the low achievement of Jordanian students on international tests such as TIMMS and PISA (The Government of Jordan, 2015). In response, the Ministry of Education (MoE) articulated the Strategic Plan (SP) 2018–2022. The legitimate question therefore is:

Why were the results of the rose-tinted reform agenda far from rosy?

The above documents (Jordan Vision 2025 and SP 2018–2022) blamed the high centralization of decision-making particularly in public schools as the main culprit to the setbacks of the education reform agenda. The SP 2018–2022 points to the persistence of centralization, the dormant standards of leadership, and the inadequate system of selecting principals as barriers to reform. The SP calls for more devolution of authorities, advanced standards of

DOI: 10.4324/9781003334835-7

leadership, and a re-authorization of Act No. 3 for the year 1994 regarding the appointment of principals.

It is obvious that the official narration presents the failure as a technical problem that could be solved through technical solutions. We questioned this official narration from cultural, political, and economic perspectives, and explored the potential applicability of the championed models of management in the Jordanian context.

Methodology

This chapter employs a document analysis methodology. We meticulously analyzed high-profile documents related to the education reform agenda, particularly the JEI (2003), ERfKI (2003–2015), and the Strategic Plan 2018–2022 (Table 7.1). Other official documents from the 20th century were used as a backdrop to our analysis. The analysis focused on the role of educational administration, management, and leadership. In addition, we employed secondary sources, previous related studies, and reports, along with drawing on our experience and expertise as insiders. We deliberately employed the document analysis methodology as this approach is missing in Arab scholarship in educational administration, management, and leadership. Bibliometric studies on Arab scholarship in EDLM found that the overwhelming majority of articles gave scant attention to the relationship between policies, politics, and education (Atari & Outum, 2019; Oplatka & Arar, 2017).

To ensure accuracy, both researchers analyzed the documents independently and derived the main themes that were related to educational leadership. After discussion and agreement, they listed the main themes (Table 7.1).

Besides the document analysis, the authors used the bibliometric methodology to describe ELA scholarship in Jordan. They analyzed (149) doctorate theses approved at Yarmouk University. They browsed every thesis, and the related data were coded by the two authors independently before being compared. The scrutiny process included the thesis title, type, sex of authors, supervisory mode, setting of the study (if applicable), research method (qualitative, quantitative, mixed method), and theme(s) (Table 7.2).

Theoretical Underpinnings

This chapter is guided by "positive psychology", the "paradox theory", and "organizational ambidexterity" literature. Positive psychology focuses on opportunities, optimism, and capabilities rather than on difficulties and problems. The paradox theory offers a polyphonic framework to unpack antithetical positions. It identifies and re-frames boundaries to create a "third space", develops opposites into a new whole, connects contentious dualities, equally values the extreme positions, deliberately engages in

Table 7.1 Themes generated from the document analysis

Reform initiatives	Involved parties	Concerns	Aspiration	Solutions	Tools	Settings	Championed leadership theories	Obstacles
JEI (2003) (later subsumed by ERIFKI)	Government of Jordan; Global Education Initiative (Originated at Davos); CISCO	The technology gap and the ability to be active in the global economy	Transforming Jordan into a regional Technology Hub and major player in global economy	Computerization of the Educational Institutions and Process	Developing and disseminating e-learning and ICT, strengthening partnerships between the private and public sector; receiving support from international stakeholders	100 "discovery schools" received new computers, textbooks, and other instructional materials		Underdevelopment of the Technology Infrastructure
ERIFKI (Phase 1- 2003-2009; Phase 2 2009-2015)	GoJ; International Donors: World, Bank, USAID, CanadaAID ….	decline of quality in education; Low results in International Tests (PISA, TIMSS) Unemployment of graduates	Schools work autonomously; Graduates equipped with critical mindset and attitudes that enable them to compete on international levels in the era of the k-based economy	Devolution of authorities to the School and Directorate of Education; Learner-centered classroom; Critical thinking, cooperation and teamwork, multilingualism, technological fluency, democratic participation, and entrepreneurship.	Computerization; Decentralization: School and Directorate of Education Development Program (SDDP). School Capacity building. School Improvement Plan (SIP), School Development Team (SDT); leadership standards;	School and Directorates of Education; classrooms	School-Based Management; Leadership Theories with sharing and democratic leanings such as the "Distribution Leadership" and "Teacher Leadership"	Deeply entrenched centralization; The prevalent rentier economy and welfare state; associating ERIFKI with neoliberalism and so-called hidden political agenda.

Educational Administration and Leadership in Jordan 117

SP 2018–2022	GoJ	Above concerns continued: Influx of Syrian refugees; reverberations of Arab Spring; Gender Disparity; Protection of people with special needs; Worsening economic situation; Commitment to the UN SDGs	Above aspirations besides inclusion of Syrian students; Narrowing the gender gap; Equity in terms of accessibility to education; facilitating access to pre-school and higher education, with arrangements for the disabled and marginalized communities	Same as above besides good governance; Busnocratic orientation; availability and accessibility to schools, the protection of the disabled, ethical and evidence-informed decision making; safety of schools that are free of violence and bullying.	Re-authorizing law 3 for 1994 on the selection of principals; Advanced leadership standards; Licensing principals; More Women Leaders; Syrian refugees; Protecting the disabled; Data-led decision-making; (EMIS software); Training and Testing principals	The educational scene throughout	Transformative leadership, distributive leadership, ethical leadership. Instructional leadership. School-based management and teacher leadership	resistance to change; weakness of school leadership; disinterest of many employees; inactivation of shared leadership; marginalizing the development teams; habits and traditions; nepotism and tribalism; disinclination of the local community to participate.

Table 7.2 Findings disaggregated by a number of quantitative indicators

Year of publication	(N=149)	%
2017	22	14.77
2018	30	20.13
2019	45	30.20
2020	44	29.53
2021	8	5.37
Type	(N = 149)	%
Doctorate	110	73.83
Master	39	26.17
Sex of authors	(N = 149)	%
Male	34	22.82
Female	115	77.18
Supervisory pattern	(N = 149)	%
Single supervisor	117	78.52
Co-supervised/panel	32	21.48
Setting	(N = 149)	%
Higher education institutions	50	33.55
Public education institutions	80	53.69
Directorate of Education	13	8.73
The Ministry of Education	4	2.69
Other settings	2	1.34
Research method	(N = 149)	%
Quantitative	145	97.32
Qualitative	1	0.67
Mixed	3	2.01
Themes	(N = 149)	%
Technology, knowledge management	5	3.36
HRM,	6	4.03
Preparation programs and training	8	5.37
Job satisfaction, loyalty, social responsibility	12	8.05
Educational policies	13	8.73
Administration creativity, management development, empowerment, TQM, excellence management,	15	10.07
Problems and obstacles	16	10.74
Leadership styles, theories, skills, roles, and processes	74	49.67

continuous learning and dialogue that open up opportunities, new interpretations, and spaces for creativity, and explores the unthought of possibility that contradictions could morph over time into new complementary integrations and repertoires that organizations can utilize to deal with contradictions (Zhang & Han, 2019; Cunha & Putnam, 2019). Organizational ambidexterity refers to the ability to strike a balance between simultaneous tensions in order to produce incremental and discontinuous innovation, just as ambidexterity refers to the use of both the left and right hand equally (Turner et al., 2013).

These approaches are not different but rather complementary and interrelated. Instead of an "either-or" approach, the organizational paradox literature advances the "both/and", "more-than", "Yin and Yang" and "at the same time, all the time" approaches. In other words, this is a sort of ambidexterity, which refers to the ability to use both the left and right hand equally instead of a preference for using one or the other. By extension, this maximizes the organizational capacity by spreading optimism and highlighting opportunities and capabilities rather than difficulties and obstacles.

The Context

Education in Jordan in the 20th Century

In 2021, modern-day Jordan celebrated its centenary. Three types of educational institutions could be identified in the then *Emirate* at the advent of 1920: The traditional private schools referred to in most Islamic countries as *Kuttab* (Plural *Katatib*) which extend back to the early centuries of Islam; the Evangelist missionary, mostly Western-based schools which spread in the 19th century in almost all of the Ottoman territories; and the modern state-administered schools which were established by the Ottoman administration as part of the reform agenda (known as the *Tanzimat* in the first half of the 19th century and the Regulations in the *Fin de Siècle*) (Emine, 2005). Being one of the peripheral territories of the Ottoman Empire, the number of modern state-administered schools in Jordan was very small. In 1918, the number ranged between 25 and 39 primary schools, enrolling a few hundred students of whom females constituted only 0.9% (Abu Al-Sha'ar, 2010). Besides schools, Jordan inherited some forms of educational organization from the Ottomans namely: the Directorate of Public Education (*Maa'ref Umumyya*), supervisory system, and the education tax (Emine, 2005).

During the era of Emir (later King) Abdulla 1 (died 1951), the legal, organizational, and physical foundations for education were laid out. Reasonable though sluggish progress was achieved. The bureaucratic apparatus has become complex with many directorates in the governorates and at the center besides the additional layer of committees and councils.

The brief era of King Talal (abdicated 1952) witnessed the issuance of the Constitution which assigned the provision of education to the Government (item 3 Article 6). Article 20 considered basic education compulsory and free in public schools, while Article 19 gave different groups the right to establish their schools within the parameters of law.

Besides expansion in school education, the era of King Hussain (1952–1999) witnessed the establishment of higher education and the issuance of education laws which culminated with the current Law No. 3 for the year 1994, which continues to regulate the educational scene today. It further streamlined educational plans to the economic and social plans and convened conferences and forums to plan for the future of education. The Conference on Educational Development in 1987 gave rise to the Jordan Education Reform Project which spanned the period from 1989 to 2005.

In the 1990s, the increasing social demand for education caused a massification of education to an extent that strained their budget allowance. Part of the response was the expansion of privatization and the internationalization of education (Atari, 2015; Atari, 2020). However, the exponential growth in the numbers of school leavers and university graduates compounded the unemployment problem. It was found that graduates, who would find jobs in the public sector or opt to migrate to Arab and foreign countries, should be equipped with capabilities, knowledge, and skills that enable them to compete on the international level in the era of K-based economies which is characterized by uncertainty and fluidity. This concern will dominate the public and educational discourse in the next decades.

Educational Reforms in Jordan in the 21st Century

In alignment with the aforementioned inter-sectoral "Economic and Social Transformation Plan", (2003), Jordan introduced ambitious plans to make the country the regional technology hub and active player in the global economy. Towards this aim, the JEI (2003) focused on developing and disseminating e-learning and ICT infrastructure, strengthening the partnership between the private and public sectors with support from international stakeholders such as CISCO (Computer Information System Company) which piloted JEI in 100 "Discovery Schools", that have received new computers, textbooks, and other instructional materials (Bannayan et al., 2012). The JEI was rolled out into the "Education Reform for Knowledge Economy" (ERfKE) which spanned the period (2003–2015) in two phases (2003–2008, and 2009–2015). ERfKI was launched with financial support by the World Bank, USAID, and other donors. It involved the promotion of critical thinking, cooperation and teamwork, multilingualism, technological fluency, democratic participation, and entrepreneurship.

Within this context, The Moe started the implementation of the School and Directorates Development Program (SDDP) to decentralize and devolve education authority to schools and education directorates of education. This was to be accompanied by capacity building to help schools function autonomously. SDDP included conducting a self-review process, surveying stakeholders' opinions, examining the school's current approach to providing services, identifying patterns of weakness that require improvement, developing "School Improvement Plan (SIP)" and forming "School Development Team (SDT)" to build and implement school's improvement plan (National Policies Team, 2010).

The Education Strategic Plan 2018–2022

The three years that followed the end of ERfKI in 2015 witnessed heated debates. Concerns regarding the quality of education were voiced. The "Royal

Letters"-inspired documents, namely "Jordan Vision 2025" (published in 2015) and The National Strategy for the Development of Human Resources 2016–2025 (NCDHR, 2015) pointed to the general decline in the education system, particularly in the public school system. The Educational Conference (2015) recommended revising Education Law No. 3 for the year 1994 and introducing new standards for appointing principals. Besides that, the country witnessed important developments that have had ramifications on the educational scene since 2011, namely the influx of spectacular numbers of Syrian refugees, the reverberations of the Arab Spring, and the worsening economic situation.

On the global level, the government declared its commitment to the UN sustainable development goals (SDGs 2016–2030), which picked up from where the Millennium Development Goals (MDGs 2000–2015) had left off. The SDGs consist of 17 aims with over 100 indicators. Those goals are indirectly or directly related to education. SDG 4 in particular calls to ensure quality, equality, equity, and accessibility to primary and secondary education, facilitating access to preschool education and higher education with a special focus on gender parity, people with special needs, and marginalized communities. The Government of Jordan prepared a national road map to streamline the SDGs in the national frameworks (The Hashemite Kingdom of Jordan, 2017).

Enlightened by all these documents and developments, the MoE articulated the Strategic Plan 2018–2022. Therefore, while building upon the previous plans including ERfKI and the JEI, the SP 2018–2022 allocated considerable space for educating Syrian refugee students, solving gender-related issues, and applying equitable and social justice measures in the form of accessible education, particularly for those with disabilities and special needs.

Educational Leadership in Jordan

Up until the 1950s, educational management in Jordan was a function informed by the wisdom and experience of practitioners who assumed "headship" of schools after a few years of service as schoolteachers. Scholarship-informed practice began in the 1960s and expanded in the succeeding decades when the departments of educational administration at Jordanian universities started to offer courses and programs leading to diplomas, master's degrees, and PhDs in educational administration. We will elaborate on ELA scholarship In Jordan in a special section in this chapter.

Legislations were upgraded to mirror the above developments. For instance, Law No. 16 for the year 1964 stipulated that a principal of a secondary school should be a university graduate with a minimum number of three years of teaching experience. Later in the century, and in accordance with Article 18 of Law No. 3 for the year 1994, all school principals were required to hold a university degree in addition to a diploma that required a year of study, and five years of experience as schoolteachers.

In response to concerns regarding the quality of education, the SP 1918–2022 emphasized the importance of good governance (the rule of law, transparency, accountability, participation, integrity, effectiveness, and sustainability), strategic planning, crisis, and risk management. It also emphasized distinction, efficiency, professionalism, and meritocracy as well as continuous assessment and follow-up plans, improving school performance, disseminating reports to local communities, and creating new positions for general supervisors to judge and rate school performance (Ministry of Education, 2018).

The SP also infused the "busnocratic" managerial terminology, inter alia: The results-based expenditure and priorities-based budget; rationalizing the available resources, cost-efficiency, and effectiveness; institutional performance appraisal; school self-reliance; strategic planning; surveying service recipients' satisfaction; and accreditation of schools and directorates of education based on internal as well as external audit, annual reports, and clear standards for assessment. In the same vein, an increased amount of attention was paid to social justice and ethical issues such as the availability and accessibility to schools, the protection of the disabled, ethical and evidence-informed decision-making, and the safety of schools that are free of violence and bullying.

Contemporary theories and approaches with sharing and participative leanings such as school-based management, distributive management, transformational leadership, ethical leadership, and instructional leadership continued to be championed. With the new concept promoting "the school as the primary unit for development", teacher leadership was emphasized (The Ministry of Education, 2016).

Decentralization has been given center stage. The document entitled "Vision 2025", which severely criticized the high centralization of decision-making in public schools, commended many private schools for their high performance. This contrast is highly indicative of the preference for the private sector management model, and by extension the promotion of the "new public management", managerialism, and neoliberalism. This aligns with the NSDHR's document entitled "Education for Prosperity" (2015) which states:

"The current centralized system does not give sufficient autonomy to school leadership and teachers to be able to implement new initiatives tailored to their local context. Furthermore, the career progression system does not promote the best or most equipped teachers into leadership positions; instead, it rewards those who have stayed the longest in the system (NCDHR, 2015, p. 105).

In concurrence, The SP 2018–2022 (p. 50) observes that the modus operandi at the school and DoE is still inclined towards centralization without clear coordination or a coherent strategic path. Therefore, the need is pressing for more delegation of authority to the DoE and school so that these entities become self-managed in order to enable the MoE to focus on developing grand effective strategies and interventions. The SP aspires for 100%

decentralization in 2022. For decentralization to work, The NCHRD's "Education for Prosperity" (2015) calls for a "data-led decision making" to enable leaders at the DoE and schools to take informed decisions:

An Education Management Information System (EMIS) has been developed in partnership with UNESCO and an "open source" version is publicly accessible online. The new system is designed to build data and management capabilities within the system to increase transparency and accountability, and inform improvement programs. For the new EMIS to be successful, it needs to be successfully integrated into current operations. This will require ongoing training to ensure teachers, school leaders, and MoE officials are able to use and input data effectively into the system. The MoE also needs to ensure stakeholders at all levels have access to dashboards containing the data they need to drive improvements (NCHRD, 2015, p. 106).

Another requirement for successful decentralization, according to SP 2018–2022, is to amend Law No. 3 for the year 1994 in order to provide for the licensing of educational leaders, pave the way for a clear professional career path for leaders, link incentives to performance, and articulate related methods for performance appraisal. By 2022, the SP aspires to have 65% of public school and 30% of private school leaders to be licensed.

Besides a sustainable PD program, SP calls to design a modified version of "Advanced Standards and Competencies" for educational leaders that would form the basis for a proposed school leadership competency exam. Aspirant, recruited and veteran leaders should sit for the school leadership competency exam to be licensed or retained as principals.

The SP identified the following challenges that may mitigate these aspirations: school leaders' resistance to the introduction of the licensing system; weakness of school leadership in many schools; disinterest of many employees to assume general supervisory positions; inactivation of shared leadership; marginalizing the development teams; habits and traditions; nepotism and tribalism which sometimes adversely affect the effectiveness of instructional leadership; disinclination of the local community to participate as they consider education the responsibility of the Government rather than a collective responsibility.

Challenging the Official Narration

It is obvious that the official narration considers the failures of the educational system in Jordan as a function of centralization and the under-qualification of school principals as leaders. The SP 2018–2022 glossed over the real factors that lie behind the centralization of educational management. It shyly touched on some cultural factors such as tribalism, habits, and traditions, as well as some malpractices that are related to them such as favoritism and nepotism; and did not show how far the values related to these factors are nested and interwoven in the local culture nor how to counter them. By the same token, the official documents present a depoliticized and a-theoretical narration.

124 *Aref Al-Attari and Eiman Essa*

We will elaborate on the cultural as well as economic and political factors in the following paragraphs.

Conflicting Values

To implement decentralization and devolve authorities to DoE and schools, the education reform agenda championed "distributed leadership", "school-based management", and similar theories with shared leadership connotations. Therefore, we start with a brief account on the notions that "distributed leadership" (DL) conjures up. DL is the outcome of the interdependent efforts and dynamic interaction of teachers and principals who share leadership responsibilities, and are held accountable for decisions. It suggests that leadership may arise anywhere in the organization and is not confined to formal leaders (Bush, 2013). It requires a democratic environment characterized by open self-expression, exchange of expertise, questioning of assumptions, and validating successful practices (Hashem, 2020; Harris & Spillane, 2008; Starr, 2014). The question is whether or not these notions cohere with the values that are embedded in the culture prevailing at Jordanian schools.

The Jordanian society, even its urbanized segments, is to a great extent, a tribal society. The tribal values, though not necessarily negative, may contradict the core values underlying the distributed leadership. According to Hashem (2018, 2020) the prevailing culture at Jordanian schools endorses the one and only, exemplary leader who is vested with exclusive authority for decision-making. This image mirrors *Shaikh Al Ashairah* (Head of the tribe) who is the father, protector, sage, and problem solver. Hashem (2018) termed this type of leadership as *Shaichoracay*, and in a subsequent article (Hashem, 2020) she termed the leadership style at Jordanian public school as *Al Faza'a*, an Arabic term that signifies the embodiment of solidarity and kinship and concomitates an emotional, explosive, and abrupt response that leads to impulsive short-term action. One negative feature of *al faza'a* is the expectation of support from one's tribe against others irrespective of the appropriateness of actions and whether or not problems are of one's own making. Participant principals in Hashem's study (2020) perceived that tribalism perpetuates dictatorship, dominance, and subordination at the school level; and normalizes nepotistic practices in workplaces. Nepotism is justified as an indication of loyalty to tribe even if it encroaches on the rule of law and the spirit of citizenship.

The contradiction between the values that underlie the tribal culture and the "distributive leadership" lends support to calls for critical examination of reform agendas and the values of the host country before program transference, failing which may lead to superficial changes. That is, educators might appear to have changed their practices to respond to reform programs while their practices still resonate with their entrenched values (Nguyen et al., 2009; Sperandio et al., 2009). Expressed otherwise, any potential tension between a proposed intervention and the prevailing leadership practices should be resolved in advance so that such intervention is not misunderstood or resisted.

Decentralizing the Classroom

Championed during ERfKI, decentralization was accompanied by a strategy to transform education from a teacher-centered to a learner-centered approach that promotes critical thinking, high-order questioning, collaborative learning, attention to the needs of individual student, and problem-solving. However, a content analysis study of primary curriculum (Sabella & Crossouard, 2018) concluded "if Jordan is to fulfill its stated aspirations, a full review of the curriculum is needed to ensure its classification and framing cohere better with a student-centered approach, p. 1". School administrators in particular and many teachers who participated in Hodges' study (2015) expressed concern over the goal of critical thinking stating that such a focus would trigger problems and disruptions, and may even be against the understanding of truth in religion. Studies conducted by Jordanian scholars reported similar findings. Al Karaki and Al-Mahhadin (2019) reported unacceptable levels of critical thinking among *Mu'ata* university students. Moreover, a study conducted by Atroz revealed average levels of awareness of critical thinking skills among school principals in the Governorate of Irbid in Northern Jordan,

On the other hand, critical thinking and learner-centered approach conflict to a great extent with the current examination-focused system which culminates in the "General Secondary School Certification Exam (GSSCE)" that directs schools to teach the exams and promotes rote learning. The GSSCE tests the average students' knowledge rather than their critical thinking. Moreover, it is the sole basis for admission at the universities. Therefore, all stakeholders (school principals, teachers, students, and guardians) are obsessed with students' performance at the GSSCE. In this case, it is almost impossible to teach "for critical thinking" and "to the test", as Kennedy (2005) put it.

Decentralization and Democratization

Decentralization at MoE was adopted as part of a "National Agenda" that included decentralizing political authority by establishing a number of regional assemblies and empowering them with many of the responsibilities enjoyed by the central government on the assumption that "political development should start at the grassroots level then move up to decision making centers, not vice-versa", as King Abdulla 11 put it when he announced the "National Agenda" in 25 January 2005. However, the Agenda did not materialize. In 2015, it was replaced by the "Decentralization Law" whereby many authorities were to be devolved to the governorates. Elections for the governorates' councils were conducted in 2017. It is premature to judge the experience but there are concerns that it would be another futile reform attempt (Jordan Strategies Forum, 2018). The latest in the series of political/administrative reform agendas is "The Plan for Upgrading the Political System" which was prepared by a blue-ribbon Royal Commission in September 2021. Its recommendations were recently passed by the Parliament, but not without much controversy. The standoff between opponents and proponents threatens to deprive it of its real intentions.

The legitimate question then is whether or not governments in Jordan are serious in their efforts towards decentralization and democratization. According to Satloff (2005), the National Agenda 2005 was a means to keep pace with the democratizing trend in the Middle East as evidenced by the first decade of the century which saw the elections in Iraq and the Palestinian territories. Therefore, it could be concluded that the Decentralization Plan in 2015 and the most recent Commission in 2021 to "upgrade the political system" were declared amidst the turbulent events which accompanied the Arab Spring in the second decade. In retrospect, "Back to the parliamentary life" in 1989 came after similar turbulences.

Thus, one assumes the existence of critical problems that impede real democratization. An ex-Interior Minister (Arar, 2020; Habashneh, 2019) attributed the failure to the hyper-bureaucracy that permeates all junctures of the deep state in Jordan. Another ex-Minister described the Decentralization Law as replete with mixed-up, vague, and incomprehensible concepts that lead to nowhere (Rbaihat, 2019). By putting critical lenses, we opine that democratization and decentralization step on some people's toes as both are vested in power, authority, and privileges. To be fair, governments and top bureaucrats are not alone in their worries about decentralization. Many segments of the Jordanian society are also concerned about fully-fledged democracy, as they relate these suggestions to the grand issues of "citizenship", the geography-demography' predicament, the ramifications of the chronic Arab-Israeli conflict, and the migration(s) from neighboring countries that are perceived as potential threats to the delicate demographic formula (Ababsa, 2011).

Although Jordan is a moderate, relatively stable country, governments always set forth limits for participation in the public sphere. Moreover, although governments have to be voted in by the Parliament, they are appointed by and survive at the discretion of the King. Members of the Parliament are not elected on the basis of programs. One result is that the government and Ministers are not held accountable before their constituencies. The current political scene in Jordan is characterized by an absence of real political life, a lack of strong political parties, and distorted representation. Ministers come and go too frequently to be able to effectively implement or monitor reform. The conclusion is that decentralization at MoE requires real democratization of political life so that governments become truly elected and accountable before the people. This is not possible without political will (Hussainy, 2014).

This public space as described above constitutes a fertile environment for nepotism, corruption, and autocracy; family and tribal connections, and tension between citizens for different considerations. This perpetuates the malpractices that the official documents decry.

The question may be: Could decentralization, participation, distributive leadership, community involvement, and all similar approaches with democratic notions work in a context shrouded by such concerns, an inflammatory neighborhood, and a hostile physical environment? Our answer is "yes", stipulated that there is a real political will undergirding it—one that perceives democracy and participation as assets rather than liabilities.

Who Owns the Agenda and Who Runs the Stage?

According to Frey (2010), Jordanian reformers claim ownership of the reform agenda, though it is anchored to a "global" discourse shaped largely by neoliberal orientations. The "JEI" grew out of the Global Education Initiative (GEI) to launch an initiative based on public-private partnership in a selected pilot developing country. Jordan was chosen as the pilot country. In 2003 "Discovery Schools" were established as a laboratory for ideas and programs that could then be rolled out nationally under ERƒKE'.

The huge role of foreign donors, particularly the United States, in initiating and funding ERfKI coincided with the rising anti-American sentiments after the invasion of Iraq in 2003 and the rise of Islamophobia in Western countries. Islamic and nationalistic/socialist critics considered the agenda as one aimed at making the educational system more Western-friendly and amenable to the liquidation of the Palestinian cause. Critics opined that the agenda was a prototype of soft power which was conceptualized as an extension of American public diplomacy (Rugh, 2017).

The agenda ownership issue is evident in research studies and reports on both the JEI and ERfKI. Based on preliminary bibliometric analysis of research and reports on the JEI and ERfKI (not tabled), we found that the studies conducted, commissioned, funded, or led by foreign donors, researchers, and external partners kept pace with the education reform agenda from the conception period till post-delivery. They were mostly multi-authored, funded, data-based, rigorous, and published in the English language. Some of these studies were done in cooperation with the MoE or the NCHRD, but universities in Jordan were totally absent from the scene despite being considered "Expert Houses". We found 28 studies in the Arabic language and nine in English on ERfKI conducted by researchers at Jordanian universities, mostly by postgraduate students. They were questionnaire studies that had been done from a distance and revealed perceptual rather than factual data, with no analysis whatsoever of the official documents or related statistics (see for instance Akour & AlShannak, 2012; Thalgi, 2020). The marginal role of the Jordan universities and academics in articulating or evaluating strategic plans and reform agendas defeats the purpose of building capacity for developing national capabilities and deepens the gap between theory and practice, which is a chronic/acute problem in Arab academia.

The absence or invisible role of Jordanian academics, practitioners, and professionals in the implementation of the agenda creates a sense of alienation and resentment along with unsubstantiated claims. For instance, a Jordanian expert claimed that Developing the Institutional Performance Project within ERfKI was prepared by Jordanian experts with a view to having national leadership cadres, but ultimately was assigned instead to a foreign profit-oriented company that excluded the national experts (Azzam, 2010). Although such claims were denied by the MoE, they lend support to the negative feelings attributed to the perceived lack of ownership of the agenda projects, particularly since the reform agenda itself is based on sharing, partnership, and cooperation.

The educational reform agenda is part of the inter-sectoral "Economic and Social Transformation Plan" of 2003, which is severely criticized by some circles as American-imposed. Critics point to the hundreds of millions of dollars from multi-donors such as USAID, World Bank, and other Western donors. There is a widely spread belief that the grand Transformation Plan was inspired by the neoliberal policies that were adopted by Jordan since the turn of the century and are perceived by many as the culprit for all the malaise that adversely affected the country and the resulting upheaval thereafter.

Economic Theoretical Underpinnings

The educational reform agenda is rooted in economic theoretical underpinnings inspired by the human capital theory, which assumes that education and formal schooling equip graduates with knowledge and skills that enable them to contribute to economic growth, increase individual incomes, and enhance national competitiveness in the global economy. However, critics (Bartlett, 2007) question these theoretical grounds, arguing that formal schooling does not necessarily transform, expand, or improve opportunities for employment; they argue that there are other social and political factors that intervene to structure opportunities and social mobility and in turn, perpetuate and broaden the gaps between different segments of society. Students and teachers in Shirazi's study were deeply skeptical of the promises of education in Jordan", pointing to *wasta* (connections) as more important than educational credentials (Shirazi, 2010).

On the other hand, the declared goal of the education reform agenda is educating graduates for the unpredictable K-based economy. However, Jordan has, for a long time, been a rentier state, depending mainly on the expatriates' remittances besides external grants (Shirazi, 2010). To transfer from a rentier economy to a K-based economy could be a paradigm-shattering development that may shake the social contract. Changing the social contract is a politically overcharged issue that may undermine the cohesion of the society in the absence of a radical change in mindset, general consensus, or visible rewards. Certain categories of Jordanians used to be "state-sponsored" through some forms of Affirmative Action's *Mukrumat* (privileges). However, the neoliberalism-based policies are meant to transform them to "self-supporters", and even consumers. But "the old model of citizen is not fading away, quite the contrary it is still an integral part of the regime's survival, therefore the consequences of the implemented reform have still to be seen (Cantini, 2012 p. 34)".

ELA Scholarship in Jordan

Knowledge production on educational administration in Jordan could be traced to the mid-1960s when the Ministry of Education issued a practitioners' journal entitled "*Rislat al Muaalem* (The Teacher's Mission)". The first refereed cross-disciplinary journal entitled "*Dirasat* (Studies)" was issued by the University of Jordan in the 1970s, the decade that also witnessed the offering of the diploma of education and MA programs at that university. In the 1980s and 1990s, more public and private universities were opened; more journals were issued; and more diploma and MA in educational administration programs were introduced. By the end of the century, the University of Jordan and Yarmouk University were licensed to operate a PhD program in educational administration. In alignment with the global trend, the University of Jordan changed the name of its doctorate program from "Educational Administration" to "educational leadership" (ELA). At the same time, an increasing number of students flocked to other Arab and foreign universities to obtain doctorates in ELA.

The above factors combined to generate a systematic accumulation of knowledge published in journals, proceedings of conferences, books, and other outlets besides non-reported research, such as theses. Bibliometric studies on Arab scholarship in ELA show that Jordanian scholars are among the most active in the Arab World (Akkari & Al-Sahib, 2019; Al Atari and Essa, 2021; Mood, 2019). However, Arab scholarship in general is small compared to international scholarship (Atari & Outum, 2019); including scholarship in some non-Western countries such as Hong Kong, Israel, and Turkey which are the most productive outside the Western, particularly Anglophone, countries (Hallinger & Chen, 2015).

Scholarship on ELA in Jordan was subject to evaluation. Ababneh (2018) conducted a basic bibliometric study on the theses in educational administration that were approved in the UoJ during the period from 2007–2016. The study generated data from quantitative indicators such as the authors' gender, research methodology, statistical treatment, and the like. Other authors (Awwad, 2013; Amr, 2015; Hiasat, 2008) used the survey method. They came up with a list of standards that are expected to be applied in thesis writing and judged (or asked academics to judge) to what extent those standards were applied in theses that were approved in their universities. These surveys generated perceptual rather than factual data. There was a general agreement among the reviewers that the theses in educational administration in Jordanian universities did not live up to expectations.

In the same way, we conducted a bibliometric study on the theses approved at Yarmouk University for the five-year period between 2017 and 2021. This is part of a project that aims to conduct a systematic review on knowledge production in ELA in Jordan that includes articles, books, and other outlets. We chose YU because, as insiders, we have first-hand information. Theses approved by Jordanian universities in the chosen five-year period are supposed to be done with more rigor as students are required to publish an extract in a refereed journal prior to their defense.

At this point, we do not aim to give thick descriptions but instead to present key features of the scholarship under review. The extracted data are displayed in Table 7.2.

The figures in Table 7.2 show that YU approved 149 theses, mostly doctorate ones (73.83%). There was a steady increase in the number of theses (from 22 in 2017 to 44 in 2020). By comparison, this number is almost double the number of theses that were annually approved at the UoJ during the period between 2006 and 2017 as reported by Ababneh (2018). The likelihood is high that the plethora of MA programs at both public and private universities, the aspiration for an academic job at universities or desire to improve one's position as a practitioner, and the influx of students from neighboring Arab countries, factored in this increase.

It is very intriguing that the theses written by females exceeded those written by males. To some extent, this finding concurs with Ababneh (2018) who reported that females outnumbered males as theses authors (56% to 44%, respectively). This finding is in sharp contrast with the findings revealed by reviews of Arab scholarship published in journals which point to a gap in favor of male authors (Atari & Outum, 2019; Atari & Essa, 2021; Hammad et al., 2020). It could be that males continue to publish in journals after obtaining their doctorates more than females do; or that females join local universities more than males who prefer to sojourn at foreign universities. This could be a function of culture that discourages females from studying abroad.

A sizeable percentage of theses (78.52%) were supervised by a single supervisor rather than by a panel. In a sense, this indicates the lack of teamwork spirit among Arab scholars. Bibliometric studies that were done on Arab scholarship in journals showed that single authorship is the norm rather than co-authorship (Atari & Essa, 2021).

The findings reveal that the majority of the theses are done on public education institutions, directorates of education, and the Ministry of Education. The private sector is given negligible attention despite its rapid burgeoning. This finding could be attributed to the fact that the vast majority of PhD students in the educational administration specialty are practitioners from the public education sector. However, a noticeable percentage of theses (33.55%) address administration in higher education institutions. It is highly probable that an increasing number of scholars find it easier to gather empirical data from university students and staff than from schools where special conditions apply.

The overwhelming majority of the theses (97.32%) are quantitative. Interviews were mostly used to provide supplementary data in a few mixed methods studies (2.01%). All reviews of journal articles on ELA revealed that the quantitative approach is the prevailing one in Arab scholarship. The underutilization of qualitative and mixed methods is worrying as it leaves much to be unearthed and hinders true triangulation, benchmarking, and approximation of reality. This means training and encouragement are needed to increase the use of qualitative methodologies. We agree with Atari and Outum (2019) that it is the duty of those in charge of postgraduate programs, teachers of methodology, supervisors, the gatekeepers (editors and reviewers of research) and the researchers themselves to promote qualitative and mixed methods. As Oplatka and Arar (2017) put it, "Listening to the authentic voices of Arab principals, teachers and other educationalists is necessary to grasp a holistic view of EDLM and the social mosaic around it. It will also allow research to trace similarities and distinctions between forms of EDLM within the Arab world" (p. 36).

Thematic analysis reveals that the vast majority of the theses are loading the themes that could be included under the rubric leadership styles, theories, roles, processes, skills, excellence, job satisfaction, loyalty, and social responsibility. A further scrutiny reveals that the prevailing trend among authors is to investigate the extent to which patterns of leadership styles and theories that originated in the West had been applied to educational settings in Jordan, the barriers faced by educational leaders in applying them and the recommendations to apply them. Other studies explored perceptions, attitudes, and practices at educational institutions. Rarely authors exceed that to establish a critique to those theories or to interrogate the applicability of them in the local cultural context.

Certain theories were very popular such as transformational leadership, ethical leadership, distributed management, and servant leadership. Almost absent are novel theories such as "Responsible Leadership" or "Sustainable leadership". It seems that authors were selective in terms of researched theories. By the same token, considerable attention was given to topics that became popular such as empowerment, organizational citizenship, and social responsibility, while many others such as refugees-related issues, cultural diversity, demographic changes, and social justice that have ramifications for educational administration were shyly addressed. A worrying trend is the reticence to undertake educational policies as a research topic. This could be attributed to the general trend of dissociation between the political and the educational, which is a disturbing phenomenon (Atari & Outum, 2019).

The Arab-Islamic legacy on administration and leadership had been totally neglected in the theses under scrutiny. This was far from congruence with the calls to explore "indigenous perspectives" to EA (Bajunid, 1996), invoke the contribution that Non-Western cultures could bring to scholarship on educational administration and create a cross-culturally valid knowledge base with global relevance (Walker & Dimmock, 2000; Dimmock, 2019).

Although beyond the scope of this chapter, it is legitimate to ask to what extent does ELA scholarship in Jordan inform practice, or shape educational policy? This is a frequently asked question in Arab academia where a gap is recognized between theory and practice; and solutions are given to bridge that gap (Atari & Awwad, 2015; Almansour, 2016). According to Arar (2021), there is "an evident gap between EA theory and research and the performance of school principals" in the Middle East countries. Pending an empirical investigation, it could be that practitioners in the educational institutions in Jordan identify their roles not in terms of research findings, but in terms of their employer(s)' expectations (mainly the Ministry of Education and Higher Education), which also oversee the operation of the private sector. Another main reason could be that the reform agendas are authored by international donors who explicitly or implicitly run the stage, as we referred to earlier. Practitioners who graduate from universities have to adapt to the reality in their institutions. But this does not preclude a "trickle-down" effect.

Will the Paradoxes Ever Meet

We presented in the above sections the development of educational policies, educational leadership, and ELA scholarship in Jordan. It is observed that reform-failure discourses are ever-present. This type of discourse is found in other studies that discuss the education reform plans in Arab countries (Akkary, 2014) and identify similar factors. Under the influence of the failure discourse, we were at first allured by the "treadmill" metaphor, but then inspired by positive psychology (Seligman et al., 2009), paradox theory, and ambidexterity scholarship. Therefore, we prefer to describe the reform efforts in Jordan as "partial success partial failure" that opens up new channels for further reforms. This is the intelligent failure referred to by Su-Keene and Bogotch (2021). Jordan unlike many surrounding countries maintained political stability; which enabled the educational system to accumulate achievements in terms of quantity, embedding gender awareness culture and reducing gender disparity; elevating literacy levels; computerization; teaching foreign languages; provision of accessible and available public education and expansion in higher education. The country is known as an early adopter of novel ideas and practices without discarding its Arab Islamic identity. However, there is much left to be accomplished in terms of quality, equity, and employability of graduates. It can build on those achievements and chart out plans to make up for shortcomings.

Following this tradition, we disagree with the positions that are based on the "either-or" approach, which generates polarized notions. For instance, Hashem (2020) associated *"al Faza"* tribal style that allegedly exists in Jordanian public schools with many negative adjectives that make it an "implicit barrier" that should be continuously disrupted pre and during the implementation of reform projects. This perspective presents the mainstream theories (i.e., distributive leadership) as the baseline models without subjecting them to criticism or examining their applicability to the Arab context.

We submit that both the mainstream theories and Arab cultural values should be critically analyzed with a view to complementarity. The mainstream theories, particularly the transformational, distributive, and teacher leadership ones, despite their "evangelical flavor", have never been perceived in the West where they originated, as normative imperatives, nor has their effectiveness been taken for granted. For instance, Slowley (2021) refers to some of the concerns that distributed leadership lacks sufficient robust evidential base, while Lumby (2013) described distributed leadership literature as littered with contradictions. By the same token, Fitzgerald and Gunter (2008) raise concerns that the term "teacher leadership" has crept into educational vocabulary without enough sophisticated debate.

Proceeding from this thesis, we treat both the Arab culture and mainstream scholarship as equally valued and engage them in deliberative learning processes. Our "both/and" approach that is promoted by the paradox theory may inform the mainstream scholarship and enable organizational ambidexterity. Rigorous investigation may reveal for instance that Islam, which is a main component of Arab culture, could be drawn upon to disrupt *al Fazaa*, and by extension fight nepotism and favoritism. That is because Islam is, by its very nature, a supra-national, non-tribal religion. For instance, verse no. 13 of *Sura* (Chapter) 49 of the Holy Quran addresses mankind irrespective of their tribes or countries "O, people! We created you from a male and a female, and We made you races and tribes, so that you may come to know one another. The best among you before Allah is the most righteous. Allah is Knowing and Aware". Therefore, we hold that transformation "from within" helps practitioners negotiate between the cultural systems and practical schemas on a daily basis. As Bajunid (1996) puts it "When new ideas are introduced which are consistent with people's a priori understandings, such ideas are acquired quickly without unnecessary cognitive dissonance ... and the trauma of 'word deep' translations, p. 4".

Such ambidextrous approaches need training. However, our investigation (Atari and Essa, 2021) found that the workshops that are offered to school principals in Jordan, particularly to the newly appointed, focus only on technical matters rather than on the cultural values that underlie new concepts and those that inform prevailing practices in schools. We also found that the content of the "advanced educational leadership diploma" which has been conducted by the University of Jordan in cooperation with the MoE and the University of Connecticut in the United States, is reticent on school-based management, distributive, transformative, and teacher leadership matters. Moreover, the content of the related training sessions is based on a translated book that is adopted in a Boston educational area filled with examples and cases pertaining to that area. This brings the issue of the "ownership" of the reform agenda to the fore, and lends support to the criticism that the reform agenda is addressing an external audience. As people at the grass-root level (i.e., practitioners) do not feel that they own the reform agenda or at the very least do not see themselves as an essential part of it, it is not surprising that they respond with indifference, resentment, or presumable resistance. Shirazi (2010) reported that teachers in his sample responded to the agenda with "performative coping strategies" such as registering for training (but not attending), paying lip service, or showing some commitment without advancing reform goals. The conclusion is that for an initiative to become a success story, it should not be perceived as imposed but rather emanate from within.

Our presentation showed that decentralization whether on the macro or micro level, is a politicized issue. In reality, educational systems exist on almost all points of the continuum that extends between two extremes. Therefore, the question is not whether to centralize or decentralize, but rather to which degree and in which domains? On the other hand, practitioners should be informed of the authorities that are vested in them and those that fall under the purview of the MoE. They should be trained to know how to practice authority and share responsibility in an ageists top-down culture. Decentralization and the sharing of both authorities and responsibilities need an "Ideal Speech Situation" as suggested by Habermas (1984), where all voices are heard and valued without fear or favor. In other words, it is not a technical issue, but rather a psychological and cultural preparedness. Decentralization depends on the examination of the practitioners' zone of interest, their self-efficacy beliefs, locus of control, and sense of empowerment. Decentralization does not work in an insecure, parochial, or patriarchal environment.

As insiders, we feel that the governments in Jordan sometimes send contradictory messages that cast doubts on their intentions towards the reform agenda including devolution of authorities. For instance, the way the government handled the standoff with the Teachers' Association in 2018–2019 which ended with delegitimizing (dare say demonizing) the Association is not conducive to teacher leadership, decentralization, and democratization. The Government was not negotiating or accommodating teachers but rather intimidating them and drawing red lines that extended beyond its permissible reach. This begs the following question: How can a shared reform agenda be implemented when teachers are forced to identify their role only within the state-sanctioned "distribution of sentiments and desires" as Hodges (2015) put it?

However, we believe that much as governments may shape education, the latter can reciprocate by augmentation of capacities, offering new insights and opening new avenues that merit exploration and in turn produce change. Expressed otherwise, power shapes and is reshaped by education, and the opposite is true.

The other side of politicizing the reform agenda is the claim of the Islamists and leftists that the education reform agenda is externally imposed by foreign powers, the United States in particular. Many scholars argue that policies imported from the dominating West are new forms of colonialism (say neo-liberalism) (Nguyen et al., 2009; Sperandio et al., 2009). It is true that many countries of the world design their educational systems in terms of the Western templates of education systems, and that this generates a sense of vulnerability among members of the subaltern (e.g., Southern) cultures. However, we believe in complementarity rather than in antagonism. We do not subscribe to either ultra-universalism or parochialism as both are equally problematic and exclude the other and the possibility of discovering alternatives. We prefer to recognize the other; unmask differences and interpret them in the context of a wider set of variations, recognizing that there are commonalities structured by the relations between "others" and between other and self (Marginson & Mollis, 2001).

Conclusions

We believe that reform is a nonlinear path that is replete with breakthroughs and breakdowns, negative and positive consequences, and partial success and partial failure. Therefore, the question is how do we deal with failure? And are we able to learn from failure? We agree with Su-Keene and Bogotch (2021) that we can learn from failure if stakeholders particularly policymakers, researchers, and school leaders work together. Passing the buck to teachers and principals, imposing technical solutions (such as the controversial licensing system of school leaders) without enlightening teachers and leaders about its benefits, introducing reform agendas that are perceived as politically dictated, and all procedures that put practitioners at a disadvantage would defeat the purpose, particularly if those measures were perceived as threatening. In other words, practitioners should feel like they are not only participants in the agenda but as productive trailblazers and owners of it. By extension, Jordanian academics should be involved in authoring, implementing, and assessing the reform agendas. This may help enhance the research-building capacities, inform practice, and bridge the "theory-practice" gap.

Moreover, there is a difference between school reformers, experts, and policymakers on the one hand and practitioners on the other regarding the way each group perceives reform. Practitioners may not have the entire school system in mind but may focus instead on their own professional scope. It is from this background that they can evaluate the value, usefulness, and scope of reform (Terhart, 2013).

References

Ababneh, S. (2018). Content analysis of academic thesis in educational administration at the University of Jordan (2007–2016). *Dirasat-Educational Studies*, 45(3), 1–13. (In Arabic).

Ababsa, M. (2011). Citizenship and urban issues in Jordan. In M. Ababsa & R. Daher (Eds.), *Cities, urban practices and nation building in Jordan* (pp. 39–64). l'Institut français du Proche-Orient.

Abu Al-Sha'ar, H. (2010). *History of trans-Jordan during the Ottoman rule*. Ministry of Culture, Amman. (In Arabic).

Akkary, R. (2014). Facing the challenges of educational reform in the Arab world. *Journal of Educational Change, 15*(2), 179–202.

Akkari, R., & Al-Sahib, N. (2019). Analytical study of *Shamaa*-documented studies on educational administration in Arab countries between 2007–2016. *Idafat, 45*, 67–91. (In Arabic)

Akour, M., & Shannak, R. (2012). Jordan education reform for the knowledge economy support project – A case study, *Journal of Management Research, 4*(4), 116–131.

Al habashneh, S. (2019). Decentralization: An overview. *Al Ra'ay Daily*, 12-12-2019. (In Arabic).

Al Karaki, W., & Al-Mahhadin, S. (2019). Critical thinking of students at Mu'ata University and its relationship to cognitive motivation. *Dirasat: Educational Studies, 64*(1), 321–343. (In Arabic).

Almansour, S. (2016). The crises of research and global recognition in Arab universities. *Near and Middle Eastern Journal of Research in Education, 7*, 11–23. 10.5339/nmerjre.2016.1

Amr, E. (2015). *Observing standards that should be applied in post graduate theses in Jordanian universities* [MA Thesis, Middle East University, Jordan]. (In Arabic).

Arar, K. (2020). Educational Administration in the Middle-East. In R. Papa (Eds.), *Oxford research encyclopedia*, Oxford Encyclopedia of Education, Oxford University Press (pp. 1–26). 10.1093/acrefore/9780190264093.013.672

Arar, K. (2021). Educational Administration in the Middle East, *Oxford research encyclopedias, education*. 23 pages. 10.1093/acrefore/9780190264093.013.672.

Atari, A., & Awwad, H. (2015). A proposed model to bridge the 'theory-practice' gap in Arab scholarship on educational administration in Arab countries. *The Educational Journal, 117*(30), 197–210 (In Arabic).

Atari, A. (2015). Privatization of higher education with special reference to Jordan. In R. Hashim, & M. Hattouri (Eds.), *Critical issues and reform in Muslim higher education*. Chapter 1. (pp. 1–19). Kuala Lumpur: IIUM Press.

Atari, A. (2020). Higher education in Jordan: At the confluence of internationalization and nationalization. In J. Thondhlana, E. Garwe, H. de Wit, J. Gacel-Avila, F. Huang, & W. Tamrat (Eds.), *The Bloomsbury handbook on internationalization of higher education in the globalized South*. Chapter 21: (pp. 325–343). USA: Bloomsbury.

Atari, A., & Essa, E. (2021). Arab scholarship in educational administration, management and leadership: An overview. *Educational Management. Administration, and Leadership*, 1–19. OnlineFirst. DOI: 17411432211012011.

Atari, A., & Outum, N. (2019). Research on educational administration published in Arabic language educational journals: A systematic review and analysis. *International Studies in Educational Administration (Commonwealth Council for Educational Administration & Management (CCEAM)), 47*(1), 61–74.

Azzam, A. (2010). ERfKI: Foreign management for a Jordanian concept, *Amon e-site*, 24-4-2010 (In Arabic).

Awwad, H. (2013). *Research behavior in generating and acquiring knowledge as perceived by professors and postgraduate students of educational administration in Jordanian universities* [Doctoral Thesis, Yarmouk University, Jordan]. (In Arabic).

Bajunid, I. A. (1996). Preliminary explorations of indigenous perspectives of educational management: The evolving Malaysian experience. *Journal of Educational Administration*, 34(5), 50–73.

Bannayan, H., Guaqueta, J., Obeidat, O., Patrinos, H. A., & Porta, E. E. (2012). *The Jordan education initiative: A multi-stakeholder partnership model to support education reform*. World Bank Policy Research Working Paper (6079). World Bank.

Bartlett, L. (2007). Human capital or human connections? The cultural meanings of education in Brazil. *Teachers College Record*, 109(7), 1613–1636.

Bush, T. (2013). Distributed leadership: The model of choice in the 21st century, *EMAL*, 41(5), 543–544.

Cantini, D. (2012). Discourses of reforms and questions of citizenship: The university in Jordan. *Revue des mondes musulmans et de la Méditerranée*, 3 (131), 147–162.

Cunha, M. P. E., & Putnam, L. L. (2019). Paradox theory and the paradox of success. *Strategic Organization*, 17(1), 95–106.

Dimmock, C. (2019). Connecting research and knowledge on educational leadership in the West and Asia: Adopting a cross-cultural comparative perspective, *Comparative Education*, 7, 5–11. DOI: 10.1080/03050068.2019.1703393

Emine, E. (2005). *The politics of late Ottoman education: Accommodating ethno-religious pluralism amid imperial disintegration* [Doctoral Thesis, The University of Arizona].

Fitzgerald, T., & Gunter, H. (2008). Contesting the orthodoxy of teacher leadership. *International Journal of Leadership in Education*, 11(4), 331–340.

Frey, C. J. (2010). The politics of education policy borrowing and lending: A study of the 'Jordan Model' of knowledge economy reforms. *World Studies in Education*, 11(1), 37–54. DOI: 10.7459/wse/11.1.05

Government of Jordan (2015). Jordan vision 2025: A national vision and strategy. Government of Jordan, Amman, Jordan.

Habermas, J. (1984). (translated by T. McCarthy). *Communication and the evolution of society*. Boston: Beacon Press.

Hallinger, P., & Chen, J. (2015). Review of research on educational leadership and management in Asia: A comparative analysis of research topics and methods, 1995–2012. *Educational Management Administration & Leadership*, 43(1), 5–27.

Hammad, W., Samier, E. A., & Mohammed, A. (2020). Mapping the field of educational leadership and management in the Arabian Gulf region: A systematic review of Arabic research literature. *Educational Management Administration and Leadership*. 1–20.

Harris, A., & Spillane, J. (2008). Distributed leadership through the looking glass. *Management in Education*, 22(1), 31–34.

Hashem, R. (2018). *Interrogating the paradox: distributed leadership and 'Sheikhocracy' in Jordanian schools' leadership*. [Doctoral dissertation, Deakin University, Australia].

Hashem, R. (2020). 'Al Faza'a' leadership: An implicit cultural barrier to distributed leadership in Jordanian public schools. *Educational Management Administration & Leadership*, 3, 1–17. 1741143220932580.

Hiasat, W. (2008). *Analysis of doctoral theses in educational administration at Jordanian universities*. [Doctoral dissertation, Yarmouk University, Jordan]. (In Arabic).

Hodges, R. M. (2015). *Transformation of sympathies: Gendered mediation of Jordanian education reform for a knowledge economy*. [Doctoral Dissertation, Washington University].
Hussainy, M. (2014). *The social impact of Jordan's electoral system*, Policy paper. Jordan: Friedrich Ebert Stiftung office in Amman.
Jordan Strategies Forum (2018). *Decentralization in its first year*, Amman: JSF. (In Arabic).
Kennedy, M. (2005). *Inside teaching: How classroom life undermines reform*. Harvard University Press.
Lumby, J. (2013). Distributed leadership: The uses and abuses of power. *Educational Management Administration & Leadership, 41*(5), 581–597.
Marginson, S., & Mollis, M. (2001). "The door opens and the tiger leaps": theories and reflexivities of comparative education for a global millennium. *Comparative Education Review, 45*(4), 581–615.
Mood, E. (2019). Knowledge sources for Arabic educational administration articles. *Idhafat, 45*, 146–173. (In Arabic).
National Policies Team (2010). *Framework for educational policies*, Amman: The Moe.
Nguyen, P. M., Elliott, J. G., Terlouw, C., & Pilot, A. (2009). Neocolonialism in education: Cooperative learning in an Asian context. *Comparative Education, 45*(1), 109–130.
Oplatka, E., & Arar, K. (2017). The research on educational leadership and management in the Arab world since the 1990s: A systematic review. *BERA Review of Education 5*(3), 267–307.
Rbaihat, S. (2019). Decentralization in Jordan. *Al Ghad Daily*. (In Arabic).
Rugh, W. (2017). American soft power and public diplomacy in the Arab world. *Palgrave Communications, 3*(1), 1–7.
Sabella, T., & Crossouard, B. (2018). Jordan's primary curriculum and its propensity for student-centred teaching and learning. *Compare: A Journal of Comparative and International Education, 48*(5), 717–732.
Satloff, R. (2005). A reform initiative in Jordan: Trying to keep pace with Iraqi and Palestinian elections. *Washington Institute for Near East Policy*.
Seligman, M. E., Ernst, R. M., Gillham, J., Reivich, K., & Linkins, M. (2009). Positive education: Positive psychology and classroom interventions. *Oxford Review of Education, 35*(3), 293–311.
Shirazi, R. (2010). Building a knowledge economy: The case of Jordan. *World Studies in Education, 11*(1), 55–70.
Slowley, D. (2021). Distributed leadership as a solution for New Zealand's education concerns. *Academia Letters, Article 1356*. 10.20935/AL1356.
Sperandio, J., Hobson, D., Douglas, R., & Pruitt, R. (2009). Does context matter? Importing US educational programs to schools overseas. *Compare: A Journal of Comparative and International Education, 39*(6), 707–721.
Starr, K. E. (2014). Interrogating conceptions of leadership: School principals, policy and paradox. *School Leadership & Management, 34*(3), 224–236.
Su-Keene, E. J., & Bogotch, I. (2021). Commentary: Can educational leadership researchers and school leaders both learn from failure? Yes, we can if together! *Journal of Educational Administration*.
Terhart, E. (2013). Teacher resistance against school reform: Reflecting an inconvenient truth. *School Leadership & Management, 33*(5), 486–500.

Thalgi, M. J. (2020). The university's role in developing the skills of the knowledge economy from the perspective of students of Yarmouk University's Faculty of Shari'a and Islamic Studies. *Journal of the Knowledge Economy, 11*(4), 1529–1537.

The Hashemite Kingdom of Jordan (2017). *Jordan's way to sustainable development, First national voluntary review on the implementation of the 2030 agenda.* The Government of the Hashemite Kingdome of Jordan https://sustainabledevelopment.un.org/content/documents/16289Jordan.pd

The Ministry of Education (2006). *Strategic plan 2006.* Amman, Jordan: The Ministry of Education (In Arabic).

The Ministry of Education (2016). *School as the primary unit for development.* Amman, Jordan: The Ministry of Education (In Arabic).

The Ministry of Education (2018). *Strategic plan 2018–2022.* Amman, Jordan: The Ministry of Education (In Arabic).

The National Center for Human Resources (2015). *Education and prosperity.* Amman, Jordan: The National Center for Human Resources.

Turner, N., Swart, J., & Maylor, H. (2013). Mechanisms for managing ambidexterity: A review and research agenda. *International Journal of Management Reviews, 15*(3), 317–332.

Walker, A., & Dimmock, C. (2000). Insights into educational administration: The need for a cross-cultural comparative perspective. *Asia Pacific Journal of Education, 20*(2), 11–22.

Zhang, Y., & Han, Y. L. (2019). Paradoxical leader behavior in long-term corporate development: Antecedents and consequences. *Organizational Behavior and Human Decision Processes, 155,* 42–54.

8 Principalship in Lebanon
The Unsung Heroes

Julia Mahfouz and Rima Karami

The Importance of Strong Educational Leaders for School Success

Decades of research on school leadership have shown how school principals in different contexts and countries have substantially impacted many aspects of education, including student performance, teacher retention, school climate and culture, and school improvement, among others (e.g., Boyd et al., 2011; Cansoy, 2019; Gómez-Leal, et al., 2022; Hallinger & Heck, 2011; Hallinger & Hammad, 2019; Huber & Muijs, 2010; Mancuso et al., 2010). Principals play a key role and have a direct impact on the effectiveness of school reforms and school improvement in general (Leithwood et al., 2020; McConnell, 2020; Oplatka & Arar, 2017). In that sense, there is wide agreement that school success, particularly in terms of teaching and learning outcomes, depends on the competencies and skills of school leaders (Arar et al., 2017; Eacott, 2019; Leithwood, et al. 2020; Leithwood and Seashore-Louis, 2011; Louis, 2022; Mahfouz et al., 2019; Robinson & Gray, 2019).

In response, the centrality of the school leadership role is mirrored by extensive institutionalization around the world of the support needed to perform the role effectively; namely in the form of nationally adopted quality standards, elaborate selection procedures, design and guidelines for pre-service training and certification, induction program, in-service training, and continuous developmental supervision, in addition to principal professional associations, and other support governmental and professional network. While the role of the school principal has gained more centrality on the international front, *there is little evidence that the role of the principal in the Lebanese educational context has undergone a similar evolution, especially in terms of the institutional support or policy adopted to train principals and frame their job expectations.* This is, unfortunately, also prevalent in other Middle Eastern countries that have witnessed constant instability, faced with a state of emergency, and/or had to deal with enduring dilemmas such as economic crises (Arar et al., 2019; Arar, 2020).

DOI: 10.4324/9781003334835-8

Shift in the School Principal Role

On the international front, especially in Western countries, the role of the school principal has shifted over time, with variances across countries and contexts (Hallinger & Heck, 1996; Kafka, 2009; Kowalski & Brunner, 2011). In the mid-20th century, school principals were primarily teachers who were assigned additional administrative work. Their formal role became increasingly shaped by a conception pushing for organizing *schools as bureaucratic organizations* capable of achieving *effectiveness and efficiency*. By the 1990s, principals functioned more as managers who focused on efficiency and on measurable school outcomes, working in isolation from each other and the teachers they managed. Later, as accountability increased and expanded beyond academic achievement, views of school principals' role included broadening the scope of their responsibility to include developing change initiatives focused on leading schools for success. The focus became on cultivating transformational leadership. At the system level, there was a shift toward decentralization and autonomy where school administrators were expected to show evidence of school improvement and were held accountable for school performance (Fullan, 2009; Hattie et al., 2015; Sahlberg, 2011). This role has been shifting further to incorporate collaborative leadership, especially with the introduction of additional national and international assessments.

While the timing of these shifts has varied across different contexts and countries, the general trend reflects a shift from bureaucratic management to more *democratic collaborative leadership* (Adams & Gaetane, 2011; Glatter, 2014; Pont et al., 2008; Roach et al., 2011; Spillane & Kenney, 2012) to *transformational leadership* (Leithwood & Jantzi, 2005). Over time, *effective schools* have been conceived as learning organizations (Fullan, 2016; Hargreaves & Connor, 2018; Harris & Jones, 2018) with broad-based leadership capacity that cultivate collaborative cultures in an attempt to build capacity for school improvement. Thus, leadership within this new organizational context has become more distributed among all stakeholders, and the term "school leadership" has transcended formal role to define the professional practice of those who lead in schools, whether it be principals, school administrators, headmasters, head teachers, or teachers.

The Systemic Role Context of the School Administrator in Lebanon—The Unsung Hero

Unlike in other contexts, the shift to more centrality and a broader scope of the principal's responsibilities that encompass leadership has been slower if at all existent in the context of the Lebanese educational system. According to the statistical report from the Center of Educational Development and Research (CRDP, 2021), there are 2796 schools that principals serve constituting 44.21% public schools, 11.84% non-profit private schools, 41.63% for-profit private schools, and 2.32% UNERWA schools. Unfortunately, additional statistical information on principals in Lebanon is very limited as the Ministry of Education does not keep track of all information in a sustainable consistent manner.

Several critical aspects of the context under which school principals work need to be highlighted and addressed in Lebanon if we are to ensure principals are adequately prepared supported and acknowledged for all the work that they do. These issues can be divided into three categories: (1) administrative processes regarding principal selection, preparation, induction, supervision, and evaluation; (2) clarification of the principal's tasks and responsibilities to teachers, students, parents, and administrators and aligning them with conception found to be effective; and (3) recognition of the contextual factors shaping the demands of the principal role while setting policies that allow for decision-making power at the school level so that they can be responsive to the demands of their particular context and teachers.

Administrative Processes Regarding Principal Selection, Preparation, Induction, Supervision, and Evaluation

In Lebanon, public school principals have prior teaching experience and many continue to teach after becoming principals. Once appointed to their positions, principals rarely change schools. Most principals work in the same school until retirement. The Lebanese government provides few guidelines and limited criteria for selecting public and private school principals to establish a pool of qualified candidates for the position. The formal selection criteria require a public school principal to be a tenured school teacher for a minimum of five years (Decree No. 1436; Decree No. 44, 1964; Decree No. 590, 1974). In private schools, principals are required to have (1) a university degree in education or educational administration, or (2) a university degree in a field other than education and at least three years of teaching experience (Decree No. 2896, 1992). In 2009, a new decree (Decree No. 73, 2009) was issued requiring principalship training as a criterion for selecting principals. However, this decree remains poorly detailed and loosely enforced and almost never applied in private schools.

The Selection Process

The formal selection process for a public school principal usually starts with a recommendation from the school's Directorate of Education and is finalized, upon approval of the recommendation by a decree from the Minister of Education (Decree No. 590, 1974). In private secondary schools, owners/operators determine the selection process, but candidates are expected to meet the government's established criteria. Private schools select principals mostly but not exclusively from their ranks of experienced teachers. It is not highly unusual to find school owners with business backgrounds assuming this role in individually owned private schools. The private school selection process for external candidates typically involves interviewing candidates and checking references; teachers and parents are rarely consulted in the process.

Except for the government's formal qualification guidelines and criteria, the selection process in both private and public schools is mostly informal and often determined by religious compatibility between the school and the principal, support from local political leaders, and personal connections. In addition, local political leaders have considerable influence on principal appointments in both public and private schools in their political districts. Sometimes, the selection process begins with a visit to a political leader in the area where the school is located. In other situations, political leaders notify chosen candidates of their endorsement, requesting them to apply for vacant positions. This alone may be sufficient to receive the appointment. Likewise, in private schools, personal connections, which often are mediated by community religious and political leaders, are key to receiving appointments. There are no term limits for principals in Lebanon; principals typically stay in their positions until retirement, with a few exceptions in private schools.

Preparation and Induction

Principals in both public and private schools usually are expected to learn their responsibilities and formulate their own conceptions about the job after assuming their role and without any formal training. Official school policies provide minimal guidance about the principal's responsibilities. While public schools have poorly elaborated policies pertaining to the principal role, private schools' policies when existent are idiosyncratic and are not monitored by the government. Primary learning about the role of the principal and associated expectations occurs "on-the-job". New principals do not receive any prior training; they must rely on their previous observations of principals when they were teachers and either emulate the same leadership skills or diverge from them. Higher education through various universities (e.g., American University of Beirut) offer principal preparation programs through leadership certificates. Since pre-training or in-service is not required by the government to assume a principal position, principal candidates do not see any added value in pursuing such degrees or certifications in school administration or participating in professional development to improve their skills and learn the profession.

Supervision and Evaluation

Moreover, principals are rarely subjected to regular formal evaluation. In public schools, evaluation processes are vague, nonexistent, or limited to inspection for attendance, abiding by decrees from the Ministry, and proper management of the school budget. Sanctions are limited to major offenses such as bribery or stealing. In private schools, principals are subject to higher accountability and tougher scrutiny mostly from demanding, tuition-paying parents. However, very few schools undergo have clearly set criteria and a formal process to evaluate their principals. In the case of schools owned by institutions or individuals other than the school principal, principals are often subjected to periodic evaluations by board members and school owners. However, in the majority of cases, the process is informal and not governed by clear standard-based criteria.

Clarification of the Principal's Tasks and Responsibilities

While administrative policies depicting this role remain very outdated, the growing global demands on schools have trickled down to the school level, pushing some principals to assume new roles and responsibilities in an attempt to respond to these demands and seek success for their schools. Unfortunately, the formal role expectations of principals in Lebanon are vague and unclear. Many aspects of a principal's responsibilities are not explicitly stated in the form of policies whether at the ministry or school level, and when they are stated, they tend to lack specificity and details. These policies can at times be restrictive that the principals navigate creative ways to go around them without actually violating them.

The stated responsibilities of principals in the private and public sectors are as follows:

1 Principals supervise all aspects of their schools' functions.
2 Principals are responsible for schedule planning and implementation.
3 Principals are the decision-makers in setting schools' tests and examinations.
4 Principals are responsible for selecting textbooks.
5 Principals are responsible for assessing school staffing and educational supply needs.
6 Principals are expected to regularly report to supervisors about their schools' finances, academic standing, and equipment and maintenance needs.

However, we know from research, interviews, and practical evidence based on the authors' experience, research studies, and observations that principals do much more than that (e.g., Arar et al., 2022; Berjaoui & Karami-Akkary, 2020; Greenfield & Akkary, 1998; Harb & Karami-Akkary, 2019; Karami-Akkary et al., 2019; Karami-Akkary & Hammad, 2019; Mahfouz et al., 2019; Mahfouz, 2021). Lebanese principals are the unsung heroes who are trying to do it all without any acknowledgment from the government of their critical role in facilitating daily operations and ensuring school success. With the absence in support the growing demands of their role can even be considered unrealistic.

As many of them answer when asked to describe the scope of their role responsibilities they indeed "do everything" around their schools. They manage budgets, play a major role in setting internal policies, make day-to-day decisions especially related to student discipline and academic problems, engage with families in endless problem-solving, and build relationships with their communities as sources of funding and support. Yet, they are not actively involved in recruiting, appointing, and evaluating teachers. All they can do is just request what they need or send recommendations that may or may not be fulfilled. All these tasks are performed in a context where there is a family-like culture making informal communication the norm. Rather than rely on well bounded formal channels of communication, the principal is expected to be ever present for all especially for parents and the community members engaged with supporting the school. As a result, formal Lebanese principals have complex, time-consuming, demanding, and evolving roles that cannot be strictly predetermined by policies but are shaped in response to emerging demands and evolving conditions. To be viewed as effective they must enact their role in a manner as role models, parent figures, and the main individuals responsible for their schools' daily functioning.

Lebanese principals develop, advocate, and enact the shared vision and core values of high-quality education at their schools to ensure positive student outcomes. They develop, support, and implement systems of curriculum, instruction, and assessment. They overview the academic and social supports, services, extracurricular activities, and accommodations to meet the different instructional needs of students.

The principal also serves as the primary link between the school and the governance body in charge of setting school policy: the central office in the case of public schools, and the school owner(s) in the case of private schools. With varying degrees of autonomy and participation, policy implementation is a major part of the principal's responsibilities in both public and private schools. However, because policies directed by the government are not clear, principals tend to be critical of their practical relevance and thus try to come up with creative interpretations that bypass or overwrite their perceived restrictions to serve the best interests of their students and institutions.

The Unrealistic Expectations and Challenges

The principals continuously struggle to create a stable educational environment while being confronted with many challenges and limited resources, and lacking substantial support. They are expected to engage with the families, communities, teachers, and students in meaningful, reciprocal, and mutually beneficial ways to ensure the success of the school. They even attend to the well-being of the whole community including parents, teachers, and students. However, they engage in these functions in a reactionary rather than proactive manner as they find strategies to overcome the many challenges they face. Given the country's unstable economic and social structures, principals are constantly struggling to provide safe, welcoming working environments for teachers and school staff. In addition to supervising teachers and staff, they try to accommodate the needs associated with balancing home responsibilities and work demands, which may be overwhelming to teachers. In many instances, principals must help resolve not only teachers' professional problems but also their personal problems. They provide constant support and guidance for novice teachers.

Principals are also responsible for managing students' academic and disciplinary problems. Many principals build relationships with students' families to help resolve problems related to academic performance and beyond. Although dealing with parents and the community is rarely stated as part of the principal's formal responsibilities, it is an important aspect of the job. They act as mediators between their schools and parents, and respond to parents' concerns, for example, regarding finances and academic standards. They work hard to encourage uninvolved parents to participate and contribute in some way. In addition, principals are actively involved in handling problematic situations with parents, as in the case of an underachieving or misbehaving student. In smaller private schools and schools serving rural communities, principals play the role of the moral authority figure, the counselor whose involvement goes beyond addressing students' academic challenges to addressing personal and family problems. They are invested in the community; some even go above and beyond. They attend funerals and weddings and are involved in the lives of members of their communities. They basically have a wholistic understanding of their school's context and their stakeholders. So, in this sense, instead of just focusing on academic performance, they spend a huge part of their times putting out fires, resolving urgent issues, and attending to the basic needs that are taken for granted in many others schools in other countries.

Principals are involved in raising funds for the school, managing routine paperwork, keeping school records and documentation regarding financial transactions, as well as reporting regularly to supervisors about their schools' finances, academic standing, and equipment and maintenance needs. Principals also are in charge of the student recruitment and admissions process. In public schools, this means contacting some families to encourage them to send their kids to school. In private schools, this aspect of the role involves setting criteria for accepting students, managing entrance examinations, and making and communicating admissions decisions.

Catalysts for School Improvement

Additionally, regardless of the type or location of the school, principals consider themselves to be the only catalysts for school improvement, despite limited resources. They are the main source of new ideas for improving instruction, organization, and facilities within their schools. Some improvements are structural and focused on ameliorating physical conditions, for example, by ensuring access to basic classroom equipment or finding administrative loopholes to avoid the dysfunctionality of the rigid bureaucratic system. Other school improvement initiatives focus directly on the effectiveness of teaching and learning, instructional programs, or the school's curriculum.

Recognition of Contextual Factors Shaping the Demands of the Principal Role

The organizational structure of the Lebanese educational system is a major factor that shapes and at times hinders the principal's work. In both public and private schools, the principal's institutional work context has the characteristics of a Weberian bureaucracy with a highly centralized authority. However, variations in the distribution of authority within the bureaucratic structure are associated with differences in school type and ownership. All schools in Lebanon are under the direct governance of the Ministry of Education and Higher Education (MEHE). The ministry is headed by a minister who is assisted by a director general of public education. The latter is assisted by a group of directors, each in charge of elementary, middle, and secondary schools. These directors of education are the immediate superiors of public school principals (Decree No. 590, 1974). As such, all secondary principals report to the director of secondary education, who in turn reports to the director of general education, who reports directly to the minister of education. All directors operate from the headquarters of the MEHE, centralized in Beirut, the capital of Lebanon. The directors of education make the main decisions affecting schools in their jurisdictions based on the policies and decrees signed by the MEHE. The decisions made by the director of secondary education are communicated to all secondary principals in the different educational districts through an internal correspondence system. Principals are only required to go to the central office to meet with their supervisors on rare occasions (Decree No. 590, 1974).

Private Versus Public Schools

In private schools, the governance structure varies from one school to another. Yet, in general, this structure gives the principal more authority in making decisions related to daily operations relative to their public school counterparts. In most cases, private school principals play a substantial role in making decisions like choosing textbooks and allocating instructional time to different subjects. They also have a major voice in decisions related to hiring and firing teachers, admitting students, setting and implementing student disciplinary policies, and setting budgetary priorities. Moreover, principals in private schools, unlike their public school counterparts, enjoy geographic proximity to their supervisors. This facilitates interaction and enhances opportunities to provide input to centralized policy decisions made by the school's owner or owner organization.

Public school principals, however, work under a highly centralized bureaucracy that limits the scope of their decision-making authority.

In addition to receiving orders from the directors of education, public school principals are accountable to the directorate of central inspection who reports to the country's prime minister (Decree No. 2460, 1959) and are independent of the MEHE. Educational, administrative, and financial inspectors visit public schools to evaluate principals' performance to ensure adherence to laws and regulations (Decree No. 2460, 1959). This inspection is the only measure for evaluating public school principals. Inspectors are the only ones who hold the authority to recommend disciplinary measures and contract termination. Under this highly centralized bureaucracy, public school principals' decision-making power is very limited. In the public sector, the central office mandates the curriculum, assigns teachers, evaluates their work, makes decisions about reprimanding incompetence, decides which equipment to send to schools, and determines how and when to allocate resources to maintain school buildings. Under these conditions, principals face difficulties in both holding teachers accountable and providing them with what they need to maintain a high level of performance within the classroom.

Relevance of MEHE Policies

Despite these differences, both public and private school principals often deal with situations where their superiors mandate regulations without adequately considering schools' individual needs. There is a major dissonance between the realities and demands at the school level and the mandates of centralized regulations and decisions, whether they originate from the ministry or school owners. Moreover, in both types of schools, there is no process set in place to initiate a review of the relevance or effectiveness of mandated decisions or to actively involve principals and consider schools' needs. In other words, while the MEHE imposes these top-down policies, principals are not included in any of these decision-making processes developed by MEHE.

Enrollment and School Location

School location is another contextual factor that influences principals' role expectations in both public and private schools. There are no policies in Lebanon that restrict enrollment to students from a certain geographic area. As a result, students in both public and private schools are free to choose which school they attend, regardless of their place of residence. However, in rural areas, and given the scarcity of schools in those areas, a school's location seems to determine the student population to a great extent. School location also shapes the resources available and school relations with the community, creating additional role expectations for the principal. Principals of both public and private schools in rural areas experience more resource shortages than their counterparts in urban areas. In many instances, public school principals in rural areas do not have school buildings with sufficient capacity and resources to properly accommodate the number of students enrolled.

Moreover, they do not receive the teaching staff they request and rarely get funding from the central office in response to their expressed needs. In some instances, principals cannot allocate space for science labs because they need every room for classroom instruction.

Thus, rather than focusing on school success, principals find themselves consumed with daily problems such as fixing broken windows, rearranging office space to serve as classroom space, substituting for absent teachers, and handling all the secretarial work within the school. Private school principals in rural areas also are affected by resource limitations, although in slightly different ways. On average, private schools are better equipped and staffed than their public counterparts. However, many rural private school parents are too poor to pay the tuition fees, which constitute the main source of funding. Consequently, fundraising becomes a major part of the principal's work. Principals end up trying to actively be involved in finding scholarships to support students' financial needs and subsidize school budgets.

Going Beyond School Duties—Playing the Political

Additionally, principals go beyond their school duties to serve students' families and community members. They exchange social visits with families. Principals, particularly in rural areas, are actively involved in the lives of their students, and spend a major part of their time interacting with students and their parents. Parents often depend on principals for advice on matters beyond school issues and seek their help to resolve their children's personal problems. Similarly, urban school principals participate in and contribute to local events, and influence critical decisions at the community level.

Local and national politics constitute a major factor shaping the work and work context of Lebanese school principals. In fact, the Lebanese educational system might best be described as a "politicized bureaucracy". The organizational structure of the system follows the characteristics of a highly centralized bureaucracy, yet closer examination reveals that the actual functioning of this system is strongly influenced by local politics grounded in religious and family structures. Religious leaders and other influential members of the community exert strong, consistent pressure on school leaders in the public and private sectors, and on senior administrators in the highly centralized educational bureaucracy. In this sense, religious/sectarian nepotism has been institutionalized in the system; it is the accepted way of doing things. Political and religious favoritism and clientelism determine, to a great degree, which teachers are hired, which students are admitted, and how many resources a school receives. Community religious leaders and other politicians also interfere in many decisions related to daily school functioning, such as promoting students, enforcing discipline rules, and reprimanding incompetent teachers. Consequently, a principal's ability to make educationally appropriate decisions within the school becomes highly constrained.

Overall, principals devote considerable time and effort to responding to and negotiating the demands of local politicians, and attempting to minimize potentially negative effects on school functioning. In the public sector, politics affect school administration at all levels. At the central ministry level, politicians' preferences and views influence, to a large degree, all major decision-making processes and outcomes pertaining to the main governance body of public schools. Religious leaders and other community politicians are actively involved in shaping decisions related to appointing new public school principals and teachers, the opening of new schools, and allocating resources among the schools. Because many policies are formulated in response to political considerations, they often result in decisions that complicate rather than facilitate the work of the principal.

The influence of politicians on educational decision-making in public schools is propagated through an institutionalized process of clientelism in hiring. Many public school principals describe how community political and religious leaders compete fiercely to ensure that their followers hold as many key leadership positions as possible at all levels. Politicians' influence is also maintained by the fact that Lebanese educators, as individuals, tend to prioritize their personal religious and political affiliations when making decisions over their professional judgment and views as educators. By ensuring that their supporters are hired for key positions, political and religious leaders appeal to the expectations of their supporters and thus reinforce and perpetuate their influence in the school system (and within their respective political and religious communities).

Principal positions seem to be leadership positions over which politicians compete. Political affiliation is a strong determinant of who gets selected to become a public school principal. Local political and religious leaders push to ensure that their supporters are selected. Once appointed, the principal is expected to allow that religious or community leader to have a say in every issue in the school. These politicians may demand personal favors from them, which in many cases violates formal policies. For example, because political and religious leaders want to please parents in their community and win their support, they sometimes ask principals to promote students who receive failing grades. In addition, political and religious leaders sometimes try to stop principals from reporting the poor performance of teachers who are allies or supporters of the central office, thereby helping them maintain their jobs despite inadequate teaching performance. In this sense, political and religious leaders are able to exert pressure on public school principals in their communities, even when they are not directly involved in supporting the hiring of a principal. As a result, most public school principals find themselves forced to choose between two evils: pledge loyalty to a certain political leader to get support when asking for resources at the risk of allowing the politician unconditional interference in the school; or avoid being associated with politicians at the risk of suffering from a lack of resources and political support, and consequently having the school's needs ignored by supervisors at the central office.

Recommendations

In Lebanon, the system sets principals to failure and abandonment. There is a lack of sustainable training, lack of presence of an entity that could provide helpful support, and abundance of challenges and barriers in their way, to name a few. Despite all that, Lebanese principals operate from an ethics of care. They have a high sense of mission toward the kids their serve, especially the ones that are left behind in the public school system. In Lebanon's times of dire, we cannot but recognize the incredible work these unproclaimed professionals do so that their students and communities thrive. As such, we propose the following recommendations to be established for clear and effective leadership:

1 *Create formal job descriptions*
2 *Continue building partnerships with communities/families*
3 *Give principals more autonomy*
4 *Ensure resources are allocated fairly and equitably, without influence from political or religious leaders*
5 *Ensure adequate principal competencies by implementing programs to support well-being, induction, training, and professional development*
6 *Supervision*
7 *Enable and expand their capacity to make decisions and lead beyond the constrictions of managerial duties*
8 *Give principals a voice in education reform.*

References

Adams, C. M., & Jean-Marie, G. (2011). A diffusion approach to study leadership reform. *Journal of Educational Administration, 49*, 354-377.
Arar, K. (2020). Educational Administration in the Middle East. In Papa, R. (Ed.) *Oxford research encyclopedia of education*. Oxford, UK: Oxford University Press.
Arar, K., Örücü, D., & Ak Küçükçayır, G. (2019). Culturally relevant school leadership for Syrian refugee students in challenging circumstances. *Educational Management Administration & Leadership, 47*(6), 960–979.
Arar, K., Örücü, D., & Mahfouz, J. (2022). Social in/justice and double marginality in educational leadership: Trajectories of three female school principals from the Middle East. In V. Showunmi, P. Moorosi, C. Shakeshaft, & I. Oplatka (Eds.), *The handbook for gender and educational leadership* (pp. 76–87). London, UK: Bloomsbury.
Arar, K., Turan, S., Barakat, M., & Oplatka, I. (2017). The characteristics of educational leadership in the Middle East: A comparative analysis of three nation-states, In D. Waite & I, Bogotch (eds.), *International handbook of leadership in education*. (pp. 355–373). John Wiley & Sons, Inc.
Berjaoui, R. R., & Karami-Akkary, R. (2020). Distributed leadership as a path to organizational commitment: The case of a Lebanese school. *Leadership and Policy in Schools, 19*(4), 610–624.

Boyd, D., Grossman, P., Ing, M., Lankford, H., Loeb, S., & Wyckoff, J. (2011). The influence of school administrators on teacher retention decisions. *American Educational Research Journal*, *48*(2), 303–333.

Cansoy, R. (2019). The relationship between school principals' leadership behaviours and teachers' job satisfaction: A systematic review. *International Education Studies*, *12*(1), 37–52.

Center of Educational Development and Research (CRDP) (2021). Statistics Bulletin. Retrieved from https://www.crdp.org/statistics-bulletin

Eacott, S. (2019). High-impact school leadership in context. *Leading and Managing*, *25*(2), 66–79.

Fullan, M. (2009). *The challenge of change: Start school improvement now!*. Thousand Oaks, CA: Corwin Press.

Fullan, M. (2016). The elusive nature of whole system improvement in education. *Journal of Educational Change*, *17*(4), 539–544.

Glatter, R. (2014). Educational administration 1969–2014: Reflections on pragmatism, agency and reform. *Journal of Educational Administration and History*, *46*(3), 351–366.

Gómez-Leal, R., Holzer, A. A., Bradley, C., Fernández-Berrocal, P., & Patti, J. (2022). The relationship between emotional intelligence and leadership in school leaders: A systematic review. *Cambridge Journal of Education*, *52*(1), 1–21.

Greenfield, W., & Akkary, R. (1998). Leadership and work context of public and private secondary schools in the Republic of Lebanon. A Paper Presented at the Annual Meeting of the American Educational Research Association San Diego, California April 13-17, 1998.

Hallinger, P., & Hammad, W. (2019). Knowledge production on educational leadership and management in Arab societies: A systematic review of research. *Educational Management Administration & Leadership*, *47*(1), 20–36.

Hallinger, P., & Heck, R. H. (1996). Reassessing the principal's role in school effectiveness: A review of empirical research, 1980–1995. *Educational Administration Quarterly*, *32*(1), 5–44.

Hallinger, P., & Heck, R. H. (2011). Collaborative leadership and school improvement: Understanding the impact on school capacity and student learning. In Townsend, T. & MacBeath, J. (Eds.) *International handbook of leadership for learning* (Vol. 25, pp. 469–485). Dordrecht: Springer.

Harb, S., & Karami-Akkary, R. (2019). Lebanese conceptions of effective school leadership: A cross-cultural analysis. *International Journal of Leadership in Education*, *24*, 126–144.

Hargreaves, A., & O'Connor, M. T. (2018). Solidarity with solidity: The case for collaborative professionalism. *Phi Delta Kappan*, *100*(1), 20–24.

Harris, A., & Jones, M. (2018). Leading schools as learning organizations. *School Leadership & Management*, *38*(4), 351–354.

Hattie, J., Masters, D., & Birch, K. (2015). *Visible learning into action: International case studies of impact*. New York, NY: Routledge.

Huber, S. G., & Muijs, D. (2010). School leadership effectiveness: The growing insight in the importance of school leadership for the quality and development of schools and their pupils. In Huber, S. (Ed.), *School leadership-international perspectives* (pp. 57–77). Dordrecht: Springer.

Kafka, J. (2009). The principalship in historical perspective. *Peabody Journal of Education*, *84*(3), 318–330.

Karami-Akkary, R., & Hammad, W. (2019). The knowledge base on educational leadership and management in Arab countries: Its current state and its implications for leadership development. In Samier, E. A. & ElKaleh, E. (Eds.), *Teaching educational leadership in Muslim countries* (pp. 77–92). Singapore: Springer.

Karami, R., Mahfouz, J., & Mansour*, S. (2019). Sustaining school-based improvement: Considering emotional responses to change. *Journal of Educational Administration*, 57(1), 50 –67. 10.1108/JEA-01-2018-0022

Kowalski, T. J., & Brunner, C. C. (2011). The school superintendent: Roles, challenges, and issues. In English, F.W. (Ed.), *Sage handbook of educational leadership: Advances in theory, research, and practice*, (pp. 142–167), Thousand Oaks, CA: Sage Publications.

Leithwood, K., Harris, A., & Hopkins, D. (2020). Seven strong claims about successful school leadership revisited. *School leadership & management*, 40(1), 5–22.

Louis, K. S. (2022). String theory and knots: A 50 year journey through organizational studies. *Journal of Educational Administration*, 60, 228–244.

Leithwood, K., & Seashore-Louis, K. (2011). *Linking leadership to student learning*. San Francisco, CA: John Wiley & Sons.

Leithwood, K., & Jantzi, D. (2005). A review of transformational school leadership research 1996–2005. *Leadership and Policy in Schools*, 4(3), 177–199.

Mahfouz, J. (2021). Neoliberalism—the straw that broke the back of Lebanon's education system. In K. Arar, D. Örücü, & J. Wilkinson (Eds.), *Neoliberalism and education systems in conflict: Exploring challenges across the globe*, (pp. 108–177), Abingdon, UK: Routledge.

Mahfouz, J., Greenberg, M. T., & Rodriguez, A. (2019). Principals' social and emotional competence: A key factor for creating caring schools. *The Pennsylvania State University*.

Mancuso, S. V., Roberts, L., & White, G. P. (2010). Teacher retention in international schools: The key role of school leadership. *Journal of Research in International Education*, 9(3), 306–323.

McConnell III, J. R. (2020). The state of educational leadership in the United States: Trends and implications for higher education and local school districts. *International Journal of Leadership in Education*, 25, 675–684.

Oplatka, I., & Arar, K. (2017). The research on educational leadership and management in the Arab world since the 1990s: A systematic review. *Review of Education*, 5(3), 267–307. 10.1002/rev3.3095

Pont, B., Moorman, H., & Nusche, D. (2008). *Improving school leadership* (Vol. 1, pp. 1–199). Paris: OECD.

Roach, V., Smith, L. W., & Boutin, J. (2011). School leadership policy trends and developments: Policy expediency or policy excellence? *Educational Administration Quarterly*, 47(1), 71–113.

Robinson, V., & Gray, E. (2019). What difference does school leadership make to student outcomes? *Journal of the Royal Society of New Zealand*, 49(2), 171–187.

Sahlberg, P. (2011). Developing effective teachers and school leaders: The case of Finland. *Effectiveness*, 13.

Spillane, J. P., & Kenney, A. W. (2012). School administration in a changing education sector: The US experience. *Journal of Educational Administration*, 50, 541–561.

9 The State of Art of Educational Leadership in Palestine
The Two Faces of the Coin

Soheil Salha and Saida Affouneh

Introduction

Educational Administration is a field where a real difference and a measurable impact can be made (Mulford, 2003) as it deals with many variables, involves people, and is a solution-oriented discipline (Darling-Hammond, 2020). Hence, Educational Administration policies and practices are always under research, improvement, and investigation (Ion & Iucu, 2015). Dos and Savas (2015) clarified the significant roles of educational administrators in leading and guiding their institutions to reach greater developmental heights.

In the Middle East, many educational administrative systems were under stress due to states of emergency that threatened students learning, school performance, and social justice for various reasons (Autin et al., 2015). In turn, these cases of emergency generated several problems for education policymakers and researchers who struggled to conduct intervention programs that would meet the needs of the local populations (Arar et al., 2021). Hence, there is an urgent need for leaders who can effectively contribute to their populations. Leadership as perceived by Brighouse and Woods (1999) should be strong, purposeful, and be an adoption of various styles at all levels. Educational leadership always generates great debate (Pont et al., 2008), especially in the context of Palestine.

The Palestinian education system provides the Palestinian community with the physical and conceptual space to sustain the nation of Palestine by enabling them to define their national identity, engage in resistance against the Israeli occupation of Palestine, and build the nation of Palestine (Bruhn, 2006).

The authors could frame the current state of educational leadership in Palestine as one crafted by a combination of history, educational and financial crises, the daily struggle against occupation, the desire for independence, and several initiatives to make tangible changes.

History of the Palestinian Education System

Education plays a fundamental and crucial role in fostering social and political change (Ramahi, 2015) especially in Palestine, which is greatly valued among

DOI: 10.4324/9781003334835-9

families. It is a treasure and a source of hope and transformation for the Palestinian people. Palestinians in Palestine and the diaspora have relied on formal education for social, economic, and political survival (Alzaroo & Hunt, 2003). After 1948, teachers and students played a significant role in building Palestinian society, when the majority of the Palestinians were forced to leave their homeland—known as the Nakba (Assaf, 1997). At that time, teachers were considered as popular and educational leaders.

Historically, education in Palestine had been administered by foreign authorities. This started with the Ottoman Empire in the 15th century and ended with the Israeli occupation in 1994. More recently, however, the Palestinian educational process has had to contend with the oppressive and often violent conditions of occupation. While most neighboring Arab states provide Palestinian refugees with access to education, in Lebanon, Palestinians are dependent on the limited services provided by the United Nations Relief and Works Agency for Palestine Refugees, and experience restrictions as a result of their political status or financial situation. Palestinians used the Jordanian and Egyptian curriculum until they established their own curriculum in 1998. A recent report by the World Bank indicated the educational system in Palestine is improved in literacy rates for the adult population.

From 1516 until 1917, Palestine was part of the Ottoman Empire (Al-Sinwar, 2019). In general, it may be said that schools at that time were not well organized and the methods of teaching were unsatisfactory. The use of foreign mediums of instruction (Turkish) even in elementary classes added to initial defects and weakened the quality of the education. The schools had no unified system as each community managed its own schools (Broco & Trad, 2011). The major Ottoman pursuit of public education began with the Ottoman Public Education Law (1869) whereby they turned to education as a means of achieving technical parity with the West. Assaf (1997) mentioned that modern formal education in Palestine developed as a reaction to Ottoman attempts to promote and impose Turkish culture. As a result, school leaders were appointed by the central body of education to keep the school harmonized with the Ottoman vision of education (Wolf, 1981).

Education under the British Mandate

The British Education policy differentiated between economic and social situations among the communities (Shanmugavelu et al., 2020). Whitehead (2007) showed that the British colonial education policy varied from one territory to another.

Palestinian education was controlled by the British mandatory government through the Department of Education. The educational system was supervised by the British mandate (Panza, 2020).

During the mandate period, the educational system for Palestinians was based on governmental schools and private institutions. Kalisman (2015) showed that the graduates of American University of Beirut were hired in leadership positions in education as they had already finished an undergraduate degree and a conducted course of teacher training.

By the end, more than 125,000 Palestinian students were enrolled in schools all over Palestine, most of them in elementary schools. About two-thirds of the students attended governmental schools, and one-third attended various religious, private, and public associations (Broco & Trad, 2011).

Education under Occupation

Prior to the finalization of the Oslo agreement in 1994, the Israeli Civil Administration managed the educational system in the occupied Palestinian territories. The Civil Administration assigned Jordanian textbooks to schools in the West Bank and Egyptian books to schools in Gaza, and much of the content was censored due to the Civil Administration's disapproval.

The Israeli occupation and the arduous conflict have extremely compromised access to education in occupied Palestine (Norwegian Refugee Council, 2020). The right to education is threatened by numerous education-related incidents such as attacks or threats of attacks on schools, student and teacher casualties, lost school time due to delays at checkpoints, military presence at school entrances, and closed military areas (UNICEF, 2017). Further threats comprise the use of tear gas in and around schools, school searches, confiscation of education items, detention of students and school staff, settler-related violence, and school demolitions and stop-work orders (Women's Centre for Legal Aid and Counselling, 2015).

The occupation damaged the education system; schools and universities were closed for a long time with some closures extending for up to four years, with large losses to the teacher workforce due to Israeli impositions. Moreover, it was prohibited to teach anything about Palestinian history, culture, and geography in class or elsewhere (Nicolai, 2007).

Education under the Palestinian Ministry of Education

There are difficulties in building an educational system under occupation, without full political, territorial, and physical freedom (Ramahi, 2015). The transfer of educational authority to the Ministry of Education (MOE) on August 28, 1994 was a historic event in terms of the development of the Palestinian nation, as the Palestinians took full responsibility over the education of their children for the first time (Assaf, 1997).

Since the establishment of the Ministry of Education and Higher Education (MOEHE) in 1994, the Ministry was tasked with the great task of structuring the educational system from the ground-up (Romahi, 2010). The first task of the MOEHE was to unify the educational systems and curricula between the West Bank and Gaza. The First Palestinian curriculum was launched in 1998 as the Ministry of Education promised to create an independent Palestinian curriculum and immediately established the Curriculum

Development Centre. It published its report on national curriculum development in 1996. The national curriculum changed the methodology adopted in schools, encouraging the promotion of critical thinking skills, problem-solving, and creativity. Preparation of the curriculum involved five consecutive stages: approving the curriculum plan by the legislative council, formulating the national teams for each subject, formulating teams of authors for specific textbooks, editing linguistic and scientific books, and piloting and evaluating the curriculum.

In 2000, after six years of struggle and trying to establish the Palestinian educational system, and as the focus began to shift to improving quality of education through learning and teaching, the second intifada—the al-Aqsa intifada—began. Even before this, the creation of the new education system occurred within an increasingly fractured geography (Nicolai, 2007).

Since 1994, the MOEHE has been spending a great amount of money and effort toward building the educational system. According to the Ministry, "Education is a human right that should be provided to all children from kindergarten to the high school" (Ministry of Education and Higher Education, 2017). It is worth noting that students in the West Bank were using Jordanian English textbooks while those in the Gaza Strip were using Egyptian English textbooks before the foundation of the MOEHE.

According to the World Bank report (2006), a total of 266 schools and 7350 classrooms were built between 1995 and 2005. The MOEHE was directly accountable for the building of 118 new schools and 2675 educational classrooms in order to decrease the school's double shifts. According to the PCBS, 41% of classes had 30 students or less in 2004–2005 and only 18% of classes had more than 40 students.

The post-intifada era highlights the tension that Palestinian children and families struggle with when accessing and attending school. While access to schools has improved since the second intifada, the potential for violence that comes with living in armed conflict zones remains (Akesson, 2015).

The structure of the Palestinian educational system consists of three stages: the primary education stage beginning in the preparatory stage, or lower basic level (grades 1–4), the middle education stage which lasts for six years, often referred to as the empowerment stage or upper basic level (5–10), and the secondary education stage which consists of the final two years of the education program that takes place at academic and technical/vocational secondary schools. At the end of this period, students sit for a national secondary education examination (*Tawjihi*) which is the portal to tertiary education in Palestine.

The Ministry of Education and Higher Education (2017) integrated its leadership approach through:

- Considering a professional diploma program in Supervisory Leadership as principals and educational leaders should be qualified to deal with all different problems, situations, and crises (Hallinger & Bridges, 2017).

- Open-minded and developed leadership that respects the other. Educational leaders contribute significantly to keep equity and justice among school members (Mulford, 2003). It's a challenging task for leaders as they face tension between their roles and the regulations of the Central Body of Education.
- Promoting leadership, creativity, and excellence among students, teachers, and support staff at all levels. Education improves through more effective school leaders. School leaders could improve the quality of thinking, learning, and management as they share their experiences with teachers and students
- Introducing specialized leadership programs for different job categories at the medium and high management levels, with the goal of reinforcing capacity building so as to include all categories. Workplace problems, miscommunication with different parties, and leading organizational change are examples of certain challenges that school leaders usually face in Palestine. Developing practical leadership programs could enable principals to drive the school to a productive organizational climate (Pérez-Vallejo, & Fernández-Muñoz, 2019)
- Improving women's participation in decision-making by creating mechanisms that provide women equal opportunities as men; this includes the approval of women's leadership programs and the removal of all hurdles that are obstructing women's full participation in social progress. Gender equity, social justice, and development are critical challenges that leaders face in the Middle East region (The World Bank, 2013). Empowering women to lead educational institutions and take decisions will guarantee real participation for women and serve more equitable leadership (Bayeh, 2016).
- Reinforcing school leadership to boost education and learning. The OECD (2010) showed that school leaders made significant differences in schools and student learning when they were granted autonomy to make their own decisions.
- Reforming the Ministry's central leadership and operational structure in line with the service delivery program of the Ministry's strategic plan.

The Bright Side of the Palestinian Educational Leadership

Education is a tool for resistance and social justice (Neri et al., 2019). Thus, after the Oslo agreement, a new role for the education system was assigned. It was expected that the education system would support the rebuilding of new authoritative institutions through empowerment, training, capacity building, and hiring skillful workers (Chard, 2005). Education is considered an important tool for reconstruction and rehabilitation since it is the only fortune in Palestine manpower (UNESCO, 2003). Hence, the education sector was made a priority by the Palestinian government.

Living under crises opened an international eye toward Palestine as an area in the transition stage (Traxler et al., 2019). Huge support was given to the

Palestinian National Authority in order to build its infrastructure and develop its human capacity. The employees in the educational sector were fortunate to be involved in many funded international professional development projects, especially in teacher training and educational management. For example, the Ministry of Education staff was given many opportunities to participate in international study visits to International Institute for Educational Planning (IIEP) through UNESCO in order to train high management-level staff on educational planning and crisis management standards. Workshops, training study visits, and expert scholars were part of the capacity-building program through different international agencies.

This training developed the knowledge and skills of the Ministry of Education staff in decentralization as a new policy for educational management, making decentralization as part of the strategic plan for many years (MOE, 2017). Unfortunately, this goal of moving towards decentralization was frozen for many years due to unqualified staff in the educational field and implementation level.

Goal 3 of the MOE strategic plan is to "promoteAccountability and results-based leadership, governance, and management" (MOE, 2017, p. 39). This goal has many sub-goals that the Ministry of Education had been trying to achieve, such as developing the job description for all staff, modifying the organizational structure, training all staff on management and financial development procedures, and improving capacity-building on measurement & evaluation (MOE, 2017, p. 100). To achieve Goal 3, the Palestinian National Educational Law was developed and published to determine the norms of accountability, leadership, governance, and management. The combination of accountability and school leadership creates a necessity of distribution of leadership (Holloway, 2021).

The only opportunity for this actual policy (Decentralization) was through times of crisis and emergency including school closures, pandemics such as COVID-19, and or bad weather situations.

Furthermore, the structure of the Ministry of Education consists of three main layers: the Ministry of Education, district directorates, and schools. The authors propose a structure as in Figure 9.1.

The Ministry of Education is usually responsible for all decision-making and policy change, since it lies at the top of the organizational hierarchy, while the district's directorates usually form a channel between the MOE and schools in order to facilitate the decisions and policy implementation in addition to following up and reporting processes.

During crises, the Center of the Ministry of Education delegates decision-making to the districts and schools, which indirectly empowers head teachers and school teachers, and enables them to choose best practices that suit their local situations. It also opens up new opportunities for local communities to help them in finding suitable solutions for their problems and challenges. This practice of leadership contributed to achieving social justice among students as school leadership collected electronic devices and provided them to

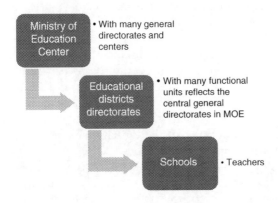

Figure 9.1 The structure of the Ministry of Education.

students who did not have any electronic tools to pursue their learning virtually (Khlaif et al., 2021).

During the Pandemic, the Ministry of Education gave more power to schools; each school developed its own way to train its teachers through distance learning and developed their schedule according to their own needs, the number of students, their teachers' capabilities, and their parents' coordination. Although there were many challenges due to delegations of power, many innovations were practiced and developed by motivated teachers who insisted on sustaining teaching and learning to offer a quality education. A great lesson can be derived from this experience in which delegations with school self-management can lead to creativity and innovations in schools.

The Dark Side of Palestinian Educational Leadership

The Ministry of Education and the Ministry of Higher Education are sometimes integrated together as one ministry and then separated as two entities which negatively reflects on policies, operations, and management levels. Therefore, in many cases, this causes an overlap in responsibilities and policymaking (International Labour Organization, 2018). The absence of a co-ordinated mechanism also affects educational outcomes, monitoring, and evaluation at schools and universities. Another challenge occurred when the two ministries were separated as this caused a need for a new structure, new leaders, and a redistribution of existing staff.

The priorities in the educational system are usually related to the priorities of foreign aid and resource are distributed accordingly. This indirectly impacts the implementation of all strategic plans and developing procedures since the financial agenda will be related to the funder policies and in many cases will be far away from the national needs and priorities.

Despite decentralization being a part of the strategic plan, it was only used for emergency situations so it was strategically used and set aside when the general situation had been improved, which left schools and districts disappointed (Mustafa et al., 2019). Another challenge was the increasing gap between the top management level as well as the middle and low levels. The Ministry of Education sent its instructions to the directorates of education in different districts, who in turn sent the same instructions to schools. Its top-down approach to management which leaves no chance for middle and low levels leads to these situations.

The financial system was not better since it was very centralized and all the resources had been distributed through the center under the authority of the Ministry of Finance. This made the situation very complicated since the absence of financial management, accountability, and transparency, the management mechanism became unclear in the different levels (Gaventa, & McGee, 2013).

There were several information systems that were used by different general directorates in the Ministry of Education with no integration systems or any type of data flow system. The result was that data had not been driven accordingly, and policy was not based on research-based outcomes. The e-governance and automation of the system suffered from weaknesses and were unable to meet the needs of the Ministry of Education requirements with its three levels (centers, districts, and schools). Several databases exist and continue to be unable to communicate with each other.

Conclusion

The Palestinian educational system changed several times and faced different challenges such as the stable financial system to keep schools open. It's also worth mentioning that 90% of educational expenditures were put toward salaries. A huge challenge is to secure teachers' salaries which depend mostly on external donations and taxes. The Israeli occupation further hinders the educational system in Palestine. Some of the destructive practices done by the Israeli military include school destruction and shootings. Flexible educational leadership has been a significant demand to overcome educational challenges and to provide quality education at the same time. Argyropoulou et al. (2021) concluded that educational leaders were among the few employees who were mandated to go to their workplace to create constant communication with their superiors in order to normalize emergencies and manage crises.

It is fair to say that Palestinian life and education are familiar with crises to the extent that crisis events have become the "new normal". The desire to live and learn creates the ability to continue against all odds. In the second intifada, schools were forced to close due to the Israeli invasion. The educational leadership reacted immediately and established popular teaching which is nearly similar to home schooling.

Despite the lack of local resources, Palestinians and their educational leadership believe in learning and teaching. Hence, community engagement is still one of the pillars that educational policies depend on. Local organizations and societies as well as parents and families support schools to achieve Palestinians' educational goals. School leaders usually formulate a common committee involving local institutions, parents, and governmental bodies to handle different unexpected cases. Arar et al. (2021) pointed out school leaders' role during uncertain conditions as this role requires high-capacity decision-making and action to ensure the safety of all and the delivery of positive results.

Palestine is still under occupation and emergency situations have become familiar. Accordingly, the field of leadership and management is the commonly utilized practice. Educational leaders, principals, and teachers are always ready to manage sudden situations like the murder of a student or a teacher, the invasion of schools, school closures, or any type of daily violence. The Ministry of Education trains the majority of principals to prepare emergency plans and asks them to work cooperatively with teachers and the local community in managing crises. Moreover, principals are trained to manage and solve conflict. (Arar 2022A) mentioned that educators work under complicated conditions due to culture, relationships, contexts, decision-making, and multiple challenges they encounter at the school level.

Finally, the authors believe that it is hard to lead in uncertain circumstances and ambiguous conditions such as in Palestine. Therefore, a state of independence and supremacy should be set. A real and strong leadership could be built, once there are applicable policies (Arar, 2022B; Scheerens, 2012). Educational leadership is a goal and a tool—a goal that we must promote and a tool to create community leaders.

Recommendations

The context of educational leadership in Palestine is a unique one. Multiple recommendations can be drawn from this content. First, designing a special program of educational leadership under crises is required to secure quality education, social justice, and effective communication. Second, it is recommended to move from centralized systems to decentralized ones to enable leaders to practice leadership skills and strengthen their abilities in leadership and management. Engaging women in leadership roles and supporting them will maximize the opportunities to create a productive and equitable educational system, especially in Palestine, where women and men share most of their daily tasks and responsibilities.

References

Akesson, B. (2015). School as a place of violence and hope: Tensions of education for children and families in post-intifada Palestine. *International Journal of Educational Development*, *41*, 192–199. 10.1016/j.ijedudev.2014.08.001

Al-Sinwar, Z. (2019). Jerusalem in the Ottoman rule (1516–1917 AD). *International Journal of Humanities Social Sciences and Education*, *6*(1), 43–51, 10.20431/2349-0381.0601005

Alzaroo, S., & Hunt, G.L. (2003), Education in the context of conflict and instability: The Palestinian case. *Social Policy & Administration*, 37, 165–180. 10.1111/1467-9515.00332

Arar, K., Sawalhi, R., Chaaban, Y., Zohri, A., & Alhouti, I. (2021). School leaders' perspectives towards leading during crisis through an ecological lens: A comparison of five Arab countries. *Journal of Educational Administration and History*, 54(2), 123–142, DOI: 10.1080/00220620.2021.1957793

Arar, K. (2022 A). Educational administration in the Middle East. Texas State University. 10.1093/acrefore/9780190264093.013.672 Published online: 27 August 2020.

Arar, K. (2022B). Understanding the educational administrator's role in a turbulent ethnic education system. *Leadership and Policy in Schools*, 21(2), 222–237. doi:10.1080/15700763.2020.1757723

Argyropoulou, E. et al. (2021). School leadership in dire straits: Fighting the virus or challenging the consequences? *International Studies in Educational Administration*, 49(1), 18–27.

Assaf, S. (1997). Educational disruption and recovery in Palestine. In S. Tawil (Ed.), *Final report and case studies of the Workshop on Educational Destruction and Reconstruction in Disrupted Societies*. Geneva, Switzerland: UN Educational, Scientific and Cultural Organization. Retrieved from http://www.ibe.unesco.org/publications/regworkshops/tawil.htm.

Autin, F, Batruch, A, & Butera, F (2015). Social justice in education: How the function of selection in educational institutions predicts support for (non)egalitarian assessment practices. *Frontiers in Psychology*, 6(707), 1–13. Doi: 10.3389/fpsyg.2015.00707

Bayeh, E. (2016). The role of empowering women and achieving gender equality to the sustainable development of Ethiopia. *Pacific Science Review B: Humanities and Social Sciences*, 2(1), 37–42, 10.1016/j.psrb.2016.09.013

Brighouse, T., & Woods, D. (1999). *How to improve your school*. London, England: Routledge.

Broco, F., & Trad, J. (2011). *Education in the Palestinian Territories*. The Centre for Middle Eastern Studies of the Foundation for the Social Promotion of Culture. Retrieved from https://cemofps.org/documents/download/education_in_the_palestinian_territories.pdf

Bruhn, C. (2006). Higher education as empowerment: The case of Palestinian universities. *American Behavioral Scientist*, 49(8), 1125–1142. 10.1177/0002764205284722

Chard, M. (2005). *The impact of capacity building for the development of the social institutions of war-torn countries: Mozambique's vision for education and its multiple partners* [Doctoral thesis, University of York].

Darling-Hammond, L., Flook, L., Cook-Harvey, C., Barron, B., & Osher, D. (2020) Implications for educational practice of the science of learning and development. *Applied Developmental Science*, 24(2), 97–140, doi: 10.1080/10888691.2018.1537791

Dos, I., & Savas, A. C. (2015). *Elementary school administrators and their roles in the context of effective schools*. SAGE Open. 10.1177/2158244014567400

Gaventa, J., & McGee, R. (2013). The impact of transparency and accountability initiatives. *Development Policy Review*, 31(51), 528–553. 10.1111/dpr.12017

Hallinger, P., & Bridges, E. M. (2017). A systematic review of research on the use of problem-based learning in the preparation and development of school leaders. *Educational Administration Quarterly*, *53*(2), 255–288. 10.1177/0013161X1665 9347

Holloway, J. (2021). *Metrics, standards and alignment in teacher policy: Critiquing fundamentalism and imagining pluralism.* Singapore: Springer. 10.1007/978-981-33-4814-1_9

International Labour Organization (2018). *The occupied Palestinian territory: An employment diagnostic study.* Genève, Switzerland: Regional Office of Arab States. International Labour Organization. Retrieved from https://labordoc.ilo.org/discovery/fulldisplay/alma994983192202676/41ILO_INST:41ILO_V2

Ion, G., & Iucu, R. (2015). Does research influence educational policy? The perspective of researchers and policy-makers in Romania. In A. Curaj, L. Matei, R. Pricopie, J. Salmi, & P. Scott, (Eds.) (2015), *The European higher education area.* Cham: Springer. 10.1007/978-3-319-20877-0_52

Kalisman, H. (2015). *Schooling the state: Educators in Iraq, Palestine and Transjordan: c. 1890–c. 1960.* PhD dissertation. Berkeley: University of California.

Khlaif, Z.N., Salha, S., Fareed, S., & Rashed, H. (2021). The hidden shadow of the coronavirus on education in developing countries. *Online Learning*, *25*(1), 269–285. 10.24059/olj.v25i1.2287

Ministry of Education and Higher Education (2017). *Education sector strategic plan 2017–2022.* Ramallah: Ministry of Education and Higher Education. Retrieved from https://planipolis.iiep.unesco.org/sites/default/files/ressources/palestine_education_sector_strategic_plan_2017-2022.pdf

Mulford, B. (2003). *School leaders: Changing roles and impact on teacher and school effectiveness.* A paper commissioned by the Education and Training Policy Division, OECD, for the Activity: "Attracting, Developing and Retaining Effective Teachers". Paris, April 2003.

Mustafa, G., Glavee-Geo, R., Gronhaug, K., & Saber Almazrouei, H. (2019). Structural impacts on formation of self-efficacy and its performance effects. *Sustainability*, *11*(3), 860. 10.3390/su11030860

Neri, R. C., Lozano, M., & Gomez, L. M. (2019). (Re)framing resistance to culturally relevant education as a multilevel learning problem. *Review of Research in Education*, *43*(1), 197–226. 10.3102/0091732X18821120

Nicolai, S. (2007). *Fragmented foundations: Education and chronic crisis in the Occupied Palestinian Territory*, (joint publication). Paris: International Institute for Educational Planning.

Norwegian Refugee Council (2020). *Raided and razed: Attacks on West Bank education.* Oslo, Norway: Norwegian Refugee Council. Retrieved from https://www.nrc.no/resources/reports/raided-and-razed/#:~:text=The%20objective%20of%20this%20report,school%20children%20in%20Area%20C.

OECD (2010). *Improving schools: Strategies for action for Mexico.* Paris: OECD Publishing. Retrieved from https://www.oecd.org/education/school/improvingschoolsstrategiesforactioninmexico.htm

Panza, L. (2020). The impact of ethnic segregation on schooling outcomes in Mandate Palestine. *Journal of Development Economics*, *146*, 10.1016/j.jdeveco.2020.102514

Pérez-Vallejo, C., & Fernández-Muñoz, J. J. (2019). Quality of leadership and organizational climate in a sample of Spanish workers. The moderation and mediation effect of recognition and teamwork. *International Journal of Environmental Research and Public Health*, 17(1), 32. 10.3390/ijerph17010032

Pont, B., Nusche, D., & Moorman, H. (2008). *Improving school leadership*. Paris: Organization for Economic Co-operation and Development.

Ramahi, H. (2015, April 25). *Empowerment and emancipation in Palestine through teacher leadership*. HertsCam Annual Conference, Cambridge, England.

Ramahi, H. (2015). *Education in Palestine: Current challenges and emancipatory alternatives*. Berlin: Rosa Luxemburg Stiftung publications.

Romahi, E. (2010). *Assessing the educational system in Palestine: An NGO perspective: Context, problems, challenges and policy recommendations*. Ramallah: Teacher Creativity Centre.

Scheerens, J. (2012). *School leadership effects revisited: Review and meta-analysis of empirical studies*. Dordrecht: Springer.

Shanmugavelu, G. et al. (2020). Development of British colonial education in Malaya, 1816–1957. *Shanlax International Journal of Education*, 8(2), 10–15, 10.34293/education.v8i2.2072

The World Bank (2013). *Opening doors gender equality and development in the Middle East and North Africa*. Washington, United States: The World Bank.

Traxler J., Khaif, Z., Nevill, A., Affouneh, S., Salha, S., Zuhd, A., & Trayek, F. (2019). Living under occupation: Palestinian teachers' experiences and their digital responses. *Research in Learning Technology*, 27, 1–18. 10.25304/rlt.v27.2263

UNESCO (2003). *Education in situations of emergency, crisis and reconstruction*. Division of Policies and Strategies of Education Support to Countries in Crisis and Reconstruction. UNESCO.

UNICEF (2017). *Right of education for 1 million Palestinian children at risk*. UNICEF for every child, State of Palestine, right of education for 1 million Palestinian children at risk (unicef.org).

Whitehead, C. (2007). The concept of British education policy in the colonies 1850–1960, *Journal of Educational Administration and History*, 39(2), 161–173, DOI: 10.1080/00220620701342296

Wolf, J. (1981). *Selected aspects in the development of public education in Palestine 1920–1946* [Doctoral thesis, Massachusetts, United States: Boston College University].

Women's Centre for Legal Aid and Counselling (2015). *Israeli settler violence in the West Bank and East Jerusalem*. Ramallah, Palestine: Women's Centre for Legal Aid and Counselling.

World Population Review (2018). Middle East population. The Middle East Population 2022 (Demographics, Maps, Graphs) (worldpopulationreview.com)

10 Educational Administration and Policy in Kuwait
A Reflection on Decades of Reform

Amal Abdulwahab Alsaleh

Kuwait is a small state located in the northwestern region of the Arabian Gulf. The Kingdom of Saudi Arabia corners it from the east, south, and southwest; and the Republic of Iraq from the north and northwest. Kuwait occupies 17,818 square kilometers and is positioned at the top of the Arabian Gulf, making it the main entry point to the Northwest Arabian Peninsula (Kuwait Government e-Gate, 2022). Kuwait shares similar educational visions, policies, and social institutions such as religion with other counties in the Gulf. However, the political context of Kuwait sheds light on education and educational leadership practices, in a more general fashion. The Kuwaiti constitution opened the door to the sharing of power and decisions by prelamins from early times. Thus, educational policies are under accountability systems and social pressure, shaping the context of the Kuwaiti educational setting.

The Development of Public Education in Kuwait

Since 1870, the independent Kuwait city-state had been nominally dependent on the Ottoman Empire, but this changed with the signed covenant of protection with the British in 1899 (Al-Rashoud, 2017). Inspired by its Islamic roots, education surfaced in Kuwait for the first time in the late 17th century (1887) with Qur'anic schools called *Katateeb* that taught the Quran, reading, writing, and mathematics [Alabdulghafoor, 1983; Ministry of Education (MoE), 2019]. *Katateeb* learning found its beginnings in mosques, but later found a separate space. It consisted of segregated schools for boys and girls (25 for boys and 10 for girls). *Katateeb* schools increased to 320 between 1887 and 1952 (Alrishidi, 2012).

The first semi-formal public schools for boys, Mubarakiya and Alahmadiya, were established in 1911 and 1922, respectively, due to demands from business people and educators influenced by Islamic modernists and Arab values. They aimed to bring the modern culture of the Arab world to their periphery, reinforced by the increased demand for a developed education system that could meet economic growth demands. Businesspeople and educators were soon active participants in the pan-Arab intellectual and political scene throughout the local press and the regional business and religious learning networks. These

DOI: 10.4324/9781003334835-10

links contributed to a lively and ambitious Arab nationalist movement with similar activists across Kuwait throughout the 1930s (Al-Rashidi, 2012; Al-Rushoud, 2017). The curriculum in the Mubarakiya school included subjects such as mathematics and geography. English, geography, and simple accounting were introduced in the Alahmadiyah school.

Gradually, these schools adapted multiple education levels, examinations, and special buildings for multi-classes. School principals governed both with businesspeople presented at individual examinations. Since their establishment, both schools have been based on citizen contributions in donations besides student registration fees. The emergence of girls' schools occurred 25 years after establishing the boys' schools. This was because the interest of men was limited to the education of boys in the first phase. The first school for girls was established in 1936, after a period of educational renaissance. This is called *Al-Wusta* (MoE, 2019). An economic crisis due to World War 1 created a lack of financial support for these schools. Hence, the Education Council (currently the MoE) annexed it in 1936 to fall under government administration (Alrishidi, 2012).

Al-Rashoud (2017) described the 1930–1950 period in Kuwait as one in which Arab countries, upon the request of Kuwait, cooperated with Kuwait in building their education systems through assistance such as the hiring of teachers from Palestine and Egypt. Based on Arab relations, Kuwait established funds in 1963 for Arabic economic development through loans and grants, including education development (Kuwait Fund, 2015). Additionally, the role of social pressure from Kuwaiti citizens and educators asking for education, sharing in decision-making, and consulting politicians is highlighted in Kuwaiti history long before independence. When Kuwait gained independence in 1961, the MoE was officially given its formal name and was established in 1965 (Alabdulghafoor, 1983).

Since the government started funding and managing the education sector, the process of developing education has been pursued continually. Kuwait University opened in 1966. Later, in 1967, a law governing private education organizations was passed, but it was not until 2000 before the first private university was established (MoE, 2019). The education system was highly affected by the war. Still, after the Iraqi occupation of Kuwait in 1990, the rebuilding of schools and human resources had been financed by reparation payments. Since then, formal education in Kuwait has been expanded and supervised by the MoE, including qualitative public education (e.g., religious and special-needs education) and private education. However, higher education institutions are supervised by the Ministry of Higher Education.

The MoE Structure

The Kuwaiti MoE was established to supervise formal education from the pre-primary level to the secondary level. It is structured as a centralized organization responsible for planning, supervising, and controlling the development of education; and the implementation of the education vision. According to the constitution, the Kuwaiti government is obligated to provide free education as a right to all its citizens and assume related expenses such as books, transportation, and meals (International Bureau of Education, 2008).

Since then, Kuwait has allocated a large budget to the MoE. For example, the MoE budget in 2017 was 10% of the country's total budget, reaching 1,692,953,413 (KWD) (almost $5,567,500,768) of total expenditures. The scope of authority and responsibility of the MoE has corresponded to the expansion of education in the state since 1983. Therefore, formal education is divided into public education, special education (e.g., religious education, special-needs education), private education, and youth and adult literacy programs (MoE, 2019). In the public education section, the MoE supervises 831 schools, consisting of 195 kindergartens, 274 elementary schools, 218 middle schools, and 144 high schools, where schools are gender-segregated starting from the elementary stage. The enrollment of students was based on the last MoE report in 2019, consisting of 400,106 students and a teaching staff of 70,317 members. Additionally, the scope of the MoE authority comprises 563 private schools (2,600,617 students), including special-needs schools and classes, 16 public special-needs schools (1,684 students), seven religious education schools (2,622 students), and 75 adult literacy educational programs (16,629 students) (MoE, 2019).

Such a large and complex organization is led by the Minister of Education appointed by the Prime Minister (and other ministers) of the Kuwaiti government in a four-year rotation after the Kuwait Parliament is elected. The Minister of Education appoints members as undersecretaries in the MoE and shapes the board of education in the MoE. The government presents its programs and plans, including the educational goals of the MoE (Alharbi, 2007).

From a structural level, the public education sector handles the following tasks: follow-up policies of the educational process in the various educational districts; studying and analyzing the reports received from them; setting requirements for occupying and assigning leadership roles; coordinating the curriculum and staff training; making decisions related to setting up schools (public and private) based on district needs; setting the yearly calendar for examinations and enrollment; and evaluating the educational process and reports (MOE, 2020).

On the other hand, education districts (or educational areas) are responsible for implementing MoE policies, reporting educational needs, and supervising schools and educational activities (Alrishidi, 2012). They were established according to a movement advocating for a more flattened decentralized education system in response to the demand for education expansion in the late 1970s and early 1980s. The ministry established five new districts: Al-Asema, Hawally, Al-Frawania, Al-Ahmadi, and Al-Jahra, corresponding to the present governorates. At the end of 1999, the sixth educational zone (Mubarak Al-Kabeer) was formed (United Nations Educational Scientific and Cultural Organization & International Bureau of Education, 2011). However, they still did not have recognizable input regarding decision-making. They merely functioned as attached units of the central ministry, rather than as independent entities.

Because of the enormous responsibilities of the MoE, its organizational structure is divided into departments to ensure workflow in such a highly centralized structure (see Figure 10.1). Kuwaiti scholars have requested a revision of the authorities responsible for granting more autonomy to districts and school principals (Almeseliem, 2012; Alsaleh, 2019). Still, more improvement is needed.

Political Reform of Public Education in Kuwait

Reforms in Kuwait have been similar to those of other Arab countries, whereby reform initiatives have been motivated by political agendas (Akkary, 2014). The Kuwaiti education system is influenced by the political context and environment. This starts with selecting the Minister of Education and high-rank leaders, who are appointed by the Prime Minister of the government; they are not elected since Kuwaiti leadership positions are neither chosen nor recruited based on qualification.

Within the MoE centralized structure (see Figure 10.1), decisions are made at the top of the hierarchy in the office of the Minister, consisting of and followed by many direct consultants of organizational units to help create the MoE vision and shape its policy (Alenizi, 2011; MoE, 2022). Such policies are crafted by the Council of Representatives, Permanent Delegation of the State of Kuwait to UNESCO in Paris, Supreme Education Council, Kuwait National Committee for Education, Science and Culture, National Center for Education Development (NCED), and the Assistant Undersecretary for Legal Affairs (MOE, 2020).

The education sector is not separate from the strategic policy of the state. The Kuwait Supreme Council for Planning and Development administers the Kuwait National Development Plan ("The Prime Minister," 2020; World Bank Group, 2021a), including MoE general guidelines. The Department of Planning and Improvement (DoPI) in the MoE receives the Supreme Council of Planning guidelines. DoPI molds teams of MoE staff members who work in several departments of this ministry for all the arrangements required for organizing the planning of procedures and requisitioning data and information necessary for the formulation of this exercise. Thus, the DoPI team manages and gathers information and writes the final report of the plan. The people who occupy high-rank levels of the MoE consist of the Minister, Undersecretary, and Assistant Secretary, who review plans and either provide approval or request further revisions. A copy is sent to the Supreme Council for the Planning and Development of the Strategic Plan document for final approval. This step includes government plans by prelamin members for legal

170 *Amal Abdulwahab Alsaleh*

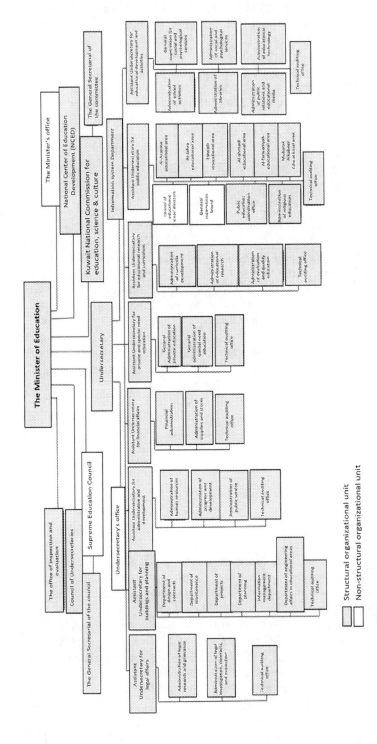

Figure 10.1 The organizational structure of the Ministry of Education (MoE, 2021).

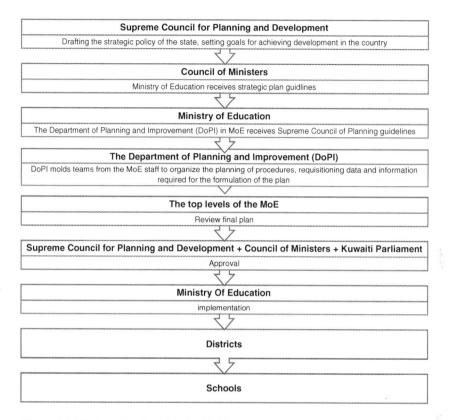

Figure 10.2 Policy planning for the MoE.

approval (Alharbi, 2007). The plans should be put into operation after their final approval, and all levels of education should follow the MoE arrangements to execute them (see Figure 10.2) (Al-hamdan, 1992 as cited in AlKandari, 2013). Nowadays, the Kuwaiti government is under obligation to implement its national development plans for the 2032 vision, for which the MoE handles projects designed to ensure a quality education system (World Bank Group, 2021a).

The main sustainable and impactable reforms are addressed in the 2035 vision target of improving the quality of education. These reforms were led by the NCED, established through Emiri Decree No. 308 of 2006. It aims to develop education by carrying out national education development projects with the help of international and local experts to achieve the best results objectively and impartially (Kuwait Local, n.d.; MoE, 2014). Developmental projects guided by the NCED include curriculum reform, the construction of national assessment systems, the enhancement of school leadership, and the establishment of professional standards (the license and formal evaluation of teachers and higher standards for promotions). Concerning the need for such reforms, the MoE established a continuous development mechanism for the education system, extending from kindergarten to university stages, linked to new developmental skills. This is necessary to develop curricula, raise the performance of teachers, and improve the learning environment available for our children and teachers (MoE 2021,MoE Development and Training Sector 2021).

However, discrepancies appeared in the implementation of these projects. Some of these developmental projects are under development, while others are suspended and understudied because of usability in political decisions. For example, Mathematics, Engineering, and Science Achievement national assessment (MESA) took slow steps toward development since its first experimental conducting in 2012 (Winokur, 2014), while the license project of teachers was still battling political obstacles. Many short-period reform projects were introduced and canceled. An unclear MoE vision results in improvised and sporadic reforms (Alsaleh, 2014). This hesitation in political decisions also appeared when COVID-19 was declared a pandemic, and public education had a delayed response causing more than six months of education suspension (Arar et al., 2022; Alsaleh, 2021a). Alsaleh (2021b) noted that the MoE was facing challenges such as weaknesses in crisis planning and educational decision-making, employment of technologies in distance learning, and difficulties in transferring to online learning. The emergency plans of the MoE were implemented for successful online learning concerning the commencement of education after a lengthy suspension.

Other prominent characteristics of Kuwaiti educational policy have been described in a few studies. AlKandari (2013) described it as "extremely centralized" (p. 222), in line with other studies that also stressed deprived lower levels of participation in decisions (Alkandari, 2013; Alsaleh, 2023; Alsharija & Watters, 2021; World Bank Group, 2019). Further, AlKandari (2013) questioned the efficiency of the education system concerning the massive MoE budget. Efforts of development by Winokur (2014) and AlAjmi (2015) referred to several of these reforms as borrowed policies that needed to be internalized and contextualized to fit the system's needs.

Calls from the previous Minister of Education Alazmi to separate the Supreme Education Council from the MoE structure are necessary to improve educational policymaking. This emphasizes the prominent role of the MoE in the process, rather than being a mere consultant unit ("The prime minister", 2020). Thus, the MoE published a proposal to develop the MoE structure to improve policymaking (MoE, 2013). The MoE's report stated the need to revise policy and development to ensure that its consistent, includes more efficient spending according to the budget, and develops a partnership with all stakeholders (MoE, 2014) (Figure 10.3).

Little is written about the formulation of Kuwaiti educational policy and its relation to EDLD studies. Alenizi (2011) explained that policy formation is a consultative process that links many organizations such as the Supreme Education Council, UNESCO, and Kuwait Supreme Council for Planning

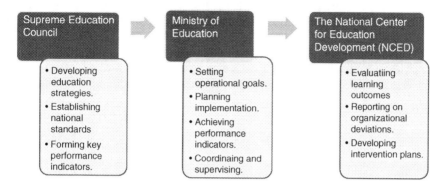

Figure 10.3 Proposal for the future development of the MoE structure (MoE, 2013).

and Development. At the same time, all opinions that come down from district and committee results do not obligate the Minister of Education to appoint MoE undersecretaries who have decision-making authority. Alenizi (2011) and Alharbi (2007) also explained that such policies did not benefit from EDLDR studies and that there was a noticeable gap between academic research and practice.

Public School Administration and Leadership in Kuwait: A Response to Reforms

The school administration formally comprises representatives at the school level. These are principals, assistant principals, and headteachers who possess formal power in supervising the school process (Alsaleh, 2014). One school principal and assistant principal (two or three) are assigned to every school structured according to their departments, consisting of teachers according to their teaching subjects. In every department, the heads of teachers responsible for implementing the subjects and curriculum work closely with teachers and students (Alsaleh, 2022). All school administration members are presented with a detailed job description, allowing them to separate and organize school tasks in the hierarchy of the school system.

School principals follow up on instructional supervision of the national curriculum based on the preliminary plans and timetables of the MoE, manage their schools by forming committees, evaluate teachers, and communicate formally with the district (MoE, 1999). Principals are promoted to leadership positions based on their experience with the MoE. Such experience includes at least five years as a successful teacher, after about another five years as a successful head of department, and promotion to vice-principal before becoming principal. The current requirements for becoming a vice-principal include specific years of teaching experience (different by major), passing a test, and completing a two-week training program. The candidate must also possess an outstanding evaluation report (for the previous two years as vice-principal). These indicate a favorable awareness of several critical leadership aspects (National Institution of Education, 2013). The MoE updated its policy for promotions to supervisory positions, resulting in heavy teacher employment in some majors (e.g., social studies, art, physical education), as well as certain levels of education. Consequently, specific teachers must wait in a long line for promotions to head departments, followed by vice-principals and principals.

School administration in Kuwait is influenced by waves of reforms and changes in school routines, instruction, and practices. Some reforms have completely changed public schools. One of these changes is seen in the school ladder from 4–4–4 years (four elementary, four middle, and four high schools) to 5–4–3 years (five elementary, four middle, and three high schools). Other reforms have had a shorter impact on schools because of their short implementation period, and many have ended without sufficient studies.

From 2010 onward, a main multi-year integrated program of reform was implemented by the MoE, addressing critical aspects (e.g., leadership, quality curriculum, effective teaching, and a quality learning environment). This reform occurred within schools supervised by the National Education Development Center (NCDC) in cooperation with the World Bank to realize the Kuwait 2025 vision (Alkhoja et al., 2014). A new school structure was proposed by assigning new assistant principals, and self-evaluation methods were adopted. Upon the first implementation of the reform within schools, AlAjmi (2015) investigated the influence of the reform on school performance and found that reformed schools experimented with growth in organizational development and the organizational environment compared to other schools. The primary structural adjustments aided organizational development (e.g., adding a third assistant principal and establishing a data gathering and analysis department). Therefore, school principals in experimental schools were more effective in the domain of the organizational environment since they had more time to focus on creating connections and leadership rather than management-based activities. It was concluded that structural modifications were designed to encourage the birth and implementation of a new reform-promoting culture. However, AlAjmi (2015) observed no differences in the instructional leadership domain. Later, Alsaleh (2019) clarified that school leaders applied the reform differently. Based on school context and obstacles school principals face, they practiced instructional leadership where some schools had high performance, and others had low performance. In her (2022) study, excellent Kuwaiti schools used data to mentor and diagnose the academic performance of students and make instructional changes due to the reform. In contrast, Alajmi (2022) showed that autonomy in Kuwaiti public schools remained constrained due to regulations and stringent accountability requirements by the MoE. This was contrary to what the school reform initiative had intended to achieve.

Regarding the newly developed competency-based curriculum that became mandatory in 2016, mixed results for success have been shown in previous studies. Al-Kendri (2020) revealed that active learning is supported by a competency-based curriculum, encouraging discussion and questioning, and enhancing technology usage by teachers. However, Mohammad (2021) revealed that science teachers face difficulties with the new curriculum in classroom implementation and related activities and evaluations. At the same time, Alshatti (2019) revealed challenges related to time and the high number of students. Teachers called for help, support, and professional training from the leaders of schools (particularly department heads and principals of higher authority) while dealing with difficulties that needed to be heard.

In 2020, a critical reform that shaped the school administration in Kuwait was online teaching conducted during the COVID-19 period. Leaders and teachers confronted a seemingly insurmountable challenge during such a time when online teaching started, on top of their poor preparation and lack of basic infrastructure in schools (Alsaleh, 2021b). During the formation of school communities, the relationship between leaders and school staff facilitated change and overcame obstacles (Alsaleh, 2021a; 2021b).

The mission of school leaders, either in Kuwait or internationally, is more complex than ever before, given these continuous and unexpected changes. They must overcome challenges, reform tasks, and build leadership capacity that influences the performance of students (Alsaeedi & Male, 2013; Alsaleh, 2019). Other challenges faced in Kuwaiti schools include low achievement of students, weak information structure, unstable Ministry decisions, and more recently, the need to cope with unexpected crises (Alsaleh, 2019, 2021; Alsharija & Watters, 2021). Thus, it was noticed in the EDLDR research that school principals' practices have been developed toward including shared and democratic forms of leadership (Al Rasheedi, 2010) or participative style (Al-Hamdan & Al-Fadli, 2008). They also practice instructional leadership to some degree (Alsaleh, 2019; 2020), distribution, or shared leadership (Alanezi, 2016; Alsaleh, 2014), and transformative leadership (Alsaeedi & Male, 2013). However, the need to pay more attention to school leadership preparation and development programs for school leaders to keep up with their continuously updated leadership roles has been recommended in many studies (Alsaleh, 2022; Alsaeedi & Male, 2013; AlAjmi, 2015; Al-Yaseen & Al-Musaileem, 2015; National Institution of Education, 2013).

Regardless of the positive aspects of reforms in improving school leadership, reforms could not contribute to removing the obstacles that school administration faced in light of the weak communication and reaction from the MoE such as limited autonomy for staff, equipment, and maintenance (Alganim, 1990; Alsaleh, 2019; 2021). Specifically, teachers do not participate in the decision-making process or shape professional development and are always responsible for supervising school leaders (Al-Yaseen & Al-Musaileem, 2015). It was shown in some studies that school leaders are typically restrained by limited autonomy and a dearth of pertinent input for major education decisions (AlAjmi, 2015; Al-Hamdan & Al-Fadli, 2008; Alsaleh, 2021; 2019; Al-Yaseen & Al-Musaileem, 2015). At the same time, the performance of Kuwaiti students reached the bottom rank in the international comparative test Trends in International Mathematics and Science Study (TIMSS) (Mullis et al., 2020). Such a result raised serious questions about the influence of educational reform policies and development.

Positive Indicators of Achievement in Educational Leadership

MoE political leaders have garnered triumphs in enhancing formal education in the country. Achievement is manifested in both quantitative and qualitative measures. The Kuwait government legislated compulsory free-of-charge education for all Kuwaiti children from the first grade of primary education (age six) up to the completion of the intermediate or preparatory level. This is regulated by Law No. 1 of 1965, in which the expansion of public education in the country is explained (United Nations Educational Scientific and Cultural Organization & International Bureau of Education, 2011). Because of such a policy, data on literacy rate growth patterns demonstrate the commitment of Kuwait to building a robust and effective education system (96.461% in 15 and above) (World Bank Group, 2021b) which is decently ranked internationally. Still, the literacy rate was only 48.3% in 1970 (Ministry of Education, 2014).

In light of political decisions moving toward the universal access to education, Kuwait has achieved pre-primary enrollment of students of 82.5% (UNESCO, 2015b), indicating the attention paid by the MoE leaders to kindergarten education in the public and private sectors. Additionally, some quality metrics were high in Kuwait such as the student–teacher ratio (with an average of seven) and pupils per class ratio (26:1) on average (MoE, 2019). Moreover, after multiple reforms and revisions, the national curriculum of Kuwait was established and published including standards for the curriculum associated with students' required skills nationally (MoE, 2021). The country ranked fourth lowest in mathematics scores internationally. In response to this fact, the political decision by MoE leaders was fruitful in increasing student performance in TIMSS international test 2015–2019 from 353 to 383 in mathematics (average score 500), 337–392 in science achievement for the fourth grade. At the same time, the gap in the Average Achievement in Mathematics test by girls was closed in Kuwait. Additionally, eighth graders' results also improved in mathematics and science (Mullis et al., 2020).

Regarding quality teaching standards, it was shown that 96.5% of teachers in the Kuwaiti education system had a bachelor's degree in 2014. Therefore, the MoE decided to provide professional training for teachers with an International Certificate of Digital Literacy (ICDL)—a computer skills certificate—before hiring them (MoE, 2014).

Based on the substantial total public expenditure on education amounting to 10% of the gross national product (GNP) (MoE, 2019), the Kuwaiti educational policy gives priority to special-needs students, and reports comprehensive data regarding such students (UNESCO, 2015b). The MoE is bound by Law No. 8 of 2010 concerning the rights of people with disabilities. In Article 4, the MoE is obligated to provide educational services at all levels for disabled students (Law No. 8, 2010). The Ministry established 16 special-needs schools (1684 students) for students with disabilities, including visual impairment, hearing, and mute impairment, Down syndrome, and autism. At the same time, the MoE also supports citizens with disabilities in their choice of private schools that provide special-needs services.

Other slow but successful steps in educational policy targeted the higher education sector, which has expanded in Kuwait. Starting with KU, this sector expanded to include 15 active higher education institutions in Kuwait: 3 public and 12 private. Besides free education for citizens of public higher education institutions, Kuwait annually provides full scholarships for nearly 4000 students who wish to study at private Kuwaiti universities. Additionally, up to 6000 Kuwaiti citizens received full scholarships to study abroad (Oxford Business Group, 2017).

Accountability is one positive feature that characterizes educational policy in Kuwait. This means that the Minister of Education is held accountable for commitment to high proficiency standards and correct deviation in the MoE performance by the Kuwaiti Parliament (National Assembly)(Herb, 2016). According to the Kuwait Constitution (Article 113), an elected member has an accountability tool to express their opinions, desires, and questions. Also, they are empowered to direct interrogations to the Prime Minister and the other ministers on matters falling within their competence (Article 100) (Kuwait Constitution, 1962). Based on this constitutional right, Kuwaiti Parliament history witnessed eight interrogations into the Minister of Education (National Assembly State of Kuwait, 2021). Al-eneze (2012) indicated the impact of parliamentary accountability on the performance of the educational administration in the MoE. This impact was shown in developing the administrative system, clarifying roles, defining responsibilities, and correcting deviations (that may exist in the actual performance) away from planned goals, besides ensuring the legalization of the new law under the accountability system.

Shortcomings and Challenges Associated with Education Policy in Kuwait

The challenges that are confronted by education in Kuwait are multifaceted. The most prominent aspect concerns political decisions that guide the entire public education system to achieve the vision 2005–2025. Though major feats have been achieved, education in Kuwait still suffers from organizational impediments.

One factor that appeared to influence the quality of education was the absence of stable political decisions and fragmented, inconsistent reforms. This point of instability in policymaking refers to changing the composition of the government (MoE, 2014). Specifically, the Ministers of Education from

2004 to 2021 (11) led the MoE, with most of them leaving without completing a regular period (four years) of duration. Such continuous instability was due to tension between opposition members of the Kuwaiti parliament and the government, which influenced the entire political status and the dynamics of the MoE. Thus, such a situation results in instability (Ulrichsen, 2014).

Additionally, political interference in educational issues raised by politicians in the National Assembly affects the general formulation of educational policies and the decisions of MoE ministers. At the same time, it does not guarantee policy implementation. The results of such accountability practices by elected members in the Kuwaiti parliament (question or interrogation) for the Minister of Education are also a question of whether to place their trust in him. This does not include the power to force the Minister to implement the planned policy—"The minister determines the Ministry's policies and supervises their execution" (Article 130) (Kuwait Constitution, 1962). Thus, changing or altering educational policies is under the power of only the Minister of Education. Such a status can be a double-edged sword. On the one hand, the Minister of Education is questioned and held accountable by members of parliament. On the other hand, the Minister of Education cannot select, replace, or be forced to implement this or that policy by parliament members. Because of a hybrid political system categorized by authoritarianism and openness (Ulrichsen, 2014), education was suspended throughout the pandemic for more than six months. This situation happened based on the decisions of the Minister, regardless of the demands of the Kuwaiti parliament and the population.

Unfortunately, educational policy in Kuwait is not based on extensive scientific studies, nor is it guided by a clear philosophy and vision (Alenizi, 2011). This makes it unclear and oriented toward management and daily operations. Besides studies about the reform, systematic documentation of educational reforms is missing (Alenizi, 2011), making it hard for researchers or academics to build cumulative experiences from previous reforms. What makes planning more efficient is internalizing reforms instead of borrowing them (Winokur, 2014) as well as focusing on sets of beliefs, values, assumptions, and norms that shape contextual factors that influence reform success (Akkary, 2014).

Additionally, the lack of capacity and structure for empowering the involvement of educators in decisions influenced the quality of political decisions. Education policies were issued in legislation by high-rank leaders in the MoE (Alharbi, 2007). Thus, Kuwaiti educators are deprived of shaping educational policy (Alkandari, 2013; Alsaeedi & Male, 2013; Alsaleh, 2014; Alsharija & Watters, 2021). Moreover, when reform is applied, the deprivation of educators from decisions might decrease their strong support, enthusiasm, adaptation, and learning. The resistance of educators and leaders to change might hinder attempts to increase education quality, relevance, and cost efficiency by preventing changes from being carried out by directors, teachers, parents, and others (AlAjmi, 2015). Thus, the building capacity for the reform is one factor that improves reform implementation in Kuwait (AlAjmi, 2015; Alsaleh, 2019; Alsharija & Watters, 2021). At the same time, educational reforms and policies in Kuwait need more autonomy for leaders to achieve reform goals. Studies have highlighted the need for school principals for more transformation, authority, and autonomy to fulfill their leadership role, not a management role. For example, control over budget, spending avenues, and staff development are essential in responding to the daily needs of schools (Alsaeedi & Male, 2013; Alsaleh, 2019; Alsharija & Watters, 2021).

Moreover, there is a shortage of community participation in educational matters in Kuwait, possibly due to the lack of a necessary structure for such involvement. According to Alharbi (2007), social and educational organizations concerned with education do not participate in the Ministry of Education's educational policy (for instance, Kuwaiti teachers' union, Arab Center for Educational Studies, and Supreme Education Council). There is an existing gap between all educational organizations that can help MoE frame national educational policy, like Kuwait University, private universities, and the teachers union.

Alharbi (2007) asserted the absence of social and educational organizations concerned about education in participation in the Ministry of Education policy (e.g., the union of Kuwaiti teachers, the Arabic Center for Educational Studies in Arab Gulf countries, and the Supreme Education Council). An existing gap is available between all educational organizations that can help MoE in framing national educational policy such as Kuwait University college education, private universities, and teacher union.

As a result, Kuwait still faces quality-related challenges in its education policies. According to the Human Capital Index Report (2020), learning-adjusted years of schooling are only 7.4 years. At the end of primary school, 51% of ten-year-olds could not read and understand a simple text. Such poor performance results need to be considered when revising educational policies, with a greater focus on factors that directly influence teaching and learning. Specifically, it focuses on learning, not schooling, by enhancing creative thinking, inquiries, and memorization (World Bank Group, 2019). The educational policy failed to shape classroom practices that rely heavily on studying for testing, which calls for emergent change.

The Emergence of EDLM in Kuwait: Knowledge Production in National and International Fields

The number of higher education institutions in Kuwait has grown in recent decades. The College of Education at Kuwait University was established in 1981 (College of Education, 2018) and consisted of an educational administration and a planning department. Since then, faculty members have increased to 16 Kuwaiti professors in 2022. These professors earned their doctorate degrees from reputable universities in EDLM, targeting many areas. Such areas include educational leadership, educational planning and development, quality management, educational supervision, educational-related law, educational communication, higher education, educational economics, and special-needs administration. Faculty members at Kuwait University published most research on EDLM in both Arabic (to target the general population of educators and leaders in Kuwait) and in English (in international journals that targeted international educators, practicians, and leaders) (e.g., Alanezi, 2016; Alajmi, 2022; AlKandari, 2012; Alsaleh, 2021, 2022). Such publications are essential to raise awareness of EDLM practices and solutions related to the Kuwaiti context. However, most articles were published in Arabic.

Kuwait University was the first and only institution in Kuwait to start an education unified Master's degree program in 2003, including educational administration and planning program specializations. In 2017, the unified Master of Education program was separated into several programs, one of which was the Master's program in Educational Administration and Planning (Dean of Graduate Studies College, 2017). The program aims to provide learners with the knowledge base and research skills needed in educational leadership practices. In 2021, 63 students were enrolled in the program. 43 students graduated from the program between 2016 and 2020 and committed to writing a Master's dissertation or a graduation study project targeting EDLDR-related topics and issues. Additionally, EDLM, as a field, can be studied abroad through scholarships provided by some institutions in Kuwait, based on institutional needs such as the Public Authority for Applied Education and Training, or the MoE. Many educators may also study abroad at their own expense at an accredited university, which can afford them many job benefits such as promotion and leadership positions.

Such substantial publication in EDLD was not benefited by the MoE guiding the policy or educational reform. Arar (2020) explained that a complete separation is available between educational policy formatting, government-driven agenda, and research development in the educational administration field. Scholars in the EDLD field call to use research results in educational policy formation. They also recommended closing this gap between policymakers at the Ministry of Education, schools, and academic institutions such as colleges of education.

Future Improvement Kuwait EDLM: Universal Values and Lessons to Learn

The globalization of education has significantly affected what is taught and tested in various educational systems in the Middle East (Arar, 2020). Kuwait still has a long way to attain a high-quality education as a developing country.

Specifically, the EDLM field in Kuwait is still evolving around balancing international values and internal challenges. The State of Kuwait has signed several international human rights agreements and treaties, including the Elimination of All Forms of Racial Discrimination, Rights of the Child, and Discrimination Against Women, Civil and Political Rights, Social, and Cultural Rights (Ministry of Foreign Affairs, n.d.). Educational organizations are obligated to follow these treaties. Still, international values, such as equity and social justice, fall short, especially in regard to the added complexity of ethnic diversity whereby the total population consists of three groups: 45% Kuwaitis, Kuwaiti Bedouin, and non-Kuwaiti (UNESCO, 2022).

The social justice issues of the Kuwaiti education system are centered on efforts to provide financial support to minorities and low-income students, such as the Bedouin (stateless people), as a response to the injustice associated with human rights calls. After the pandemic, a noticeable gap was found in the learning of the students depending on socioeconomic status, since some families could not provide an internet connection or devices for their children (Alsaleh, 2021a). However, more studies are required to discover and analyze this achievement gap. Regarding gender equality, a UNESCO (2022) study revealed a considerable gender gap in education in Kuwait, placing males at a disadvantage. Males have lower levels of achievement than females, especially in reading, science, and mathematics, as well as higher rates of repetition, poorer participation in higher education, and a shorter school life expectancy. Regardless, most leadership positions are occupied by males. Specifically, in the EDLDR field, women fulfill many roles such as Minister of Education, undersecretary of Education, supervisors, and school leaders. Leadership positions held by women are set back due to cultural issues. For example, Al-Suwaihel (2010) showed that Kuwaiti males have more chances of getting nominated to leadership positions since they have greater social relationships and a wider social network. Thus, females have to work harder to show their capabilities for top positions in organizations. From 1962 to 2022, 23 Ministers of Education led the MoE, but only two were females. This may raise serious questions about gender equity and invite the need for solutions in order to offer equal opportunities for women to occupy leadership positions.

Regarding internal challenges, educational policies and reforms must be seen as systematic. Additionally, sustainable improvements should be based on a common mission instead of fragmented projects. In practice, educational policy in Kuwait lacks consistency. Besides outside political pressure on the ministers of education, the continuous change of ministers of education are factors that shape fragmented policies. It is recommended that a Minister of Education stay in their formal position for at least ten years to demonstrate an individual commitment to implement the policies.

Benefiting from the expertise of researchers in the EDLDR field, extensive studies must be conducted before any educational reform is adopted, ensuring that contextual and cultural factors are considered to guarantee its success. Reforms must be studied, evaluated, and explained to raise success and failure factors. They should also be thoroughly and systematically documented to shape a valuable source of information that speaks to the context of Kuwaiti education. Thus, they would open doors and activate partnerships between the MoE and higher education institutions, such as Kuwait University, which is the keystone in combining academic research with field experience that would guide education in the country.

Participation in decision-making is necessary to draw a realistic picture of schools regarding the performance of students and human needs. It is recommended that the MoE create a structure that facilitates building capacity at the school (e.g., school leaders and educators) and district levels. Such a structure will encourage their participation in new policies. A graduate transformation toward more autonomous schools is needed. Additionally, revisions of the school skills of principals and more significant efforts in their selection, preparation, and professional development to make them more successful are needed.

Additionally, social and professional communities, such as the unions of teachers and students, parent groups, and the participation of politician unions, in educational decision-making must correspond to a general interest in education. When education faces crises or new changes, the skills of national experts, education professors, and other educators in their respective fields must be leveraged to achieve an optimal outcome. Additionally, opportunities should be provided to guide education for future success.

A comprehensive roadmap is needed for the overall system assessment, especially concerning the low results in the international TIMSS comparative test (Mullis et al., 2020). Thus, developing accreditation for the national MESA evaluation is recommended to evaluate the performance of the students in the main subjects in public schools and indicate the overall system performance.

Moreover, the activation of the role of the Supreme Education Council as an independent unit to develop education strategies gives it the power to supervise the implementation of educational strategies. Consequently, it would be able to guarantee its continuity and protect educational policies and decisions from deviating from the education vision, planned goals, and agreed values. An overall evaluation of the educational system taking into consideration equality, social justice, and gender equity is needed to provide education for all.

References

Al eneze, M. (2012). Athar masayilih albarlaman alkuaytiu ealaa "ada" aladarat altarbawiat min khilal alai [The impact of accountability of the Kuwaiti Parliament of the Minister of Education and Higher Education on the performance of management education: An analytical study]. *Journal of Childhood and Education*, 4(10), 105–146.

Al-Hamdan, J. (1992). *Altakhtit altarbawiu fi alkuayt'ahamiyatuh wawaqieuh [Educational planning in Kuwait: Its importance and reality]*. Kuwaiti Teachers' Assembly, Kuwait University.

Al-Hamdan, J., & Al-Fadli, K. (2008). Al'anmat alqiadiat alsaayidat ladaa mudiri madaris altaelim aleami bidawlat alkuayt bihasab alnazariat almawqifia [Leadership styles for Kuwait public school principals according to situational theory]. *King Saud University Journal for Educational and Islamic Science*, 20(2), 606–605.

Al-Kendri, K. (2020). Min almanhaj alqayim ealaa al'ahdaf 'iilaa almanhaj alqayim eali alkifayat fi dawlat alkuayti: min wijhat nazar muealimat altarbiat al'iislamia [From objectives-based curriculum to competencies-based curriculum in Kuwait Islamic studies teachers' perspectives]. *Educational Journal-Kuwait University*, 34(135), 13–47.

Al-Suwaihel, O. (2010). Kuwaiti female leaders' perspectives: The influence of culture on their leadership. *Contemporary Issues in Education Research*, 3(3), 29–40.

Al Rasheedi, A. (2010). *Al'anmat alqiadiat fi almarhalat almutawasitat fi dawlat alkuayt waealaqatiha bialwala' altanzimii lilmuealimin [School leadership styles in Kuwaiti middle schools and its relation to teachers' organizational commitment from their viewpoint perception]*. [Unpublished Master's thesis. Middle East University].

Al-Rashoud, T. (2017). *Modern education and Arab nationalism in Kuwait* [Doctoral dissertation, SOAS University of London]. https://eprints.soas.ac.uk/24384/1/Al-Rashoud_4381.pdf

Al-Shatti, Y. (2019). Waqie tatbiq manhaj aleulum alqayim ealaa alkifayat min khilal muealimat aleulum fi almarhalat alaibtidayiyat bidawlat alkuayt: dirasat wasfiatan tahliliatan [The reality of applying the competency-based science curriculum through the opinions of science teachers at the primary stage in the State of Kuwait: A descriptive and analytical study]. *Journal of Gulf and Arabian Peninsula Studies*, 45(173), 319–362.

Al-Yaseen, W., & Al-Musaileem, M. (2015). Teacher potential as an important component of job satisfaction: A comparative study of teachers' perspectives in Al-Farwaniya District, Kuwait. *Compare*, 45(6), 863–885. 10.1080/03057925.2013.855006

Akkary, R. K. (2014). Facing the challenges of educational reform in the Arab world. *Journal of Educational Change*, 15(2), 179–202. 10.1007/s10833-013-9225-6

Alabdulghafoor, F. (1983). *Tatawur altaelim fi alkuayt [The development of education in Kuwait]*. Alfalah Publisher

Alajmi, M. (2015). *The impact of a pilot program aimed at developing effective school leadership in Kuwait*. [PhD dissertation, The Pennsylvania State University]. https://eric.ed.gov/?id=ED584193

Alajmi, M. (2022). School principals' experiences of autonomy and accountability: Outcomes of the school education quality improvement project in Kuwait. *International Journal of Educational Management*, 36(4), 606–617. 10.1108/IJEM-09-2021-0366

Alenizi, K. (2011). Dawr buhuth al'iidarat altaelimiat fi sune alsiyasat altaelimiat fi dawlat alkuayt [*The role of educational management research in making educational policy in the state of Kuwait*]. [Unpublished Master's dissertation]. Kuwait University. http://catalog.library.kuniv.edu.kw/ipac20/ipac.jsp?session=C58M4414354B5.37669&profile=ara&uri=full%3D3100027%7E%21244786%7E%210&booklistformat=

Alanezi, A. (2016). The relationship between shared leadership and administrative creativity in Kuwaiti schools. *Management in Education*, 30(2), 50–56.

Alganim, A. (1990). Aladarat almadrasiat waealaqatuha balundart altarbawiat fi dawlat alkuayt [The relationship between school administration and educational administration in the State of Kuwait]. *Educational Studies*, 5(25), 214–246.

Alharbi, S. (2007). *Ruyat tahliliat naqdiat fi mushkilat fi alsiyasat altaelimiat fi dawlat alkuayt [A critical analytical view of a problem in educational policy in the State of Kuwait]*. Unpublished document. Ministry of Education Library

AlKandari, E. M. (2013). *Perceptions of the effectiveness of Kuwait strategic education planning policy and processes*. [Doctoral dissertation, University of Leads].

AlKandari, N. (2012). Students' communication and positive outcomes in college classrooms. *Education, 133*(1), 19–30.

Alkhoja, G., Halabi, S., Abdullah, M., & Al-Shamali, F. (2014). *Kuwait education program achievement report: School Education Quality Improvement Program*. The world Bank.

Almeseliem, M. (2012). Difficulties facing empowering school principals from the viewpoint of school district leaders in the State of Kuwait. *Educational Journal in Kuwait, 2*(103), 53–87.

Alrishidi, G. (2012). *Alnizam altarbawii waltaelimii fi dawlat alkuayt [The education and educational system in the State of Kuwait]*. Alfalah Publisher.

Alsaeedi, F, & Male, T. (2013). Transformational leadership and globalization: Attitudes of school principals in Kuwait. *Educational Management Administration & Leadership, 41*(5), 640–657. 10.1177/1741143213488588

Alsaleh, A. (2014). The relationship between the perception of distributed leadership and the degree of participation in ministry decision on teachers' organizational commitment in the State of Kuwait [The Pennsylvania State University]. *Pennsylvania State University* (Issue May). https://www.proquest.com/docview/1826352873?pq-origsite=gscholar&fromopenview=true

Alsaleh, A. (2019). Investigating educational leadership in Kuwait's educational reform context: School leaders' perspectives. *School Leadership and Management, 39*(1), 96–120. 10.1080/13632434.2018.1467888

Alsaleh, A. (2022). The influence of heads of departments' instructional leadership, cooperation, and administrative support on school-based professional learning in Kuwait. *Educational Management Administration & Leadership, 50*(5), 832–850. 10.1177/1741143220953597

Alsaleh, A. (2021a). The roles of school principals and head teachers in mitigating potential learning loss in the online setting: Calls for change. *International Journal of Educational Management, 35*(7), 1525–1537

Alsaleh, A. (2021b). Professional learning communities for educators' capacity building during COVID-19: Kuwait educators' successes and challenges. *International Journal of Leadership in Education*, 1–20. 10.1080/13603124.2021.1964607

Alsaleh, A. (2023). Investigating the use of data to inform instructional leadership and build data-use capacity: Case studies in Kuwaiti context. *Leadership and Policy in Schools, 22*(3), 746–764. 10.1080/15700763.2021.2019791

Alsharija, M., & Watters, J. (2021). Secondary school principals as change agents in Kuwait: Principals' perspectives. *Educational Management Administration & Leadership. 49*(6), 883–903. 10.1177/1741143220925090

Arar, K., Sawalhi, R., Chaaban, Y., Zohri, A., & Alhouti, I. (2022). School leaders' perspectives towards leading during crisis through an ecological lens: A comparison of five Arab countries. *Journal of Educational Administration and History, 54*(2), 123–142.

Arar, K. (2020). Educational Administration in the Middle East. In *Oxford Research Encyclopedia of Education*. Retrieved 18 Aug. 2023, from https://oxfordre.com/education/view/10.1093/acrefore/9780190264093.001.0001/acrefore-9780190264093-e-672

Coates Ulrichsen, K. (2014). Politics and opposition in Kuwait: Continuity and change. *Journal of Arabian Studies, 4,* 214–230.
College of Education (2018). *Mubdhat tarikhiat ean alkulia* [The history of the college] http://kuweb.ku.edu.kw/COE/ar/CollegeManagement/index.htm.
Dean of Graduate Studies College (2017). Unpublished official document.
Herb, M. (2016). The origins of Kuwait's national assembly. *LSE Kuwait Program Paper Series, 39,* 1–26. https://eprints.lse.ac.uk/65693/1/39_MichaelHerb.pdf
International Bureau of Education, U. K. N. C. for E. and S. (2008). The national report development of education in the State of Kuwait 2004–2008. http://www.ibe.unesco.org/fileadmin/user_upload/archive/National_Reports/ICE_2008/kuwait_NR08.pdf
Kuwait's Constitution of 1962, https://www.constituteproject.org/constitution/Kuwait_1992.pdf?lang=en
Kuwait Fund (2015). https://kuwait-fund.org/en/web/kfund/general-information
Kuwait Government e-gate (2022). *Open data.* https://e.gov.kw/sites/kgoenglish/Pages/OtherTopics/OpenData.aspx
Kuwait Local (n.d.). The National Center for Education Development. https://kuwaitlocal.com/ar/business/national-center-for-education-development-sharq.
"Law no 8." (2010). *Law number 8 of 2010 for the rights of people with disabilities.* https://www.ilo.org/dyn/natlex/docs/ELECTRONIC/89501/102841/F-1202766234/KALD20110318.pdf
MoE website (n.d).
MoE (1999). *Dalil Alwaseef Alwadifi [Guide for job description].* Development Department in MoE.
MoE (2014). *Alkuaytu: taqrir aliastierad alwatanii liltaelim liljamie bihulul eam 2015 [Kuwait: Education for all 2015 National Review Report].* https://unesdoc.unesco.org/ark:/48223/pf0000229886
MoE (2019). *Almajmueat alahisayiyat liltaelim [Educational statistical group]. Educational facilities and planning sector.* Planning Department.
MoE (2020). *Aikhtisasat qitae altaelim aleami [Specializations in the public education sector].* https://moe.edu.kw/about/Pages/MinistryHierarchy/ges.aspx
MoE (2022). *Alaikhtisasat alrayiysiat limaeali wazir altarbia [The main functions of his highness the Minister of Education].* https://moe.edu.kw/about/Pages/Ministry%20Hierarchy/MinisterOffice.aspx
MoE (2021) *Alwehdat Altandimiyah lilwezara* [Organizational structure for the Ministry of Education]. https://moe.edu.kw/about/Pages/Ministry%20Hierarchy/MinisterOffice.aspx
MoE (2013). *Al'iitar almarjieii waltanfidhii libarnamaj wizarat altarbiat nahw tatwir almanzumat altaelimiat fi alkuayt [The reference and implementation framework for the Ministry of Education program toward developing the educational system in Kuwait].* https://moe.edu.kw/docs/Wathaiq/ReferenceFram/ReferenceFram.pdf
MoE Development and Training Sector (2021). *Khutat albaramij altadribia [Training programs plan].Kuwait Ministry of Education publication.* https://moe.edu.kw/employee/Pages/trainingSchedule.aspx
Ministry of Foreign Affairs (n.d.). *State of Kuwait's efforts in the field of human rights.* Retrieved from: https://www.mofa.gov.kw/en/kuwait-state/state-kuwaits-efforts-field-human-rights/

Mohammad, A. (2021). Mueawiqat al'ada' altadrisii alati tuajih muealimi almarhalat alaibtidayiyat fi dawd almanhaj alwatanii aljadid alkifayat [*Teaching performance obstacles that facing elementary school teachers in the new national school curriculum (competencies) in the State of Kuwait*]. Journal of Education-Ain Shams, 44(4), 321–376.

Mullis, I. V. S., Martin, M. O., Foy, P., Kelly, D. L., & Fishbein, B. (2020). *TIMSS 2019: International results in mathematics and science*. TIMSS & PIRLS International Study Center, Lynch School of Education and Human Development, Boston College and International Association for the Evaluation of Educational Achievement (IEA).

National Assembly State of Kuwait (2021). *Integration in the history of Kuwaiti parliamentary life.* http://www.kna.kw/clt-html5/run.asp?id=1971

National Institution of Education (2013). A diagnostic study of education in Kuwait. https://www.nie.edu.sg/nienews/jun13/18-02.html

Oxford Business Group (2017). Government reforms to change Kuwait's education sector. https://oxfordbusinessgroup.com/overview/time-transition-extensive-government-reforms-signal-change-kuwait%E2%80%99s-education-sector

The Prime Minister: An important role of the Supreme Council for Planning in drawing up the strategic policy (2020, July). Alanba Newspaper. https://www.alanba.com.kw/ar/kuwait-news/978471/02-07-2020

The Minister of Education stresses the necessity of the independence of the Supreme Education Council from education (2019, April 11). Kuwait News Agency. https://www.kuna.net.kw/ArticleDetails.aspx?id=2788003#

UNESCO (2022). Leave no child behind: Boy's disengagement from education Kuwait case study. Retrieved from https://unesdoc.unesco.org/ark:/48223/pf0000381174

UNESCO (2015a). *Education for all 2000–2015: Achievements and challenges.* In EFA Global Monitoring Report.

UNESCO (2015b). Education for all 2015 regional review. https://unesdoc.unesco.org/ark:/48223/pf0000232941

United Nations Educational, Scientific and Cultural Organization & International Burial of Education (2011). *World data on education.* In World Data on Education. http://www.ibe.unesco.org/en/document/world-data-education-seventh-edition-2010-11

Winokur, I. K. (2014). From centralized education to innovation: Cultural shifts in Kuwait's education system. In *International Perspectives on Education and Society*, 24. Emerald Group Publishing Limited. 10.1108/S1479-3679201400024013

World Bank Group (2019). *Expectations and aspirations: A new framework for education in the Middle East and North Africa.* Overview booklet. World Bank. Retrieved from https://openknowledge.worldbank.org/handle/10986/30618

World Bank Group (2021a). State of Kuwait; World Bank country engagement framework 2021–2025. Retrieved from https://thedocs.worldbank.org/en/doc/06a7eba0bc51a01f8b1e4ba80be0bcdf-0280012021/state-of-kuwait-world-bank-country-engagement-framework-2021-2025

World Bank Group (2021b). Literacy rate, adult total (% of people ages 15 and above) https://data.worldbank.org/indicator/SE.ADT.LITR.ZS?most_recent_value_desc=true

11 K-12 Educational Leadership and Administration in Qatar

Lessons Learned

Abdellatif Sellami, Rania Sawalhi, and Asmaa E. Al-Fadala

The Context of Qatar

Qatar is the second-smallest country in the Arabian Gulf, with an approximate land area of 11,500 km² which has made considerable efforts to channel oil and gas wealth to the improvement of the quality of its educational system in order to achieve its national priorities on par with international standards (Brewer et al., 2007). Under the British Protectorate and before the discovery of oil in Qatar, the country did not have a formal educational system. The Kuttab, also known as the "traveling educators," mostly ran education, teaching Arabic and the Quran (Alkhater, 2016; Nasser, 2017). The first school was opened in 1948 for boys in Doha, the capital of Qatar. More public schools were gradually opened, and, in the mid-1950s, the Ministry of Education, called *Wizarat Al-Maarif*, was established and became one of the first government ministries in Qatar (Alkhater, 2016).

Historically, the system of education in Qatar was imported from Egyptian and Kuwaiti systems (Alfadala et al, 2021). In its earliest stages, schooling was mainly provided for boys, with girls' education supported by opening the first school for girls in 1956 (Al-Banai & Nasser, 2015). All school subjects were taught in Arabic, except English. At present, K-12 education in Qatar is compulsory and schools are segregated based on gender. The educational sector consists of primary (grades 1–6), preparatory (grades 7–9), and secondary (grades 10–12) divisions. Students attend school five days a week, beginning at the age of six. The number of school days and hours has increased from 130 days in the 1980s and 1990s to five to seven hours per day, i.e., 180 at present.

While Qatar succeeded in eradicating illiteracy with the expansion of its school system throughout the 1970s and 1980s, by the late 1990s concerns about the quality of education started to emerge. The school system was struggling to produce quality outcomes in academic achievement, college enrollment, and entry into the labor market (Nasser, 2017). In the late 1990s, the Ministry of Education (MoEHE) established scientific schools, called the "Developed Schools" or *Al-Madaris Al-Mutawara* in Arabic. These schools "had complete independence from the Ministry of Education. The idea

DOI: 10.4324/9781003334835-11

started with two segregated secondary schools – one for boys and one for girls – that were inspired by the Canadian schooling system and were designed and implemented with the help of Canadian experts" (Alkhater, 2016, p. 99). These schools taught mathematics and science in English as models of change and gained a great reputation for quality education in Qatar (Al-Banai & Nasser, 2015). Due to the results achieved by these scientific schools compared to the government schools, and with many other concerns related to the public educational system, the Qatari government commissioned Research and Development (RAND) Cooperation to conduct an objective assessment of the Qatari education system and suggest remedial solutions (Al-Banai & Nasser, 2015; Al-Fadala, 2012; Alkhater, 2016; Zellman et al., 2009).

With increased revenue from oil and gas resources helping to propel economic growth, Qatar's leadership began to prioritize improvement of the education system so that young people could gain the skills needed to diversify the country's economy and enhance knowledge creation. An initial step was commissioning the RAND Corporation to conduct a comprehensive assessment of the educational system. The next section provides an overview of the educational reform in Qatar before discussing how educational and management policies are developed in Qatar and the factors that influence them.

The aim of this chapter is to explore K-12 educational leadership and administration in the State of Qatar with a view to identifying salient influences affecting school leadership and lessons to be learned. The significance of this study lies in that it presents a portrait of existing educational leadership policies and practices in the context of Qatar, focusing on the perspectives key school and MoEHE leaders in the country. In so doing, it seeks to fill the gap in existing knowledge and thus extend the relevant literature. While extant scholarship provides ample evidence of different aspects of international school leadership (for example, Sawalhi & Tamimi, 2023; Lee et al., 2012; Mahfouz et al., 2019), not enough is known about K-12 educational leadership and administration in Qatar, the Gulf Cooperation Council (GCC) countries, and the larger Arab region.

Background: Education for a New Era

The RAND report identified a series of weaknesses in Qatar's school system. For example, schools lacked a vision and a mission, and the organizational structure of schools was very hierarchical. School facilities were not suitable for teaching and learning. Zellman et al. (2009) noted the RAND report's claim that schools relied on higher authority and top-down decisions. The curriculum from the MoEHE needed to be reviewed to support a student-centered approach and the number of target-specific professional development programs needed to be increased.

RAND asserted that all the options that were studied (Brewer et al., 2007) required the endorsement of four basic principles:

Autonomy, meaning schools would operate according to specific conditions in a time-limited agreement.

Accountability, meaning schools would be evaluated regularly based on measures that would be available to all stakeholders.

Variety, meaning each school would be free to develop its own educational plan and policies.

Choice, meaning parents would use schools' evaluation reports to select the best school for their children's needs.

Eventually, the Supreme Educational Council (SEC) was launched to clarify the objectives of the new education system. At the same time, MoEHE continued to supervise and run government schools. Private schools were run by investors, and community schools were run mainly by embassies and vocational schools.

The Need to Revisit K-12 Educational Policies in Qatar

The reform provided a tremendous amount of knowledge and generated opportunities to apply new information and skills. Yet, applying systems borrowed from Western countries without a clear translation of terminology left educators perplexed (Sellami et al., 2019). However, this chapter is not an evaluation of the reform and aims only to clarify the context in which this study was conducted. The next section is a detailed summary of the history of education in Qatar which is necessary as many terms are used differently than in other countries, e.g., policy to provide the context of teachers' and school leaders' practices and policies and sharing the insights from reviewing the documents and our interviewees.

Despite an intense, albeit brief, history of borrowing Western educational polices, many aspects of educational leadership remain largely underdeveloped in Qatar, including teacher leadership (Sawalhi & Sellami, 2021). Against this background, it is crucial to shed light on the importance of how educational leadership and management policies are developed and implemented in Qatar as a country that has developed a reputation for its massive educational reform and recognized educational initiatives such as the World Innovation Summit for Education (WISE) and Education Above All (EAA).

This chapter aims to explore three key areas:

How do K-12 educational leaders in Qatar define educational leadership?

How has K-12 public school leadership developed over the years in Qatar?

What influences shape current educational policies governing K-12 school leadership in Qatar?

The chapter focuses on public schools in Qatar, looking at the evolution and various changes the schooling system has gone through over the last 70 years.

Only recently has the private schooling system gained importance and is still developing, especially during the last ten years. According to Sawalhi and Tamimi (2021), zigzagging decisions and the restructuring of the MoEHE affect private schools' policies and systems. The scope of this chapter does not permit examining higher education.

Methodology

Research Design

In order to review Qatar's efforts in developing educational management and leadership policies, a qualitative research methodology was utilized as the most suitable tool for two main reasons. First, choosing a qualitative method was deemed the most appropriate for this study as it would help to improve our understanding of how school leadership is conceptualized in public (school leaders') and official (Ministry of Education officials') discourse. Second, using a qualitative approach would also aid in gathering in-depth and robust data on the how and why of school leaders' viewpoints and perspectives rooted in "real life"' contexts. These two reasons make for, a qualitative research methodology was deemed the most appropriate to adopt (Bryman, 2008; Flick, 2007; Given, 2008). As Merriam and Tisdell (2015) contended, "Qualitative researchers are interested in understanding how people interpret their experiences, how they construct their worlds, and what meaning they attribute to their experiences" (p. 6).

Research Instruments

To attain the goals set for this study, a qualitative approach was adopted to collect the data using semi-structured interviews conducted with six school principals, educational leaders and policy makers, and teachers, in both formal and informal leadership roles in Qatar. Interview data would help to elicit insights on school leaders' roles, practices, expectations, and the issues they encounter, as well as implications for education policies.

A review of Qatar's national education policies was also carried out in order to analyze the development and implementation of education policies in the country and examine the involvement of the MoEHE and stakeholders in designing and developing such policies. In doing so, a review of education policy was implemented in order to analyze how reports undertaken by the MoEHE and other government organizations are designed and developed. This was also useful in gleaning information about educational policy changes following the reforms adopted over the past two decades in Qatar.

Participants

Semi-structured interviews were conducted with six school principals, educational leaders, policymakers, and teachers, in both formal and informal leadership roles in Qatar. To maintain the anonymity of the interviewees and ensure the confidentiality of their responses, pseudonyms are used to identify them in the ensuing discussion. In addition, the three researchers have different experiences in the education sector in Qatar. One of the researchers had previously assumed the role of educational programs manager at Qatar Foundation. He then worked as a senior researcher and a faculty member at the College of Education, Qatar University. Currently, he occupies a managerial position as director of Educational Research Center at the same university.

Another serves as the Director of Research and Content Development at WISE, an initiative of the Qatar Foundation for Education, Science and Community Development. She has extensive professional experience in K-12 education and higher education and was an associate policy analyst at the RAND-Qatar Policy Institute. Previously, she had taught in the College of Education at Qatar University and worked at Qatar's Ministry of Education and Higher Education (MoEHE) as a teacher and then as the head of the science department.

The third researcher worked as teacher and academic vice principal in independent schools since the first cohort and witnessed all the changes. She also worked as a strategic and project development manager in an educational group in Qatar to develop private schools. In addition, she worked in the College of Education as a student teachers supervisor while she also continued to train teachers and school leaders in schools. Her PhD thesis explored teacher leadership in Qatar's government schools where around 3000 teachers participated and she interviewed 96 teacher leaders. She uses the conducted studies and her personal experiences and reflections to provide insights into this chapter.

Data Analysis

For the purpose of this study, in-depth, semi-structured interviews were used to collect the required data. After securing all necessary approvals, interviews were carried out in Arabic, audio-recorded and translated into English. In analyzing the interview data, a thematic content analysis is adopted. This involved the use of content analysis, an approach that is very common in qualitative research. Themes and codes, key components of our analyses, were identified in this study.

What Is the Nature of the New ERA?

The SEC started the first group of independent schools that taught the new curriculum in 2004 (Brewer et al., 2007). The Independent schools – a modified version of charter schools – were funded by the government, but each school could apply a different system based on the contract signed between the SEC and the school operator and according to the educational plan submitted by the independent school operator. From 2004 until 2010, Qatar began a new cohort of independent schools to replace the MoEHE schools gradually. The educational system came to provide different policies and guidelines related to hiring, teaching and learning, assessment, student discipline, appraisal system, and professional development according to each school operator/ principal.

New Professional Development Opportunities

In 2003, the SEC placed an advertisement in the local newspapers to receive applications for school operators. As Alkhater (2016) suggested, "The school operator is not necessarily the school principal; in fact, one operator can have several school principals reporting to him/her depending on the number of the contracted schools that the operator could get" (p. 101). Each school operator had the freedom to select, hire, determine salaries, and even dismiss teachers and staff; the professional development plan was left to each school according to its educational programs and system. This required massive training provided for senior school leaders and many preparation programs. The school support organizations (SSOs) also made efforts to build capacity and train coordinators, using the Training of Trainers model to reach the largest number of teachers (Nasser, 2017). This approach to training can be effective if there is an evaluation process, a follow-up, and a sound selection of master teachers (Katzenmeyer & Moller, 2009; Levin & Schrum, 2016).

Most of the professional development programs offered by the SEC were meant to enhance student-centered approaches. Teacher and school leader preparation programs were offered, including (1) teacher-training programs for new teachers entitled the Teacher Preparation and Certification Program (TPCP), which offered different modules to enable teachers to plan in line with the curriculum standards; (2) SSO teams that supported schools in their first year of operation; (3) a variety of professional development workshops, some offered by the Education Institute's Professional Development Office and others provided by international contractors (Zellman et al., 2009); and (4) a teacher training agenda introduced in 2003 by the SEC and Qatar University in collaboration with Texas A&M University-Qatar (Nasser, 2017). This training program was provided because a vast number of newly recruited teachers lacked teaching qualifications or experience and were expected to teach mathematics and science in English (Alkhater, 2016).

In 2006, the Qatar National Professional Standards for Teachers and Leaders (QNPSTL) were launched, providing a benchmark for teachers and school leaders in Qatar. The Education Queensland International of Australia outlined these guidelines (Brewer et al., 2007). The QNPSTL identified the type of knowledge, disposition, and skills required of teachers and administrators (Table 11.2). Because all teachers were compelled to register with the Qatar Office for Registration, Licensing, and Accreditation, certification procedures were developed (Brewer et al., 2007; Ellili-Cherif et al., 2012; Zellman et al., 2009).

In 2016, the MoEHE reduced the number of QNPSTL standards for teachers and educational leaders (teachers were required to meet 12 standards, which were subsequently reduced to six. For educational leaders, the standards were reduced from seven to five.) Romanowski and his colleagues (2018, p. 4) identify four main reasons for this review. The first involves more focus on the impact of teaching on students' learning, progress, and achievement. The second entails refining and improving standards, so they are realistic. The third refers to standards and licensing based on relevant, authentic classroom-based practices. The fourth involves increasing the capability of teachers, school leaders, and system leaders through programs of professional development aligned to the achievement of the standards.

Teachers' Autonomy

Alfadala and others (2021) clarified that autonomy was identified as one of the key driving themes in the Education for a New Era reforms and was translated into teachers' ability to make autonomous choices about instructional practices (Brewer et al., 2007). Undoubtedly, the reform created a great demand for and high expectations of teachers (Zellman et al., 2009) (see Table 11.1). Teachers' contribution in any reform is vital to ensure improving schools and students' performance, whether these efforts are called leadership or agency or empowerment or any formal or informal efforts. Teachers' autonomy allows them to innovate and develop their identity and improve their skills.

All this considered, teachers were given many responsibilities and the autonomy to implement initiatives during the educational reform, e.g., designing the curriculum, selecting the resources, and assessing the students. Yet, these responsibilities were changed into more centralized top-down decisions in less than a decade. Moreover, teachers began to plan their lessons collaboratively, and these lessons had to be approved by the SEC, and, at present, by the MoEHE (see Table 11.2, which summarizes the main changes during the reform).

Between 2011 and 2016, the MoEHE opened new schools also called independent, but with a different level of authority given to the school operator based on centralized decisions from the MoEHE. Any teacher or school leader who was hired after 2011 did not have the same experiences and training as those hired before.

Back to the MoEHE (After the Reform)

In line with Emiri Decision No. 9 of 2016, the SEC was disbanded and the MoEHE again became responsible for all aspects of education in Qatar (Doha News, 2016). The use of the term *independent school* was discontinued, and all MoEHE schools were called "Government schools" by 2017. The MoEHE hired school operators who espoused the MoEHE vision and mission (*The Peninsula*, 2016). These changes were made in response to the voices of society and decision-makers and their dissatisfaction with the results and impact of Independent schools (Nasser, 2017). Reflecting on critical lessons

Table 11.1 MoEHE school teachers' responsibilities compared to those of independent school teachers 2004–2010

Teachers in MoEHE schools	Teachers' responsibilities in independent schools
• The MoEHE provided its teachers with textbooks and teachers did not have to add or use their own resources to develop the curriculum.	• The SEC trained teachers to plan according to curriculum standards. They were required to develop textbooks, or schools could purchase textbooks or materials. • Independent schoolteachers performed many duties related to curriculum development and material selection outside of the classroom. These duties expanded the scope of their responsibilities and were often quite time-consuming.
• The MoEHE curriculum was based on a lecture and recitation format, which primarily required students to memorize content and teachers to mainly lecture in a teacher-centered approach. The curriculum changed only about once a decade, so new preparations were relatively uncommon. • The MoEHE curriculum did not incorporate the use of information technology	• The standards-based reform was designed to encourage teachers to employ student-centered teaching practices in the classroom. • Teaching in independent schools required the use of information technology to prepare for classes, communicate with students, conduct research, and make presentations • Independent schools required that a large portion of mathematics and science instruction be conducted in English.
• A MoEHE school teacher's day often began at 7:00 a.m. but ended around noon. Teachers worked for a maximum of 130 days.	• The workload in independent schools often meant long hours for teachers, with days lasting from 7:00 a.m. to 3:00 or 4:00 p.m. and a longer academic year (180 days). • Independent school teachers attended professional development courses that were sometimes offered after school hours and in the evening. • Non-Qatari teachers' feeling of insecurity was based on the perception that hiring and firing decisions were in the hands of only one person, the school operator (who was, after the policy change, also the principal).

Note: Adapted from Zellman et al., 2009, pp. 31–33 taken from Chaaban and Sawalhi, 2020.

Table 11.2 Samples of continuous changes and decisions made by the SEC 2004–2015 (adopted from Sawalhi, 2019)

Year	Changes					
2004–2005	First cohort of independent schools launched	Teachers and school leaders can design and select their own resources	Science and math taught in English	Any candidate can apply to teach in independent schools	School support organization teams (SSO) support school leaders and teachers in the first year	Each school can have its own structure to operate	Each school may apply its own training program for teachers and staff
2006–2007	Teachers and school leaders must select resources from a list approved by the SEC					
2010–2011	All schools shifted to become independent schools	The SEC began hiring teachers in coordination with school principals				
2015–2016	SEC disbanded and all schools placed under MoEHE					

from Qatar and GCC countries, Al-Fadala and others (2021, p. 174) contend that MOEHE "expanded to meet problems as they emerged, failing to evaluate the system and take opportunities to develop coherent strategies. Furthermore, the MoEHE lacked purposeful organizing principles."

Other countries were looking forward to seeing the results of Qatar's educational reform, and many studies have been conducted to explore the impact and results of this reform (Al-Banai & Nasser, 2015; Fadlemula & Koc, 2016; Romanowski et al., 2013). In fact, the United Arab Emirates publicized its approval of the principles of the educational reform program established in Qatar (Ghafir, 2012). In 2017, the MoEHE reverted to a centralized system, curtailing the greater freedom earlier schools had experienced in operating and managing their budgets. As was stated above, recruitment constituted an area that underwent the most important changes in order to ensure a secure environment for employees. The newly created positions including having an activities coordinator, a public relations coordinator, a year coordinator or leader, and a resource coordinator were innovative for teachers and educators in general. They provided a formal leadership organization, and teachers who were promoted to leadership positions were compensated with extra allowances.[1]

Figure 11.1 shows how administrative roles are separated from teaching and academic ones and summarizes the unified positions. Interestingly, the MoEHE classifies teaching assistants as administrative roles not related to academic supervision because most of them have secondary certificate qualifications, and because of the tasks assigned to them.

Backward or forward!

The following sections present the main findings that answer our questions and clarify how educational leaders reflect on the designing and implementation of educational leadership policies.

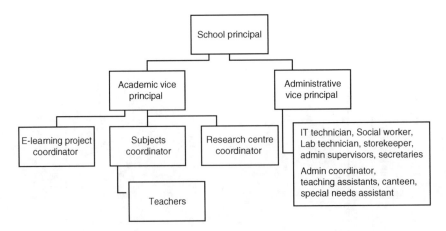

Figure 11.1 MoEHE unified school structure in 2016 (developed by the researchers).

Educational Leadership and Arab Educators

For many decades, major international organizations and agencies have played a major role in shaping global educational actions and discourses. The International Monetary Fund (IMF), the Organisation for Economic Co-operation and Development (OECD), the United Nations (UN), the United Nations Educational, Scientific and Cultural Organization (UNESCO), the World Bank, and the World Trade Organization (WTO) have all contributed in orienting educational policies, programs, and practices (Auld et al., 2019; Mundy & Manion, 2014; Spring, 2014). In parallel with this global course, national systems of education have become "increasingly attuned to global models of what constitutes quality education" (Ramirez, Schofer & Meyer, 2018, p. 356). Within the realm of education, an area where the impact of this global trend is clearly manifest is the reliance of many countries on international yardsticks to benchmark the quality of their systems of education. It is not surprising that the educational performance of those countries is often assessed against international standards such as PISA and TIMSS.

In particular, the pressures of globalization have had an enormous impact on educational leadership and decision-making (Litz, 2011). In the words of Apple (2011), "Globalization can have a critical influence on core educational decisions such as 'what counts as responsive and effective education, what counts as appropriate teaching ... and who benefits from it throughout the world' (pp. 222–223)." The bulk of research done on the impacts of globalization in the domain of education has largely focused on neoliberal influences affecting local educational practice and delivery (Apple, 2011; Gandin, 2006; Gupta, 2018). Central to neoliberal globalized education are the principles of "deregulation, privatization, and liberalization".

Many researchers highlight that there is a dearth of studies related to educational leadership and management in Arab countries (Arar et al., 2017; Oplatka & Arar, 2017; Hallinger & Hammad, 2019; Hammad & Alazmi, 2020) although schooling and educational systems were well-known in early Islamic centuries. Sellami and others (2019) show that defining the term education in Arabic causes lots of confusion and affects educators' practices, especially with policy borrowing and relying on Western theories related to educational policies (Arar & Haj-Yehia, 2018).

As education policy includes laws as well as processes and policies that educational organizations, local districts, states, and nations put in place and follow to achieve academic goals, educational leadership policies show the law and processes that educational leaders follow to achieve educational goals. However, it is important to clarify what is meant by educational leadership as some educators might confuse it with school leadership (Gunter, 2016). Educational leadership has been defined and conceptualized by researchers in myriad ways, evolving chronologically from "educational administration" and "educational management" to a more recent view of the concept as "educational leadership" (Bush, 2011). Commenting on the developments the construct has witnessed over the years, Adams, Kutty and Zabidi (2017) argue that "The language of leadership has joined or rather superseded the concept of management" (p. 1), suggesting that there is no single correct definition of leadership (Arar & Oplatka, 2022).

To use Allix and Gronn's (2005) description, educational leadership is a "notoriously perplexing and enigmatic phenomenon" (p. 181). This view corroborates a similar stance echoed in other research treating definitions of leadership as subjective, arbitrary, and capricious (for example, Botha (2013), Connolly, James & Fertig (2019), Hallinger (2018), Hallinger & Hammad (2019), McKimm & Swanwick (2010), Morrison (2013)) Oplatka & Arar, 2022. In this study, educational leadership is viewed as the process of developing an individual as a whole person and unleashing their potential in formal and informal educational organizations (Sawalhi, 2019). We also believe that everyone can lead from where they stand as we define leadership as influencing others. Therefore, educational leadership includes principals, formal school leadership, teacher leadership, student leadership, and educational community leaders.

Educational Leadership Policies in Qatar

Overall, a chronological overview of the evolution of education in Qatar reveals three prominent phases that characterize critical changes underlying the education system in country. First, prior to 2001, the system of education was predominantly centralized, focusing primarily on the management of schools. Second, the period from 2001 to 2017 witnessed ambitious educational reform and zigzagging decisions, including a decentralized system, teachers' and school leaders' autonomy, and many newly introduced concepts such as standard, professional development, independent schools, school operator, professional standards, school policies, and school accreditation. Finally, from 2017 to the present time now, there has been a return back to centralized systems with some noticeable achievements such as professional development and professional standards.

Having said this, we need to highlight that major educational leadership policies are issued by the Emir (the Head of the State), including the establishment of the SEC and the creation and structure of the MoEHE (see Figure 11.2). The Emir's decision specified the roles and responsibilities of MOEHE departments, while the MoEHE would issue internal policies such as professional standards. The following section discusses the main findings driven from reviewing relevant policies in Qatar, interviewing MoEHE staff, school leaders, and teachers, in addition to our own reflections and insights.

K-12 Educational Leadership and Administration in Qatar 199

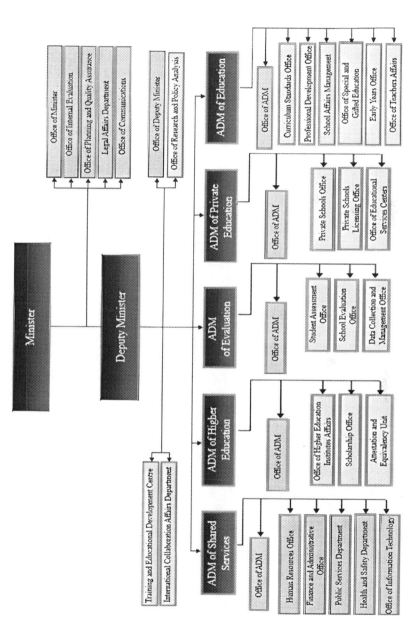

Figure 11.2 MoEHE structure 2016 taken from Koç & Fadlelmula (2016).

Lost in Translation

Despite all the professional development provided and all the changes that Qatar's educational system has undergone owing to and during the reform in addition to borrowing from Western models and working with support organizations, educational leaders have not been able to define what is meant by policy and how it can be developed. Looking at the interview data, the respondents were generally of the view that there is no clear understanding of what policy means. Indeed, many reported that no access is available to previous educational policies and that there are no standards or templates for developing policies. Similarly, respondents stated that there is no internal communication among the MoEHE departments. As one respondent reported, "Educational policy is a very broad concept ... When I use the term policy during my discussions with different administrators, I use it correctly. When you mention policy, it may simply refer to an instructional guide and it may just as well mean a set of instructions. Therefore, you may not really capture the construct of educational policy ... It is difficult for me to define the concept."

An interviewee noted: "No, because you may classify the tasks and duties at the MoEHE as policies or otherwise. When drafting policies, does one know that there are basic rules 1, 2, 3, and 4? From a theoretical standpoint, what does educational policy mean? What are its components? You will not find a definite answer as there are different names. What you will find are various perceptions, views, types and forms of how policies are written and revised that are delineated according to the different MoEHE offices and based on spatial and temporal influences." Other respondents reiterated similar opinions, indicating that they find the term unclear, ambiguous, and interpretable in various ways.

Based on the accounts reported in the interviews, it appears that educational leadership is not governed by any policy unlike educational management, which is defined and delineated by specific policies. For example, school principals report to school office, while academic vice principals are guided by the supervision office. Respondents feel lost in translation and often complained that some departments have put in place a set of actions that they adopt as policies. In the words of one respondent, "Very often, there is a committee consisting of employees from the different MoEHE departments and we always make sure that a representative from the Policy Department is a member of the committee." Some policies are designed by specific departments and come to us for review. For example, early childhood education policies originate from the MoEHE's Early Years Education Department and other departments might not know about these policies.

The confusion is in using terms not only related to what is meant by policy but also what is meant by educational leadership (Chaaban et al., 2021). Interviewees often considered educational leadership a new term; as one pointed out, "The concept of educational leadership is new to us and has been introduced to the MoEHE in the last ten years and it is not yet embedded in the system." Another mentioned that "There are departments in the Ministry; they are specialized in administrative affairs. I mean, the administration of the

Ministry, such as human resources, is related to administrative matters more, but in departments that have more to do with the field, such as instructional supervision, curricula, teachers and teacher affairs, or there may be an overlap between their roles."

This is consistent with the findings of a study conducted by Sellami and colleagues (2019), which revealed different understandings of the concept of educational leadership and its impact on educational practices starting with the alteration of the Arabic name of the MoEHE from *Tarbiyyah* (education) to *At-Ta'leem wa At-Ta'leem Al-'Aali* (education and higher education). In the same vein, Sawalhi (2019) argued that teacher leadership was not introduced to teachers in Qatar despite the massive educational reform and mentioned that interviewees in her study used Arabic terms such as *Murrabi* (educator) to describe the role of teacher leaders.

We claim that this confusion has increased as Qatar has witnessed many phases of developing educational management and leadership policies and many restructurings without a clear archiving system. This is especially the case since many departments have not been included in the new structure. In addition, MoEHE staff members are not aware of the history or evaluation of the department's experiences (Sawalhi & Tamimi, 2021). In addition, a dominant feature that emerged from the interviews is the feeling that there is a lack of internal communication regarding developing and implementing educational leadership policies in Qatar. As was reported by an interviewee, "I am in the advisory committee, but there is no announcement that, for example, the policy of principal appraisal policy will change, it is assumed that you are the first person to be notified of the policy or the model and the mechanism but that is not the case." Another voice indicated that "We are working on developing a guide to design and review a policy. Cooperation between departments means that all departments and personnel will work together."

Walking the Talk and Not Another Piece of Art

Over the past two decades, school leadership has shifted from a focus on leading schools during the reform to managing mundane day-to-day work due to centralized practices and different professional development opportunities. These barriers have caused a gap between the level of knowledge and level of practices. In the words of an interviewee, "Policies have been developed but the problem lies in implementing them, meaning in many cases the policies are present but ink on paper. If the person responsible for implementing these policies does not adopt and relate to them, he/she will not deal with them with a broad horizon, an open mind and an unclosed mindset. So these policies have no real value. The root of development is the development of mentalities and individuals more than the development of policies."

The comment above is not only about formal educational leadership but also shows to what extent the MoEHE identifies educational leaders:

What categories can be identified as educational leaders. I mean, I had a teaboy, and I was in the public school, may God bless them. He was making tea, but he was a leader, do you understand me? While I had a manager, in the administration, and he was a positive man, and he loved meaningful change, he was a manager. It is not about the position.

Sawalhi (2019), for instance, highlighted the importance of differentiating between school leadership and educational leadership. Furthermore, she emphasized the need to redefine school leadership, for example by allowing teachers to practice leadership in an outside school to meet the main purpose of education as mentioned earlier in this chapter, and to consider students' part of school leadership.

Interestingly, a critical element that is crippling educational leadership is the issue of *Wasta* (nepotism and personal connections) which continues to control the process of selecting educational leaders such as school principals. One of the interviewees, for example, mentioned that selecting a principal is a sensitive role and she highlighted that despite the selection criteria, there is bias in the selection process:

You, for example, enter the schools and see, and you will certainly notice the differences between this principal and that principal. I mean, see in all schools, whether independent or governmental. The issue needed awareness. For example, people were selected based on their relationship or being a relative of..!

Wasta is a widespread social practice in Arab countries. Despite personal qualifications, the selection and recruitment criteria are affected by myriad influences. For example, research by Ali, Raiden, and Kirk (2015), Forstenlechner, Madi, Selim, Rutledge (2012), and Iles, Almhedie, and Baruch (2012) has shown that social and cultural factors shape the process of hiring employees in Arabian Gulf states. With specific reference to the education sector, research by Sawalhi and Sellami (2021) reveals that the principal selection of teachers to practice leadership is largely affected by their nationality.

The MoEHE and school personnel still do not differentiate between leadership and managerial roles. A comment by an interviewee indicates that "There is a time when people do what they are told to do and what to avoid and because of the annual evaluation or because of something else. This is not a big change, because as you know, changing cultures takes time." This raises a real concern not only about the selection but also about the quality of the practices and the ability to achieve the educational objectives to guide action. In addition, to what extent do the MoEHE's educational policies help MoEHE and school personnel to lead for learning? An example related to transferring a bus supervisor without taking into consideration the need of the school or the potential impact on students was mentioned. An interviewee highlighted that the MoEHE departments "pout their policies in schools without considering the field or the need of these schools"

The gap identified above between educational policy and implementation has caused a lack of trust between MoEHE leaders and school leaders, and even the community. A recent example during the COVID-19 pandemic MoEHE is the issuing of many memos and declarations. One of these memos was related to principals' and teachers' working hours, which caused many complaints that generated trends on Twitter. Earlier in this chapter, we provided many examples of how the MoEHE has changed policies continuously in a manner that has impacted educational leadership, management policies, and the quality of implementations.

Three interviewees mentioned the role of women's leading roles in educational leadership and management policies. Interestingly, it is clear that most of the formal positions in the MoEHE are occupied by women. The interviewees mentioned that the lack of stability in decision-making is due to women's nature and the bias in selection is due to women's jealousy. We believe that emotional agility is an important factor in educational leadership and our claim agrees with that of other researchers who highlight the importance of emotional leadership (Arar, 2017; Ball, 2011; Hallinger & Kovačević, 2019; Khan et al., 2016). However, we do not see that gender is behind these practices as much as it is related to the lack of experience and knowledge, especially that the gender factor shows mixed results in previous studies.

Conclusion

This chapter sought to explore and provide a critical perspective on how K-12 educational leadership policies have evolved over the years in Qatar. It also aimed to discuss the influences shaping current educational policies governing K-12 in the country. Findings showed that before the reform, the concept of educational leadership was not employed in wide currency in Qatar. The MoEHE and school principals are required to manage day-to-day tasks in schools within a very centralized system. The reform brought new terms and perspectives not only to Qatar but also to the region more broadly, including policies, educational leadership, and standards. However, this sudden shift did not achieve the expected outcomes. In 2017, a new educational chapter was started in Qatar based on many assumptions. For example, educators in Qatar are aware and capable of designing policies and implementing them due to the intensive professional development programs provided to them which was not the case and affected many departments and schools' performance. In addition, many departments have no clear vision or policies to guide their work such as private school's office.

As was pointed out by Alfadala and others (2021, p. 173), educational policies and reform were "fragmented rather systemic and were not part of an integrated vision for the education system." There is therefore a need to document the reform's experience and provide clear standards and guidelines that will guide educational policies. The interviews disclosed that there is a need to develop and further improve educational policies so that attention is focused on developing leadership instead of focusing on administrative matters. This can help educational leaders in dealing with teachers and students in a productive matter, which in turn will enhance the teaching-learning process.

The MoEHE needs to clarify the terms used and what is expected, including the terms educational leadership and educational leadership policies. This covers not only clarifying the terms but also helping the MoEHE personnel understand what the components of educational policy are and how they are to be implemented. Findings also showed the need for developing professional development programs. Additionally, the interviews identified educational policies as varied and multiple, covering a wide spectrum. More specifically, the field of professional development for teachers and educational leaders was identified as one of the most important policies that need addressing because professional development policies are still deficient.

Policymakers, researchers, and practitioners need to reflect and work on how educational leaders, including school leadership, are prepared and what professional development opportunities are provided. Educational leadership preparation programs might not need a new framework as much as focusing on leadership for learning and leadership for action. There is a need to provide a supportive environment to equip principals to encourage teacher leadership and empower teachers through developing an ecosystem to include teachers and students' well-being and agency through progressive education to support innovation like WISE initiatives. Indeed, Qatar's journey reveals the need to clearly identify the destination while humanizing educational leadership policies and practices. Unleashing human potential including educational leaders, school principals, teachers, and learners of all ages is worth every effort and moment.

Note

1 Teachers who held formal leadership roles were given extra allowance until the time of writing.

References

Adams, D., Kutty, G. R., & Zabidi, Z. M. (2017). Educational leadership for the 21st century. *International Online Journal of Educational Leadership*, *1*(1), 1–4. 10.22452//iojel.vol1no1.1â€‹

Al-Banai, N., & Nasser, R. (2015). The educational reform in Qatar: Challenges and success. *INTCESS15 – 2nd international conference on education and social science*, 678–683. Retrieved from http://www.ocerint.org/intcess15_epublication/papers/293.pdf

Alfadala, A. (2012). *How do school leaders' perceptions of education for a new era affect the implementation of the reform in primary schools in Qatar?* Doha, Qatar: Hamad bin Khalifa University Press (HBKU Press). 10.5339/qfarf.2012.AHPS4

Alfadala, A., Yiannouka, S., & Zaki, O. (2021). Qatar's road to education reform. In C. McLaughlin, & A. Ruby (Eds.), *Implementing educational reform: Cases and challenges (Cambridge Education Research)* (pp. 171–192). Cambridge: Cambridge University Press. doi:10.1017/9781108864800.010

Ali, S. A., Raiden, A., & Kirk, S. (2015). Social capital in Jordan: Wasta in employment selection. *The international conference on organization and management (ICOM)*. Retrieved from https://eprints.worc.ac.uk/4699/1/Social%20capital%20in%20Jordan%20-%20wasta%20in%20employment%20selection.pdf

AlKhater, L. R. M. (2016). Qatar's borrowed K-12 education reform in context. In M.N. Tok, L. AlKhater, & L.A. Pal (Eds.), *Policy-making in a transformative state. The case of Qatar* (pp. 97–130). UK: Palgrave Macmillan.

Allix, N., & Gronn, P. (2005). 'Leadership' as a manifestation of knowledge. *Educational Management Administration & Leadership*, 33(2), 181–196. 10.1177/1741143205051052

Apple, M. (2011). Global crises, social justice, and teacher education. *Journal of Teacher Education*, 62(2), 222–234. 10.1177/0022487110385428

Arar, K. (2017). Emotional expression at different managerial career stages. *Educational Management Administration & Leadership*, 45, 929–943.

Arar, K., & Haj-Yehia, K. (2018). Perceptions of educational leadership in medieval Islamic thought: A contribution to multicultural contexts. *Journal of Educational Administration and History*, 50(2), 69–81. https://doi.org/10.1080/00220620.2017.1413341

Arar, K., & Oplatka, I. (2022). Advanced theories of educational leadership. Springer.

Arar, K., Turan, S., Barakat, M., & Oplatka, I. (2017). The characteristics of educational leadership in the Middle East: A comparative analysis of three nation-states, In D. Waite & I, Bogotch (eds.), *International handbook of leadership in education*. (pp. 355–373). John Wiley & Sons, Inc.

Auld, E., Rappleye, J., & Morris, P. (2019). PISA for development: How the OECD and World Bank shaped education governance post-2015. *Comparative Education*, 55(2), 197–219. 10.1080/03050068.2018.1538635

Ball, S. J. (2011). A new research agenda for educational leadership and policy. *Management in Education*, 25(2), 50–52. DOI: 10.1177/0892020611399488

Botha, R. J. (2013). Epistemological beliefs and leadership approaches among South African school principals. *Educational Studies*, 39(4), 431–443. 10.1080/03055698.2013.776944

Brewer, D. J., Augustine, C. H., Zellman, G. L., Ryan, G. W., Goldman, C. A., Stasz, C., & Constant, L. (2007). *Education for a new era: Design and implementation of k-12 education reform in Qatar*. Santa Monica, CA: Rand Corp.

Bryman, A. (2008). *Social research methods*. Oxford: Oxford University Press.

Bush, T. (2011). *Theories of educational leadership and management* (4th edn.). London: Sage.

Chaaban, Y., & Sawalhi, R. (2020). Student teachers' development as teacher leaders during the practicum experience. *Journal of Applied Research in Higher Education*, 12, 927–942.

Chaaban, Y., Sawalhi, R., & Du, X. (2021). Exploring teacher leadership for professional learning in response to educational disruption in Qatar. *Professional Development in Education*, 1, 1–18. 10.1080/19415257.2021.1973070

Connolly, M., James, C., & Fertig, M. (2019). The difference between educational management and educational leadership and the importance of educational responsibility. *Educational Management Administration & Leadership*, 47(4), 504–519. 10.1177/1741143217745880

Ellili-Cherif, M., Romanowski, M. H., & Nasser, R. (2012). All that glitters is not gold: Challenges of teacher and school leader licensure licensing system in Qatar. *International Journal of Educational Development*, 32(3), 471–481. 10.1016/j.ijedudev.2011.11.010

Flick, U. (2007). What is qualitative research? In U. Flick (Ed.), *Designing qualitative research* (pp. 2–16). London: SAGE Publications. 10.4135/9781849208826.n1

Forstenlechner, I., Madi, M. T., Selim, H. M., & Rutledge, E. J. (2012). Emiratisation: determining the factors that influence the recruitment decisions of employers in the UAE. *The International Journal of Human Resource Management*, 23(2), 406–421. 10.1080/09585192.2011.561243

Gandin, L. A. (2006). Creating real alternatives to neoliberal policies in education: The citizen school project. In M.W. Apple, & K.L. Buras (Eds.), *The subaltern speak: Curriculum, power, and educational struggles* (pp. 217–241). New York: Routledge.

Ghafir, H. (2012). *Education reform in Qatar for K-12 school*. Chicago: National Opinion Research Center.

Given, L. M. (Ed.). (2008). *The SAGE encyclopedia of qualitative research methods*. London: SAGE Publications.

Gunter, H. M. (2016). *An intellectual history of school leadership practice and research*. London: Bloomsbury Publishing.

Gupta, G. (2018). How neoliberal globalization is shaping early childhood education policies in India, China, Singapore, Sri Lanka and the Maldives. *Policy Futures in Education*, 16(1), 11–28. 10.1177/1478210317715796

Hallinger, P. (2018). Surfacing a hidden literature: A systematic review of research on educational leadership and management in Africa. *Educational Management Administration & Leadership*, 46(3), 362–384. 10.1177/1741143217694895

Hallinger, P., & Hammad, W. (2019). Knowledge production on educational leadership and management in Arab societies: A systematic review of research. *Educational Management Administration & Leadership*, 47(1), 20–36. 10.1177/1741143217717280

Hallinger, P., & Kovačević, J. (2019). A bibliometric review of research on educational administration: Science mapping the literature, 1960 to 2018. *Review of Educational Research*, 89(3), 335–369. 10.3102/0034654319830380

Hammad, W., & Alazmi, A. A. (2020). Research on school principals in the Gulf states: A systematic review of topics and conceptual models. *Management in Education*, 1, 0892020620959748. 10.1177/0892020620959748

Iles, P., Almhedie, A., & Baruch, Y. (2012). Managing HR in the Middle East: Challenges in the public sector. *Public Personnel Management*, 41(3), 465–492. 10.1177/009102601204100305

Katzenmeyer, M., & Moller, G. (2009). *Awakening the sleeping giant: Helping teachers develop as leaders* (3rd ed). Thousand Oaks, CA: Corwin Press.

Khan, M., Ro, H., Gregory, A. M., & Hara, T. (2016). Gender dynamics from an Arab perspective: Intercultural service encounters. *Cornell Hospitality Quarterly*, 57(1), 51–65. 10.1177/1938965515581397

Koç, M., & Fadlelmula, F. (2016). *Overall review of education system in Qatar*. Moldova: Lambert Academic Publishing.

Lee, M., Hallinger, P., & Walker, A. (2012). Leadership challenges in international schools in the Asia Pacific region: Evidence from programme implementation of the International Baccalaureate. *International Journal of Leadership in Education*, 15, 289–310.

Levin, B. B., & Schrum, L. (2016). *Every teacher a leader: Developing the needed dispositions, knowledge, and skills for teacher leadership*. London: Corwin Press.

Litz, D. (2011). Globalization and the changing face of educational leadership: Current trends and emerging dilemmas. *International Education Studies*, 4(3), 47–61.

Mahfouz, J., Sausner, E., & Kornhaber, M. (2018). US international schools overseas and the Common Core. *International Journal of Leadership in Education*, 22, 406–420.

McKimm, J., & Swanwick, T. (2010). Educational leadership. In T. Swanwick (Ed.), *Understanding medical education: Evidence, theory and practice* (pp. 419–437). Oxford: Wiley-Blackwell. 10.1002/9781444320282

Merriam, S. B., & Tisdell, E. J. (2015). *Qualitative research: A guide to design and implementation*. San Francisco, CA: John Wiley & Sons.

Ministry of Development Planning and Statistics (MDPS). (2016). *Education in Qatar: Statistical profile 2016*. Doha, Qatar: Ministry of Development Planning and Statistics. Retrieved from https://www.psa.gov.qa/en/statistics/Statistical%20Releases/Social/Education/2016/Education_Statistical_Pro%EF%AC%81le_2016_En.pdf

Morrison, A. R. (2013). Educational leadership and change: Structural challenges in the implementation of a shifting paradigm. *School Leadership and Management*, 33(4), 412–424. 10.1080/13632434.2013.813462

Mundy, K., & Manion, C. (2014). Globalization and global governance in education. In N.P. Stromquist, & K. Monkman (Eds.), *Globalization and education: Integration and contestation across cultures* (2nd edn., pp. 39–53). Lanham, MD: Rowman and Littlefield.

Nasser, R. (2017). Qatar's educational reform past and future: Challenges in teacher development. *Open Review of Educational Research*, 4(1), 1–19. 10.1080/23265507.2016.1266693

Oplatka, I., & Arar, K. (2017). The research on educational leadership and management in the Arab world since the 1990s: A systematic review. *Review of Education*, 5(3), 267–307. 10.1002/rev3.3095

Ramirez, F. O., Schofer, E., & Meyer, J. W. (2018). International tests, national assessments, and educational development (1970–2012). *Comparative Education Review*, 62(3), 344–364. 10.1086/698326

Romanowski, M. H., & Amatullah, T. (2014). The impact of Qatar national professional standards: Teachers' perspectives. *International Journal of Research Studies in Education*, 3(2), 97–114.

Romanowski, M. H., Ellili-Cherif, M., Al Ammari, B., & Al Attiya, A. (2013). Qatar's educational reform: The experiences and perceptions of principals, teachers and parents. *International Journal of Education*, 5(3), 108–135. 10.5296/ije.v5i3.3995

Sawalhi, R., & Sellami, A. L. (2021). Factors influencing teacher leadership: Voices of public school teachers in Qatar. *International Journal of Leadership in Education*, 1–8. 10.1080/13603124.2021.1913238

Sawalhi, R., & Tamimi, A. (2021). Leading outstanding international schools in Qatar: Lessons learned. *Leadership and Policy in Schools*, 1–13. 10.1080/15700763.2021.1894455

Sellami, A. L., Sawalhi, R., Romanowski, M. H., & Amatullah, T. (2019). Definitions of educational leadership – Arab educators' perspectives. *International Journal of Leadership in Education*, 3, 1–20. 10.1080/13603124.2019.1690701

Spring, J. (2014). *Globalization of education: An introduction*. London: Routledge.

Stasz, C., Eide, E. R., & Martorell, P. (2008). *Post-secondary education in Qatar: Employer demand, student choice, and options for policy*. Santa Monica, CA: RAND Education.

The Peninsula (2016, January 29). Independent schools to see major changes. Retrieved from https://thepeninsulaqatar.com/article/29/01/2016/Independent-schools-to-see-major-changes

Walker, L. (2016). Qatar Emir: Reforms must continue, but 'no room for panic'. *Doha News*. Retrieved from Qatar Emir: Reforms must continue, but 'no room for panic' – Doha News | Qatar

Zellman, G. L., Karam, R., Constant, L., Salem, H., Gonzalez, G., Orr, N., ... & Al-Obaidli, K. (2009). *Implementation of the k-12 education reform in Qatar's schools. Monograph*. Santa Monica, CA: RAND Corporation. 90407-2138. Retrieved from http://www.rand.org/pubs/monographs/2009/RAND_MG880.pdf

12 Exploring the Omani Educational Administration and Leadership Literature

Hidden Gems or Concerns to Be Addressed?

Yara Yasser Hilal and Muna Khamis Al-Alawi

Introduction

Educational administration and leadership (EAL) continues to receive scholarly attention since the 1990s (e.g., Garratt & Forrester, 2012), which has translated into a growing knowledge base of the field. However, this growth does not show an even distribution between the Global North and the Global South, where a dominance of Anglo-American culture has been documented in several regional and international systematic reviews (Castillo & Hallinger, 2017; Hallinger & Hammad, 2017; Hammad et al., 2020; Hammad & Hallinger, 2017). Such an uneven distribution of knowledge production can be problematic for a number of reasons. Leadership is a cultural, social, and intersubjective construct and hence is expected to be conceptualized and enacted differently across different cultures (e.g., Dimmock & Walker, 2000). This dominance has resulted in the use of mainly Anglo-American leadership theories in research and practice conducted in the Global South despite logical concerns about the applicability of these theories to the respective culture and context (Bajunid, 1996; Belchetz & Leithwood, 2007; Hallinger, 1995). Moreover, the dominance of imported EAL knowledge and practices resonates with a documented growth of postcolonial research and the lack of accessible indigenous knowledge needed to develop culturally responsive educational leadership (Arar et al., 2017; Lopez, 2020; Samier, 2016).

The Arab region lies at the heart of this discourse, where several reviews reveal a number of concerns related to its knowledge production in terms of quality, quantity, and its contribution to the international EAL literature (Atari & Outum, 2019; Hallinger & Hammad, 2017; Hammad & Hallinger, 2017; Karami-Akkary & El Sahib, 2019; Oplatka & Arar, 2017b). One of the challenges facing these reviews is in their framing of the "Arab world" as one single entity, whereas actually, Arabs differ in culture, history, ethnicities, and religion (Hammad & Hallinger, 2017; Salibi, 1988). Therefore, trying to understand the contributions of different nations in the Arab world as a collective whole may not provide an accurate representation of the contribution of these

DOI: 10.4324/9781003334835-12

different countries to the global EAL literature; more importantly, such a collective approach may not be conducive to understanding the contextual and idiosyncratic factors contributing to the different patterns of EAL literature in different countries including Oman, which is the focus of this chapter.

The Sultanate of Oman is one of the six states constituting the Gulf Cooperation Council (GCC). It has a young, yet rapidly changing education system. Since the early 1990s, the system has witnessed dramatic changes aimed at raising its overall quality as part of the modernization and nation-building plans set by the country's leadership (Al Balushi & Griffiths, 2013; Nasser, 2019).

The Renaissance period in 1970 marks the beginning of the development of the formal educational sector in Oman. In 1970, there were only three schools in the Sultanate with only 900 students and 30 teachers (Ministry of Education, 2010). Since then, the educational sector in general and K-12 in particular have witnessed significant developments where the number of schools increased to reach 1182 with 603,797 students and 678,350 teachers (Ministry of Education, 2021).

The education system in Oman is a centralized system where the Ministry of Education is responsible for policymaking, implementation, and the supervision of the overall educational processes in both the private and public educational sectors and hence many of the contributions to the development of the EAL field is associated with the Ministry of Education.

Contributions to the EAL field in Oman can be traced to the establishment of a number of EAL programs and the development of different policies and legislations by the Ministry of Education. The establishment of the Department of Educational Foundations and Administration (DEFA) in 1997, as a separate unit in the College of Education, in the first university in Oman, Sultan Qaboos University (SQU) (Sultan Qaboos University, n.d.), marks the first attempt of the government to keep abreast with the rapid developments of the educational field in Oman. DEFA's mission is focused on contributing to the research and knowledge production in the field of leadership, administration, and foundations of education, and also providing services for all practitioners in the educational field in Oman.

Later years showed the establishment of more universities in Oman with their respective EAL departments and programs. In 2001, University of Sohar, the first private university in Oman launched its Master's program in Educational Foundations and Administration in its Education and Arts College (Sohar University, 2021). The academic year 2004–2005 marked the opening of the University of Nizwa and its Master's in Educational Administration program (Nizwa University, 2021). In 2004, Dhofar University was established and began offering a master's in educational administration in its education department (Dhofar University, 2021). In the academic year 2008–2009, the Arab Open University opened its doors and began offering a master's in educational leadership (Arab Open University, 2021). The most recent development of the EAL field in terms of university programs happened in 2021, as the A'Sharqiyah University began offering a master's in educational administration comprising three different emphases: educational leadership, planning and educational policies, and instructional supervision (A'Sharqiyah University, n.d.).

On another front, EAL has experienced development in regard to the ministry's efforts toward the professional development of school leaders. The year 1999 marked the first initiative of the Ministry of Education toward the development of school leaders with the introduction of the Diploma in School Administration for school principals who hold a bachelor's degree (Ministry of Education, 2005). This was followed by the introduction of a bachelor program in educational administration in 2003, where both programs were executed in collaboration with Sultan Qaboos University (SQU), and specifically its DEFA (Ministry of Education, 2005). In 2014, the Ministry of Education established The Specialized Institute for Professional Training of Teachers and launched the Educational Leadership program as part of this institute (Ministry of Education, 2016). The program is designed for school principals and their assistants and focuses primarily on improving school principals' instructional leadership skills (Ministry of Education, 2016).

On the other hand, the development of the EAL field in Oman was accompanied by a significant increase in policy planning, revision, and implementation. An example of this increased activity at the policy level is the development of detailed job descriptions for school principals and their assistants, as well as criteria for their appointment and evaluation (Ministry of Education, 2015). Moreover, in an effort to support school principals, the Ministry of Education issued a decree creating the job of an "administrative supervisor" whose job is to provide guidance and support for school principals (Ministry of Education and the Federation of New Zealand Educational Organizations, 2017).

We argue that, as the country continues to implement educational reform, there is a need for a high-quality, contextually relevant EAL knowledge base that can inform these efforts. Based on previous EAL research reviews in the region (Hammad et al., 2020; Hammad & Hallinger, 2017), it is not clear to what extent the existing EAL scholarship in Oman will live up to this challenge. It is within this framework that the current review is conducted. The chapter seeks to explore the EAL literature about Oman published in both Arabic and English language journals between 2000 and 2021. The Arabic EAL literature was identified by searching the Dar Al-Mandhuma database, while core EAL and international journals indexed in Scopus were used to identify the English-language literature. The chapter employs systematic review methods to quantitatively identify the key features of the Omani EAL literature, including publication volume, authorship trends, types of research studies, the composition of research topics, and the research methods employed.

The chapter is organized into three sections. The first section explains the methodology used in the review with specific reference to source identification, data extraction, and analysis. The second section discusses the results of the present review in light of the global literature. The third section presents the conclusion and proposes areas that future scholars in the field might focus on to help build a more balanced EAL literature in Oman with reference to the key features that emerged from the review.

Reviewing the Omani EAL Knowledge Base

The chapter follows the guidelines of systematic reviews of research (Gough, 2007; Hallinger, 2013). The review focused on finding patterns in the EAL literature in Oman, specifically with reference to volume of publication, study types, authorship trends, topical coverage, and research methods. The review was guided by the following research questions:

1 What is the volume of the Omani EAL research literature published between 2000 and 2021?
2 What authorship trends characterize the Omani EAL literature?
3 What research topics were used by scholars contributing to this literature?
4 What are the research methods used by scholars contributing to this literature?

This section discusses the procedures related to source identification, data extraction, and data analysis.

Identification of Sources

As a starting point, the review took prior reviews conducted in the Arab world in general (Hallinger & Hammad, 2017; Hammad & Hallinger, 2017; Karami-Akkary & El Sahib, 2019) and those done in the Gulf region (Hammad et al., 2020b; Hammad & Alazmi, 2022); the researchers use these reviews as a guiding lens to help identify and extract the sources. The chapter reports, exclusively, on published research articles and hence excludes books, book chapters, dissertations, or parts of dissertations published in journals. In order to provide an accurate display of the EAL scholarship published about Oman, the researchers decided to include research published in English and Arabic. Such a decision resonates with studies showing that scholars in the Global South continue to publish in their native language due to their lack of knowledge of the English language (Getahun et al., 2021).

Locating the EAL literature published in Arabic began with identifying sources on Dar Al-Mandhouma database using keywords such as principal, leadership, administration, supervision, decision-making, and organizational. Each of these words was used in conjunction with the keyword "Oman". The Dar Al-Mandhouma database was chosen because it is more comprehensive, comprising a number of databases specializing in social sciences and humanities such as EduSearch, EcoLink, IslamicInfo, AraBase, and Humanindex. This search yielded more than 2000 articles. These articles were scanned and with their abstracts occasionally read to make sure that they fit the following criteria; (1) articles about Oman; (2) articles that have a clear focus on EAL;

(3) articles that are *not* about EAL in higher education; (4) articles that are not excerpts from students' dissertations; and (5) articles that are available in full-text format. This left us with a total of 206 articles. In locating the Arabic literature, and based on previous systematic reviews conducted in the region (Attari & Essa, 2021; Hallinger & Hammad, 2017; Hammad & Hallinger, 2017; Karami-Akkary & El Sahib, 2019), the researchers had concerns regarding the quality of the published research. Therefore, an additional filter was added whereby articles to be included in the review had to publish in journals affiliated with universities or educational societies such as the Egyptian Society for Comparative Education and Educational Administration. The addition of this filter reduced the number of articles to 134.

In locating the English articles, the search began by looking for articles published in ten core EAL journals, namely *Educational Administration Quarterly (EAQ), Journal of Educational Administration (JEA), School Effectiveness and School Improvement (SESI), Educational Management, Administration and Leadership (EMAL), International Journal of Leadership in Education (IJLE), International Journal of Educational Management (IJEM), School Leadership and Management (SLM), Leadership and Policy in Schools (LPS), International Journal of Educational Administration & History (IJEAH),* and *International Studies in Educational Administration (ISEA).* The researchers scanned each issue to find articles about Oman; this resulted in eight articles. In the next stage, we expanded the search to include sources published in international journals indexed in the Scopus database.

In this stage, the researchers applied the same keywords used in identifying the EAL literature published in the Arabic language. This stage yielded six additional articles, raising the total of English articles to 15. Out of the 15, one article was removed as it did not have a clear focus on EAL. This brought the total number of Arabic and English articles in the review database to 148. When we began the data extraction process, the first author noticed that it was difficult to extract data pertaining to the research methods and data collection in ten out of 134 Arabic articles. This difficulty prompted the first author to read these articles very thoroughly. These ten articles were found to lack the methodological rigor to qualify them to be research articles. At this stage, these articles were removed from the review. The scanning of abstracts, at this stage, also led the first author to remove six additional articles from the review database, five of which were found not to have a clear EAL focus despite having a title that indicates this, and one was found to be part of a dissertation which does not align with the inclusion criteria delineated in the source identification stage. The total number of articles in the review database is now 132, of which 118 are in Arabic and 14 are in English.

Data Extraction and Analysis

During this stage, 132 articles were carefully scanned to extract the data relevant to answering the research questions. These data included article titles, authors' names, year of publication, types of studies, research topics, research methods, data collection tools, and statistical analyses. While the researchers were able to extract much of the data by simply reading the abstract, many instances required reading the full text. This was particularly true for the Arabic articles. In fact, it is important to note here that the aim of this review is not to judge the quality of the research articles. However, the removal of the articles from the Arabic database was necessary because the ten articles that were removed, due to their lack of methodological rigor, made it impossible for the researchers to code the research methods and data collection tools used in these articles; and the six articles removed did not meet the inclusion criteria. Therefore, the data extraction in this review served as an additional filter. The extracted data were entered into a Microsoft Excel spreadsheet and codes were used to identify the different areas in the articles that were needed to answer the research questions. For example, "paper type" was coded as empirical (=1), and non-empirical (=2). The choice of the codes was based on previous reviews done in the region (Hammad et al., 2020; Hammad & Hallinger, 2017) but was modified according to the database. For example, we removed commentaries and reviews as these were not present in any of the 132 articles. Research methods were coded as follows: quantitative = 1, qualitative = 2, and mixed = 3.

Quantitative data analysis was used to identify the general trends in the EAL literature in Oman where descriptive statistics were employed to generate tables and describe the salient features in the literature. We were keen on grounding our data in previous systematic reviews especially those done in the region (Ahmed, 2020; Atari & Outum, 2019; Hallinger & Hammad, 2017; Hammad et al., 2020b; Hammad & Hallinger, 2017; Karami-Akkary & El Sahib, 2019; Oplatka & Arar, 2017b), in addition to reviews done at the international level (Bridges, 1982; Castillo & Hallinger, 2017; Hallinger, 2018; Hallinger & Chen, 2015). This grounding provides a conceptual lens that enables a more critical analysis of the data.

The Status Quo of the EAL Knowledge Base in Oman

This part of the chapter delineates the results of the present systematic review of articles published in English and Arabic language journals. However, before proceeding, it is important to ground the EAL literature of Oman within the Arab and Gulf production of EAL knowledge. Systematic reviews consistently describe the production of EAL in the Arab region as being on the developing end (Oplatka & Arar, 2017), and that its volume constitutes a very small percentage of the EAL international literature (Atari & Outum, 2019; Hallinger & Hammad, 2017). It is within this context that the data of this systematic review in Oman are analyzed.

Volume of the Production

With reference to the volume of production, there are two aspects that this section will look at: the overall number of articles produced in Oman, and how this number is distributed between Arabic and English language publication outlets. The overall number of 132 articles published over a period of 22 years may be considered low; however, this number resonates with Hammad's et al. (2020) systematic review in the Gulf region where Oman's contribution to the total number of articles published was 20%. Such a moderate percentage may be understood within the fewer number of universities in Oman compared, for example, with KSA which is the largest producer of EAL knowledge in the Gulf region. The number of universities and the type of research that these universities produce remain important indicators for knowledge production (Hanafi & Arvanitis, 2015).

Despite the moderate contribution of Oman to the Gulf EAL knowledge production, there is a promising finding. The number of articles produced in the last ten years (between 2011 and 2021) with 119 out of 132 articles reviewed comprises 90.15% percent of the total number of articles showing a striking increase of 80%. Such a result is also consistent with reviews in the Arab World, which shows that the number of research publications is increasing in the region (Hammad et al., 2020; Hammad & Hallinger, 2017; Karami-Akkary & El Sahib, 2019; Oplatka & Arar, 2017). As for the literature published in English language journals, this comprised only 10.6% of the Omani EAL literature. While the percentage is alarmingly low, it can be expected as it aligns with systematic reviews indicating that the contribution of Arab scholars to the international literature remains very low (Hammad et al., 2020; Hammad and Alazmi, 2022; Hammad & Hallinger, 2017). There are several reasons for this: one is the language barrier as many of the Arab scholars residing in the Arab region do not have a good command of the English language, making it challenging for them to publish in international journals (Getahun et al., 2021). Another reason could be the less stringent review processes of the Arab journals (El-Amine, 2021). Like other scholars around the globe, scholars in the Arab world are under increasing pressure to publish, elegantly seen in the infamous "publish or perish" culture (Smith, 1990). Academia, as a field, has the rule of "publish or perish" which scholars need to adhere to or they risk losing their "habitus", borrowing the concept from Bourdieu (2020). Therefore, the language, review process, and increasing pressure on academicians to publish are all factors that help explain the significantly higher number of articles published in Arabic journals.

Authorship Trends

Analysis for authorship trends included articles, whether articles were single-authored or co-authored, and the gender of the authors. The analysis revealed that 78% ($N = 103$) of the articles reviewed are co-authored as shown in Table 12.1. This result represents a deviation from the other systematic reviews where single-authored articles were the dominant feature (e.g., Hammad et al., 2020) and where the gap between single-authored and co-authored articles was not wide (e.g., Attari & Essa, 2021; Atari & Outum,

Table 12.1 Authorship trends in the review

	Authorship in all articles in the review (%)	Authorship in Arabic articles (%)	Authorship in English articles (%)
Single author	21.97	22.88	14.29
Co-authored	78.03	77.12	85.71

2019). Within the international scholarship, the high percentage of co-authored articles may be explained in two ways. First, the language barrier that some researchers may encounter might be mediated by teaming up with colleagues who have a better command of the English language. Second, the complexity of the topics seen in the international journal articles advocates for collaboration and teamwork.

With reference to gender, 47.73% ($N = 63$) of the articles were written by male scholars, 26% ($N = 26$) by female scholars, and 32.58% ($N = 43$) were written by teams comprising both male and female authors. The results indicate a dominance of the male authorship on the Omani EAL literature which concurs with systematic reviews in the Gulf region, Arab world, and on the international level (Atari & Outum, 2019; Attari & Essa, 2021; Hammad et al., 2020).

Types of Paper

All 132 articles reviewed in this chapter were empirical in nature and, despite this being an alarming result, it aligns with a number of systematic reviews in the region where empirical studies continue to show the highest percentage of paper types (El-Amine, 2021; Hallinger & Hammad, 2017; Hammad et al., 2020; Karami-Akkary & El Sahib, 2019; Oplatka & Arar, 2017).

There are a number of ways to interpret this result. One is that the EAL field in the Arab world is on the developing end (Attari & Essa, 2021; Oplatka & Arar, 2017) and therefore data-driven analyses and conclusions about leadership practices, developed from empirical studies, are very much needed to help develop a grounded understanding of the field in the Omani context. Hence, this might be a positive indication showing that the field is developing away from researchers' opinions and commentaries; such an argument is supported by systematic reviews that tried to explain the dominance of empirical research on the Arab EAL scholarship (Hallinger & Hammad, 2017). However, within the frame of our study, adopting this argument is not without its challenges, as the argument makes the assumption that the empirical studies do indeed make a contribution to the EAL knowledge base. Within the research articles published in Arabic journals, such an assumption is questioned as a number of educational scholars have voiced concerns regarding the quality of published research articles and the review process adopted by these journals. In fact, El-Amine (2021) refers to this trend as "empty empiricism" that does not contribute to any knowledge production, but rather to the production of "void" output. While it is not within the scope of this chapter to adopt or reject El-Amine's (2021) position of the status quo of the Arab scholarship, this chapter does acknowledge that empty empiricism may be a challenge facing knowledge production in the Arab world, which calls for qualitative systematic reviews seeking to critically synthesize the result of these studies.

Therefore, within this framing, the result of paper types in the Omani EAL literature is one of significance comprising two contradicting interpretations. One interpretation carries a positive connotation of the EAL field in Oman moving toward the production of data-driven contextual knowledge, while the other interpretation can be quite alarming signaling a field that is growing in the direction of producing redundant empirical studies that fail to make a meaningful contribution to the EAL Omani knowledge base. The latter direction becomes a more pressing notion to allude to as we consider that empirical studies might be preferred by scholars because these studies follow a more systematic and predictable path and therefore might have better chances of being published (see Getahun et al, 2021), hence allowing scholars stuck in the notorious 'publish or perish' culture to advance.

Therefore, while the dominance of empirical studies in the field might be in line with the manner in which other EAL literatures are emerging in developing countries, researchers need to be careful about the absence of critiques and conceptualizations of leadership practices in the Arab world (Attari & Essa, 2021; Oplatka & Arar, 2017); and the Omani EAL field developing into a field of empty empiricism branded by numbers, graphs, and tables that are void of any meaningful contribution to the EAL scholarship (El-Amine, 2021).

Research Methods

This section focuses on three main areas: the research methods employed, the data collection tools used, and the level of statistical analysis applied in the Omani EAL. Results of the present systematic review showed an uneven distribution in all three areas. All 132 articles were analyzed for research methods since all 132 articles were empirical in nature. The analysis of the data extracted revealed that 120 articles out of the total 132 articles (91%) reviewed employed quantitative research methods, and only seven articles (5.3%) employed qualitative research methods as demonstrated in Figure 12.1. This result resonates with prior reviews showing the dominance of quantitative research methods (Atari & Outum, 2019; El-Amine, 2021; Hammad & Hallinger, 2017) in the Arab region.

Results of data collection methods were consistent with the pattern of research methods used as 90% ($N = 124$) of the total number of articles in the review used surveys, and a shy 9% ($N = 12$) used interviews. This aligns with

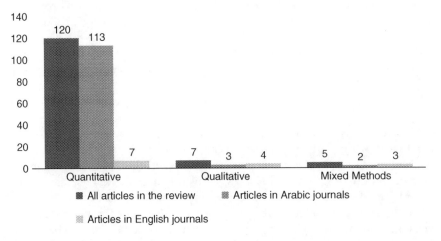

Figure 12.1 Distribution of articles by research methods.

Hammad & Hallinger's (2017) review where 63% of the Arab articles published in core EAL journals were found to have used surveys. However, once again, the dominance of surveys was much more prominent in the articles published in Arabic, with the vast majority of these studies (i.e., 115 out of 118) having used surveys as a data collection tool. Only one study used document analysis (Al-Ani, 2013), and five studies used interviews (e.g., Al-Ani et al., 2018; Salah El-Din, 2020). In parallel to this, nine English language articles used surveys (Imran et al., 2017; Shindi et al., 2020), and seven articles used interviews (Al-Kiyumi & Hammad, 2019; Hammad & Bush, 2021), thus showing a more even distribution between surveys (64.28%) and interviews (50%), which is consistent with the research methods used in these articles. Figure 12.2 shows the distribution of data collection in both Arabic and English journals.

Interestingly, none of the articles reviewed in this chapter used observation as a means of collecting data. This is also consistent with prior reviews which showed that the use of observation is rare in the Arab EAL scholarship (Attari & Essa, 2021; Hammad et al., 2020; Hammad & Hallinger, 2017).

The third aspect in this section is concerned with the statistical tests used for data analysis in the subset of quantitative and mixed research methods articles. The review employed a rubric developed by Bridges (1982) for assessing the level of statistical analysis used. Using a rubric that has been used in a number of other systematic reviews enabled us to compare the results of our analysis with other studies (see Ahmed, 2020; Hallinger, 2011; Hallinger & Chen, 2015; Hallinger & Hammad, 2017; Hammad & Hallinger, 2017). The rubric (Bridges, 1982) delineates the four levels of statistical analysis:

1 Level 1: is limited to descriptive statistics such as calculating means and standard deviations.

Educational Administration and Leadership in Oman 219

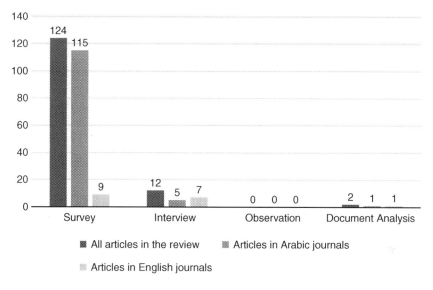

Figure 12.2 Distribution of articles by data collection methods.

2 Level 2: Includes statistical test to relate to single causal factor/correlational statistics such as the t-test and Pearson's correlation.
3 Level 3: Involves having control with the single causal factor/correlational statistics that are used (e.g., one-way analysis of variance)
4 Level 4: statistical analysis at this level includes multiple factor and advanced modeling (e.g., structural equation modeling, multiple regression, MANOVA).

The statistical level was extracted for the 125 articles that used either quantitative or mixed research methods. As depicted in Figure 12.3, 73% ($N = 93$ articles) of the articles reviewed in this chapter used level 2 and 3 analyses (e.g., Al-Bandari, 2021; Al-Zadjali, 2020; Al-Saeedi, 2019), while only 13% (N = 17) used Level 4 statistical tests (Al-Harthyi et al., 2021; Ahmed & Al-Ani, 2020; Al-Mahdy et al., 2016). Figure 12.4 shows a comparison between Arabic and English language articles with regard to the distribution of articles by level of statistical analysis.

With reference to the use of multivariate analysis (level 4), a difference was noted between articles published in Arabic journals and those published in English journals, where level 4 was employed by 60% of the English articles and only 7.8% of Arabic articles. Our results, therefore, show a prevalence of simple quantitative statistical analyses in Omani EAL with reference to articles published in Arabic. This result is in sync with reviews of early EAL literature which showed a heavy reliance on simple statistical tests (Bridges, 1982; Haller, 1979). The result is also consistent with the description of the broader

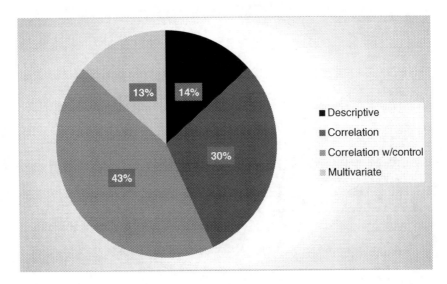

Figure 12.3 Overall distribution of articles by level of statistical analysis.

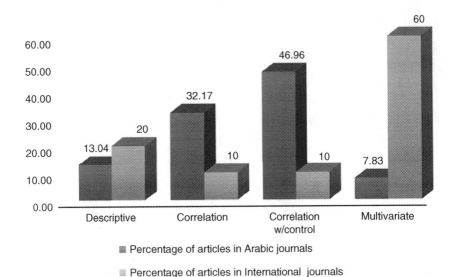

Figure 12.4 The distribution, by percentage, of articles in Arabic and English journals by level of statistical analysis.

Arab EAL scholarship as an emerging field (Attari & Essa, 2021; Hallinger & Hammad, 2017; Oplatka & Arar, 2017). Moreover, this finding also resonates with the review done by Hammad et al. (2020) on the Arabic language EAL literature published in the Gulf which showed that 73% of the articles used level 2 and level 3 statistical tests. Conversely, the analysis reveals the predominance of advanced statistical analyses in the subset of English language articles which is not consistent with the emerging nature of the field in the region, despite being aligned with previous reviews done in the region (Hammad & Hallinger, 2017). Such a prevalence of advanced statistical analyses may be an indication that the stringent review processes employed in English journals in addition to university promotion criteria requiring faculty members to publish in indexed and high-ranking journals (Getahun et al., 2021; Lee, 2014) may serve as factors accelerating the development of the EAL field in developing societies.

Research Topics Covered in the Omani EAL Literature

The analysis focused on classifying the topics addressed in the research articles reviewed. The chapter employed a typology adapted from previous EAL reviews (Atari & Outum, 2019; Gümüş et al., 2020; Hallinger & Chen, 2015; Hammad et al., 2020; Karami-Akkary & El Sahib, 2019); a number of topics were added and others were removed to suit the database identified. The topical coverage of Omani EAL literature shows an uneven distribution, as some topics are heavily researched, and others are either under-researched or not researched at all. Specifically, the topical coverage in both English and Arabic scholarship showed an eclectic and dispersed pattern, where even topics that were heavily researched did not show a focused trajectory. Such a pattern in coverage, while being consistent with previous reviews on emerging contexts (e.g., Bridges, 1982; Hallinger & Chen, 2015), does not help accumulate knowledge in a particular area (Hanafi & Arvanitis, 2015) which results in leaving behind a clear "footprint".

Data shown in Table 12.2 indicate that the number of studies done on leadership was the highest ($N = 75$) with a percentage of 56.8%. Not very far from this number were the 65 studies about school principals (49.2%), followed by studies on instructional supervision and teacher evaluation (19.6%), and then school management roles, practices, and processes at 18.9% ($N = 25$). Studies addressing human resources and organizational behavior, and climate and culture were also common with 12.8% ($N = 17$) and 12.12% ($N = 16$), respectively. This general pattern aligns with prior reviews done in the region (Hammad et al., 2020; Hammad & Hallinger, 2017; Karami-Akkary & El Sahib, 2019; Oplatka & Arar, 2017).

Table 12.2 Gender authorship trends in the review

	Gender authorship in all articles in the review (%)	Gender authorship in Arabic articles (%)	Gender authorship in English articles (%)
Male	47.73	50.00	28.57
Female	19.70	19.49	21.43
Mixed	32.58	30.51	50.00

The analysis also looked for differences in the pattern of topical coverage between Arabic and English language articles. While both leadership and principals topped the chart for English and Arabic EAL, this was not the case for instructional supervision which had only been addressed in two out of the 14 English language articles compared to 24 articles in Arabic journals. This specific result resonates with Hammad et al.'s (2020) review in the Gulf region and Karami-Akkary & El-Sahib's (2019) review in the Arab region.

Within the Arabic scholarship, leadership was addressed in 64 out of the 118 articles. A number of these articles focused on diverse leadership styles such as servant leadership (Al-Siyabi et al., 2021), spiritual leadership (Al-Shuhoomi, 2020), transformational leadership (Al-Obaidani & Hashem, 2020), and distributed leadership (Al-Ani, 2013). Therefore, the results of the review did not indicate a prevalence of one particular style of leadership in the topical coverage. Moreover, many of the articles addressed the leadership aspect of instructional supervision (e.g., Khamis & Al-Shukaili, 2019; Al-Sayed & Saar, 2020; Al-Mahdy & Al-Harthi, 2021). In the articles published in English journals, 11 out of the 14 articles addressed leadership in a rather eclectic manner. There were articles that focused on the leadership aspect in instructional supervision (Al-Kiyumi & Hammad, 2019, 2020) and this is similar to the trend seen in the Arabic EAL scholarship. There were also studies that addressed the relation between leadership and a number of different variables such as collective teacher agency (Al-Mahdy et al., 2018), teachers' attitudes (Al-Mahdy & Emam, 2018), school effectiveness (Al-Harthi & Al-Mahdy, 2017), and teachers' professional learning (Al-Mahdy et al., 2021). Studying the relationship between leadership and different aspects of teacher development is a promising finding as it interjects with understanding the impact of leadership as a complex phenomenon contributing to the development and improvement of different areas in teaching and learning. However, despite the emphasis given to both leadership and principals in the Omani EAL literature, leadership preparation was completely *absent* from the Arabic publications and heavily under-researched in the English literature with an orphan article published by Hammad and Bush (2021).

Studies on school principals were common in both Arabic ($N = 57$) and English scholarship ($N = 8$). Studies published in Arabic journals focused primarily on the degree of practice of certain functions of administration by school principals (Al-Ghafri et al., 2020; Al-Hashemi et al., 2020; Al-Maaytah & Al-Rajhi, 2017), while other studies addressed the role school principals play in teachers' attitudes and professional development (e.g Al-Shuaili & Ibrahim, 2020; Al-Harthi et al., 2021; Ibrahim & Al-Shahoumi, 2018). The eight articles in the English journals that addressed school principals showed a diverse coverage of the topic as some focused on studying principals' perceptions (Al-Ani & Al-Harthi, 2017; Al-Harthi, 2017; Hammad & Bush, 2021), while others focused on studying the relation between principals' role and different teacher-related variables (Al-Mahdy et al., 2021; Al-Mahdy &

Emam, 2018). The predominance of leadership and school principals in the topical coverage of the EAL Omani literature aligns with previous systematic reviews (Hammad et al., 2020; Hammad & Hallinger, 2017).

The analysis also revealed a difference (Table 12.3) in the overall distribution of topics between Arabic and English scholarship in the Omani EAL, primarily with reference to two categories: emotions: commitment, motivation,

Table 12.3 Topical coverage (The total number of topics exceeded 132 because most of the articles addressed more than one topic)

	Articles in both Arabic and Int. journals	Articles in Arabic journals	Articles in Int. journals
Leadership	75	64	11
Principals	65	57	8
Instructional supervision and teacher evaluation	26	24	2
School management roles, practices, and processes	25	24	1
Emotions: commitment, motivation, satisfaction	20	14	6
Human resources: selection, preparation, and development	18	16	2
Organizational behavior, climate, and culture	16	12	4
ICT	11	10	1
Quality and accreditation	8	8	0
Change, school performance, and improvement	7	4	3
Values, ethics, and social Justice	6	5	1
Superintends, districts, and directorates	5	4	1
Governance: SBM, decentralization, accountability, and empowerment	3	3	0
Inclusive education	3	1	2
Curriculum and teaching	3	3	0
Parents and community	2	2	0
Proposed frameworks and models	2	2	0
Decision-making	1	1	0
Entrepreneurship	1	1	0
Gender	0	0	0
Middle-Level Leadership	0	0	0
Finance	0	0	0
Cultural contexts	0	0	0

(I agree but was not sure how to this).

satisfaction; and organizational behavior, climate, and culture as shown in Table 12.3. Six out of the 14 (42.8%) English articles addressed emotions including commitment and motivation (Al-Mahdy et al., 2016; Al-Mahdy & Emam, 2018; Imran et al., 2017), while only 14 out of the 118 (11.86%) Arabic articles addressed these topics (e.g., Al-Dhafri & Al-Saeedi, 2020; Al-Bandari & Al-Atoum, 2002; Attari et al., 2006). A similar pattern was seen in the organizational behavior, climate, and culture as the topic was addressed by four English articles (28.5%) (Al-Mahdy et al., 2021; Al-Mahdy et al., 2016; Shindi et al., 2020) and only 12 (10.2%) Arabic articles (e.g., Al-Jaraydah, 2021; Al-Mahdy et al., 2018; Al Balushi, 2014). This difference between Arabic and English scholarship might be understood with respect to the statistical analysis level used. Multivariate analysis was much more commonly used in the articles published in English journals, and within these two topical categories, *all* the English articles used this level of analysis, while seven out of the 12 Arabic articles used this level of analysis.

Quite interestingly no studies were found on gender, middle-level leadership, finance, and cultural contexts despite being topics of interest at the international level. These results are consistent with previous systematic reviews (Hammad & Hallinger, 2017; Hammad et al., 2020). Unlike the review of Hammad et al. (2020), results of this review show a shy emergence of topics such as social justice and values ($N = 6$), which aligns with Atari and Outum's (2019) review.

Conclusion and Implications

The current review represents a response to recent calls from EAL scholars (e.g., Hallinger & Bryant, 2013), which recommends conducting national reviews of research to help expand and understand the knowledge base of EAL, especially in countries with a relatively modest contribution to the global EAL literature. The purpose of this chapter was therefore to examine the EAL knowledge base in Oman by systematically reviewing 132 Arabic and English language EAL research articles published between 2000 and 2021. The chapter applied quantitative methods to identify the salient features of the articles reviewed, with reference to publication volume, types of articles, authorship trends, topical coverage, and research methods. The analysis revealed interesting results that largely mirror those reported for the broader Arab EAL scholarship. It is expected that these results will enrich the global EAL literature and enhance our understanding of how the production of EAL knowledge develops in different parts of the world. However, before proceeding, it is appropriate to indicate that these findings should be understood in light of the limitations of the review. First, the review only analyzed research articles, thus excluding other potential sources of EAL literature such as students' dissertations, books, book chapters, and conference proceedings. Second, the review adopted a quantitative approach to analyzing the articles that did not allow for in-depth analysis.

The main implication for this chapter is the need to develop a mature EAL scholarship in Oman, which in turn requires the development of a research agenda that can bridge the gap between EAL research, educational policy, and practice in the country. As a field that is relatively young, EAL in Oman has been on a steep learning curve that aims to remain abreast with the global developments in the field. The development of policies, research centers, and departments of EAL in universities represents concerted efforts materializing the advancement of Oman's EAL. However, scholars agree that this development requires creating solid bridges between research agenda and policymaking (Ball, 2011). Therefore, exploring the current knowledge base of EAL in Oman represents an important and critical step toward identifying areas in which the relation between research, practice, and policymaking can be strengthened, which would lead toward a contextual and critical development of the EAL field in Oman.

Within this context, methodological limitations need to be recognized. There are a number of ways in which this can happen. First, our results indicate a need to employ more complex/multivariate designs, especially in Arabic language research, as this will help better understand leadership and administration as complex notions affected by a number of different variables. Second, there is a need to encourage EAL scholars to adopt diverse research methods, especially qualitative research. The review performed in this chapter found a concerning scarcity in qualitative studies. Conducting such studies is needed to provide an in-depth critical analysis of the leadership practices and educational administration processes in Oman. In the same vein, this review sees a need to conduct large-scale surveys that study the attitudes, characteristics, and beliefs of school leaders in Oman in addition to the theory-informed studies that connect to the global literature to help scholars develop culturally grounded theories of leadership, taking into account the historic, ethnic, and religious context of the country. Third, the review also showed that topical coverage is dispersed and eclectic and does not facilitate the development of a well-balanced EAL scholarship. Therefore, there is a need for scholars to focus on the under-researched topics such as gender, middle-level leadership, finance, and cultural contexts, especially since these topics are of interest at the international level and are much needed within development at policy and legislation levels. For example, researching the topic of gender in educational leadership is of importance, especially within the context of Oman as studies indicate that a gender gap exists in the representation of women in critical and policymaking positions (AlWahaibi, 2020). This comes at odds with royal decrees and legislations delineating women as equal to men in rights (Al-Lamky, 2007). This is one example of the importance of cultural grounding as scholars continue to question the applicability of many of the models and theories of EAL with their intellectual roots being in North America (Oplatka & Arar, 2017c).

Our findings show that the research produced in Oman is on the developing end and has the potential to contribute to the knowledge base and, hence, inform practice and policy provided that attention is given to concerns raised in this review, especially with regard to the research methods and data analysis employed, and the research topics being explored. Such a concern resonates with studies showing EAL literature is scant in the Middle East region (Arar, 2020). Therefore, scholars are encouraged to use data from systematic reviews and educational reform initiatives to develop research agendas that are relevant and respond to the needs of their contexts.

However, it is vital that these findings are understood within both the regional and national contexts of EAL knowledge production. The production of culturally relevant knowledge is not a challenge particular to Omani EAL literature but extends to include the Arab region as documented by a number of scholars referring to the relevance and contextualization of knowledge produced in the area (Alazmi & Hammad, 2021; Attari & Essa, 2021; Hanafi & Arvanitis, 2015). Said's (2014) traveling theory helps us understand the overuse of Western theories in Arab scholarship which comes at the expense of producing knowledge that is relevant, useful, and grounded in societies and culture. Said (2014) contends that theories are unidirectional in their travel, traveling from dominating societies (Global North) to the dominated societies (Global South). This domination is also seen in the pressure to publish in international journals (Lee, 2014; Smith, 1990) that have their own readership in terms of scope which may be different from the needs of Arab societies and lack relevance; needs and relevance are two points that Hanafi and Arvanitis (2015) advocate for in order to help improve knowledge production in the Arab world. On the other hand, the lack of qualitative research and publication in international journals may be understood within the idiosyncratic challenges facing scholars in Oman (Hammad & Al-Ani, 2021) and the region (Getahun et al., 2021), where both studies advocate for the need to place greater emphasis on research capacity building. This capacity building may help scholars in the field adopt research methods and data collection tools that may have been otherwise outside their comfort zone.

Nonetheless, assuming that the capacity building and scholars' adoption of diverse research methods will be sufficient to address the implications that this chapter presents would be naïve. Scholars in the Arab world, in general, are working within challenging conditions; some of these may be common to challenges at the international level, while other conditions may be particular to the Omani context. One of these challenges is the impact of "publish and perish" on the quality and contribution of EAL research published in the Arab world to the global EAL knowledge base. While this might be an international concern (Lee, 2014; Smith, 1990), it is more pressing in the scholarship published in the Arab world as journals lack a ranking system and citation index (El-Amine, 2021; Hallinger & Hammad, 2017; Hammad et al., 2020), in addition to concerns about the rigor of review processes in Arabic journals (El-Amine, 2021). Therefore, improving the contribution of Arab scholarship does not *only* fall on the shoulders of Arab scholars, but it is also a concerted effort that includes publication venues, criteria for promotion in universities, in addition to researchers' capacity building.

Last but not least, and stemming from the limitations that the review acknowledges, our chapter calls for qualitative reviews of the EAL literature in Oman. Such a call aligns with Hammad et al.'s (2020) discussion on the importance of carrying out quality reviews in the Arabian Gulf in order to better understand the nature of the EAL literature produced in this region, using a critical lens for this understanding. In carrying out these qualitative reviews, the chapter advocates for the use of models developed by a number of scholars (e.g., Attari & Essa, 2021; Gunter et al., 2013; Hallinger, 2019) that ask critical questions about what, who, where, and, why EAL knowledge is produced in the Arab world. Asking these critical questions will pave the way to understanding the critical mass of the knowledge produced, problematize it, ground it in reference to global knowledge, and suggest future research foci. Therefore, Omani EAL scholarship has a number of promising features that may qualify as gems to be capitalized on provided that the concerns raised in this review are addressed.

References

Ahmed, A., & Al-Ani, W. (2020). The practices of school principals in applying entrepreneurial education as an entry point towards a knowledge society: "An applied study on post-basic education in the Sultanate of Oman". *Journal of Educational Administration: The Egyptian Association for Comparative Education and Educational Administration, 7*(25), 13–103. DOI: 10.21608/emj.2020.92451

Ahmed, E. I. (2020). Systematic review of research on educational leadership and management in Muslim societies. *Educational Management Administration & Leadership, 51*, 52–74. 10.1177/1741143220973658

Al-Ani, W. (2013). Employing the approach of distributed leadership and work teams in the development of basic education schools in the Sultanate of Oman. *Journal of the Faculty of Education: Beni Suef University - Faculty of Education, 10*(65), 291–329.

Al-Ani, W. T., & Al-Harthi, A. S. (2017). Perceived educational values of Omani school principals. *International Journal of Leadership in Education, 20*(2), 198–219.

Al-Bandari, A. (2021). The effectiveness of time management from the point of view of school principals in Al Batinah Governorate, North, Sultanate of Oman. *Educational and psychological studies: Zagazig University- Faculty of Education, 110*, 221–274.

Al-Bandari, M., & Al-Atoum, A. (2002). The nature of personal relationships between principals and teachers and their relationship to job satisfaction in secondary school teachers in the Sultanate of Oman and Jordan. *Journal of Educational and Psychological Sciences: University of Bahrain - Scientific Publishing Center, 3*(3), 90–121.

Al Balushi, H. (2014). New teachers' awareness of organizational support for school principals in the Sultanate of Oman: A field study. *University Performance Development Magazine: Mansoura University - University Performance Development Center, 3*(1), 187–230.

Aldhafri, S., & Alsaidi, D. (2020). Organizational silence and its relation to organizational justice among school workers in Sultanate of Oman. *Journal of Educational and Psychological Sciences*, 21, 373–401. 10.12785/jeps/210111

Al-Harthi, A. S. A. (2017). Technological self-efficacy among school leaders in Oman: A preliminary study. *Journal of Further and Higher Education*, 41(6), 760–772.

Al-Harthi, A. S. A., & Al-Mahdy, Y. F. H. (2017). Distributed leadership and school effectiveness in Egypt and Oman: An exploratory study. *International Journal of Educational Management*, 31(6), 801–813. 10.1108/IJEM-05-2016-0132

Al-Harthi, K., Al-Mahdi, Y., & Ihab, M. (2021). Modeling the impact of school principals' leadership on teachers' professional learning in public schools in the Sultanate of Oman. *International Journal of Educational Research - United Arab Emirates University*, 45(3), 131–157.

Al-Hashemi, A., Muhammad, A., & Jawhar, Y. (2020). The degree of practicing strategic planning processes in basic education schools in the Sultanate of Oman from the point of view of school principals. *Fayoum University Journal of Educational and Psychological Sciences*, 14, 105–172. 10.21608/jfust.2020.119375.

Al-Ghafri, H., Ibn Samah, R., & Abdul Rahman, A. (2020). The level of practice of school principals in the Sultanate of Oman of educational leadership. *Journal of Educational and Psychological Sciences: The National Research Center Gaza*, 4(47), 76–105.

Al-Jaraydah, M. (2021). Relationship between organizational prowess and the quality of the organizational climate in the schools of AlDakhiliyah Governorate in the Sultanate of Oman. *Arab Research Journal in the Fields of Specific Education: Association of Arab Educators*, 22, 267–29010.21608/raes.2021.160704.

Al-Kiyumi, A., & Hammad, W. (2019). Instructional supervision in the Sultanate of Oman: Shifting roles and practices in a stage of educational reform. *International Journal of Leadership in Education*, 22(2), 237–249.

Al-Kiyumi, A., & Hammad, W. (2020). *Preparing instructional supervisors for educational change: Empirical evidence from the Sultanate of Oman*. SAGE Open, 10(2), 2158244020935905.

Al-Mahdy, Y. E. H., Emam, M. M., & Hallinger, P. (2018). Assessing the contribution of principal instructional leadership and collective teacher efficacy to teacher commitment in Oman. *Teaching and Teacher Education*, 69, 191–201.

Al-Mahdy, Y. F. H., Al-Harthi, A. S., & Salah El-Din, N. S. (2016). Perceptions of school principals' servant leadership and their teachers' job satisfaction in Oman. *Leadership and Policy in Schools*, 15(4), 543–566.

Al-Mahdy, Y. F. H., & Emam, M. M. (2018). 'Much ado about something' how school leaders affect attitudes towards inclusive education: The case of Oman. *International Journal of Inclusive Education*, 22(11), 1154–1172. 10.1080/13603116.2017.1417500

Al-Mahdy, Y., Hallinger, P., Emam, M., Hammad, W., Alabri, K. M., & Al-Harthi, K. (2021). Supporting teacher professional learning in Oman: The effects of principal leadership, teacher trust, and teacher agency. *Educational Management Administration & Leadership*. 10.1177/17411432211064428Incomplete

Al-Maaytah, A., & Al-Rajhiyi, S. (2017). The practice job performance evaluation skills by principals of post-basic education from the teachers' point of view in AlDakhiliyah Governorate in the Sultanate of Oman. *Zarqa Journal of Researchand Human Studies: Zarqa University - Deanship of Scientific Research*, 17, 453–470.

Al-Lamky, A. (2007). Feminizing leadership in Arab societies: The perspectives of Omani female leaders. *Women in Management Review, 22*(1), 49–67

Al Balushi, S., & Griffiths, D. (2013). The school education system in the Sultanate of Oman. In G. Donn, & Y. Al Manthri (Eds.), *Education in the broader Middle East: Borrowing a baroque arsenal* (pp. 107–126). Symposium Books.

Alazmi, A. A., & Hammad, W. (2021). Modeling the relationship between principal leadership and teacher professional learning in Kuwait: The mediating effects of Trust and Teacher Agency. *Educational Management Administration & Leadership*, 1–20. 10.1177/17411432211038007

Al-Obaidani, K., & Hashem, N. (2020). The application of transformational leadership by instructional supervisors in the Sultanate of Oman: A descriptive and analytical study. *Journal of Educational and Psychological Sciences: The National Research Center Gaza, 4*, 67–80.

Al-Saeedi, H. (2019). The role of school principals in developing civic education in basic education schools in the Sultanate of Oman. *Educational Magazine: Sohag University - Faculty of Education, 67*, 123–144.

Al-Shuhoomi, H. (2020). The reality of school principals' practice of spiritual leadership in the Wilayat of Ibri, Al Dhahirah Governorate, in the Sultanate of Oman. *Arab Research Journal in the Fields of Specific Education: Association of Arab Educators, 20*, 313–333.

Al-Shuaili, S., & Ibrahim, H. (2020). The role of school principals in building professional learning communities in basic education schools in the North Sharqiyah Governorate in the Sultanate of Oman from the point of view of teachers. *Arab Studies in Education and Psychology: The Arab Educators Association, 126*, 465–491.

Al-Sayed, A. & Saar, S. (2020). Studying the differences in administrative empowerment among educational supervisors in the Sultanate of Oman. *Educational Sciences:Cairo University - Faculty of Postgraduate Studies for Education, 28*(3), 311–347.

Al-Siyabi, N., Al-Fahdi, R., & Al-Mahdi, Y. (2021). The reality of the practice of servant leadership for principals from the point of view of teachers in basic education schools in the Sultanate of Oman. *Journal of Educational and Psychological Research: University of Baghdad - Educational and Psychological Research Center, 70*, 214–248.

AlWahaibi, A. N. (2020). Women's empowerment from the perspective of female Omani academic leaders. *Handbook on promoting social justice in education*, pp. 1759–1777. Springer.

A'Sharqiyah University (n.d.). *Student handbook for postgraduate studies.* https://www.asu.edu.om/Page/55?College%20of%20Arts%20and%20Humanities

Arab Open University (2021). *Student handbook for postgraduate studies 2021–2022.* Arab Open University. https://www.aou.edu.om/ar/students/guide/Pages/default.aspx

Arar, K., Turan, S., Barakat, M., & Oplatka, I. (2017). The characteristics of educational leadership in the Middle East: A comparative analysis of three nation-states, In D. Waite & I, Bogotch (eds.), *International handbook of leadership in education.* (pp. 355–373). John Wiley & Sons, Inc.

Arar, K. (2020). Educational administration in the Middle East. In *The Oxford encyclopedia of education.* Oxford University Press. 10.1093/acrefore/9780190264093.013.672

Atari, A., & Outum, N. (2019). Research on educational administration published in Arabic language educational journals: A systematic review and analysis. *International Studies in Educational Administration (Commonwealth Council for Educational Administration & Management (CCEAM)), 47*(1).

Attari, A. T. M. Al., & Essa, E. B. (2021). Arab scholarship in educational administration, management and leadership: An overview. *Educational Management Administration & Leadership, 51*, 849–867. 10.1177/17411432211012011

Al-Zadjali, A. (2020). The status quo of training programs offered to principals of private schools in the North Al Batinah Governorate in the Sultanate of Oman. *Journal of Educational and Psychological Sciences: The National Research Center Gaza, 4*, 21–43.

Bajunid, I. A. (1996). Preliminary explorations of indigenous perspectives of educational management. *Journal of Educational Administration, 34*(5), 50–73. 10.1108/09578239610148278

Ball, S. J. (2011). A new research agenda for educational leadership and policy. *Management in Education, 25*(2), 50–52.

Belchetz, D., & Leithwood, K. (2007). *Successful leadership: Does context matter and if so, how?* (5, pp. 17–138). Dordrecht: Springer Netherlands. 10.1007/1-4020-5516-1_8

Bourdieu, P. (2020). Outline of a theory of practice. In B.B. Lawrence, & A. Karim (Eds.), *On violence* (pp. 189–198). Duke University Press. 10.1515/9780822390169-024

Bridges, E. M. (1982). Research on the school administrator: The state of the art, 1967–19801. *Educational Administration Quarterly, 18*(3), 12–33.

Castillo, F. A., & Hallinger, P. (2017). Systematic review of research on educational leadership and management in Latin America, 1991–2017. *Educational Management Administration & Leadership, 46*(2), 207–225. 10.1177/1741143217745882

Dimmock, C., & Walker, A. (2000). Developing comparative and international educational leadership and management: A cross-cultural model. *School Leadership & Management, 20*(2), 143–160. 10.1080/13632430050011399

Dhofar University (2021). *Postgraduate studies catalogue 2021–2022*, Dhoar University, Retrieved June 20, 2022, from http://caas.du.edu.om/en/master-of-education-in-education-admin/

El-Amine, A. (2021). *The production of void: The traditions of research in the Arab world*. Arab Scientific Publishers, Inc.

Garratt, D., & Forrester, G. (2012). *Education policy unravelled*. Continuum.

Getahun, D. A., Hammad, W., & Robinson-Pant, A. (2021). Academic writing for publication: Putting the 'international' into context. *Research in Comparative and International Education, 16*(2), 160–180.

Gough, D. (2007). Weight of evidence: A framework for the appraisal of the quality and relevance of evidence. *Research Papers in Education, 22*(2), 213–228.

Gümüş, S., Bellibaş, M. Ş., Gümüş, E., & Hallinger, P. (2020). Science mapping research on educational leadership and management in Turkey: A bibliometric review of international publications. *School Leadership & Management, 40*(1), 23–44. 10.1080/13632434.2019.1578737

Gunter, H., Hall, D., & Bragg, J. (2013). Distributed leadership: A study in knowledge production. *Educational Management Administration & Leadership, 41*(5), 555–580. 10.1177/1741143213488586

Haller, E. J. (1979). Questionnaires and the dissertation in educational administration. *Educational Administration Quarterly, 15*(1), 47–66.

Hallinger (1995). Culture and leadership: Developing an international perspective in educational administration. *UcEa Review, 36*(1), 3–7.

Hallinger, P. (2011). A review of three decades of doctoral studies using the principal instructional management rating scale: A lens on methodological progress in educational leadership. *Educational Administration Quarterly, 47*(2), 271–306. 10.1177/0013161X10383412

Hallinger, P., & Bryant, D. (2013). Mapping the terrain of educational leadership and management in East Asia. *Journal of Educational Administration, 51*(5), 618–637.

Hallinger, P. (2018). Surfacing a hidden literature: A systematic review of research on educational leadership and management in Africa. *Educational Management Administration & Leadership, 46*(3), 362–384.

Hallinger, P. (2019). A systematic review of research on educational leadership and management in South Africa: Mapping knowledge production in a developing society. *International Journal of Leadership in Education, 22*, 1–19. 10.1080/13603124.2018.1463460

Hallinger, P., & Chen, J. (2015). Review of research on educational leadership and management in Asia: A comparative analysis of research topics and methods, 1995–2012. *Educational Management Administration & Leadership, 43*(1), 5–27.

Hammad, W., & Al-Ani, W. (2021). Building educational research capacity: Challenges and opportunities from the perspectives of faculty members at a national university in Oman. *SAGE Open, 11*(3), 21582440211032668.

Hammad, W., & Alazmi, A. A. (2022). Research on school principals in the Gulf states: A systematic review of topics and conceptual models. *Management in Education, 36*(3), 105–114.

Hammad, W., & Bush, T. (2021). Exploring the perceptions of Omani school principals about their leadership preparation: A mixed-methods study. *Leadership and Policy in Schools, 22*, 1–16. 10.1080/15700763.2021.1931348

Hammad, W., & Hallinger, P. (2017). A systematic review of conceptual models and methods used in research on educational leadership and management in Arab societies. *School Leadership & Management, 37*(5), 434–456. 10.1080/13632434.2017.1366441

Hammad, W., Samier, E. A., & Mohammed, A. (2020). Mapping the field of educational leadership and management in the Arabian Gulf region: A systematic review of Arabic research literature. *Educational Management Administration & Leadership, 50*, 6–25. 10.1177/1741143220937308

Hanafi, S., & Arvanitis, R. (2015). *Knowledge production in the Arab world: The impossible promise*. Routledge.

Ibrahim, H., & Al-Shahoumi, S. (2018). The role of school principals in building professional learning communities in the Sultanate of Oman from the point of view of school administration supervisors. *Journal of the Faculty of Education: Benha University - Faculty of Education, 29*, 335–376.

Imran, R., Allil, K., & Mahmoud, A. B. (2017). Teacher's turnover intentions: Examining the impact of motivation and organizational commitment. *International Journal of Educational Management, 31*(6), 828–842.

Karami-Akkary, R., & El Sahib, N. (2019). A review of studies on educational administration in Arab countries (Shamaa Database 2007–2017). *Idafat, 45*, 67–90.

Khamis, A. & Al-Shukaili, M. (2019). The degree of practice of participatory instructional supervision in basic education schools and its relationship to teachers' job commitment in Al Dhahirah Governorate in the Sultanate of Oman. *Journal of Educational Knowledge: The Egyptian Association for Pedagogy, 7*, 65–116.

Lee, I. (2014). Publish or perish: The myth and reality of academic publishing. *Language Teaching, 47*(2), 250–261.

Lopez, A. E. (2020). *Decolonizing educational leadership: Exploring alternative approaches to leading schools.* Springer International Publishing.

Ministry of Education (2005). *Guide to professional development studies.* Ministry of Education in the Sultanate of Oman.

Ministry of Education (2010). *The educational renaissance in the Sultanate of Oman in numbers: 1970–2010.* Ministry of Education in the Sultanate of Oman.

Ministry of Education (2015). *School job description and workload guide.* Ministry of Education in the Sultanate of Oman.

Ministry of Education (2016). *The handbook of the Specialized Institute for Professional Training of Teachers.* Ministry of Education in the Sultanate of Oman.

Ministry of Education (2021). *Educational statistics for the academic year 2020/2021.* Ministry of Education in the Sultanate of Oman.

Ministry of Education and the Federation of New Zealand Educational Organizations (2017). *Evaluation of the educational system in the Sultanate of Oman: Grades 1–12.* Ministry of Education in the Sultanate of Oman.

Nasser, R. (2019). Educational reform in Oman: System and structural changes. In G. Porto Jr. (Ed.), *Education systems around the world* (pp. 75–92). IntechOpen.

Nizwa University (2021). *Program guide.* https://www.unizwa.edu.om/program_details.php.

Oplatka, I., & Arar, K. (2017). Context and Implications Document for: The research on educational leadership and management in the Arab world since the 1990s: A systematic review. *Review of Education, 5*(3), 308–310.

Oplatka, I., & Arar, K. (2017b). The research on educational leadership and management in the Arab world since the 1990s: A systematic review. *Review of Education, 5*(3), 267–307. 10.1002/rev3.3095

Oplatka, I., & Arar, K. (2017c). The field of educational administration as an arena of knowledge production: Some implications for Turkish field members. *Research in Educational Administration & Leadership, 1,* 161–186. 10.30828/real/2016.2.1

SalahEl-Din, N. (2020). Improving the professional performance of teachers in basic education schools in the Sultanate of Oman using integrated instructional supervision. *Journal of Scientific Research in Education: Ain Shams University - College of Arts, Sciences and Education for Girls, 21,* 27–97.

Said, E. (2014). *Orientalism.* Routledge.

Salibi, K. S. (1988). *A house of many mansions: The history of Lebanon reconsidered.* I.B. Tauris.

Samier, E. A. (2016). *Ideologies in educational administration and leadership.* Routledge. 10.4324/9781315661155

Shindi, Y. A. A., Al Omari, A. A., & Alabri, K. M. (2020). Omani short version of organizational health inventory: Application of item response theory. *Opción: Revista de Ciencias Humanas y Sociales, 27,* 90.

Smith, P. (1990). *Killing the spirit: Higher education in America.* ERIC.

Sohar University (2021). *Postgraduate student handbook 2021–2022,* Sohar University, https://www.su.edu.om/index.php/ar/study/postgraduate/handbookpg-ar

Sultan Qaboos University (n.d). *Postgraduate student handbook* Sutlan Qaboos University, https://www.squ.edu.om/education.

13 Revisiting and Reimagining Educational Leadership and Administration in the Middle East and North Africa

Khalid Arar, Selahattin Turan, Sedat Gümüş, Abdellatif Sellami, and Julia Mahfouz

In our introductory chapter, we noted that our intent in this book was to provide readers with insights about the development of educational leadership and administration (ELA) as a discipline in the Middle East and North Africa (MENA) region, how it is constructed in this region, and how the social and political stances of governments have a great influence on the ELA field. In this concluding chapter, we take a more macro view and consider some of the challenges and promises of some of the current trends we have observed in the ELA field in the MENA region based on the chapters that have important implications for systemic improvement. In contrast to the rest of the book, where each chapter aimed to provide a deep understanding of how ELA in each presented country has been developed and contributed to policy, practices, and research, our intent in this chapter is to offer more questions than answers, that is, we aim to highlight issues for researchers, practitioners, and policymakers that are important for extending and deepening the ELA field in the MENA region.

This book presents the historical development and the current situation of ELA in 11 countries from the MENA region considering research, policy, and practice perspectives. Each country case provides detailed information about ELA in the respective country, paying particular attention to the national and social-cultural context and how the context has interacted with the global norms and changes. Besides, discussions related to social justice, equity, and political inclusion have been included in most chapters given the high level of diversity regarding ethnic and religious backgrounds as well as numerous political and contextual challenges in the region. Overall, this book provides rich discussions on ELA in the region and demonstrates many commonalities as well as some similarities across different countries regarding the developments, challenges, and opportunities in research, policy, and practice.

It is clear from country cases that ELA as a research field has been growing in many countries, such as Egypt, Jordan, and Qatar, while it is more advanced and well-integrated with the ELA field internationally in a few

DOI: 10.4324/9781003334835-13

countries such as Turkey and Oman. However, there are also countries like Iraq, where there is a need for great efforts to establish and flourish ELA as a research field. While the research production shows great diversity across countries in the region, the lack of connection between research, policy, and practice has been raised as an important issue even in countries where the research is relatively strong (e.g., Chapters 2, 3, and 6). As one of the most common educational features of all countries in the region, the central and hierarchical government structure seems to play a role in such a lack of connection. Informing existing policies and practices of ELA with relevant research is one area that needs to be developed across all countries.

Country cases in this book also show that the quality and the quantity of education and training opportunities for educational leaders have been improved over the years while they are still not at the desired level in most countries. Overall, established structures for such opportunities and appointment processes are missing. This is even the case for Turkey, where the ELA departments at public universities have been well-established across the country. Consistently changing political influences on educational policies and institutions as well as clientelism seem to play roles in this, besides the lack of human resources in most countries. The situation is even worse regarding both the competencies of school leaders and informal requirements, such as having connections to certain groups, in some countries like Iraq where the political instability and internal conflicts have been lasting for a while.

Another trend in many countries in the region is securing financial and/or expert support from international organizations for the development and implementation of educational reforms. While such reforms have built some infrastructural and human capacity, the relevance of those reforms to the cultural and policy contexts has been a concern in some countries (e.g., Chapters 5 and 11). In addition, the sustainability of the established capacity through those external organizations is questionable. Therefore, building internal capacity through contextually relevant research and education/training activities could be suggested for a long-term improvement of educational reforms and ELA implementations in the region.

It is clear that despite the achievements mentioned in these chapters, educational leadership as a field in the MENA region is still far from its desired ends. The disconnect between policy, practice, and research is a fundamental roadblock to improvement. We need to build our understanding and development of ELA on evidence-informed research by MENA region experts who have a clear understanding of their governments and systems. The scarcity of research on ELA will not enable governments to make informed decisions. They may revert to only what the Western research says about the MENA region. This research should be based on the uniqueness of each country highlighting specific implications and recommendations that are fit to the school conditions of the particular countries' studies. We hope that such research is based on the funds of knowledge of the peoples of the countries and stems from a deeper understanding of ELA, its policies, and practices.

It is also important to note that educational leadership experts from outside the MENA region might not know how contextually and culturally diverse part of this world is. While educational systems ranging from countries in the context of fully centralized government control to other countries whose schools operate within an explicitly competitive market model seem to be similar, the day-to-day work of educational leaders from one country to the other varies greatly. First, we simply cannot ignore the social and political influences of each country on their schooling and educational leadership in particular. One size fits all, as a result, does not work in such a context. Second, educational leaders in the MENA region may hold various statuses within their societies that are not reflected in literature. Understanding this multilayered professional presence and its impact on their communities is important.

While salient issues are being addressed, depending heavily on imitating Western experiences or adopting policies from the West does not yield too much improvement. Each country needs to address its own issues and thus adopt specific strategies that account for the unique needs and particularities of each country. Policies to inform the field of ELA need to be locally developed. For example, a principal who is considered one of the most prominent figures in their communities and thus is expected to engage with parents, families, and students on a more personal level cannot be deprived of such privilege because Western research does not include such interaction among other stakeholders. In that sense, the related research and policies have been almost entirely based on Western conceptualizations, with some limited, but increasing, efforts to take unique cultural and policy contexts into account in recent years. It is, therefore, also important to contextualize future research to make it more relevant to ELA policies and practices in the region.

As we bring this book to a close, our hope is that the exposure to the work shared by the authors in this book has provided fuel for thought for readers' efforts. Throughout this book, we are rooted in the research that brings variation in thought and perspectives and appreciates the voices of the region that are much needed to be heard if we are to improve the ELA field. The future of this work requires the effort of not only researchers but also practitioners and policymakers ideally working collaboratively to bring forth a better understanding of how we want the ELA domain to look like and be operated within the different geographical, political, and social contexts. Thus, we are left with questions more than answers: How can we ensure that the impact of their knowledge and activism is embraced and included in not only how they are perceived but also how they are given the voice to play that part and contribute to the communities they're in? They are the creative innovators who have navigated systems that may have outdated policies, traditional mentalities, or corrupt institutions. How can we recognize their invaluable work and contributions to our societies through systemic changes? With limited resources or power, they've been hardworking to lift up their communities and transform the lives of their students and staff. How do we recognize their efforts and streamline the great work to become part of principal licensure programs in higher education? How do we continue to enhance their skills and knowledge by facilitating partnerships, social networks for collaborations, communities of practice, professional learning, and network improvement communities across countries? How can we sustain processes that ensure they are being heard, included, and supported?

What we can confidently say, however, is that we now have very strong evidence on the value of ELA for schooling in general, and school improvement in particular. This evidence is only becoming stronger with time, and this means we need a clearer vision for how we create ELA higher education programs, training, policies, and practices that are in synergy with each other bringing forth a well-established ELA program within each of the countries described. Our hope is that those of you reading this book will join the effort to further advance knowledge and practices and even contribute to the making of policies. Our call to action is that we work together to create conditions for ELAs on government, community, and school levels that will help improve the state of the field.

Index

Ababneh, S. 129, 130
academic leadership 28, 99
accountability, in Kuwait 177
Adams, D. 198
administrative and pedagogical leadership, in Algeria 98–102
Administrative Behavior in Education (Campbell & Gregg) 4
Advancing Learning and Employability for a Better Future (ALEF) (2004–2009) 82
Alajmi 172, 174
ALECSO *see* The Arab Organization for Education & and Science
ALEF *see* Advancing Learning and Employability for a Better Future
Al eneze, M. 177
Alenizi, K. 172, 173
Alfadala, A. 193, 196, 203
"*al Faza*" tribal style 132
Algeria, ELA in 95; administrative and pedagogical leadership 98–102; educational leaders 107; higher education reforms 98–102; key features of education 97–98; leadership, administration and bureaucracy 102–103; leadership and "ethics of intimacy" 108–110; organisation and administration 97–98; policy, culture and leadership 105–108; small- and medium-sized companies (SMEs) 108; theoretical perspectives and research methods 96–97; working environment and conflicts of interests 103–105
Algerian Constitutions 96
Algerian National Education 99
Alharbi, S. 173, 179

Ali, S. A. 202
AlKandari, E. M. 172
Al Karaki, W. 125
Al-Kendri, K. 175
AlKhater, L. R. M. 192
Allix, N. 198
Al-Madaris Al-Mutawara 187
Al-Mahhadin, S. 125
Almhedie, A. 202
Al-Rashoud, T. 167
Alsaleh, A. 172, 174
Al-Shatti, Y. 175
Al-Suwaihel, O. 181
Al-Wusta 167
ambidexterity scholarship 132
American University of Beirut 155
ANOVA 30
Apple, M. 197
Arabisation policy 99
Arab-Islamic legacy 131–132
Arab Open University 101, 210
The Arab Organization for Education & and Science (ALECSO) 101
Arab scholarship 115, 129–132, 217, 226
Arar, K. 52, 54, 131, 132, 162, 180
Arar, K. H. 106
Argyropoulou, E. 161
Arvanitis, R. 226
A'Sharqiyah University 210–211
Assaf, S. 155
Atari, A. 77, 88, 131, 224
Attari, A. T. A. 51
authorship trends: in Egypt 45; in Oman 215–216
Avolio, B. J. 106

Bajunid, I. A. 133
Ball, D. L. 106

238 Index

Baruch, Y. 202
Basic Education Policy Support Activity (BEPS) 82
Bass, A. 106
Bass and Avolio's (1994) conceptualisation of transformational leadership 106
Bates' and Foster's critical theory of educational administration 4
Ba'th Party 64, 67–69
Bellibaş, M. Ş. 28
Benzagho Committee 98
BEPS see Basic Education Policy Support Activity
The Bergen Communiqué 106
Besma 104, 105
Bogotch, I. 132, 135
Bourdieu, P. 215
Bridges, E. 49
Bridges, E. M. 218
Brighouse, T. 154
British Education policy 155
Brough, R. 84
Bryant, D. A. 38
Bush, T. 222

capacity building, in Morocco 75, 83, 84–87, 89, 90
Center of Educational Development and Research (CRDP) 141
Cheikha 104–105
CISCO see Computer Information System Company
Civil Administration 156
Classroom Council 81
Cohen, D. K. 106
CoHE see Council of Higher Education
colonial education 2, 155
community religious leaders, in Lebanon 149
Computer Information System Company (CISCO) 120
Conference on Educational Development in 1987 119–120
Council of Higher Education (CoHE) 12, 15, 27
COVID-19 pandemic 172, 175, 203
CRDP see Center of Educational Development and Research
critical thinking 125, 157
Curriculum Development Centre 156–157

Dar Al-Mandhuma database 211, 212
Darülfünun 14

Daun, H. 78
decentralization: in Jordan 122–123, 125–127, 134; in Morocco 78, 80, 84, 87; in Palestine 159
Decentralization Law 125, 126
DEFA see Department of Educational Foundations and Administration
democratic collaborative leadership 141
democratization: in Jordan 125–127; in Morocco 78
Department of Educational Foundations and Administration (DEFA) 210
Department of Planning and Improvement (DoPI) 169
Developed Schools in Qatar 187
Dewey, J. 19
distributed leadership (DL) 124, 133
distributive leadership 114, 124, 127, 133
DL see distributed leadership
DoPI see Department of Planning and Improvement
Dos, I. 154
"double hermeneutic" notion 96
Drucker, P. 84, 89

EAA see Education Above All
Economic and Social Transformation Plan (2003) 114, 120, 128
Education Above All (EAA) 189
The Educational Conference 121
educational leaders: in Algeria 107; in Egypt 40–41; in Lebanon 140
educational leadership and communities, in Iraq 67–69
Educational Management Certificate Program 18
"Education for Prosperity" 122, 123
Education Framework Act (EFA) (2019) 78
Education Management Information System (EMIS) 123
education policy, in Kuwait 177–179
Education Queensland International of Australia 192
Education Reform for Knowledge Economy 114, 120, 125, 127, 128
Education Strategic Plan, in Jordan 120–121
EFA see Education Framework Act
effective schools 141

Egypt, EAL in 37; authorship trends 45; context 38–39; data extraction and analysis 43; educational leaders, current challenges to 40–41; educational leadership, route to 39–40; implications 50–54; journals publication 44–45, 44f; knowledge production 43–50; reform initiatives 41; research methods employed in EAL literature of 47–50; research topics 46–47; sources, identification of 42–43; structure and administration 39; studies, types of 45–46; topical coverage 46, 48t

Egyptian Society for Comparative Education and Educational Administration (ESCEEA) 42, 45, 51
El-Amine, A. 217
El Sahib, N. 222
EMIS *see* Education Management Information System
EMOETE 39
empty empiricism 217
ESCEEA *see* Egyptian Society for Comparative Education and Educational Administration
Essa, E. B. 51
European Union Education Commission 14
Evers, C. W. 4

facility capacity 85
Fadlelmula, F. 199
Fitzgerald, T. 133
Forstenlechner, I. 202
Frey, C. J. 127

GEI *see* Global Education Initiative
General Competencies for Teaching Profession 16
General Secondary School Certification Exam (GSSCE) 125
Giddens, A. 96
Global Education Initiative (GEI) 127
globalization of education 1, 2, 80
governing bodies in Iraq 65–67
Government schools, in Qatar 188, 189, 191, 193
Greenfield, T. B. 3, 4
Greenfield's critique of logical empiricism 3

Grissom, J. A. 52
Gronn, P. 198
GSSCE *see* General Secondary School Certification Exam
Gunter, H. 133
Gümüş, S. 28

Habermas, J. 134
Hadjer 102
Hallinger, P. 38, 44, 48, 53, 77, 218
Hammad, W. 44, 45, 48, 53, 77, 215, 218, 220, 222, 224, 227
Hanafi, S. 226
Hashem, R. 124, 132
HCETSR *see* High Council for Education, Training, and Scientific Research
HICD *see* Human and Institutional Capacity Development
High Council for Education, Training, and Scientific Research (HCETSR) 75, 79, 85, 86, 88
higher education reforms, in Algeria 98–102
Hodges, R. M. 125, 134
Human and Institutional Capacity Development (HICD) 85, 86
Human Capital Index Report 179

ICDL *see* International Certificate of Digital Literacy
IIEP *see* International Institute for Educational Planning
Iles, P. 202
IMF *see* International Monetary Fund
Improving Training for Quality Advancement in National Education (ITQANE) 2009–2014 82, 83
Instructional Council 81
International Certificate of Digital Literacy (ICDL) 176
International Institute for Educational Planning (IIEP) 159
International Monetary Fund (IMF) 197
Iraq, ELA in 62; educational leadership and communities 67–69; governing bodies 67; school leaders 71–72; school leadership evaluation 69–71; schools administrations 63–65; schools governing bodies 65–67

Israeli Civil Administration 156
ITQANE *see* Improving Training for Quality Advancement in National Education

JEI *see* Jordan Education Initiative
Jordan, EAL in 114; decentralization and democratization 125–127; decentralizing the classroom 125; economic theoretical underpinnings 128–129; educational leadership 121–123; education strategic plan 2018–2022 120–121; knowledge production on educational administration 129; methodology 115; official narration, challenging 123–129; paradox theory 132–135; reform agenda, ownership of 127–128; scholarship on ELA 129–132; theoretical underpinnings 115–119; 20th century, education in 119–120; 21st century, educational reforms in 120–121; values, conflicting 124–125
Jordan Education Initiative (JEI) 114, 127
journals publication in Egypt 44–45

K-12 education in Qatar 187, 189–190
Kalisman, H. 155
Karami-Akkary, R. 222
Katateeb schools 166
K-based economies 120, 128
Kennedy, M. 125
Kirk, S. 202
knowledge production: in Egypt 43; in Jordan 129, 130; in Kuwait 179–180; in Morocco 89; in Oman 215, 217, 226
Koç, M. 199
Kuttab 119, 187
Kutty, G. R. 198
Kuwait, education in 166; accountability 177; educational leadership and management (EDLM) 179–180; education policy 177–179; future improvement Kuwait EDLM 180–182; Ministry of Education structure 167–169, 170, 171; positive indicators of achievement in educational leadership 176–177; public education, political reform of 169–173; public education development 166–167; public school administration and leadership 173–176; school administration 174; Supreme Education Council 172, 182
Kuwait National Development Plan 169
Kuwait Supreme Council for Planning and Development 169
Kuwait University 179–180

Lakomski, G. 4
Law of Unification of Education 14
leadership, task of 84, 89
learner-centered approach 125
Lebanon, principalship in 140; community religious leaders 149; enrollment to students 148–149; Ministry of Education and Higher Education (MEHE) policies, relevance of 148; preparation and induction 143; principals going beyond school duties 149–150; principal's tasks and responsibilities, clarification of 144–145; private school selection process 142–143; private versus public schools 147–148; public school principals 142; recommendations 151; religious/sectarian nepotism 149; school improvement, catalysts for 146–147; school location 148–149; school principal role, shift in 141; strong educational leaders for school success 140; supervision and evaluation 143–144; systemic role context of school administrator 141–150; unrealistic expectations and challenges 145–146
Leila 103
linguistic duality 97
Lumby, J. 133

Madi, M. T. 202
Management Council (MC) 81, 86
MC *see* Management Council
MDGs *see* Millennium Development Goals

MEG *see* Morocco Education for Girls
MEHE policies *see* Ministry of Education and Higher Education policies
Mellahi, K. 108, 109
Meriem 104
Merriam, S. B. 190
MESRS *see* Ministry of Higher Education and Scientific Research
Millennium Challenge Account, Morocco 83
Millennium Development Goals (MDGs) 121
Ministry of Education (MoE) 8; in Iraq 63, 64, 68, 72; in Jordan 114, 129; in Kuwait 167–169, 170f, 171f; in Morocco 80; in Oman 210–211; in Palestine 156–158, 159–160; in Qatar 187, 190–196
Ministry of Education and Higher Education (MEHE) policies, in Lebanon 147–148
Ministry of Education and Higher Education (MOEHE), in Palestine 156, 157
Ministry of Education and Technical Education (MOETE), in Egypt 39
Ministry of Education Strategic Plan 114
Ministry of Higher Education and Scientific Research (MESRS), in Algeria 96, 98
Ministry of National Education (MoNE) 12, 15t, 25, 27, 96
Ministry of Planning and International Cooperation 114
MOEHE *see* Ministry of Education and Higher Education
MoE *see* Ministry of Education
MOETE *see* Ministry of Education and Technical Education
Mohammad, A. 175
MoNE *see* Ministry of National Education
Morocco, ELA in 75; capacity building, areas for 84–87; learning improvement imperative 75–77; operational embodiment 80–84; policy, practice, and research implications 87–90; policy inception 77–80; School Development Project 80–84, 81f
Morocco Education for Girls (MEG) 82

Naima 105
National Agenda 2005 126
National Center for Education Development (NCED) 171
National Charter for Education and Training (NCET) 77, 78
National Committee for the Reform of the Educational System 98
National Education Basic Law 22, 23
National Education Development Center (NCDC) 174
National Index on the Development of Education (NIDE) 75, 76f, 80
National Strategy for the School Development Project (NSSDP) 80, 81, 85
National Universities Symposium 99, 100
NCDC *see* National Education Development Center
NCED *see* National Center for Education Development
NCET *see* National Charter for Education and Training
nepotism 123, 124, 133, 149
New Model for Development (NMD) (2021) 78–79
NIDE *see* National Index on the Development of Education
NMD *see* New Model for Development
Normand, R. 89
NSSDP *see* National Strategy for the School Development Project

OECD *see* Organisation for Economic Co-operation and Development
Oman, EAL in 209; authorship trends 215–216; data extraction and analysis 213–214; education system 210; identification of sources 212–213; implications 224–227; paper, types of 216–217; Renaissance period in 1970 210; research methods 217–221; research topics covered in Omani EAL literature 221–224; status quo of EAL knowledge base 214–224; volume of the production 214–215
operational embodiment of ELA in Morocco 80–84
Oplatka, E. 131
Oplatka, I. 52, 54, 106, 107

242 Index

Organisation for Economic Co-operation and Development (OECD) 15, 16–17, 18, 21, 158, 197
organizational ambidexterity 115, 118, 133
Oslo agreement in 1994 156, 158
Ottoman Public Education Law 155
Outum, N. 77, 88, 131, 224

PAGESM *see* Project for Assistance for the Management of Schools
Palestinian educational leadership 154; bright side of 158–160; British mandate, education under 155–156; dark side of 160–161; history of education system 154–158; Ministry of Education (MoE) 156–158; occupation, education under 156
Palestinian National Authority 159
Palestinian National Educational Law 159
Pan-Arab 38
paradox theory 115, 132, 133
PAT *see* Professional Academy for Teachers
Pedagogical Council 81
pedagogical leadership, in Algeria 98–102
performance capacity 85, 86
personal capacity 85, 86
PIRLS *see* Progress in International Reading Literacy Study
The Plan for Upgrading the Political System 126
policy, culture and leadership in Algeria 105–108
policy inception in Morocco 77–80
policy-makers 83, 87
political reform of public education, in Kuwait 169–173
politicized bureaucracy 149
positive psychology 115, 132
Potter, C. 84
Potter and Brough's hierarchy of system capacity 84, 84f
principals going beyond school duties, in Lebanon 149–150
principal's tasks and responsibilities, in Lebanon 144–145
Private Education Institutions Law 16
private school selection process, in Lebanon 142–143
private versus public schools, in Lebanon 147–148

PROCADEM *see* Project for the Reinforcement of the Institutional Capacities of the Moroccan Educational System
Professional Academy for Teachers (PAT) 39, 40
professional development opportunities, in Qatar 192–193, 201
Progress in International Reading Literacy Study (PIRLS) 76–77
Project for Assistance for the Management of Schools (PAGESM) 83
Project for the Reinforcement of the Institutional Capacities of the Moroccan Educational System (PROCADEM) 83
public education development in Kuwait 166–167
Public Personnel Selection Examination 16
public school administration and leadership, in Kuwait 173–176
public school principals, in Lebanon 142

Qatar, ELA in 187; context of 187–188; data analysis 191; educational leadership and Arab educators 197–198; educational leadership policies 198; Government schools 193; K-12 education 187; K-12 educational leaders 189; K-12 educational policies, revisiting 189–190; Ministry of Education (MoEHE) 187, 190–191, 192, 193–196; new era, education for 188–189; new ERA, nature of 191–192; new professional development opportunities 192–193; participants 190–191; research design 190; research instruments 190; teachers' autonomy 193; translation, lost in 200–201
Qatar National Professional Standards for Teachers and Leaders (QNPSTL) 192
QNPSTL *see* Qatar National Professional Standards for Teachers and Leaders

Raiden, A. 202
Ramdani, B. 107

RAND Cooperation *see* Research and Development Cooperation
reform-failure discourses 132
religious/sectarian nepotism, in Lebanon 149
Renaissance period, in Oman 210
Research and Development (RAND) Cooperation 188
research methods employed in Egyptian EAL literature 47–50
Responsible Leadership 131
role capacity 85
Romanowski, M. H. 193
Rutledge, E. J. 202

Sadat, A. 41
Said, E. 226
Saito, F. 78
Satloff, R. 126
Savas, A. C. 154
Sawalhi, R. 190, 201, 202
scholarship on ELA in Jordan 129–132
school administration: in Iraq 65, 66; in Kuwait 173, 174; in Lebanon 141–150
School and Directorates Development Program (SDDP) 120
school-based management 114; in Jordan 114, 124; in Morocco 80, 86
School Development Project (SDP), in Morocco 75, 80–84, 81f
School Development Team (SDT) 120
school improvement: in Lebanon 146–147; in Morocco 80, 81, 90
School Improvement Plan (SIP) 120
school leadership: in Egypt 40, 54; in Iraq 64–65, 69–71; in Jordan 123; in Kuwait 175; in Lebanon 140, 141; in Qatar 188, 202
school leaders in Iraq 71–72
school location, in Lebanon 148–149
school principal role, in Lebanon 141
school principalship in Turkey 16–18
schools administrations, in Iraq 63–65
schools governing bodies, in Iraq 65–67
school support organizations (SSOs) 192
SCU *see* Supreme Council of Universities
SDDP *see* School and Directorates Development Program
SDGs *see* sustainable development goals
SDP *see* School Development Project
SDS *see* The Sustainable Development Strategy

SDT *see* School Development Team
SEC *see* Supreme Education Council
the Secondary School of Challenge 83
Selim, H. M. 202
Sellami, A. L. 197, 201, 202
Shaichoracay 124
SHEMERA project 109
Shirazi, R. 134
SIP *see* School Improvement Plan
Sirine 102
Şişman, M. 33
Slowley, D. 133
small- and medium-sized companies (SMEs), in Algeria 108
SMEs *see* small- and medium-sized companies
Soumia 104
Specialized Institute for Professional Training of Teachers 211
SP *see* Strategic Plan
SQU *see* Sultan Qaboos University
SSOs *see* school support organizations
Strategic Plan (SP) 2018–2022 114, 121, 122
Strategic Vision for Reform (SVR) (2015–2030) 78
structural capacity 85
students enrollment, in Lebanon 148–149
Su-Keene, E. J. 132, 135
Sultan Qaboos University (SQU) 210, 211
supervisory capacity 85, 86
support capacity 85
Supreme Council for the Planning and Development of the Strategic Plan 169
Supreme Council of Universities (SCU), in Egypt 42
Supreme Education Council (SEC): in Kuwait 172, 182, 189; in Qatar 189
sustainable development goals (SDGs) 121
The Sustainable Development Strategy (SDS) 38
sustainable leadership 131
SVR *see* Strategic Vision for Reform
system capacity 84, 85

TALIS *see* Teaching and Learning International Survey
Tamimi, A. 190

Tanzimat Period 14
teacher leadership 8, 114, 122, 133, 134, 189, 204
Teacher Preparation and Certification Program (TPCP) 192
teachers' autonomy, in Qatar 193
Teacher Training and Development 16, 18
teacher training process in Turkey 16
Teaching and Learning International Survey (TALIS) 16
teaching profession in Turkey 16–18
theory movement 3–4
TIMSS *see* Trends in International Mathematics and Science Study
Tisdell, E. J. 190
TODAIE *see* Turkey Middle East Public Management Institute
TPCP *see* Teacher Preparation and Certification Program
transformational leadership 28, 106, 122, 131, 141
Trends in International Mathematics and Science Study (TIMSS) 76–77, 76f, 176
Trow's developmental theory of HE classification 101
t-tests 30
Turan, S. 28, 29, 33
Turkey, EDLM in 12; deepening years (1997–2014) 24–26; educational context 14–18; emergence and development of EDLM 19; establishment and search years (1953–1982) 22; mass and compulsory national education (1869–1953) 19–20; modernization efforts, EDLM and (1773–1869) 19; scientification of education and school management and educational management (1953–present) 21–22; social, cultural, and political context 13–14; state of the art in research on EDLM in Turkey 27–31; teaching profession and school principalship 16–18; years of inquiry (2014–present) 26–27; years of spread (1982–1996) 23–24
Turkey Middle East Public Management Institute (TODAIE) 21, 22, 31

UNESCO *see* United Nations Educational, Scientific and Cultural Organization
United Nations Educational, Scientific and Cultural Organization (UNESCO) 123, 159, 169, 181, 197
United Nations Relief and Works Agency for Palestine Refugees 155
United States Agency for International Development (USAID) 82
University Academies 99
the University Map 99
USAID *see* United States Agency for International Development

Wasta 108, 109, 128, 202
Western research 234, 235
Whitehead, C. 155
Winkler, D. R. 78
Winokur, I. K. 172
WISE *see* World Innovation Summit for Education
Wizarat Al-Maarif 187
Wolman, H. 78
Wood, G. T. 108, 109
Woods, D. 154
workload capacity, in Morocco 85
World Bank 75, 197
World Innovation Summit for Education (WISE) 189
World Trade Organization (WTO) 197
WTO *see* World Trade Organization

Yılmaz, K. 28, 29

Zabidi, Z. M. 198
Zahira 103, 105
Zellman, G. L. 188
Zeyneb 102, 103, 104

Printed in the United States
by Baker & Taylor Publisher Services